ROUTLEDGE LIBRARY EDITIONS: SLAVERY

Volume 3

ANTISLAVERY POLITICAL WRITINGS, 1833–1860

ANTISLAVERY POLITICAL WRITINGS, 1833–1860

A Reader

Edited by
C. BRADLEY THOMPSON

Routledge
Taylor & Francis Group
LONDON AND NEW YORK

First published in 2004 by M.E. Sharpe

This edition first published in 2023
by Routledge
4 Park Square, Milton Park, Abingdon, Oxon OX14 4RN

and by Routledge
605 Third Avenue, New York, NY 10158

Routledge is an imprint of the Taylor & Francis Group, an informa business

© 2004 Taylor & Francis

All rights reserved. No part of this book may be reprinted or reproduced or utilised in any form or by any electronic, mechanical, or other means, now known or hereafter invented, including photocopying and recording, or in any information storage or retrieval system, without permission in writing from the publishers.

Trademark notice: Product or corporate names may be trademarks or registered trademarks, and are used only for identification and explanation without intent to infringe.

British Library Cataloguing in Publication Data
A catalogue record for this book is available from the British Library

ISBN: 978-1-032-30942-2 (Set)
ISBN: 978-1-032-32805-8 (Volume 3) (hbk)
ISBN: 978-1-032-32810-2 (Volume 3) (pbk)
ISBN: 978-1-003-31684-8 (Volume 3) (ebk)

DOI: 10.4324/9781003316848

Publisher's Note
The publisher has gone to great lengths to ensure the quality of this reprint but points out that some imperfections in the original copies may be apparent.

Disclaimer
The publisher has made every effort to trace copyright holders and would welcome correspondence from those they have been unable to trace.

ANTISLAVERY POLITICAL WRITINGS, 1833–1860

ANTISLAVERY POLITICAL WRITINGS, 1833–1860

A READER

EDITED BY C. BRADLEY THOMPSON

LONDON AND NEW YORK

First published 2004 by M.E. Sharpe

Published 2015 by Routledge
2 Park Square, Milton Park, Abingdon, Oxon OX14 4RN
711 Third Avenue, New York, NY 10017, USA

Routledge is an imprint of the Taylor & Francis Group, an informa business

Copyright © 2004 Taylor & Francis. All rights reserved.

No part of this book may be reprinted or reproduced or utilised in any form or by any electronic, mechanical, or other means, now known or hereafter invented, including photocopying and recording, or in any information storage or retrieval system, without permission in writing from the publishers.

Notices
No responsibility is assumed by the publisher for any injury and/or damage to persons or property as a matter of products liability, negligence or otherwise, or from any use of operation of any methods, products, instructions or ideas contained in the material herein.

Practitioners and researchers must always rely on their own experience and knowledge in evaluating and using any information, methods, compounds, or experiments described herein. In using such information or methods they should be mindful of their own safety and the safety of others, including parties for whom they have a professional responsibility.

Product or corporate names may be trademarks or registered trademarks, and are used only for identification and explanation without intent to infringe.

Library of Congress Cataloging-in-Publication Data

Antislavery political writings, 1833–1860 : a reader / C. Bradley Thompson, editor.
    p. cm.
Includes bibliographical references (p.) and index.
ISBN 0-7656-0402-7 (cloth: alk. paper) — ISBN 0-7656-0403-5 (pbk.: alk. paper)
    1. Antislavery movements—United States—History—19th century—Sources. 2. Slavery—Political aspects—United States—History—19th century—Sources. 3. Abolitionists—United States—Political activity—History—19 century—Sources. 4. United States—Politics and government—1815–1861—Sources. I. Thompson, C. Bradley.

E449.A62374 2003
326'.8'0973—dc21   2003042760

ISBN 13: 9780765604033 (pbk)
ISBN 13: 9780765604026 (hbk)

To Henry, Samuel, and Islay

Contents

Preface	ix
Introduction	xiii

I. Slavery and Freedom

1. *The Patriarchal Institution,* ... (1860) *Lydia Maria Child*	3
2. "Lecture on Slavery, No. 1" (1850) *Frederick Douglass*	24
3. Selections from *Slavery* (1836) *William E. Channing*	31

II. Immediate Emancipation

4. "Declaration of Sentiments ..." (1833) *American Anti-Slavery Society*	41
5. Selections from *Lectures on Slavery and its Remedy* (1834) *Amos A. Phelps*	46

III. Moral Suasion and Politics

6. "An Address to the Abolitionists of Massachusetts, ..." (1838) *Massachusetts Anti-Slavery Society*	63
7. "A Letter on the Political Obligation of Abolitionists, ..." (1839) *James G. Birney*	75
8. "Talk About Political Party" (1842) *Lydia Maria Child*	98

IV. The Liberty Party

9. "Lecture Showing the Necessity for a Liberty Party, ..." (1844) *Arnold Buffum*	107
10. "Address of the Macedon Convention" (1847) *William Goodell*	114

V. Slavery and the Constitution

11. Slavery and the Constitution (1849) — 133
    William I. Bowditch
12. "The Constitution of the United States: Is It Pro-Slavery or Anti-Slavery? (1860) — 144
    Frederick Douglass

VI. Free-Soil and Fugitive Slaves

13. "The Two Altars; Or, Two Pictures in One" (1851) — 159
    Harriet Beecher Stowe
14. "Speech on Our Present Anti-Slavery Duties" (1850) — 170
    Charles Sumner

VII. Impending Crisis

15. "Moral Responsibility of Statesmen" (1854) — 187
    Joshua R. Giddings
16. "What Is My Duty as an Anti-Slavery Voter?" and "Fremont and Dayton" (1856) — 202
    Frederick Douglass
17. "House Divided" Speech (1858) — 212
    Abraham Lincoln

VIII. Disunion and Revolution

18. "Address to the Slaves of the United States of America" (1843) — 223
    Henry Highland Garnet
19. "No Compromise With Slavery" (1854) — 230
    William Lloyd Garrison
20. "No Rights, No Duties: Or, Slaveholders, as Such, Have No Rights; Slaves, as Such, Owe No Duties" (1860) — 246
    Henry C. Wright
21. A Plan for the Abolition of Slavery (1858) — 261
    Lysander Spooner

Selected Bibliography — 265
Index — 269
About the Editor — 291

Preface

The purpose of this anthology is threefold: first, to present the best writings and speeches of the most influential antislavery thinkers, activists, and statesmen in the years between 1830 and 1860; second, to demonstrate the range of theoretical and political choices open to antislavery advocates during the antebellum period; and finally, to introduce students to the general problem associated with reconciling theory and practice. Hopefully, the lessons learned from this volume will point students beyond the specific historical issue of antislavery reform to the general relationship between principles and practice in the modern world. By studying the antislavery movement, we can see more clearly how men and women who share a common moral principle can develop radically different strategies and tactics to achieve that principle.

Sooner or later, all political and social movements guided by deeply held moral principles must confront the problem of how to realize those principles in a world that may not share the same values—that is, they must confront the problem of how to convert principle into practice. More precisely, they must address certain difficult questions. Is compromise ever permissible in a conflict between two antagonistic moral systems, or is it inherently corrupting? Under what conditions is compromise permissible? How much compromise is acceptable? Does moral absolutism inspire or hinder reform? What constitutes prudence in the pursuit of long-range values? Is it possible to advance a moral cause politically without diluting one's principles? Does political victory require appealing to the lowest common denominator, and, if it does, how can one do it without corrupting one's goals? In other words, is compromise a fact of reality or is it inherently self-defeating?

From the beginning, American abolitionists confronted these questions on a specific issue (i.e., slavery) and in a specific context (e.g., the fact that approximately only 5 percent of Northern opinion favored immediate abolition, 5 percent favored slavery, 20 percent were opportunists who followed the drift of public opinion, and 70 percent were opposed to slavery but would not defy the Constitution). The very particular questions and the range of alternatives they confronted in dealing with the related questions of expediency and tactics were complex and many. Should abolitionists engage in politics or should they remain faithful to moral conversion? Is an antislavery political movement legitimate or even helpful if a majority of citizens do not accept antislavery principles? Should they work within the context of the traditional two-party system or should they form a third party? If abolitionists opted for a third party, should it be a one-plank arty devoted exclusively to the abolition of slavery, or should it adopt a multi-planked platform that might appeal to a larger audience? How should they respond to non-abolitionist, antislavery parties such as the Free-Soil Party? Is the Constitution a pro- or antislavery document? If it is a proslavery document, what course of action is required of antislavery men? If it is an antislavery document, what course of action is required of these same men? What is the moral status of an abolitionist who compromises with the slave power once in a while? If slavery cannot be abolished, is it the moral responsibility of those who believe in freedom and natural rights to secede from the Union? Is violence justified in abolishing slavery? Could emancipation have been achieved without a civil war?

Selecting the essays for this volume has proved to be both a labor of love and a burden of regret. The overarching theme that defined the project and which guided my choices was the relationship of moral principle to political practice. Even within this context I have been forced to make difficult choices. This volume could very easily have been doubled in length without diminishing its quality. By definition, then, I have also excluded essays that take religion, economics, women's civil rights, or Northern racism as their principal themes. There are several extant volumes that deal with these issues very nicely. The criteria that I used in choosing from among the scores, even hundreds, of antislavery books, pamphlets, and speeches were two: first, that the essays selected represent the deepest and most influential expressions of antislavery thought; and second, that they represent the broad spectrum of antislavery solutions to the problem of slavery. Early on, I also decided to publish full texts or lightly edited texts. Rather than following the current trend of publishing a large number of very short, highly edited essays, I am presenting a smaller selection of longer pieces. Pedagogically, I reject the claim that MTV–inspired television has reduced our students' capacities to read and to think through sustained arguments. All of this is to say that there are still more volumes of antislavery writings to be collected and published using a variety of different themes and criteria. My hope is that this volume will inspire other scholars to do just that.

The idea for this volume was first inspired by Paul Finkelman, who suggested that I turn my course readings packet into a published book. I have also profited from the wise suggestions of Bertram Wyatt-Brown, John L. Thomas, Brendan McConville, and my colleague John Lewis. I should also like to thank William B. Weiss, director of the Ashland University Library, for his invaluable assistance in helping me to acquire many of these old documents. I owe a particular debt of gratitude to John McCaskey and the Anthem Foundation for Objectivist Studies, who provided me with a fellowship to complete this project. Finally, to my wife Sidney and my children Henry, Samuel, and Islay, I promise to pay back time borrowed.

Introduction

On January 1, 1831, William Lloyd Garrison published the first issue of *The Liberator*. He there announced to the world a new kind of crusade to abolish slavery in America. He promised his readers that he would be "as harsh as truth, and as uncompromising as justice." On January 1, 1863, exactly thirty-two years later, Abraham Lincoln signed the Emancipation Proclamation, that declared "all persons held as slaves within any State or designated part of a State . . . shall be then, thenceforth and forever free." Thus began and ended one of the truly heroic episodes in American history. Over the course of three decades, thousands of men and woman actively dedicated themselves to the antislavery cause. This volume tells their story in their own words.

Slavery and Freedom

In 1831, the year that an organized movement to abolish slavery began, chattel slavery had existed in United States for at least 170 years. The exact origins of American slavery are shrouded in mystery, but what it was and what it became are well known. By the early years of the new republic, and particularly since the introduction of the cotton gin, slavery had become a thriving economic institution. Between 1790 and 1830 the number of slaves in America increased from approximately 694,280 to roughly 2,000,000, despite federal law that prohibited the importation of African slaves. That number would increase to 4 million by 1860. Slaveholding and slave production became the major form of Southern wealth. More importantly, slavery had become a way of life deeply embedded in all Southern institutions.

Prior to the 1830s, slavery was viewed by many Southerners as an unfortunate but necessary evil. After 1830, Southern intellectuals and statesmen began to defend slavery more aggressively as a positive good, as "the cornerstone of our Republican edifice." John C. Calhoun, speaking on the floor of the United States Senate in 1838, bellowed that "Many in the South *once* believed that slavery was a moral and political evil; but *that folly and delusion are gone*. We now see it in its true light, and regard it as the most *safe and stable basis for free institutions*." George Fitzhugh, a leading Southern intellectual described a free society as a "monstrous abortion" and the slave system as the "healthy, beautiful, and natural state of being." Slavery, he continued, is "the oldest, the best, and the most common form of socialism." Explicitly rejecting the principles of the Declaration of Independence as a self-evident lie, Southern defenders of slavery scoffed at the idea that liberty is unalienable or that men are entitled to equal rights. The fact of the matter is, Fitzhugh argued, "that some are born with saddles on their backs, and others booted and spurred to ride them." Slavery was right, just, and for the good of civilization; it is, they argued, "the natural and normal condition of the laboring man, white or black."

As an institution and as a way of life, slavery can be viewed from a variety of perspectives—e.g., political, economic, social, religious, etc.—but, at its core, it defines a relationship between a master and his slave. Defined by the "chattel principle"—i.e., the ownership of the body and labor of another human being as property—slavery was first and foremost a moral issue. The slave system sanctioned the ownership of human beings; it gave one man complete and arbitrary power over the lives of others; it permitted the master to flog and sell his slaves as he would horses, sheep, and swine; and it denied to the slave the moral and legal right to a wife or husband, to children, to education, to chastity, to a home, and to property.

To those nineteenth-century Americans who took the principles of the Declaration of Independence seriously and who dreamed of living in the free society that it envisioned, the anomaly of slavery was a threat to their most cherished moral and political ideals. Abolitionists confronted American slavery as a moral question. In fact, no issue more clearly demonstrated the objectivity of morals. Slavery was a moral abomination because it denied the self-evident fact that blacks are human beings, which means that it violated the first law of human morality—i.e., the law of self-ownership—and which finally means that it denied to black slaves the natural rights that inhere in all men *qua* men. Thus it became the moral responsibility of all Americans to purge the land of this evil sickness.

Immediate Emancipation

To most Americans of the early republic, the problem of slave emancipation was vividly summarized by Thomas Jefferson. In his *Notes on the States of Virginia*, Jefferson explained why he regarded the emancipation of slaves and their integration into American society as impossible: "Deep rooted prejudices entertained by the whites; ten thousand recollections, by the blacks, of the injuries they have sustained; new provocations; the real distinctions which nature has made; and many other circumstances which will probably never end but in the extermination of the one or the other race." Thirty-five years later, in the middle of the Missouri crisis, he stated the dilemma even more succinctly: "We have the wolf by the ears, and we can neither hold him, nor safely let him go. Justice is on one scale, and self-preservation in the other." Like most Americans at the time, Jefferson favored gradual emancipation and the expatriation of the slaves to Africa. The American Colonization Society, founded in 1816, was the first national organization dedicated to emancipation. Its goal was gradual manumission and the establishment of a colony in Liberia for freed blacks.

During the early 1830s, antislavery thought took a radical turn. Inspired by the Enlightenment natural-rights philosophy of the Declaration of Independence and the religious revivals of the Second Great Awakening, a new moral sensibility—indeed, a moral revolution—swept over the American landscape that promoted an uncompromising vision of good and evil. Seemingly overnight, a new generation of antislavery reformers began to reexamine the moral aspects of slavery and to search for radical solutions to America's blight. They found their mission in the cause of "immediate emancipation." Led by William Lloyd Garrison in Boston and Lewis and Arthur Tappan in New York, antislavery reformers became abolitionists—that is, they now called for immediate, unconditional, uncompensated emancipation. Their movement was non-violent, non-revolutionary, and it was based on voluntary conversion.

In December 1833, sixty-two abolitionists—a heterogeneous group of whites and blacks, men and women from all walks of life—met in Philadelphia to establish the American Anti-Slavery Association. From the beginning, the meeting was dominated by Garrison's vision for immediate, non-violent emancipation. The grand strategy of the new organization was to initiate a moral revolution in America that would alter the nation's social, religious, and political institutions. This new generation of abolitionists consciously and strategically assumed a moral posture that was unequivocating and uncompromising. They understood that non-violent emancipation and a workable post-emancipation society were not possible unless a vast majority of Americans (i.e., both slaveholding Southerners and free Northerners) were prepared morally to establish a just society for all.

That was the unconditional first premise of the abolitionist movement. Emancipation was not possible, they argued, until the entire nation, or at least a vast majority of Americans, were converted to this moral premise. Once the nation had been sufficiently enlightened and was willing to act in order to excise the tumor of slavery, then and only then did the abolitionists think it possible to actually begin the political process of decommissioning slavery as an institution. As uncomfortable as they made others feel, the abolitionists were right in suggesting that those individuals who closed their eyes and evaded the crime of slavery implicitly sanctioned and bore responsibility for its continued existence. Despite claims to the contrary, the abolitionists were not idle dreamers, nor were they irresponsible fanatics. They knew full well, for instance, that immediate and unconditional emancipation would take decades to fully implement, but they also understood that the issue had to be agitated immediately and without compromise. Moral conversion might take a long time but it was the only non-violent means of ending slavery and of establishing a just and integrated society. They therefore rejected range-of-the-moment political compromises with the "Slave Power" as impractical and imprudent. In other words, they believed that in any compromise between good and evil, it is only the evil that profits.

The American Anti-Slavery Society devoted its early years to establishing an organizational structure and elevating its moral stature as a grassroots movement. But abolitionists were confronted by two undeniable facts: that slavery was deeply embedded in America's political, religious and economic institutions, and that race prejudice was ingrained in American manners and mores. Abolitionists therefore directed their activities toward what they called "moral suasion"—a nation-wide process of moral conversion and regeneration. The instruments of moral suasion employed by the American Anti-Slavery Society included the following: first, sponsoring agents and lecturers to evangelize the countryside on the evils of slavery; second, shaping public opinion by circulating antislavery pamphlets and newspapers to clergymen, editors, politicians, and slaveholders; third, organizing and supporting antislavery societies in every state, city, town, and village; and fourth, petitioning federal and state governments to abolish slavery or to remove its political supports.

The fruits of moral suasion are seen most clearly in two abolitionist activities that occurred in the mid-1830s. One of the first and most successful activities of the American Anti-Slavery Society was their project to flood the country with abolitionist mailings (primarily sent to ministers, politicians, and newspaper editors). Remarkably, by 1838, over a million pieces of antislavery literature were mailed. Abolitionists also launched a "petition" campaign that merged moral suasion with politics. Working at the grassroots level, hundreds of state and local antislavery societies throughout the North and West sent their volunteers door-to-door with petitions protesting against slavery in the District of Columbia, the interstate slave trade, the "three-fifths compromise," and the admission of new slave states. Remarkably, by 1838 some 415,000 petitions had been sent to Washington. The repercussions were felt immediately: A moral earthquake was shifting the tectonic structures of America's political system.

By 1838, after five years of exponential growth and great successes in proselytizing the nation, there can be little doubt that the abolitionist movement had jolted Northerners and Southerners out of their dogmatic slumbers. Increasingly, the violent reaction to abolitionist agitation by Northern mobs and the repression and aggressiveness of the Slave Power awakened many to the merits of a moderate form of antislavery sentiment. Many Northerners were shocked into adopting antislavery sentiments through their disgust at mob action against abolitionists in the North, mail searches in the South, "gag" rules in Congress preventing the discussion of antislavery petitions, censorship, vandalized newspaper offices, and, most importantly, by the murder of Elijah Lovejoy, an abolitionist newspaperman in Alton, Illinois. More generally, many came to fear what they saw as the increasing aggression and expansionism of the planter aristocracy and its threat to the freedom of all Americans. Ultimately, abolitionism's greatest success was in convincing many white Northerners that a conspiracy existed between the slave aristocracy and their "doughface" supporters in the North (doughface was a term of disapprobation for Northern men with Southern principles) to deface Americans of their constitutionally guaranteed liberties, including the right of petition, free speech, free assembly, and a free press. Most of these people, conventional in their attitudes toward the union and blacks, were not advocates of immediate emancipation, but they were willing to challenge the imperialistic designs of Southern politicians. Abolitionists were therefore confronted with a dilemma: How could they take advantage of moderate, non-immediatist antislavery Northern sentiment without compromising their principles?

Moral Suasion and Politics

By 1838, the leaders of the American Anti-Slavery Society responded to this question in very different ways. For some abolitionists—the Garrisonians in particular—moral suasion had been a ringing success and should be continued unabated. It was achieving the kind of moral awakening that was a necessary precondition for emancipation. Others, however, argued that moral suasion had reached its natural limits, but also that its ideas had circulated widely enough for abolitionists to pursue newer and more ambitious forms of agitation. With time, many began to realize that moral and political action were, and must be, intimately connected. Why abandon Congress to the Slave Power, some asked? The advocates of moral suasion responded by charging that party politics, with its corruption, treachery and intrigue, would pollute and waste the moral vision of their movement. Thus came the first major breach in the abolitionist movement.

Most abolitionists, including Garrison and his followers, did engage in some form of political agitation, if only indirectly. The most obvious strategy was to organize and vote as a bloc for antislavery candidates from either of the two major parties—the Democrats and Whigs. Their tactical goal was to elect either antislavery candidates or to influence the platforms and nominations of the two major parties by wielding a balance of power. Abolitionists adopted and employed a method to identify the views of candidates on the slavery question known as "interrogation." Abolitionists would send questionnaires to all nominees for important political offices asking them to publicly declare their positions on a range of issues dealing with slavery such as the right of abolitionists to petition Congress and the authority of Congress to abolish slavery in the District of Columbia. If neither candidate supported emancipation, abolitionists would either refuse to vote or they would "scatter" their votes by writing in the name of a known antislavery proponent. Initially, abolitionists thought these methods would allow them to influence elections and legislation without having to compromise their moral principles in the dirty world of party politics. In the end, however, the interrogation method was unreliable and limited in its effectiveness. A common problem was that many abolitionists couldn't shake off their ingrained party loyalties and voted for one of the two-party candidates in order to affect the other great issues of the day.

In 1838–39, a debate erupted amongst abolitionists over the expediency of direct political action. Essentially, the division pitted the "ultraist" Garrison and his followers against the more conservative abolitionists, men such as the Tappan brothers, James G. Birney, William Goodell, and Geritt Smith. The central issue that divided abolitionists came down to this question: Do all abolitionists have a moral duty to vote? Put another way: Can those who refuse to vote for the slave be members of the American Anti-Slavery Society? The resulting clash over the morality and expediency of political action led to a civil war within the ranks of the abolitionist movement.

Garrison's official position was that the American Anti-Slavery Society should be open to all men and women who pronounced slavery a sin and who were willing to work for immediate emancipation. Membership would therefore include men and women like himself who had taken on a host of other causes such as equal rights for women and a principled aversion to all government and party politics. During the late 1830s Garrison had come to believe that slavery was created and sustained by government and that only a policy of political "non-resistance"—that is, a withdrawing of one's sanction from America's immoral political institutions—could achieve the desired end of emancipation. When Garrison committed himself to the doctrine of "non-resistance" in 1838, he thereafter abstained from voting and boycotted active political action altogether. The Garrisonians rejected pragmatic appeals to piecemeal and short-term gains for a long-range, bottom-up strategy that sought broad-based moral reform as the necessary condition for political emancipation. Without the moral authority of public opinion standing squarely behind them, the Garrisonians worried that a premature entry into politics would dilute and corrupt their long-range goal.

By contrast, the more conservative wing was appalled by Garrison's social radicalism and by what they saw as his attempt to highjack the abolitionist movement for his broader vision of universal reform. They were repulsed by his harsh attacks on orthodox religion and America's political institutions, and they saw in Garrison and his followers a band of eccentric fanatics that were unnecessarily alienating potential antislavery supporters who held conventional moral, religious, and political beliefs. They worried that their message would never be accepted by the majority of Americans because of its association with Garrisonian anarchism. Finally and most importantly, conservative abolitionists genuinely believed that effective action required united and concerted pressure on and within the political system. They believed that they were on the verge of organizing an antislavery constituency that could affect American politics in a meaningful way. They insisted therefore that the society be limited only to abolitionists who accepted the moral duty to vote for antislavery political candidates. The future of the abolitionist movement lay with politics, and the time had come, they argued, for direct political action, for an explicitly antislavery political party to challenge the Whigs and Democrats.

The Garrisonians responded by denouncing the political abolitionists on four counts. First, they argued that political action was at best premature because the American political system was gerry-rigged to support slavery. Second, they continued to argue that successful antislavery politics could only be an effect of a national moral revolution. Third, they warned that without this moral revolution, antislavery politicians would be forced to compromise their moral principles in order to gain votes and win elections, thereby watering down and betraying their ultimate goal of emancipation. Fourth, without moral regeneration, any future political emancipation would be meaningless if race prejudice effectively segregated and disenfranchised the newly freed slaves. Abolitionism, by definition, would mean substantial numbers of freed blacks migrating to the North. Racist Northerners would not accept the abolition of slavery if they thought that they would now have to live and work with blacks.

After two years of ideological skirmishes, the warring factions of the American Anti-Slavery Society met in New York City in 1840 for their annual meeting and for their final showdown. In short, the Garrisonians defeated the conservatives' proposal to restrict Society membership to those who publicly swore a moral duty to vote for antislavery political candidates. Defeated and bitter, the conservatives left the national organization and formed a new one, the American and Foreign Anti-Slavery Society. More importantly, however, the "politicized" abolitionists who left the American Anti-Slavery Society were now convinced as never before that the antislavery movement must actively engage in politics or become irrelevant. Slavery, they argued, was sustained by the political system and its ultimate destruction could only be achieved through reforming and purifying the political system. Many now directed their greatest energies toward the formation of a new, strictly abolitionist political party that could elevate and broadcast moral suasion from a higher vantage.

The Liberty Party

The creation of the Liberty Party in 1840 was a watershed in the history of abolitionism. The new party nominated James G. Birney as their presidential nominee, and it offered voters a single-plank, "one idea" platform. The party's mission was simple: it supported immediate emancipation while recognizing that the federal government did not have the authority to abolish slavery in the states where it existed. The Liberty Party program to denationalize slavery included, first, directing Congress to eliminate slavery where it had constitutional authority to do so (e.g., in the District of Columbia); second, preventing the interstate slave trade and the extension of slavery into the territories; third, opposing the admission of any new slave states into the union; and finally, electing antislavery candidates to high political office. The great unanswered question, though, was whether the party could maintain its moral purity while pursuing political power and vote-getting.

Measuring the success of the Liberty Party is tricky business. Electorally, it was a failure. In 1840, the Liberty Party received only 7,059 votes, and in 1844 it improved only slightly to 62,000 votes. But the Liberty Party's long-term successes cannot be measured in vote totals. The party had an effect on American politics that far outweighed its electoral numbers. While it is true that Birney's vote count in 1840 and then again in 1844 was small, the Liberty Party did succeed in driving slavery to the forefront of American politics and it also forced the major parties to accommodate antislavery sentiment. Eventually, the Whigs and Democrats smuggled in some of the Liberty platform and eventually each party developed an antislavery wing.

Still, political abolitionists wanted to be more than just a party of moral conscience. Gradually, a shift began to occur in abolitionist political strategy during the mid-1840s—a shift predicted by the Garrisonians. The heady doctrines of moral regeneration and immediate emancipation were being quietly supplanted by a new strategy that sought to advance the party's political fortunes by appealing to the broadest antislavery common denominator—that is, by de-emphasizing the plight of the slave and emphasizing the invidious designs of the Slave Power to expand slavery into the territories and to deny white Northerners their civil liberties. In other words, political success at the polls, they thought, required either an expanded platform or doctrinal compromise. Furthermore, by 1848, the context in which the Liberty Party would develop its strategy and tactics changed dramatically. The annexation of Texas, the war with Mexico in 1846–47, and the furor over the "Wilmot Proviso" reignited for the first time since the Missouri Compromise the explosive question of the status of slavery in the newly acquired territories. From approximately 1844 to the outbreak of the Civil War, the defining political question of the era was this: Would the vast Western territories be reserved for slaveholders or for free labor settlers?

Ironically, the question of whether slavery should be allowed into the territories worked both for and against the Liberty Party. On the one hand, Liberty Party supporters were able to use this issue to demonstrate that the Slave Power was using the federal government—and therewith the North—to create new slave states out of Western territories, thereby extending and perpetuating their political control over the Union. This played to the strengths of the Liberty Party. Increasingly, though, Liberty Party supporters were willing to downplay their abolitionist principles, to broaden their platform, and to unite with antislavery Whigs and Democrats around a common banner. Thus began the end of the Liberty Party.

In preparation for the presidential election of 1848, the Liberty Party found itself at a crossroads: either it could compromise its abolitionist principles and become a broad-based antislavery party allied with antislavery Whigs and Democrats concerned primarily with the non-extension of slavery into the territories, or it could remain true to its founding principle of immediate emancipation. Those advocating alliance argued that the party had to confront and defeat an immediate threat, which meant compromise. Party purists remained deeply skeptical of any alliance that did not openly advocate the immediate abolition of slavery as its primary goal. What good is the principle of non-extension to existing slaves, they asked? For the most part, non-extension only works for and applies to slaves not yet born.

The party also had to decide whether or not to extend its one-idea platform. The weakness of the Liberty Party at the polls in 1840 and 1844 inspired some Liberty Men to abandon "one ideaism" and their "balance-of-power" strategy for a multi-planked platform on a wide range of issues in order to appeal to a larger Northern audience. The move to nominate a presidential candidate on a platform of universal reform came to a head in 1847, when a break-away faction of Liberty Party men, led by Gerrit Smith and William Goodell, met at a convention held at Macedon Lock, New York. The platform of the newly formed "Liberty League," mirroring the limited-government platform of locofoco democrats, included, in addition to the immediate abolition of slavery, the following planks: the abolition of all legalized monopolies, reducing the size of government, the establishment of free trade, and opening of government lands to free labor.

At this point, students confronting the history of abolitionism for the first time must ask themselves some difficult questions. Did those abolitionists who joined the Free-Soil Party compromise their principles beyond recognition for short-term gain, or was their decision to form a new party the prudent choice in order to achieve their long-range goals? Likewise, were the Liberty Leaguers imprudent and foolish idealists sacrificing immediate political gains, or was their strategy farsighted and the best long-range means for abolishing slavery? Did the merging of the Liberty Party into the Free-Soil movement represent the downfall of political abolitionism for mere nonextension? Was the moral purpose of abolitionism replaced by vote seeking? Was Garrison right all along?

Slavery and the Constitution

In America, all political action is shaped and guided by the Constitution. This fact was particularly true with regard to antislavery strategies for abolishing slavery. It is not surprising, then, that abolitionist political strategy was ultimately guided and shaped by one simple question: Is slavery constitutional or unconstitutional? And around this fundamental question orbited several others that related directly to the question of how slavery should be abolished. Did the Constitution give Congress power to abolish slavery in the states? Does the slaveholder have a legal and constitutional right to the slave? Does an oath to support the Constitution oblige one to work for or against slavery? If the Constitution does support slavery, should it be amended or overthrown? How one answered these questions determined one's response to slavery and therefore one's political tactics.

Not surprisingly, abolitionists divided three ways over the fundamental question. Some, the Garrisonians in particular, argued that the Constitution was proslavery in purpose and effect. They denied that the Constitution gave Congress direct power over slavery. Others, such as William Goodell, Lysander Spooner and Frederick Douglass, believed that the Constitution was antislavery in word, spirit, and intention, which meant of course that the federal government could and should be used to help abolish slavery, even in those states where it existed. Finally, moderate abolitionists and most Free Soilers interpreted the Constitution as guaranteeing slavery where it existed but giving Congress the authority to prevent its extension into the territories (We shall here only discuss the pro and antislavery interpretations).

The Garrisonian argument that the Constitution guaranteed slavery rested on their interpretation of four clauses: Article 1, sec. 2, allowing slave-holding states to count three-fifths of their slaves for purposes of representation in the House of Representatives, gave the Slave Power an unjust political advantage in Congress; Article 1, sec. 9, permitting the slave trade until 1808, encouraged slaveholders to aggressively import slaves for twenty years and left open the possibility that the slave trade might be continued in perpetuity; Article IV, sec. 2, requiring fugitive slaves to be returned to their owner, made the "whole union a vast hunting ground for slaves!"; and Article 1, sec. 8, supposedly authorizing Congress to call forth the militia for purposes of suppressing slave rebellions, sanctioned the coercive power of the national government to be used against any slave who fought for his freedom. In support of his interpretation of the Constitution as proslavery, William Bowditch cited evidence of the framers' intent, of the practice of the federal government for sixty years, and the decisions of the Supreme Court as confirming the constitutionality of slavery. And it was on this basis, according to Bowditch, that "radical abolitionists refuse to vote or take office under it."

Men like Frederick Douglass who argued that the Constitution was antislavery in word and deed met the Garrisonian argument toe-to-toe on its own ground. In response to the Garrisonian claim that Article 1, sec. 2. gives the slave states added representation, Douglass argued that it actually gives free blacks in the North two-fifths more representation than those enslaved in the South thereby depriving the slave states of their natural basis of representation. In response to the claim that Article 1, sec. 9. sanctioned slavery by permitting the African slave trade, Douglass argued that it conclusively demonstrates just the opposite, that the Constitution regarded slavery as an evil to be abolished as soon as possible. In response to the claim that Article 1, sec. 8. enlists the federal government in putting down slave insurrections, Douglass argued that an antislavery national government might do just the opposite, that it might determine slavery to be the cause of insurrectionary behavior and therefore determine to excise the cause rather than the effect. Finally, in response to the claim that Article 4, sec. 2. pressed the federal government to support the return of fugitive slaves, Douglass replied that it does no such thing, that the clause refers not to fugitive slaves but to indentured servants. The very purpose of law is to protect freedom and ensure justice, which means that constitutions and laws should be interpreted in light of their ultimate purposes.

Interpreting the Constitution benevolently—that is, interpreting it to have innocent rather than wicked purposes—removed the taint of its being proslavery. The more difficult intellectual task, however, was to demonstrate that it was profreedom, that it actually gave Congress the power to abolish slavery. Douglass argued that the animating spirit of the Constitution's Preamble, its promise of habeas corpus and republican government, and, most importantly, the Fifth Amendment's insistence that no person "be derived of life, liberty, or property, without due process of law" made the Constitution profreedom. "If the South has made the Constitution bend to the purposes of slavery," said Douglass, "let the North now make that instrument bend to the cause of freedom and justice." The time had come for the free men of the North, "who have the power in their hands, and who can make the American Government just what they think fit," Douglass argued, "resolve to blot out for ever the foul and haggard crime, which is the blight and mildew, the curse and the disgrace of the whole United States."

Free-Soil and Fugitive Slaves

In August 1848, Free-Soil coalitionists from all three parties called a convention to meet in Buffalo, New York, in order to forge a new party and to nominate men that could actually win the election. Those Liberty Party men who had not gone with the Liberty Leaguers—men such as Joshua Leavitt and Frederick Douglass—chose the path of least resistance and maximum compromise to ally themselves with the antislavery wings of the two major parties —i.e., Barnburner Democrats and Conscience Whigs. The coalition created a new party known as the Free-Soil Party, nominated Martin Van Buren as its presidential candidate, and took "Free Soil, Free Speech, Free Labor, and Free Men" as its motto. The party's strategy followed a three-step process: first, they would prevent slavery's extension into new territories; second, they would abolish it wherever constitutionally possible (e.g., the District of Columbia); and finally, they would slowly strangle it to death by eliminating all supports from the federal government. By quarantining slavery, Free Soilers believed that slaveholders would be left with no choice but to emancipate their slaves. Noticeably absent, however, was an open declaration for abolitionism.

By 1850, leaders in the major parties sought to permanently remove slavery from the front burner of American politics and to neutralize the growing Free-Soil Party. The Compromise of 1850—designed by Henry Clay and supported by Daniel Webster—proved the trick. Within a few short years, the Free-Soil Party was gone and the Whigs were imploding. The collapse of an explicitly antislavery third-party did not mean, however, that antislavery politics was dead. In fact, quite the opposite was true. With time, the Compromise would prove a watershed in the development of a Northern antislavery majority. At first, antislavery men and women saw Clay's compromise legislation as a moral abomination and a loss in their battle with the Slave Power. The gains for freedom in the compromise—i.e., the admission of California as a free state, the abolition of the slave trade in the District of Columbia—were outweighed by the egregious concessions to the Slave Power—i.e., organizing the territories of Utah and New Mexico on the basis of popular sovereignty and a stringent fugitive slave law. Here was a prime example, argued abolitionists, of why any compromise between good and evil can only benefit evil.

But the unintended effect of the Compromise was to radicalize and bring more new people into the antislavery cause. Northern imaginations were repulsed at the thought of a panting runaway slave as he fled from his captors and their gnarling dogs. They were also shocked that the new statute denied to *alleged* fugitives the protection of habeus corpus, jury trial, and the right to give evidence. More invidiously, the Fugitive Slave Law imposed on Northerners a legal duty to assist in the capture and return of runaway slaves by giving federal marshals the power to organize local *posses*. Free men would now be coerced into complicity with the Slave Power. For many, the immorality of the Slave Power was now at their doorstep. Within a few years the fault line in American politics shifted away from the party contest between Whigs and Democrats to a sectional divide between the free North and the slave South.

Impending Crisis

In 1854 Stephen A. Douglas introduced a bill in Congress calling for the organization and settlement of the immense Nebraska territory. Douglas's bill applied the doctrine of popular sovereignty to the territories (i.e., allowing the citizens of each territory to vote up or down on whether to allow or ban slavery), thereby repealing the Missouri Compromise ban on the migration of slavery north of 36°30'. The moral and political effect of Douglas's Kansas–Nebraska bill was volcanic. Morally, it had the effect of radicalizing those Northerners who had formerly resisted the call of the antislavery movement, but who now saw clearly the aggressiveness and imperialistic designs of the Slave Power. Northerners who had hitherto remained politically agnostic on the slavery issue began to understand the abolitionist message: that compromise with the Slave Power was not only immoral, but impossible. For many, America was now engaged in a great struggle between freedom and slavery. In the wake of Kansas–Nebraska and the events of 1856, antislavery men reduced the moral issue to one simple question: Would freedom or slavery be nationalized?

The immediate political effect of Douglas's bill was the creation of the Republican Party in 1856, a powerful new coalition of antislavery Whigs, Democrats, and the remnants of the Free-Soil and Liberty parties. In the short run, the Republicans fought to repeal the Kansas–Nebraska Act, but their ultimate goal was to put slavery on the ultimate road to extinction by divorcing the federal government from slavery, prohibiting the extension of slavery and the creation of new slave states, and repealing the Fugitive Slave Law. The party's lowest common denominator was that freedom be made national and slavery sectional. The last act of this great national drama was about to begin.

By 1858, the most nuanced moral and political vision of the Republican Party was being developed by Abraham Lincoln during and after his famous debates with Stephen A. Douglas. It was in Lincoln—and not an abolitionist—that most Northerners found a common voice to enunciate a shared principle. Lincoln had been roused from his political hibernation, he said, by the passage of the Kansas–Nebraska Act and Douglas's application of the policy of "popular sovereignty" to the question of slavery in the territories—that is, the philosophy of not caring whether slavery was "voted down or voted up." Lincoln thought Douglas's "don't care" philosophy, his "declared indifference" to the status of slavery in the territories, morally dangerous because it anesthetized the moral judgment of ordinary Americans. He charged Douglas with being an *agent provocateur* for the Slave Power, with attempting to instill in the minds of Northerners an attitude of moral relativism toward slavery, thus preparing the way for new laws and new court decisions that would nationalize the South's "peculiar institution." From this point forward, Lincoln became increasingly convinced that slavery and a free society were absolutely incompatible. By 1858, he predicted that the Union could not "endure, permanently half *slave* and half *free*. . . . It will become *all* one thing, or *all* the other." Lincoln simultaneously stated a moral principle and predicted the future.

Disunion and Revolution

Meanwhile, during the years of the rise and decline of the Liberty, Free-Soil, and Republican parties, the Garrisonians quietly and patiently continued their moral agitation and warned against the imprudence of political compromise. By the mid-1840s, however, radical abolitionists began to shift their position as well. The most important development in radical abolitionist thought and tactics was Garrison's endorsement of the idea that the free states should secede from the Union. Garrison first advanced the idea of "disunionism" in 1842 and the American Anti-Slavery Society officially proclaimed "No Union

With Slaveholders" in 1844. Based on their reading of the Constitution as proslavery, Garrison and his followers argued that slavery was sanctioned, protected, and sustained by the Federal Government. And given that a constitutional amendment to abolish slavery was a politically hopeless quest, abolition was impossible in the context of the Union. The Constitution was, he therefore concluded in words that shocked the nation, "a covenant with death and an agreement with hell."

The logic of Garrisonian disunionism served several principled and strategic purposes. First, Garrison genuinely believed that antislavery politics was doomed to failure. The system was gerry-rigged to support the Slave Power, which meant that antislavery forces would always be required to compromise. Second, given that slavery was empowered by the Union, the death of slavery could only be achieved by destroying its life-giving source. Remove the sanction and support, Garrisonians argued, and the South's "peculiar institution" would collapse of its own weight. Finally, disunionism shocked public opinion, publicized the abolitionist cause, and brought to new people the message of moral suasion. On July 4, 1854, Garrison, in one the most sensational acts in the history of abolitionism, publicly burned a copy of the American Constitution. Garrison's ritual was less a statement of political action than it was an act of performance art, the purpose of which was to dramatize the imperial designs of the Slave Power to moderate Northerners.

By the mid-1850s the Garrisonian policy of peaceful moral conversion began to give way to a new doctrine that flirted with resistance and violence as the only means by which to confront proslavery violence and to eradicate unjust laws. The crucial events that spurred an advancing militancy among white abolitionists were the Fugitive Slave Law of 1850, proslavery guerilla warfare against Free-Soil settlers in Kansas, and the beating of Charles Sumner of the floor of the Senate in 1856. These were ominous signs for abolitionists. Militant abolitionists increasingly advocated new tactics to meet a radically altered political landscape.

For a small but influential group of abolitionists the time had come to meet force with force. Moderate antislavery politicians and radical abolitionists joined together on several occasions during the early 1850s to forcibly resist the federal government's enforcement of the Fugitive Slave Law. Some organized vigilance committees to obstruct slave-catchers. Others worked on the underground railroad. In 1856, even moderate abolitionists were willing to send "Beecher's Bibles" (i.e., rifles) to antislavery settlers in Kansas. By the end of the 1850s, some abolitionists had completely abandoned moral suasion and nonviolence for direct action against the Slave Power. The most famous attempt at revolutionary change was John Brown's ill-fated raid on the Federal Arsenal at Harper's Ferry.

By the late 1850s, abolitionists were pulled in seemingly opposite directions: They could moderate their principles and join the mass political movement led by Abraham Lincoln, or they could radicalize their principles and join John Brown's small band of freedom fighters. In either case, violence and war would be the final result. In a sense, history had now caught up to the abolitionists and was racing past them. Their only path to relevance was to follow Lincoln with their ballots or Brown with their bullets. Very quickly, history decided for them. Brown's cataclysmic failure and Lincoln's stunning success drove most abolitionists to support Lincoln's Union armies.

In the end, however, the differences between radical abolitionists and Lincoln's Republican Party were not as great as some might suggest. Lincoln refused to be publicly identified with the abolitionists, but his message was understood and supported by millions of Northerners only because of the moral integrity and unceasing dedication of abolitionists over the course of the previous thirty years. They prepared the road for Lincoln and he knew it. Just before his assassination in April 1865, Lincoln acknowledged his debt to Garrison and the antislavery movement: "I have been only an instrument. The logic and moral power of Garrison, and the antislavery people of the country and the Army, have done all." Garrison likewise recognized the melding of his life's work with that of Lincoln: "Of one thing I feel sure, either he has become a Garrisonian abolitionist or I have become a Lincoln Emancipationist, for I know that we blend, like kindred drops, into one." And so it was.

I

Slavery and Freedom

1

The Patriarchal Institution, as Described by Members of Its Own Family (1860)

Compiled by Lydia Maria Child

Lydia Maria Child (1802–1880) was already a successful novelist when she enlisted as one of William Lloyd Garrison's first recruits in the abolitionist movement. Her best known abolitionist writing, An Appeal in Favor of that Class of Americans Called Africans *(1833), was widely read and converted many people to the abolitionist movement. In the early 1840s, she was the editor of the official newspaper of the American Anti-Slavery Society, the* National Anti-Slavery Standard. *She published several other abolitionist tracts, including* Anti-Slavery Catechism *(1839),* The Right Way, the Safe Way, Proved by Emancipation in the British West Indies, and Elsewhere *(1860), and* Correspondence between Lydia Maria Child and Gov. Wise and Mrs. Mason of Virginia *(1860).*

In the selection that follows, The Patriarchal Institution, *Child compiles first-hand accounts of slavery by its defenders and witnesses. The pamphlet is a stinging indictment of the hypocrisy, immorality, and cruelty of slavery. In her concluding remarks, Child reminds her readers that proslavery advocates have imperialistic designs to nationalize slavery.*

Southern Prophecies

"Can the liberties of a nation be thought *secure*, when we have removed their *only firm basis*, a conviction in the minds of the people that these *liberties are the gift of God*?"—Thomas Jefferson

"That the dangerous consequences of this system of bondage have not as *yet* been felt, does not prove that they never *will* be. To me, nothing, for which I have not the evidence of my senses, is more clear than that *it will one day destroy that reverence for liberty, which is the vital principle of a Republic*."—William Pinkney, of Maryland, in 1789

"Is it not amazing, that at a time when the rights of humanity are defined with precision, in a country above all others fond of liberty, that in such an age, and in such a country, we find men, professing a religion the most humane and gentle, adopting a principle as repugnant to humanity, as it is inconsistent with the Bible, and *destructive to liberty*? I could say many things on this subject, a serious view of which *gives a gloomy prospect for future times*."—Letter of Patrick Henry, of Virginia

"Slavery is inconsistent with the genius of republicanism, and has a tendency to *destroy those principles on which it is supported; as it lessens the sense of the equal rights of mankind, and habituates us to tyranny and oppression*."—Luther Martin, of Maryland, in 1787

"It is a fact too well known, at least by the poor, to admit of successful controversy, that the man who will oppress and abuse his own slaves, will also, when an opportunity is afforded, oppress his indigent neighbor, or any one else, over whom he may have gained an advantage. *This principle strikes at the root of our Republican institutions, and if suffered to become sufficiently strong, it will overturn even our liberty itself.*"—Address of William Swaim, Guildford Co., N.C., 1830

Southern Fulfilment of the Preceding Prophecies

"Many in the South *once* believed that slavery was a moral and political evil; but *that folly and delusion are gone*. We now see it in its true light, and regard it as *the most safe and stable basis for free institutions*."—Hon. John C. Calhoun, of S.C., U.S. Senate, 1838

"The substance of the wild and extravagant notions which many seem to entertain respecting liberty is contained in that *rhetorical flourish* of Mr. Jefferson, in which he says: 'We hold these truths to be self-evident; that all men are created equal; that they are endowed by their Creator with certain unalienable rights; that among these are life, liberty, and the pursuit of happiness.' Upon this proposition, *false as it is*, rests the *wild theories of liberty* held by so many. We are told that men are not only born equal, but free. The very reverse of this is true."—*The Southern Christian Herald*, Columbia, S.C.

"In all social systems, there must be a class to do the menial duties, to perform the drudgery of life; a class requiring but a low order of intellect, and little skill. It constitutes the *mud-sill* of society and of political government.* * * *Your whole class of manual hireling laborers at the North, and your 'opera-*

tives,' as you call them, are essentially slaves."—Mr. Hammond, of South Carolina, Speech in Congress

"Domestic slavery is the only institution I know of which can secure the spirit of equality among freemen, so necessary to the true and genuine feeling of republicanism, without propelling the body politic into the dangerous vices of agrarianism, and *legislative intermeddling between the laborer and the capitalist*."—George McDuffie, Governor of South Carolina, 1835

"Slavery is the corner-stone of our Republican edifice. * * * It supersedes the *necessity* of an order of nobility."—Gov. McDuffie

"I endorse, without reserve, that much-abused sentiment of Gov. McDuffie, that 'Slavery is the corner-stone of our Republican edifice'; while I repudiate, as ridiculously absurd, that much-lauded, but nowhere accredited, dogma of Mr. Jefferson, that 'all men are born equal.'"—Gov. Hammond, of South Carolina

"The Declaration of Independence is exuberantly false and arborescently fallacious. Life and liberty are *not* unalienable. Men are *not* born entitled to equal rights. It would be far nearer the truth to say, that some are born with saddles on their backs, and others booted and spurred to ride them; and the riding does them good; they *need* the reins, the bit, and the spur."—George Fitzhugh, of Virginia

"Two hundred years of liberty have made *white laborers a pauper banditti*. Free society is a failure. We slaveholders say you must recur to domestic slavery, the oldest, the best, and the most common form of socialism."

"Free society is a monstrous abortion, and slavery is the healthy, beautiful, and natural state of being."—"Sociology for the South; or the Failure of Free Society"; published at Richmond, Virginia, 1854, by George Fitzhugh

"Make the laboring man the slave of one man, instead of the slave of society, and he would be far better off." "Slavery, *black or white*, is right and necessary." "*Nature has made the weak in mind or body for slaves.*"—"Sociology for the South," by George Fitzhugh, of Virginia

"The great evil of Northern Society is, that it is burdened with a servile class of mechanics and laborers, unfit for self-government, and yet clothed with the attributes and powers of citizens. Master and slave is a relation in society as necessary as that of parent and child, and the Northern States will yet have to introduce it. The theory of free government is a delusion. Slavery is the natural and normal condition of the laboring man, white or black."—A Democratic paper in South Carolina, 1856

"Free society! We sicken of the name. What is it but a conglomeration of greasy mechanics, filthy operatives, small-fisted farmers, and moon-struck theorists? All the Northern States, and especially the New England States, are devoid of society fitted for well-bred gentlemen. The prevailing class one meets with is that of mechanics struggling to be genteel, and small farmers, who do their own drudgery; and yet who are hardly fit for association with a gentleman's body servant. That is your free society!"—*The Muscogee Herald*, a Democratic paper in Alabama

"Free society has failed; and that which is *not* free must be substituted." —Senator Mason, of Virginia

"We have got to hating every thing with the prefix *free*; from free negroes, down and up, through the whole catalogue. Free farms, free labor, free society, free will, free thinking, free children, and free schools, all belong to the same brood of damnable *isms*. But *the worst of all these abominations* is the modern system of *free schools*. The New England system of free schools has been the cause and prolific source of the infidelities and treasons that have turned her cities into Sodoms and Gomorrahs, and her land into the common nestling-places of howling bedlamites. We abominate the system, *because the schools are free*."—*Richmond Examiner*, Virginia, 1856

"The Northern States, in dispensing with slavery, have destroyed order, and removed the strongest argument to prove the existence of Deity, the author of that order."—*Richmond Enquirer*, 1855

Southern Statements of the Happiness of Slaves

"Our slaves are well compensated. There is no starvation, no begging, no want of employment, and not too much employment either." "The status in which we have placed them is an elevation. They are happy, contented, and unaspiring."—Mr. Hammond, of South Carolina, in Congress

"It is now almost universally believed, in the South, that slavery is ennobling to both races, white and black."—Mr. Mason, of Virginia, in U.S. Senate [He subsequently stated that *elevating* would have been a more appropriate word than *ennobling*.]

"Civilization and Christianity have spread over slavery their humanizing influence."—*Charleston Courier*, South Carolina

"The slave population of the South are peculiarly susceptible to religious influences. Their mere residence among Christian people has wrought a great and happy change in their condition. They have been raised from the night of heathenism to the light of Christianity."—Judge Baker, of Virginia

"Under this relation of master and slave, the two races have long lived in peace and prosperity."—Hon. J.C. Calhoun, of South Carolina, U.S. Senate, 1836

"Among no people in the world are the *affections of the heart* more *cherished* and more *gratified*, than among the *slaves* at the South."—Mr. Preston, of South Carolina

"Domestic slavery contributes to form and preserves the chivalrous and high-minded character of our people, and gives to the African race, domesticated among us, Christianity, civilization, and peace."—*Charleston Courier*, South Carolina

"Slavery is with us a parental relation."—Ditto

"The tender care and protection of the master elicit an affectionate attachment from the slave, which will be looked for in vain from the hired servant of a more Northern clime."—Ditto

"The slaves are governed far better than the free laborers of the North. Our slaves are not only better off as to physical comfort than free laborers, but their moral condition is better."—*Richmond Enquirer*, Virginia

"Contrasting the condition of *white slaves* in New England with our slaves in the South, is like comparing Egyptian bondage with millennial glory. Mild slavery at the South is heaven on earth, compared to the tyranny of the spindle at the North."—Rev. J.C. Postell, of South Carolina

Southern Proofs That Slaves Are "Happy and Contented"

"In case any person shall wilfully cut out the tongue, put out the eye, cruelly scald, burn, or deprive any slave of any limb, or member, or shall inflict any other cruel punishment, *otherwise than by whipping, or beating, with a horsewhip, cowskin, switch, or small stick, or by putting on irons, or confining, or imprisoning such slave*, every such person, for every such offence shall forfeit one hundred pounds, current money."—Law of South Carolina

"Vicinity to non-slaveholding States must for ever render this sort of property *precarious and insecure*."—Judge Upshur, of Virginia, in Convention, 1829

Hon. Bushrod Washington, nephew of Gen. Washington, and Supreme Judge of the United States, sold fifty-four slaves, to be carried to Louisiana, in 1831. In a letter published in the *Baltimore Telegraph*, Sept. 18, 1831, he says: "I had good reason to anticipate the *escape to the Northern States of all the laboring men of any value*, as soon as I should leave home."

"For the past month, the journals from different Southern States have been filled with numberless alarms respecting contemplated risings of the negro population. In Tennessee, Missouri, Virginia, and Alabama, the danger has been deemed so imminent, that the most severe measures have been adopted to prevent their congregating, or visiting, after night; to suppress their customary attendance at neighborhood preachings; and to keep a vigilant watch upon all their movements, by an efficient patrolling system. This is, assuredly, a most lamentable condition for the slave States; for *nothing causes such terror upon the plantations as the bare suspicion of these insurrections*."—*Missouri Democrat*, Dec. 4, 1856

"$100 Reward for my negro Glasgow, and Kate, his wife. Glasgow is twenty-four years old; has *marks of the whip on his back*. Kate is twenty-six years old; has a *scar* on her cheek, and *several marks of the whip*." —L.E. Cooner. From the *Macon Messenger*, South Carolina, May 25, 1837

"Ranaway, my negro man Frederic, about twenty years of age. He is no doubt near the plantation of G.W. Corprew, Esq., of Noxubee Co., Mississippi, as *his wife belongs to that gentleman, and he followed her from my residence*."— Kerkman Lewis. From the *Southern Argus*, Ala., Oct. 31, 1837

"If any person, or persons, shall cut or break any *iron collar*, which any master of slaves shall have used, in order to prevent the running away, or escape, of any such slave or slaves, such person or persons, so offending, shall, on conviction, be fined not less than $200, nor more than $1000, and suffer imprisonment for a term not exceeding two years, nor less than six months."—Louisiana Act of Assembly, 1819

"$25 Reward. Absconded from the subscriber, a negro man named Ned. He is *branded on the forehead* with the letters A.M., and on each cheek with the letters J.G."—Anthony M. Minter. From the *Free Press*, Ala., Sept. 18, 1846

"Negro Dogs. The undersigned having an excellent pack of hounds for trailing and catching runaway slaves, informs the public that his prices will be," &c. P. Black—From the *Dadeville Banner*, Ala., Nov. 10, 1852

"*Any* person may *lawfully* kill a slave who has been *outlawed* for running away, lurking in swamps," &c.—Haywood's Manual of the Laws of North Carolina

"Ranaway, my negro man Richard. A reward of $25 will be paid for his apprehension, *dead or alive*. Satisfactory proof will only be required of his having been *killed*. He has with him, in all probability, *his wife*, Eliza, who ran away from Col. Thompson, now a *resident in Alabama*."—Durant H. Rhodes. From the *Wilmington Advertiser*, July 13, 1838

"Ranaway, my man Fountain. He has *holes in his ears, a scar on his forehead, has been shot in the hind part of his legs, and is marked on the back by the whip*."—Robert Beasly. From the *Georgia Messenger*, July 27, 1837

"Dealing in slaves has become a large business. Establishments are made at several places in Maryland and Virginia, at which they are sold like cattle. These places are strongly built, and well supplied with *thumbscrews, gags, cowskins, and other whips, oftentimes bloody*. But the *laws* permit the traffic, and it is suffered."—*Niles's Register*, published in Baltimore, vol. 35, p. 4

"In the ordinary course of the business of the country, the punishment of relations frequently happens on the same farm, and in view of each other. The father often sees his beloved son, the son sees his venerable sire, the mother sees her much loved daughter, the daughter sees her affectionate parent, the husband sees the wife of his bosom, and she sees the husband of her affection, cruelly bound up, *without delicacy or mercy, and punished with all the extremity of incensed rage, and all the rigor of unrelenting severity*, while they dare not interpose in each other's behalf. All is silent horror."—From the *Maryland Journal and Baltimore Advertiser*, May 30, 1788

"There are now in our land two millions of human beings exposed, *defenceless*, to every insult and every injury, short of maiming or death, which their fellow-men may choose to inflict. They suffer all that can be inflicted by wanton caprice, grasping avarice, brutal lust, malignant spite, and insane anger. Their happiness is the sport of every whim, and the prey of every passion, that may occasionally, or habitually, infest the master's bosom. If we could calculate the amount of woe endured by ill-treated slaves, it would overwhelm every compassionate heart, and move even the obdurate to sympathy. Brothers and sisters, parents and children, husbands and wives, are torn asunder, and permitted to see each other no more. These acts are *daily occurring* in the midst of us. The shrieks and the agony often proclaim, with trumpet tongue, the iniquity and cruelty of our system."—Address of the Presbyterian Synod of Kentucky, 1836

"In the slave system, the laborer himself is property. The man himself is a negotiable chattel. His *soul* is ignored. He is a brute. He can be sheared like a sheep, branded like a mule, yoked like an ox, hobbled like a horse, marked like a hog, and maimed like a cur; he can be butchered like a beef, skinned like a buck, or scalded like a shear; he can be hurled into a fish-pond, to fatten and flavor lampreys, or smeared with tar and set on fire to light ungodly dances."—Report of the Southern Commercial Convention, at Vicksburg, Mississippi, May 10, 1859

"It is *slavery itself*, and not *cruelties* merely, that makes slaves unhappy. Even those that are the most kindly treated are generally far from happy. The slaves in my father's family are almost as kindly treated as slaves can be; but they pant for liberty."—William T. Allen, son of a Presbyterian clergyman in Huntsville, Ala., 1839

Southern Proofs of the "Chivalrous and High-Minded Character" Produced by Slavery

"A slave shall be deemed a chattel personal, in the hands of the owner, *to all intents, constructions and purposes whatsoever*."—Stroud's Laws of the Slave States

"I have lately *purchased four women and ten children*, in whom I thought I had a great bargain; for I supposed they were my own *property*, as were my *brood-mares*."—Mr. Gholson, of Virginia, in the Legislature, 1832

"For sale, *a girl about twenty years of age, raised in Virginia*; remarkably strong and healthy; with her two *female children, one four years old, the other two years*; fine, healthy children. *She is very prolific in her generating qualities*, and affords a rare opportunity to any person who wishes *to raise a family of strong and healthy servants."* —From the *Charleston Mercury*, South Carolina, May 16, 1839

"Raffle. The celebrated dark bay horse, Star, age five years, square trotter, and warranted sound; with a new, light trotting-buggy and harness; also, the stout mulatto girl, Sarah, age about twenty; general house-servant; valued at $900; will be raffled for, at any hotel selected by the subscribers."—Joseph Jennings. From the *True Delta*, New Orleans, Jan. 11, 1853

"The subscriber has just arrived *from Petersburg, Virginia*, with 120 likely *young* negroes; among them, several *women with children; small girls*, suitable for nurses; and *small boys without their mothers*."—Benjamin Davis, Hamburg, S.C., Sept. 28, 1838. A standing advertisement in the Charleston papers

"A negro woman, belonging to George M. Garrison, of Polk Co., killed four of her children, by cutting their throats while they were asleep. Her master knows of no cause for the horrid act, unless it be that she heard him speaking of *selling her and two of her children, and keeping the others*."—This paragraph went the rounds of the Southern papers in 1853

"$20 Reward. Ranaway from the subscriber, a negro *woman and two children*. A few days before she went off, *I burnt her with a hot iron* on the left side of her face; I tried to make the letter M. Her children are both boys; the oldest in his 7th year; he is a *mulatto*, and has *blue eyes*. The youngest is black, and is in his 5th year."—Micajah Ricks, Nash Co. From the *North Carolina Standard*, July 18, 1838

"$50 Reward. Ranaway, a negro girl, *named Caroline, eighteen years of age; far advanced in child-bearing*. The above reward will be paid for her delivery at either of the jails of the city."—J.H. Leverick & Co. From the *New Orleans Bulletin*, Jan. 22, 1839

Sale of Women. "Girl is sound, I suppose?" carelessly inquired a purchaser. "Wind and limb," responded the trader; "but strip her naked and examine every inch of her, if you wish; I never have any disguises with my customers."—Conversation in Mr. Corbin Thompson's negro yard, at St. Louis, Missouri, June, 1856

"A negro woman, *twenty-four years old*, with her two *children, one eight years old, the other three years*; said negroes will be sold together, or *sepa-*

rately, as desired. The woman is a good seamstress. She will be sold low for cash, or *exchanged for groceries*."—Mayhew Bliss & Co. From the *New Orleans Bulletin*, June 2, 1838

"Will be sold before the Court House door, in the town of Irwinton, one negro *girl, about two years old*, named Rachel, belonging to the estate of William Chambers, deceased. Sold for the benefit of the heirs and creditors of said estate."—Samuel Bell and Jesse Peacock, Executors. From the *Milledgeville Journal*, Geo., Dec. 26, 1837

"To be sold, one negro girl, *eighteen months old*, belonging to the estate of William Chambers, deceased. Sold for the purpose of *distribution*."—Jethro Dean and Samuel Beall, Executors. From the *Georgia Journal*, Nov. 7, 1837

"Mr. Hedding, of Chatham County, held a slave woman. In order to prevent her running away, *a child about seven years of age was connected with her by a long chain fastened to her neck*. In this situation, she was compelled, all the day, to grub up the roots of herbs and saplings, to prepare ground for the plough. I travelled past Heddings' as often as once in two weeks, in the winter of 1828, and I always saw her."—Hiram White, of Chatham Co., North Carolina, now in Illinois

"My uncle used to tie his 'house wench' to a peach tree in the yard, and whip her till there was no sound place to lay another stroke; and he repeated it so often, that her back was continually sore. *Whipping females round the legs was a favorite mode of punishment* with him. They must stand and hold up their clothes, while he plied his hickory."—William Leftwich, of Virginia, now in Ohio

"A handsome mulatto woman, eighteen or twenty years of age, whose independent spirit could not brook the degradation of slavery, was in the habit of running away. For this offence, she had been repeatedly sent by her master and mistress to be whipped by the keeper of the Charleston Work House. *This had been done with such inhuman severity as to lacerate her back in the most shocking manner. A finger could not be laid between the cuts*. But the love of liberty was too strong to be annihilated by torture. As a last resort, she was whipped at several different times, and kept a close prisoner. *A heavy iron collar, with three long prongs projecting from it, was placed round her neck, and a sound front tooth was extracted*, to serve as a mark to describe her, in case of escape. Her sufferings were agonizing. She could lie in no position but on her back, which was sore from scourgings, as I can testify from personal inspection; and her only place of rest was the floor, on a blanket. These outrages were committed in a family where the mistress daily read the Scriptures, and assembled the family for worship. She was a charitable woman, tenderhearted to the poor, so far as alms-giving was concerned. Yet this suffering slave, who was the seamstress of the family, was sitting in her chamber, with her bleeding back, her mutilated mouth, and her heavy iron collar, without, so far as appeared, exciting any feelings of compassion."—Sarah M. Grimke, daughter of Judge Grimke, of South Carolina

Southern Proofs That Slavery Is a "Parental Relation"

"The child shall follow the condition of the mother."—Laws of the Slave States

"Ranaway, a *light mulatto* woman; has long, black, *straight hair*, and usually keeps it in good order. She generally dresses neatly, is *very intelligent*, converses well, and can read print."—U. McAllister. From the *Southern Standard*, Mississippi, Oct. 16, 1852

"$100 reward will be given for my *negro*, Edmund Kenny. He has *straight hair, and a complexion so nearly white that it is believed a stranger would suppose there was no African blood in him.* A short time since, he was in Norfolk with my boy Dick, and *offered him for sale*. He was apprehended, but *escaped under pretence of being a white man*."—Anderson Bowles. From the *Richmond Whig*, Va., Jan. 6, 1836

"Runaway from me, a negro woman, named Fanny. *She is as white as most white women; with straight light hair, and blue eyes, and can pass herself for a white woman.* She is *very intelligent*; can read and write, and so forge passes for herself. She is *very pious*, prays a great deal, and was, as supposed, *contented and happy*. I will give $500 for her delivery to me."—John Balch, Tuscaloosa, Alabama, May 29, 1845

"On my way from Washington to Richmond, not long Since, I found in the cars a negro trader, with half a dozen sons and daughters of the descendants of Ham, whom he had purchased in Maryland, and was on his way with them to the New Orleans market. I was particularly struck by the beauty of *a white girl, about seventeen years old, with white, rosy, transparent complexion, finely chiselled features, and auburn tresses.* I concluded she must be the young and handsome daughter of the trader; but he told me he had paid $1200 for her up in Maryland, to a man *whose wife had become jealous of her*. This story fully explained the mystery of the gold rings that hung from her ears and encircled her fingers."—Correspondent of the *Wheeling Intelligencer*, Va., Jan., 1860

14 SLAVERY AND FREEDOM

"A steamer, on her way from this place to Natchez, had, on her last trip, forty-seven slaves on board. Our informant states that among these was a beautiful young girl of thirteen, who, he learned with astonishment and pity, was a slave; hopelessly in slavery as the blackest of her companions, all of whom were in charge of traders, on their way to New Orleans. *The girl was nearly white, with straight hair, blooming complexion, attractive shape, and gentle bearing.* She is the daughter of a merchant on the Missouri river, whose well-known intention was to emancipate her. But he died, and his executors, or heirs, thought it would not do any longer to bring her up together with the merchant's other daughter, her white sister; therefore she has been sold away into the South."—*St. Louis Democrat,* Mo., Feb., 1860

"We had, not long since, a striking illustration of the Patriarchal Institution of Slavery. A Mississippi gentleman came to this State to supply his plantation, and made his head-quarters in this city. Among the two or three dozen he bought was a little girl, about nine years old, *whose complexion was as fair as the average of white children.* She attracted some attention, and the purchaser related her history. She was the child of a handsome mulatto woman, and her father was the Hon. Mr.—*Member of Congress from this State. Her mother was not the slave of Mr.—, but was owned by a neighbor. I believe it is a custom among the Patriarchs to make an interchange of civilities of this kind. A strange coincidence happened in bringing her to this city. She came with her master down the river in a steamboat, and among the passengers was her father. He conversed with her owner about her, and said *he would have bought her himself, were it not for his wife.* I had this information from the owner of the girl. She was kept in a slave-pen on Sixth street, and was visited by numbers, who learned her history. Here was a child of *tender age, apparently white*, driven off with a gang of slaves to a distant land, never again to know a mother's love, but to be thenceforth the victim of a tyrant's lash or lust, while her father, in the august Senate of the United States, declaims of Liberty!"—Correspondent of the *N.Y. Tribune,* St. Louis, Missouri, Oct. 31st, 1859. [Note: * Our correspondent, who is a most reliable man, gives the name in full, which will be imparted to any one entitled to ask for it."—Editor *Tribune.*]

Southern Proofs That "The Moral Condition of Slaves Is Better Than That of Northern Laborers"

Laws of Virginia. Section 31. "Every assemblage of negroes for the purpose of *religious worship*, when such worship is conducted by a negro, and every assemblage of negroes for the purpose of *instruction in reading or writing,* shall be an *unlawful assembly*. Any Justice may issue his warrant to any officer, or other person, to enter any such assemblage and seize any negro therein; and he or any other Justice may order such negro to be *punished with stripes*."

Section 32. "If a white person assemble with negroes for the purpose of *instructing them to read or write*, or if he associate with them, in an *unlawful assembly*, he shall be confined in jail not exceeding six months, and fined not exceeding one hundred dollars."

"Mrs. Margaret Douglass, formerly of Charleston, S.C., was arraigned one day last week and tried before Judge Baker, at Norfolk city, on a charge of teaching negro children to read and write, contrary to the statute made and provided, and against the *peace* and *dignity* of the Commonwealth."—From the *Petersburg Express*, Va., Nov. 30, 1853

Mrs. Douglass, from motives of benevolence, instructed, at her own house, a few *free* colored children, who greatly desired to learn to read and write. For that offence "against the *peace* and *dignity* of the Commonwealth," she was imprisoned a month in Norfolk jail; the term prescribed by law being shortened, in consideration of her being a woman. . . .

No places of worship are built for negroes. By sufferance of indulgent masters, when no peculiar cause for alarm exists in the community, religious slaves meet at each other's cabins to sing and pray; or they listen to the rude eloquence of some brother slave, preaching from a stump in the fields. In pious white families, there is sometimes a chaplain employed, part of whose duty it is to give *oral* instruction to the slaves on the plantation; to teach them to *read* would be offensive to the community. House servants are not unfrequently allowed a place in the same church where their masters attend. How carefully the instruction they receive is adapted to their peculiar circumstances, is shown by the following extracts from the published Sermons of Bishop Meade, an Episcopal clergyman in Virginia: "You are to be obedient and subject to your masters in *all* things. * * When correction is given you, whether you deserve it or not, it is your duty, and God Almighty requires, that you bear it patiently. * * Your masters and mistresses are God's *overseers*. If you are faulty toward them, God himself will punish you severely for it in the next world, unless you repent of it, and strive to make amends by your faithfulness and diligence for the time to come. * * Almighty God hath been pleased to make you slaves here, and to give you *nothing but labor and poverty* in this world, which you are obliged to submit to, as it is *His* will that it should be so. Your bodies, you know, are not your own; they are at the disposal of those you belong to. But your precious souls are still your own, which nothing can take from you, if it be not your own fault. Think within yourselves what a terrible thing it would be, after all your *labors and sufferings* in this life, to be turned into hell in the next life, and after wearing out your bodies in service here, to go into a far *worse slavery* when this is over, and your poor souls be delivered over into the possession of the Devil, to become *his slaves* for ever in hell, without any hope of ever getting free from it!"—Rev. C.C. Jones, of Savannah, Ga.

"In our State, many Christians no more think of instructing their *slaves*, than they do their *horses*. This may seem a strong expression, and it is; but it just contains the simple truth, and nothing more."—From the *St. Louis Observer*, Missouri, May 7, 1835

"Seeing his master wholly engrossed by his own advantage, the slave naturally pursues the same selfish course, and, when not restrained by higher principle, becomes deceitful and thievish. The master takes no pains to conceal that he takes it for granted the negro will steal and lie; and when the slave is tempted to do either, he feels that he has no character to lose."—Thomas Clay's Address before the Presbytery of Georgia

"Thousands of fellow-creatures within our State are destitute of every real protection afforded them by law, either in their persons or property; *without any law to guard their marriage rights, and without the law's having any knowledge of marriage among them.* Such is the fact with regard to the whole slave-population among us."—Oration by Amos Weaver, of North Carolina, 1829

"Negro marriages are neither recognized by law nor protected by law. The negroes receive no instruction on the nature, sacredness, or perpetuity of the system."—Rev. C.C. Jones, of Savannah, Ga.

"How important for Southern Sultans that the objects of their criminal passions should be kept in utter ignorance and degradation! They must not read the Bible, because that teaches them the sin of their masters. They must not learn to read and write, for every mental and moral improvement tends to bring out and improve those feelings and emotions that already repel this gross system of sensuality and licentiousness. Is it to be supposed that the ordinary teachings of nature do not tell the sable sons and daughters of the South that this custom is inhuman and ungodly? Will not the natural impulses rebel against what becomes with them a matter of force? For the female slave knows she *must* submit to the caprices of her master; that there is no way of escape. And when a man, black though he be, knows that he may be compelled, at any moment, to hand over his wife, his sister, or his daughter, to the loathed embraces of the man whose chains he wears, how can it be expected he will submit without feelings of hatred and revenge taking possession of his heart?"—Mrs. Margaret Douglass, of South Carolina

Southern Proofs That "The Physical Condition of Slaves Is Better Than That of Northern Laborers"

Laws. "All that a slave possesses belongs to his master. He possesses nothing of his own, except the sum of money, or the moveable estate, which *his master chooses he should possess*." "The earnings of slaves, and the price of their service, belong to their owners." The law prescribes a fine for any master who permits a slave to hire himself out for his own benefit; and it is "made the duty of the Sheriff to apprehend such slave." Slaves have no legal right to any bequest or donation. Slaves can make no contract; and no contract with them is binding by law. "The testimony of no colored person, bond or free, is ever received against any white person."—Stroud's Laws of the Slave States

"Benjamin James Harris, a wealthy tobacconist of Richmond, Va., whipped a slave girl, fifteen years old, to death. The verdict of the Coroner's Inquest was, 'Died of excessive whipping.' He was tried in Richmond, and *acquitted*. I attended the trial. Some years after, this same Harris whipped a slave man to death. He was tried, and *again acquitted, because none but blacks saw it done*."—Testimony, in 1839, of William Poe, a native of Virginia

The amount of labor performed by a slave practically depends on the master's will; but there is a law imposing a fine on any master who keeps a slave at work "*more than fifteen hours*" a day in summer, or "*more than fourteen hours*" a day in winter. The law has the following preamble: "Whereas, *many* owners of slaves, and others who have the management and overseeing of slaves, *do confine them so closely to hard labor, that they have not sufficient time for natural rest*," &c.

In North Carolina, the law prescribes "a quart of corn a day" for the food of a field slave. In Louisiana, if a master does not allow his slaves a bit of land to cultivate on their own account, the law requires him to give each of them "*one shirt and pair of pantaloons for* summer, and *one shirt, one pair of woollen pantaloons, and a woollen great coat for winter.*" In most of the States, food and clothing are not regulated by law, but left to the will of the master. Some laws have been passed to guard against an insufficient supply of food and clothing; but there are two obstacles in the way of carrying such laws into effect: *No colored person is allowed to testify*; and if a man is accused by his white neighbors of starving his negroes, the law allows him, in the absence of *evidence*, to exculpate himself on *his own oath.*

"A single peck of corn a week, or the like measure of rice, is the ordinary quantity of provision for a *hard-working slave*; to which a small quantity of meat is occasionally, though *rarely*, added."—*Maryland Journal and Baltimore Advertiser*, May 30, 1788

"The slaves, *naked and starved*, often fall victims to the inclemency of the weather."—Dr. George Buchanan, of Maryland; Oration at Baltimore, 1791

"It is an every-day sight to see women, as well as men, with no *other covering than a few filthy rags fastened above the hips*, reaching midway to the ankles. Children of both sexes, from infancy to ten years, are seen in companies, on the plantations, in a state of perfect nudity. This was so common, that the most refined and delicate beheld them unmoved. * * I know the slaves are overworked. It was customary for the overseer to call out the gangs *long before day*; say three o'clock, in the winter, while dressing out the crops. Such work was provided as could be done by firelight."—W.C. Gildersleeve, a native of Georgia

"From dawn till dark, the slaves are required to bend to their constant toil, wrung out by fear. Their food is scanty, and taken without comfort. The young children, until they can work, often go naked until warm weather. The dwellings of the slaves are log huts, ten or twelve feet square, often without windows, doors, or floors. They have neither chairs, table, nor bedstead. I have lived in Alabama, Tennessee and Kentucky, and I *know* the condition of the slaves to be that of *unmixed wretchedness and degradation*; and on the part of the slaveholders, there is cruelty untold."—Wm. Leftwich, a native of Virginia

"When they return to their miserable huts at night, they find there no means of comfortable rest. They must lie on the cold ground, and shiver while they slumber."—Rev. John Rankin, a native of Tennessee

Southern and Northern Democrats Now Leagued for the Extension of Slavery

"The determination of the South is fixed and unalterable, that they will have an *expansion* of Slave Territory." * * "There is but one mode by which, in my humble judgment, the institution of slavery can be perpetuated for any considerable number of years, That mode is by *expansion*."—Hon. Mr. Singleton, of Mississippi

"Free society has failed, and *that which is not free must be substituted.*"—Senator Mason, of Virginia

"Policy and humanity alike *forbid the extension of the evils of free society to new people and coming generations.*"—*Richmond Enquirer*, Virginia

"*Slavery should pour itself abroad without restraint, and find no limit but the Southern Ocean.*" "*I would introduce it into the very heart of the North.*"—Hon. Henry A. Wise, of Virginia

"We will call the roll of our slaves on Bunker Hill."—Hon. Mr. Toombs, of Georgia

"I want Cuba, I want Tamaulipas, Potosi, and one or two others of the Mexican States; and I want them all for the same reason: *for the planting and spreading of slavery. I would spread the blessing of slavery, like the religion of the Divine Master, to the uttermost ends of the earth.* Rebellious and wicked as the Yankees have been, I would extend it even to them." * * "I would make a refusal to acquire territory, because it was to be slave-territory, a cause for disunion."—Hon. Mr. Brown, of Mississippi

"The Democrats of the South, in the present canvass, cannot rely on the old grounds of defence and excuse for slavery; for they seek not merely to retain it where it is, *but to extend it into regions where it is unknown.* Much less can they rely on the mere Constitutional guarantees of slavery; for such reliance is pregnant with the admission that slavery is wrong, and, *but for the Constitution, should be abolished.* If we stop there, we weaken our cause; for *we propose to introduce into new Territory human beings, whom we assert to be unfit for liberty, self-government, and equal association with other men.* We must go a step further. We must show that African slavery is a moral, religious, natural, and probably, in the general, a necessary institution of society. This is the only line of argument that will enable Southern Democrats to maintain the doctrines of State equality and slavery extension." * * "Northern Democrats need not go thus far. They do not seek to extend slavery, but only to agree to its extension, as a matter of right on our part."—*Richmond Enquirer*, Virginia

"I trust that the day will come when the principles of Democracy, *as understood and practised at the South,* will prevail over the entire country." —Senator Evans, of S.C. . . .

"The Democracy is the same every where—North, South, East and West. It seeks the ascendancy of the same principles, and the success of the same measures, in all sections."—The Washington Union, D.C.

Concluding Remarks

Human nature is essentially the same in all nations and ages; being modified only by the laws that control and regulate it, and the social conditions under which it is developed. Hence laws and social institutions are of immense importance. In *all* countries, there are men who do not scruple to build up their own fortunes at the expense of their neighbors. Anger, lust and avarice are powerful passions, and glaring manifestations of them abound *every where*. But every intelligent and reflecting reader of the preceding pages will readily perceive that countries blest with the institution of slavery have an advantage *peculiar to themselves*. In all such communities, capital is irresponsible *by law*. Encroachments on the laborer cannot be *punished by law*, for the simple reason that the laborer is a chattel, and *having no legal rights*, he can have no wrongs that can be *legally redressed*. It is true that the degree of Patriarchal discipline is regulated by law, when it is administered *in public*; that inconvenience is, however, trifling; for history shows that Judge Lynch rides over all such regulations, whenever he sees fit; and as for discipline in *private*, over that the law assumes no control whatsoever. Slaves cannot testify in court, even if murder is committed in the presence of a dozen of them. This circumstance renders the regulation of labor exceedingly convenient; it being placed entirely in the hands of "unchecked, unregulated, and irresponsible capital."

Communities incommoded by free institutions cannot enjoy these inestimable advantages. The enlightened and chivalrous minority have no such facilities for compelling "greasy mechanics, filthy operatives, and small-fisted farmers," to toil for them without wages. Doubtless, some of them would *like* such facilities extremely well; nor would they object to including within their privileges the possession of their neighbors' wives and daughters, as "brood mares." But, unfortunately, in Free States, the *laws* come in the way of such arrangements; and when such experiments are attempted, both *law* and *public opinion* become troublesome. No wonder that state of society is pronounced a "complete failure," where there are so many impediments in the way of "capital," that seeks to be "unchecked, unregulated, and irresponsible"!

To *laborers*, also, the "Patriarchal Institution" offers many inducements, though they are not so obvious as the advantages to *capitalists*. In the first place, the South sets a high value upon them. The *Greenville Enterprise*, a paper published in South Carolina, lately announced that "George, a likely fellow, said to be a *good joiner and carpenter*, was bought by the Rev. J.P. Boyce for $3,500; and Mr. Boyce was afterward offered $4,000 for him." How satisfied and proud laborers must be in a community that estimates them so highly!

Don't your mouth water for the situation? It is true you would receive no wages for your valuable services; but, to balance that, you would be relieved from all the cares and responsibilities entailed upon property. Your dwellings might not be the most comfortable; but then you would have neither rent nor taxes to pay. If you should happen to have a generous master, you might be dressed as fine as "Dandy Jim"; and if your owner deemed a "few tattered rags about the loins" sufficient, you would at least have the advantage of having no tailor's bills to pay. "A peck of corn a week" half the year, and sweet potatoes the other half, might seem rather monotonous provender; but then you would be almost sure not to die of repletion, or dyspepsia. The frequency and severity of your floggings would depend entirely on the temper and disposition of your master and mistress, or of the overseer they employed; but if you should happen to be killed in the course of customary discipline, it would be a great satisfaction to surviving friends to know that you "died of moderate correction." A chattel has also the advantage of being relieved from all family cares and expenses. He who is allowed to hold no property will not be troubled with bills for crinolines or new-fashioned bonnets. It might be a little unpleasant to see your wife examined on the auction-block; but you would soon conquer prejudices on that point, knowing that the proceeding was according to law. She might happen to be sold into a State far distant from the place where your own lot was cast; but the separation would offer advantages to both. The proverb says, "Variety is the spice of life"; and you could both forthwith form new connections, without the formality or expense of weddings. You would have neither law nor public opinion to trouble you; for you would not be "persons," in the eye of the law, and your characters would belong to your masters. It would be for his *interest* to lend you one of his handmaids, that you might raise up a crop of children, whose market value would be increased by the infusion of Anglo-Saxon blood. This would be peculiarly the case if they were girls; for the virtuous horror of amalgamation is entirely overcome by the consideration that "crossing the breed" often produces specimens of rare beauty. It might at first pain you a little to see your daughters held as property; but if they were good-looking, they might find so much favor in the eyes of the master, that he would bestow upon them gold rings for ears and fingers; symbols of a connection "ennobling to both" parties. If this arrangement should excite the jealousy, of his wife, the worst that could happen would be the having your daughter sold to some trader, making up a herd of "brood mares" for the market; and he would be sure to treat her respectfully and kindly, modesty and tender-heartedness being the inevitable results of his dignified vocation. Your grand-children might be sold by the sheriff, at "eight months old"; but then the blessings of involuntary servitude would be just as safely secured to them, as if they remained with their mothers. As for scruples on any of these subjects, you would soon be effectually taught that the whole of *religious* and moral obligation is comprised in the injunction, "Servants, obey your masters in all things." What a convenience to have all questions of conscience thus simplified to a unity! It might at first trouble you to have your children forbidden to learn to read and write, under penalty of "twenty lashes"; but you know it is a time-honored maxim that "ignorance is bliss"; and in their situation, they would have no use for knowledge. If they knew how to read about free countries, it might excite "dissatisfaction in their minds"; for, to the young and inexperienced, freedom *appears* to be a blessing, though in reality it is not. If they knew how to write, they might be tempted to forge permissions from their masters to go and see their mothers, or sisters; and it is a great inconvenience to have mechanics, laborers, or house-servants, form a taste for travelling about; they might carry it *too far*.

You of course perceive there would be no need of their learning arithmetic; for those who can make no contracts, and hold no property, are released from all necessity of ciphering.

Don't despair because it happens to be your misfortune to be born under free institutions! That can be remedied; if not for yourselves, at least for your children; and measures are actively in train for it. Neither your *complexion* nor your *intelligence* need to be any hindrance. The Power that rules the nation has announced its decision, that the right to hold slaves "does not depend on difference of complexion"; and advertisements show that "very intelligent" men and women, with "clear white complexions, blue eyes, and sandy hair," are continually sold upon the auction-block. In 1834, I talked with a blue-eyed Irish girl, named Mary Gilmore, who was claimed as a slave, and was with difficulty proved to have been free-born. A few weeks ago, I saw a notice in the papers of an Irishman in the Western States, who was claimed as a slave, and was foolishly trying to prove himself free. In 1855, a white girl, fourteen years old, daughter of Mr. Samuel Goodshall, of Downington, Chester Co., Penn., while walking in the road, was seized by two men, a plaster put upon her mouth, hurried into a carriage, and driven furiously toward Maryland. They threatened to kill her if she made any noise. But she was taken from them by a company of colored men on the road, and was restored to her parents. About the same time, an attempt was made to carry off, by violence, a white lad of fifteen; but he succeeded in making his escape, after the darkness of evening came on.

It is very possible that our opportunities for enjoying the beneficent institution of slavery will not long be limited to the chances of kidnapping successfully. The blessing seems to be in a fair way to be universally disseminated. Gov. Wise, of Virginia, wants it to have "no limit but the ocean," and kindly wishes to carry it into "the heart of the North." Mr. Toombs, of Georgia, holds out to us the cheering prospect of "calling the roll of his slaves on Bunker Hill"; and Mr. Brown, of Mississippi, is so benevolent, that, "rebellious and wicked as the Yankees have been, he would extend the blessings of slavery even to *them*." We know also the encouraging fact that the Democratic Party, North and South, are leagued together, to "stop the extension of the evils of free society."

But those who are impatient to become slaves need not wait for the result of political movements. I dare say Gov. Wise and Mr. Brown would kindly raise a subscription for paying their expenses South. Would it not be a judicious move for our "greasy mechanics, filthy operatives, and small-fisted farmers," to apply to them immediately for the privileges of the auction-block? How happy they would be, having enlightened *owners* to *vote* for them, and with no necessity of troubling their own heads about laws or elections! With no wives to clothe, and no families to care for! Knowing that their children will be sure to grow up in blessed ignorance, and that their daughters will be cared for as tenderly as "brood mares"! How enviable would be their situation, working in those sunny fields from dawn till dark, with the fragrance of orange blossoms on the air, and the varied melodies of the mocking bird, occasionally accompanied by the quick staccato movement of a kind driver's whip!

The question is fairly before the American people. It is for them to decide whether our fathers were mistaken in considering Freedom a blessing; whether our Declaration of Independence embodies eternal principles, or is a mere "rhetorical flourish." Slavery and Freedom are antagonistic elements. One must inevitably destroy the other. Which do you choose? Momentous issues are at stake on your decision. . . .

2
"Lecture on Slavery, No. 1" (1850)

Frederick Douglass

Frederick Douglass (ca. 1817–1895), an ex-slave, a brilliant orator, and a prolific writer, was the best known and certainly the most influential black abolitionist. Soon after his escape from slavery, Douglass joined ranks with William Lloyd Garrison, but eventually broke with Garrison for personal, intellectual, and tactical reasons. He then established his own abolitionist newspaper The North Star, *in Rochester, New York, helped to establish the Free-Soil Party in 1848, and later served three presidents, including Abraham Lincoln. He is best remembered today for his three autobiographical narratives:* Narrative of the Life of Frederick Douglass, an American Slave, Written by Himself *(1845),* My Bondage and My Freedom *(1855), and* The Life and Times of Frederick Douglass *(1881).*

Douglass' Lectures on Slavery *brought to Northern audiences a first-hand account of the brutality of slavery. He draws a vivid picture of the relationship between masters and slaves, the inhumanity of that relationship, and its contradiction to the principles on which the United States was founded. Douglass is particularly powerful in demonstrating to his Northern audience the responsibility they share for eradicating evil.*

I come before you this evening to deliver the first lecture of a course which I purpose to give in this city, during the present winter, on the subject of American Slavery....

I shall deal, during these lectures, alike with individuals and institutions—men shall no more escape me than things. I shall have occasion, at times, to be even personal, and to rebuke sin in high places. I shall not hesitate to arraign either priests or politicians, church or state, and to measure all by the standard of justice, and in the light of truth. I shall not forget to deal with the unrighteous spirit of *caste* which prevails in this community; and I shall give particular attention to the recently enacted fugitive slave bill. I shall keep my eye upon the Congress which is to commence to-morrow, and fully inform myself as to its proceedings. In a word, the whole subject of slavery, in all its bearings, shall have a full and impartial discussion.

A very slight acquaintance with the history of American slavery is sufficient to show that it is an evil of which it will be difficult to rid this country. It is not the creature of a moment, which to-day is, and to-morrow is not; it is not a pigmy, which a slight blow may demolish; it is no youthful upstart, whose impertinent pratings may be silenced by a dignified contempt. No: it is an evil of gigantic proportions, and of long standing.

Its origin in this country dates back to the landing of the pilgrims on Plymouth rock.—It was here more than two centuries ago. The first spot poisoned by its leprous presence, was a small plantation in Virginia. The slaves, at that time, numbered only twenty. They have now increased to the frightful number of three millions; and from that narrow plantation, they are now spread over by far the largest half of the American Union. Indeed, slavery forms an important part of the entire history of the American people. Its presence may be seen in all American affairs. It has become interwoven with all American institutions, and has anchored itself in the very soil of the American Constitution. It has thrown its paralysing arm over freedom of speech, and the liberty of the press; and has created for itself morals and manners favorable to its own continuance. It has seduced the church, corrupted the pulpit, and brought the powers of both into degrading bondage; and now, in the pride of its power, it even threatens to bring down that grand political edifice, the American Union, unless every member of this republic shall so far disregard his conscience and his God as to yield to its infernal behests.

That must be a powerful influence which can truly be said to govern a nation; and that slavery governs the American people, is indisputably true. If there were any doubt on this point, a few plain questions (it seems to me) could not fail to remove it. *What* power has given this nation its Presidents for more than fifty years? *Slavery.* What power is that to which the present aspirants to presidential honors are bowing? *Slavery.* We may call it "Union," "Constitution," "Harmony," or "American institutions," that to which such men as Cass, Dickinson, Webster, Clay and other distinguished men of this country, are devoting their energies, is nothing more nor less than American slavery. It is for this that they are writing letters, making speeches, and promoting the holding of great mass meetings, professedly in favor of *"the Union."* These men know the service most pleasing to their master, and that which is most likely to be richly rewarded. Men may "serve God for nought," as did Job; but he who serves the devil has an eye to his reward. "Patriotism," "obedience to the law," "prosperity to the country," have come to mean, in the mouths of these distinguished statesmen, a mean and servile acquiescence in the most flagitious and profligate legislation in favor of slavery. I might enlarge here on this picture of the slave power, and tell of its influence upon the press in the free States, and upon the condition and rights of the free colored people of the North; but I forbear for the present.—Enough has been said, I trust, to convince all that the abolition of this evil will require time, energy, zeal, perseverance and patience; that it will require fidelity, a martyr-like spirit of self-sacrifice, and a firm reliance on Him who has declared Himself to be *"the God of the oppressed."* Having said thus much upon the power and prevalence of slavery, allow me to speak of the nature of slavery itself; and here I can speak, in part, from experience—I can speak with the authority of positive knowledge. . . .

First of all, I will state, as well as I can, the legal and social relation of master and slave. A master is one (to speak in the vocabulary of the Southern States) who claims and exercises a right of property in the person of a fellow man. This he does with the force of the law and the sanction of Southern religion. The law gives the master absolute power over the slave. He may work him, flog him, hire him out, sell him, and, in certain contingencies, *kill* him, with perfect impunity. The slave is a human being, divested of all rights—reduced to the level of a brute—a mere "chattel" in the eye of the law—placed beyond the circle of human brotherhood—cut off from his kind—his name, which the "recording angel" may have enrolled in heaven, among the blest, is impiously inserted in a *master's ledger,* with horses, sheep and swine. In law, the slave has no wife, no children, no country, and no home. He can own nothing, possess nothing, acquire nothing, but what must belong to another. To eat the fruit of his own toil, to clothe his person with the work of his own hands, is considered stealing. He toils that another may reap the fruit; he is industrious that another may live in idleness; he eats unbolted meal, that another may eat the bread of fine flour; he labors in chains at home, under a burning sun and a biting lash, that another may ride in ease and splendor abroad; he lives in ignorance, that another may be educated; he is abused, that another may be exalted; he rests his toil-worn limbs on the cold, damp ground, that another may repose on the softest pillow; he is clad in coarse and tattered raiment, that another may be arrayed in purple and fine linen; he is sheltered only by the wretched hovel, that a master may dwell in a magnificent mansion; and to this condition he is bound down as by an arm of iron.

From this monstrous relation, there springs an unceasing stream of most revolting cruelties. The very accompaniments of the slave system stamp it as the offspring of hell itself. To ensure good behavior, the slave-holder relies on *the whip;* to induce proper humility, he relies on *the whip;* to rebuke what he is pleased to term insolence, he relies on *the whip;* to supply the place of wages, as an incentive to toil, he relies on *the whip;* to bind down the spirit of the slave, to imbrute and to destroy his manhood, he relies on *the whip,* the chain, the gag, the thumb-screw, the pillory, the bowie-knife, the pistol, and the blood-hound. These are the necessary and unvarying accompaniments of the system. . . .

Nor is slavery more adverse to the conscience than it is to the mind.

This is shown by the fact that in every State of the American Union, where slavery exists, except the State of Kentucky, there are laws, *absolutely* prohibitory of education among the slaves. The crime of teaching a slave to read is punishable with severe fines and imprisonment, and, in some instances, with *death itself.*

Nor are the laws respecting this matter, a dead letter. Cases may occur in which they are disregarded, and a few instances may be found where slaves may have learned to read; but such are isolated cases, and only prove the rule. The great mass of slaveholders look upon education among the slaves as utterly subversive of the slave system. I *well* remember when my mistress first announced to my master that she had discovered that I could read. His face colored at once, with surprise and chagrin. He said that "I was ruined, and my value as a slave destroyed; that a slave should know nothing but to obey his master; that to give a Negro an inch would lead him to take an ell; that having learned how to read, I would soon want to know how to write; and that, bye and bye, I would be running away." I think my audience will bear witness to the correctness of this philosophy, and to the literal fulfilment of this prophecy.

It is perfectly well understood at the South that to educate a slave is to make him discontented with slavery, and to invest him with a power which shall open to him the treasures of freedom; and since the object of the slaveholder is to maintain complete authority over his slave, his constant vigilance is exercised to prevent everything which militates against, or endangers the stability of his authority. Education being among the menacing influences, and, perhaps, the most dangerous, is, therefore, the most cautiously guarded against.

It is true that we do not often hear of the enforcement of the law, punishing as crime the teaching of slaves to read, but this is not because of a want of disposition to enforce it. The true reason, or explanation of the matter is this, there is the greatest unanimity of opinion among the white population of the South, in favor of the policy of keeping the slave in ignorance. There is, perhaps, another reason why the law against education is so seldom violated. The slave is *too* poor to be able to offer a temptation sufficiently strong to induce a white man to violate it; and it is not to be supposed that in a community where the moral and religious sentiment is in favor of slavery, many martyrs will be found sacrificing their liberty and lives by violating those prohibitory enactments.

As a general rule, then, darkness reigns over the abodes of the enslaved, and "how great is that darkness!"

We are sometimes told of the contentment of the slaves, and are entertained with vivid pictures of their happiness. We are told that they often dance and sing; that their masters frequently give them wherewith to make merry; in fine, that that they have little of which to complain. I admit that the slave *does* sometimes sing, dance, and appear to be merry. But what does this prove? It only proves to my mind, that though slavery is armed with a thousand stings, it is not able entirely to kill the elastic spirit of the bondman. That spirit will rise and walk abroad, despite of whips and chains, and extract from the cup of nature, occasional drops of joy and gladness. No thanks to the slaveholder, nor to slavery, that the vivacious captive may sometimes dance in his chains, his very mirth in such circumstances, stands before God, as an accusing angel against his enslaver.

But *who* tells us of the extraordinary contentment and happiness of the slave? What traveller has explored the balmy regions of our Southern country and brought back "these glad tidings of joy"? Bring him on the platform, and bid him answer a few plain questions, we shall then be able to determine the weight and importance that attach to his testimony. Is he a minister? Yes. Were you ever in a slave State, sir? Yes. May I inquire the object of your mission South? To preach the gospel, sir. Of what denomination are you? A Presbyterian, sir. To whom were you introduced? To the Rev. Dr. Plummer. Is he a slaveholder, sir? Yes, sir. Has slaves about his house? Yes, sir. Were you then the guest of Dr. Plummer? Yes, sir. Waited on by slaves while there? Yes, sir. Did you preach for Dr. Plummer? Yes, sir. Did you spend your nights at the great house, or at the quarter among the slaves? At the great house. You had, then, no social intercourse with the slaves? No, sir. You fraternized, then, wholly with the *white* portion of the population while there? Yes, sir. This is sufficient, sir; you can leave the platform.

Nothing is more natural than that those who go into slave States, and enjoy the hospitality of slaveholders, should bring back favorable reports of the condition of the slave. If that ultra republican, the Hon. Lewis Cass could not return from the Court of France, without paying a compliment to royalty simply because King Louis Phillippe patted him on the shoulder, called him "friend," and invited him to dinner, it is not to be expected that those hungry shadows of men in the shape of ministers, that go South, can escape a contamination even more beguiling and insidious. Alas! for the weakness of poor human nature! "Pleased with a rattle, tickled with a straw!"

Why is it that all the reports of contentment and happiness among the slaves at the South come to us upon the authority of slaveholders, or (what is equally significant) of slaveholder's friends? *Why* is it that we do not hear from the slaves direct? The answer to this question furnishes the darkest features in the American slave system.

It is often said, by the opponents of the anti-slavery cause, that the condition of the people of Ireland is more deplorable than that of the American slaves. *Far* be it from me to underrate the sufferings of the Irish people. They have been long oppressed; and the same heart that prompts me to plead the cause of the American bondman, makes it impossible for me *not* to sympathize with the oppressed of all lands. Yet I must say that there is no analogy between the two cases. The Irishman is poor, but he is *not* a slave. He *may* be in rags, but he is *not* a slave. He is still the master of his own body, and can say with the poet, "The hand of Douglass is his own." "The world is all before him, where to choose," and poor as may be my opinion of the British Parliament, I cannot believe that it will ever sink to such a depth of infamy as to pass a law for the recapture of Fugitive Irishmen! The shame and scandal of kidnapping will long remain wholly monopolized by the American Congress! The Irishman has not only the liberty to emigrate from his country, but he has liberty at home. He can write, and speak, and co-operate for the attainment of his rights and the redress of his wrongs.

The multitude can assemble upon all the green hills, and fertile plains of the Emerald Isle—they can pour out their grievances, and proclaim their wants without molestation; and the press, that "swift-winged messenger," can bear the tidings of their doings to the extreme bounds of the civilized world; They have their "Conciliation Hall" on the banks of the Liffey, their reform Clubs, and their newspapers; they pass resolutions, send forth addresses, and enjoy the right of petition. But how is it with the American slave? *Where* may he assemble? *Where* is his Conciliation Hall? Where are his newspapers? Where is his right of petition? Where is his freedom of speech? his liberty of the press? and his right of locomotion? He is said to be happy; happy men can speak. But ask the slave—*what* is his condition?—*what* his state of mind?—*what* he thinks of his enslavement? and you had as well address your inquiries to the *silent dead*. There comes no *voice* from the enslaved, we are left to gather his feelings by imagining what ours would be, were our souls in his soul's stead.

If there were no other fact descriptive of slavery, than that the slave is dumb, this alone would be sufficient to mark the slave system as a grand aggregation of human horrors.

Most who are present will have observed that leading men, in this country, have been puting forth their skill to secure quiet to the nation. A system of measures to promote this object was adopted a few months ago in Congress.

The result of those measures is known. Instead of quiet, they have produced alarm; instead of peace, they have brought us war, and so must ever be.

While this nation is guilty of the enslavement of three millions of innocent men and women, it is as idle to think of having a sound and lasting peace, as it is to think there is no God, to take cognizance of the affairs of men. There can be no peace to the wicked while slavery continues in the land, it will be condemned, and while it is condemned there will be agitation; Nature must cease to be nature; Men must become monsters; Humanity must be transformed; Christianity must be exterminated; all ideas of justice, and the laws of eternal goodness must be utterly blotted out from the human soul, ere a system so foul and infernal can escape condemnation, or this guilty Republic can have a sound and enduring Peace.

3

Selections from *Slavery* (1836)

William E. Channing

William E. Channing (1780–1842) was one of the most respected and influential Unitarian clergymen and intellectuals of the antebellum period. Never a radical abolitionist, Channing was nonetheless a staunch antislavery man who inched closer and closer in the years just before his death to the abolitionist position.

The selection that follows is drawn from the chapter on "Property" in Channing's best known antislavery work entitled Slavery. *Channing went deeper than virtually any other antislavery thinker in defining and explicating the nature of property and rights from a natural law perspective. He attempted to reconcile the most advanced Enlightenment thinking with the natural religious teachings of Unitarianism.*

The slave-holder claims the slave as his Property. The very idea of a slave is, that be belongs to another, that he is bound to live and labour for another, to be another's instrument, and to make another's will his habitual law, however adverse to his own. Another owns him, and, of course, has a right to his time and strength, a right to the fruits of his labour, a right to task him without his consent and to determine the kind and duration of his toil, a right to confine him to any bounds, a right, to extort the required work by stripes, a right, in a word, to use him as a tool, without contract, against his will, and in denial of his right to dispose of himself or to use his power for his own good. "A slave," says the Louisiana code, "is in the power of the master to whom he belongs. The master may sell him, dispose of his person, his industry, his labour; he can do nothing, possess nothing, nor acquire anything, but which must belong to his master." "Slaves shall be deemed, taken, reputed, and adjudged," say the South Carolina laws, "to be chattels personal in the hands of their masters, and possessions to all intents and purposes whatsoever." Such is slavery, a claim to man as property.

Now this claim of property in a human being is altogether false, groundless. No such right of man in man can exist. A human being cannot be justly owned. To hold and treat him as property is to inflict a great wrong, to incur the guilt of oppression.

This position there is a difficulty in maintaining on account of its exceeding obviousness. It is too plain for proof. To defend it is like trying to confirm a self-evident truth. To find arguments is not easy, because an argument is something clearer than the proposition to be sustained. The man who, on hearing the claim to property in man, does not see and feel distinctly that it is a cruel usurpation, is hardly to be reached by reasoning, for it is hard to find any plainer principles than what he begins with denying. I will endeavour, however, to illustrate the truth which I have stated.

1. It is plain, that, if one man may be held as property, then every other man may be so held. If there be nothing in human nature, in our common nature, which excludes and forbids the conversion of him who possesses it into an article of property; if the right of the free to liberty is founded, not on their essential attributes as rational and moral beings, but on certain adventitious, accidental circumstances, into which they have been thrown; then every human being, by a change of circumstances, may justly be held and treated by another as property. If one man may be rightfully reduced to slavery, then there is not a human being on whom the same, chain may not be imposed. Now let every reader ask himself this plain question: Could I, can I, be rightfully seized, and made an article of property; be made a passive instrument of another's will and pleasure; be subjected to another's irresponsible power; be subjected to stripes at another's will; be denied the control and use of my own limbs and faculties for my own good? Does any man, so questioned, doubt, waver, look about him for an answer? Is not the reply given immediately, intuitively, by his whole inward being? Does not an unhesitating, unerring conviction spring up in my breast, that no other man can acquire such a right in myself? Do we not repel indignantly and with horror the thought of being reduced to the condition of tools and chattels to a fellow-creature? Is there any moral truth more deeply rooted in us, than that such a degradation would be an infinite wrong? And if this impression be a delusion, on what single moral conviction can we rely? This deep assurance, that we cannot be rightfully made another's property, does not rest on the hue of our skins, or the place of our birth, or our strength, or wealth. These things do not enter our thoughts. The consciousness of indestructible rights is a part of our moral being. The consciousness of our humanity involves the persuasion that we cannot be owned as a tree or a brute. As men we cannot justly be made slaves. Then no man can be rightfully enslaved. In casting the yoke from ourselves as an unspeakable wrong, we condemn ourselves as wrong-doers and oppressors in laying it on any who share our nature.—It is not necessary to inquire whether a man, by extreme guilt, may not forfeit the rights of his nature, and be justly punished with slavery. On this point crude notions pre-

vail. But the discussion would be foreign to the present subject. We are now not speaking of criminals. We speak of innocent men, who have given us no hold on them by guilt; and our own consciousness is a proof that such cannot rightfully be seized as property by a fellow-creature.

2. A man cannot be seized and held as property, because he has Rights. What these rights are, whether few or many, or whether all men have the same, are questions for future discussion. All that is assumed now is, that every human being has *some* rights. This truth cannot be denied, but by denying to a portion of the race that moral nature which is the sure and only foundation of rights. This truth has never, I believe, been disputed. It is even recognised in the very codes of slave legislation, which, while they strip a man of liberty, affirm his right to life, and threaten his murderer with punishment. Now, I say, a being having rights cannot justly be made property; for this claim over him virtually annuls all his rights. It strips him of all power to assert them. It makes it a crime to assert them. The very essence of slavery is, to put a man defenceless into the hands of another. The right claimed by the master, to task, to force, to imprison, to whip, and to punish the slave, at discretion, and especially to prevent the least resistance to his will, is a virtual denial and subversion of all the rights of the victim of his power. The two cannot stand together. Can we doubt which of them ought to fall?

3. Another argument against property is to be found in the Essential Equality of men. I know that this doctrine, so venerable in the eyes of our fathers, has lately been denied. Verbal logicians have told us that men are "born equal" only in the sense of being equally born. They have asked whether all are equally tall, strong, or beautiful; or whether nature, Procrustes-like, reduces all her children to one standard of intellect and virtue. By such arguments it is attempted to set aside the principle of equality, on which the soundest moralists have reared the structure of social duty; and in these ways the old foundations of despotic power, which our fathers in their simplicity thought they had subverted, are laid again by their sons.

It is freely granted that there are innumerable diversities among men; but be it remembered, they are ordained to bind men together, and not to subdue one to the other; ordained to give means and occasions of mutual aid, and to carry forward each and all, so that the good of all is equally intended in this distribution of various gifts. Be it also remembered, that these diversities among men are as nothing in comparison with the attributes in which they agree; and it is this which constitutes their essential equality. All men have the same rational nature and the same power of conscience, and all are equally made for indefinite improvement of these divine faculties, and for the happiness to be found in their virtuous use. Who, that comprehends these gifts, does not see that the diversities of the race vanish before them? Let it be added, that the natural advantages, which distinguish one man from another, are so bestowed as to counterbalance one another, and bestowed without regard to rank or condition in life. Whoever surpasses in one endowment is inferior in others. Even genius, the greatest gift, is found in union with strange infirmities, and often places its possessors below ordinary men in the conduct of life. Great learning is often put to shame by the mother-wit and keen good sense of uneducated men. Nature, indeed, pays no heed to birth or condition in bestowing her favours. The noblest spirits sometimes grow up in the obscurest spheres. Thus equal are men; and among these equals who can substantiate his claim to make others his property, his tools, the mere instruments of his private interest and gratification? Let this claim begin, and where will it stop? If one may assert it, why not all? Among these partakers of the same rational and moral nature, who can make good a right over others, which others may not establish over himself? Does he insist on superior strength of body or mind? Who of us has no superior in one or the other of these endowments? Is it sure that the slave or the slave's child may not surpass his master in intellectual energy or in moral worth? Has nature conferred distinctions which tell us plainly who shall be owners and who be owned? Who of us can unblushingly lift his head and say that God has written "Master" there? or who can show the word " Slave" engraven on his brother's brow? The equality of nature makes slavery a wrong. Nature's seal is affixed to no instrument by which property in a single human being is conveyed.

4. That a human being cannot be justly held and used as property, is apparent from the very nature of property. Property is an exclusive right. It shuts out all claim but that of the possessor. What one man owns cannot belong to another. What, then, is the consequence of holding a human being as property? Plainly this. He can have no right to himself. His limbs are, in truth, not morally his own. He has not a right to his own strength. It belongs to another. His will, intellect, and muscles, all the powers of body and mind which are exercised in labour, he is bound to regard as another's. Now, if there be property in anything, it is that of a man in his own person, mind, and strength. All other rights are weak, unmeaning, compared with this, and in denying this all right is denied. It is true that an individual may forfeit by crime his right to the use of his limbs, perhaps to his limbs, and even to life. But the very idea of forfeiture implies that the right was originally possessed. It is true that a man may by contract give to another a limited right to his strength. But he gives only because he possesses it, and gives it for consider-

ations which he deems beneficial to himself; and the right conferred ceases at once on violation of the conditions on which it was bestowed. To deny the right of a human being to himself, to his own limbs and faculties, to his energy of body and mind, is an absurdity too gross to be confuted by anything but a simple statement. Yet this absurdity is involved in the idea of his belonging to another.

5. We have a plain recognition of the principle now laid down, in the universal indignation excited towards a man who makes another his slave. Our laws know no higher crime than that of reducing a man to slavery. To steal or to buy an African on his own shores, is piracy. In this act the greatest wrong is inflicted, the most sacred right violated. But if a human being cannot without infinite injustice be seized as property, then he cannot without equal wrong be held and used as such. The wrong in the first seizure lies in the destination of a human being to future bondage, to the criminal use of him as a chattel or brute. Can that very use, which makes the original seizure an enormous wrong, become gradually innocent? If the slave receive injury without measure at the first moment of the outrage, is he less injured by being held fast the second or the third? Does the duration of wrong, the increase of it by continuance, convert it into right? It is true, in many cases, that length of possession is considered as giving a right, where the goods were acquired by unlawful means. But in these cases the goods were such as might justly be appropriated to individual use. They were intended by the Creator to be owned. They fulfil their purpose by passing into the hands of an exclusive possessor. It is essential to rightful property in a thing, that the thing from its nature may be rightfully appropriated. If it cannot originally he made one's own without crime, it certainly cannot be continued as such without guilt. Now the ground, on which the seizure of the African on his own shore is condemned, is, that he is a man, who has by his nature a right to be free. Ought not, then, the same condemnation to light on the continuance of his yoke? Still more. Whence is it that length of possession is considered by the laws as conferring a right? I answer, from the difficulty of determining the original proprietor, and from the apprehension of unsettling all property by carrying back inquiry beyond a certain time. Suppose, however, an article of property to be of such a nature that it could bear the name of the true original owner stamped on it in bright and indelible characters. In this case, the whole ground, on which length of possession bars other claims, would fail. The proprietor would not be concealed or rendered doubtful by the lapse of time. Would not he, who should receive such an article from a robber or a succession of robbers, be involved in their guilt? Now the true owner of a human being is made manifest to all. It is Himself.

No brand on the slave was ever so conspicuous as the mark of property which God has set on him. God, in making him a rational and moral being, has put a glorious stamp on him, which all the slave legislation and slave-markets of worlds cannot efface. Hence, no right accrues to the master from the length of the wrong which has been done to the slave.

6. Another argument against the right of property in man, may be drawn from a very obvious principle of moral science. It is a plain truth, universally received, that every right supposes or involves a corresponding obligation. If, then, a man has a right to another's person or powers, the latter is under obligation to give himself up as a chattel to the former. This is his duty. He is bound to be a slave; and bound not merely by the Christian law which enjoins submission to injury, not merely by prudential considerations or by the claims of public order and peace; but bound because another has a right of ownership, has a moral claim to him, so that he would be guilty of dishonesty, of robbery, in withdrawing himself from this other's service. It is his duty to work for his master, though all compulsion were withdrawn; and in deserting him he would commit the crime of taking away another man's property, as truly as if he were to carry off his owner's purse. Now do we not instantly feel, can we help feeling, that this is false? Is the slave thus morally bound? When the African was first brought to these shores, would he have violated a solemn obligation by slipping his chain, and flying back to his native home? Would he not have been bound to seize the precious opportunity of escape? Is the slave under a moral obligation to confine himself, his wife, and children, to a spot where their union in a moment may be forcibly dissolved? Ought he not, if he can, to place himself and his family under the guardianship of equal laws? Should we blame him for leaving his yoke? Do we not feel, that, in the same condition, a sense of duty would quicken our flying steps? Where, then, is the obligation which would necessarily be imposed, if the right existed which the master claims? Time absence of obligation proves the want of the right. The claim is groundless. It is a cruel wrong.

7. I come now to what is to my own mind the great argument against seizing and using a man as property. He cannot be property in the sight of God and justice, because he is a Rational, Moral, Immortal Being; because created in God's image, and therefore in the highest sense his child; because created to unfold godlike faculties, and to govern himself by a Divine Law written on his heart, and republished in God's Word. His whole nature forbids that he should be seized as property. From his very nature it follows, that so to seize him is to offer an insult to his Maker, and to inflict aggravated social wrong. Into every human being God has breathed an

immortal spirit, more precious than the whole outward creation. No earthly or celestial language can exaggerate the worth of a human being. No matter how obscure his condition. Thought, Reason, Conscience, the capacity of Virtue, the capacity of Christian Love, an Immortal Destiny, an intimate moral connection with God,—here are attributes of our common humanity which reduce to insignificance all outward distinctions, and make every human being unspeakably dear to his Maker. No matter how ignorant he may be. The capacity of Improvement allies him to the more instructed of his race, and places within his reach the knowledge and happiness of higher worlds. Every human being has in him the germ of the greatest idea in the universe, the idea of God; and to unfold this is the end of his existence. Every human being has in his breast the elements of that Divine, Everlasting Law, which the highest orders of the creation obey. He has the idea of Duty; and to unfold, revere, obey this, is the very purpose for which life was given. Every human being has the idea of what is meant by that word, Truth; that is, he sees, however dimly, the great object of Divine and created intelligence, and is capable of ever-enlarging perceptions of truth. Every human being has affections, which may be purified and expanded into a Sublime Love. He has, too, the idea of Happiness, and a thirst for it which cannot be appeased. Such is our nature. Wherever we see a man, we see the possessor of these great capacities. Did God make such a being to be owned as a tree or a brute? How plainly was he made to exercise, unfold, improve his highest powers, made for a moral, spiritual good! and how is he wronged, and his Creator opposed, when he is forced and broken into a tool to another's physical enjoyment!

Such a being was plainly made for an End in Himself. He is a Person, not a Thing. He is an End, not a mere Instrument or Means. He was made for his own virtue and happiness. Is this end reconcileable with his being held and used as a chattel? The sacrifice of such a being to another's will, to another's present, outward, ill-comprehended good, is the greatest violence which can be offered to any creature of God. It is to degrade him from his rank in the universe, to make him a means, not an end, to cast him out from God's spiritual family into the brutal herd.

Such a being was plainly made to obey a Law within Himself. This is the essence of a moral being. He possesses, as a part of his nature, and the most essential part, a sense of Duty, which he is to reverence and follow, in opposition to all pleasure or pain, to all interfering human wills. The great purpose of all good education and discipline is, to make a man Master of Himself, to excite him to act from a principle in his own mind, to lead him to propose his own perfection as his supreme law and end. And is this highest purpose of man's nature to be reconciled with entire subjection to a foreign will, to an outward, overwhelming force, which is satisfied with nothing but complete submission?

The end of such a being as we have described, is, manifestly, Improvement. Now it is the fundamental law of our nature, that all our powers are to improve by free exertion. Action is the indispensable condition of progress to the intellect, conscience, and heart. Is it not plain, then, that a human being cannot, without wrong, be owned by another, who claims, as proprietor, the right to repress the powers of his slaves, to withhold from them the means of developement, to keep them within time limits which are necessary to contentment in chains, to shut out every ray of light and every generous sentiment which may interfere with entire subjection to his will?

No man, who seriously considers what human nature is, and what it was made for, can think of setting up a claim to a fellow-creature. What! own a spiritual being, a being made to know and adore God, and who is to outlive the sun and stars! What! chain to our lowest uses a being made for truth and virtue! convert into a brute instrument that intelligent nature, on which the idea of Duty has dawned, and which is a nobler type of God than all outward creation! Should we not deem it a wrong which no punishment could expiate, were one of our children seized as property, and driven by the whip to toil? And shall God's child, dearer to him than an only son to a human parent, be thus degraded? Everything else may be owned in the universe; but a moral, rational being cannot be property. Suns and stars may be owned, but not the lowest spirit. Touch anything but this. Lay not your hand on God's rational offspring. The whole spiritual world cries out, Forbear! The highest intelligences recognise their own nature, their own rights, in the humblest, human being. By that priceless, immortal spirit which dwells in him, by that likeness of God which he wears, tread him not in the dust, confound him not with the brute.

We have thus seen that a human being cannot rightfully be held and used as property. No legislation, not that of all countries or worlds, could make him so. Let this be laid down, as a first, fundamental truth. Let us hold it fast, as a most sacred, precious truth. Let us hold it fast against all customs, all laws, all rank, wealth, and power. Let it be armed with the whole authority of the civilised and Christian world.

II
Immediate Emancipation

4

"Declaration of Sentiments of the National Anti-Slavery Convention" (1833)

American Anti-Slavery Society
[William Lloyd Garrison]

In December 1833, sixty-two men and women, black and white, met in New York City to launch the first national organization dedicated to the principle of immediate emancipation. The establishment of the American Anti-Slavery Society marks the official beginning of an organized movement to abolish slavery in America. Over the course of the next seven years, the Anti-Slavery Society would dedicate itself to transforming America through moral conversion. Their favorite tactics included the establishment of regional, state, and local antislavery societies, mailing antislavery literature to the South, petition campaigns, and evangelizing antislavery lecturers who traveled throughout the North.

The founding document of the American Anti-Slavery Society is its "Declaration of Sentiments" written by William Lloyd Garrison. Garrison (1805–1879), the most famous of all radical abolitionists, is generally recognized as the movement's leader and spiritual light. He devoted himself entirely to the cause for over thirty-five years. Garrison grew up in poverty in Newburyport, Massachusetts, the son of an alcoholic, ne'er-do-well sailor who abandoned the family when William was a young boy. Garrison struggled in his early years as an apprentice in a print shop, but eventually elevated himself to write for, and then edit, a series of reformist newspapers. In the late 1820s, Garrison converted to the doctrine of immediate emancipation and then started The Liberator, *the most famous and influential of abolitionist newspapers.*

The "Declaration of Sentiments" states succinctly and clearly the organization's founding principles and the tactics it would pursue to achieve the end of immediate emancipation. In later years, abolitionists would split over interpreting the "Declaration's" tactical recommendations. Those who left the organization in 1840 founded the American and Foreign Anti-Slavery Society.

The Convention assembled in the city of Philadelphia, to organize a National Anti-Slavery Society, promptly seize the opportunity to promulgate the following Declaration of Sentiments, as cherished by them in relation to the enslavement of one-sixth portion of the American people.

More than fifty-seven years have elapsed, since a band of patriots convened in this place, to devise measures for the deliverance of this country from a foreign yoke. The corner-stone upon which they founded the Temple of Freedom was broadly this—'that all men are created equal; that they are endowed by their Creator with certain inalienable rights; that among these are life, LIBERTY, and the pursuit of happiness.' At the sound of their trumpet-call, three millions of people rose up as from the sleep of death, and rushed to the strife of blood; deeming it more glorious to die instantly as freemen, than desirable to live one hour as slaves. They were few in number—poor in resource; but the honest conviction that Truth, and Right were on their side, made them invincible.

We have met together for the achievement of an enterprise, without which that of our fathers is incomplete; and which, for its magnitude, solemnity, and probable results upon the destiny of the world, as far transcends theirs as moral truth does physical force.

In purity of motive, in earnestness of zeal, in decision of purpose, in intrepidity of action, in steadfastness of faith, in sincerity of spirit, we would not be inferior to them.

Their principles led them to wage war against their oppressors, and to spill human blood like water, in order to be free. Ours forbid the doing of evil that good may come, and lead us to reject, and to entreat the oppressed to reject, the use of all carnal weapons for deliverance from bondage; relying solely upon those which are spiritual, and mighty through God to the pulling down of strong holds.

Their measures were physical resistance—the marshaling in arms—the hostile array—the mortal encounter. Ours shall be such only as the opposition of the moral purity to moral corruption—the destruction of error by the potency of truth—the overthrow of prejudice by the power of love—and the abolition of slavery by the spirit of repentance.

Their grievances, great as they were, were trifling in comparison with the wrongs and sufferings of those for whom we plead. Our fathers were never slaves—never bought and sold like cattle—never shut out from the light of knowledge and religion—never subjected to the lash of brutal taskmasters.

But those, for whose emancipation we are striving—constituting at the present time at least one-sixth part of our countrymen—are recognized by law, and treated by their fellow-beings, as marketable commodities, as goods and chattels, as brute beasts; are plundered daily of the fruits of their toil without redress; really enjoy no constitutional nor legal protection from licentious and murderous outrages upon their persons; and are ruthlessly torn asunder—the tender babe from the arms of its frantic mother—the heartbroken wife from her weeping husband—at the caprice or pleasure of irresponsible tyrants. For the crime of having a dark complexion, they suffer the pangs of hunger, the infliction of stripes, the ignominy of brutal servitude. They are kept in heathenish darkness by laws expressly enacted to make their instruction a criminal offence.

These are the prominent circumstances in the condition of more than two millions of our people, the proof of which may be found in thousands of indisputable facts, and in the laws of the slaveholding States.

Hence we maintain—that, in view of the civil and religious privileges of this nation, the guilt of its oppression is unequaled by any other on the face of the earth; and, therefore, that it is bound to repent instantly, to undo the heavy burdens, and to let the oppressed go free.

We further maintain—that no man has a right to enslave or imbrute his brother—to hold or acknowledge him, for one moment, as a piece of merchandize—to keep back his hire by fraud—or to brutalize his mind, by denying him the means of intellectual, social and moral improvement.

The right to enjoy liberty is inalienable. To invade it is to usurp the prerogative of Jehovah. Every man has a right to his own body—to the products of his own labor—to the protection of law—and to the common advantages of society. It is piracy to buy or steal a native African, and subject him to servitude. Surely, the sin is great to enslave an American as an African.

Therefore we believe and affirm—that there is no difference, in principle, between the African slave trade and American slavery:

That every American citizen, who detains a human being in involuntary bondage as his property, is, according to Scripture, (Ex. xxi. 16) a man-stealer:

That the slaves ought instantly to be set free, and brought under the protection of law:

That if they had lived from the time of Pharaoh down to the present period, and had been entailed through successive generations, their right to be free could never have been alienated, but their claims would have constantly risen in solemnity:

That all those laws which are now in force, admitting the right of slavery, are therefore, before God, utterly null and void; being an audacious usurpation of the Divine prerogative, a daring infringement on the law of nature, a base overthrow of the very foundations of the social compact, a complete extinction of all the relations, endearments and obligations of mankind, and a presumptuous transgression of all the holy commandments; and that therefore they ought instantly to be abrogated.

We further believe and affirm—that all persons of color who possess the qualifications which are demanded of others, ought to be admitted forthwith to the enjoyment of the same privileges, and the exercise of the same prerogatives, as others; and that the paths of preferment, of wealth, and of intelligence, should be opened as widely to them as to persons of a white complexion.

We maintain that no compensation should be given to the planters emancipating their slaves:

Because it would be a surrender of the great fundamental principle, that man cannot hold property in man:

Because slavery is a crime, and therefore is not an article to be sold:

Because the holders of slaves are not the just proprietors of what they claim; freeing the slave is not depriving them of property, but restoring it to its rightful owner; it is not wronging the master, but righting the slave—restoring him to himself:

Because immediate and general emancipation would only destroy nominal, not real property; it would not amputate a limb or break a bone of the slaves, but by infusing motives into their breasts, would make them doubly valuable to the masters as free laborers; and

Because, if compensation is to be given at all, it should be given to the outraged and guiltless slaves, and not to those who have plundered and abused them.

We regard as delusive, cruel and dangerous, any scheme of expatriation which pretends to aid, either directly or indirectly, in the emancipation of the slaves, or to be a substitute for the immediate and total abolition of slavery.

We fully and unanimously recognise the sovereignty of each State, to legislate exclusively on the subject of the slavery which is tolerated within its limits; we concede that Congress, under the present national compact, has no right to interfere with any of the slave States, in relation to the momentous subject:

But we maintain that Congress has a right, and is solemnly bound, to suppress the domestic slave trade between the several States, and to abolish slavery in those portions of our territory which the Constitution has placed under its exclusive jurisdiction.

We also maintain that there are, at the present time, the highest obligations resting upon the people of the free States to remove slavery by moral and political action, as prescribed in the Constitution of the United States. They are now living under a pledge of their tremendous physical force, to fasten the galling fetters of tyranny upon the limbs of the millions in the Southern States; they are liable to be called at any moment to suppress a general insurrection of the slaves; they authorize the slave owner to vote for three-fifths of his slaves as property, and thus enable him to perpetuate his oppression; they support a standing army at the South for its protection; and they seize the slave, who has escaped into their territories, and send him back to be tortured by an enraged master or a brutal driver. This relation to slavery is criminal, and full of danger: IT MUST BE BROKEN UP.

These are our views and principles—these our designs and measures. With entire confidence in the overruling justice of God, we plant ourselves upon the Declaration of our Independence and the truths of Divine Revelation, as upon the Everlasting Rock.

We shall organize Anti-Slavery Societies, if possible, in every city, town and village in our land.

We shall send forth agents to lift up the voice of remonstrance, of warning, of entreaty, and of rebuke.

We shall circulate, unsparingly and extensively, anti-slavery tracts and periodicals.

We shall enlist the pulpit and the press in the cause of the suffering and the dumb.

We shall aim at a purification of the churches from all participation in the guilt of slavery.

We shall encourage the labor of freemen rather than that of slaves, by giving a preference to their productions: and

We shall spare no exertions nor means to bring the whole nation to speedy repentance.

Out trust for victory is solely in God. We may be personally defeated, but our principles never! Truth, Justice, Reason, Humanity, must and will gloriously triumph. Already a host is coming up to the help of the Lord against the mighty, and the prospect before us is full of encouragement.

Submitting this Declaration to the candid examination of the people of this country, and of the friends of liberty throughout the world, we hereby affix our signatures to it; pledging ourselves that, under the guidance and by the help of Almighty God, we will do all that in us lies, consistently with this Declaration of our principles, to overthrow the most execrable system of slavery that has ever been witnessed upon the earth; to deliver our land from its deadliest curse; to wipe out the foulest stain which rests upon our national escutcheon; and to secure to the colored population of the United States, all the rights and privileges which belong to them as men, and as Americans—come what may to our persons, our interests, or our reputation—whether we live to witness the triumph of Liberty, Justice and Humanity, or perish untimely as martyrs in this great, benevolent, and holy cause.

5

Selections from *Lectures on Slavery and its Remedy* (1834)

Amos A. Phelps

Amos A. Phelps (1804–1847) was one of the earliest members of the Boston clerical establishment to join the cause of immediate abolition. He was a founding member of the American Anti-Slavery Society, and he later served as one of its traveling agents in 1837 and 1838. Phelps was a close friend of Garrison's during the early years of the abolition movement, but eventually the two broke their association over the role of the clergy in the abolition cause and over the admission of women to the Massachusetts and American Anti-Slavery societies. He briefly edited the anti-Garrisonian newspaper The Abolitionist *during the 1840s.*

Phelp's Lectures on Slavery and its Remedy *provides one of the very best definitions of, and clearest arguments for, immediate emancipation.*

I have already spoken of the sin of slavery. I come now to the question of remedy. On this point, I hope to be able to tell you, what the new doctrine we speak of is, and what the strange things we utter mean, even if I do not succeed in convincing you of their correctness.

And here, let me say, that the time has evidently come, when this subject is to undergo a new and thorough investigation, among all classes of the community. Men are springing up, in every section of the land—men too, who are not to be cashiered as 'babblers,' or in the parlance of modern philosophers, as 'visionary enthusiasts,' 'reckless incendiaries,' &c.—men, whose sentiments are not to be set aside, or sneered out of existence, as being the result of fanaticism and overheated zeal—who tell us, that their former views upon the subject have been wrong, radically wrong, and that some new and more efficient means of remedy must speedily be adopted. They have re-investigated the subject. They have done it with fervent prayer for guidance from on high; and they have come to results at variance, or at least in advance of their former views. They now regard the matter of slaveholding as a sin, not merely in the abstraction of theory, but in actual and present practice.

They are beginning to preach, and print, and talk of it as a sin; and laugh at them as it may, the whole community feels the effect thereof. Attention is awakened, discussion is elicited,—the right kind of discussion too, and not that of apology merely—the press and the pulpit are speaking, and the time has gone by, when the subject of slavery and its remedy can avoid the light, or escape the scrutiny of strict and general examination. The community will not and cannot be lulled to sleep much longer with cries of 'hush,' hush,' 'careful,' 'careful.' Nor will it much longer be imposed on by cries of 'fanatic,' 'incendiary,' 'firebrand,' &c. on the one hand, or be frightened on the other by cues of 'danger,' 'insurrection,' 'blood.' On the contrary, it will claim the right of seeing for itself; on the subject; and if it be true, indeed, that slavery has grown up to such frightful maturity, as that remedy is out of the question, and we therefore are a ruined people, the community will insist on knowing it; or if there be yet a remedy, the community will insist on knowing what it is, and on its speedy application. The subject cannot escape a thorough and rigid investigation. It must and will be thoroughly sifted. The investigation is begun. It is going on, and cry 'hush' as much as you will, there is no stopping it.

And farther, the investigation has begun just where it ought, and just where we should expect it to begin. To my mind, it amounts almost to an axiom, that *the people of the North are better qualified to judge of the true nature, and hit upon the true and best remedy of slavery, than are the people of the South.* To be sure they have no power, and I trust, no desire to force any remedy on the South, without its own consent. Still they are most favorably situated to give an impartial judgment in the case, and therefore best qualified to hit upon and recommend the true and only remedy; and then they have the power and the right, nay, it is their solemn duty to urge that remedy on the voluntary acceptance of the South in every possible and lawful way. . . .

The true remedy, therefore, if it is ever hit upon, must, as a matter of course, originate with those that are not personally interested or implicated in the sin, and be recommended by them to slaveholders, and pressed on their acceptance, by every possible consideration of duty and of interest.

But to the question of remedy, what is it? I remark,

1. *That whatever it be, it is to be determined on general principles, and not on the supposition of excepted cases.* How much reasoning there is of this kind, on this subject, you need not be told. One can hardly whisper the doctrine of immediate emancipation, but he is met at once by the supposition of some extreme case, in which it is always *taken for granted*, that such emancipation would be certain ruin both to master and slave; and then, starting with this extreme case—the creature of interest, or a panic-struck imagi-

nation, by which all sorts of frightful things are conjured up—starting with this, as a fair representation of the slave-holding community generally, and a correct basis of reasoning, it is gravely inferred that such emancipation cannot be duty! Was ever reasoning more absurd? . . .

So in the present ease—the remedy for slavery is to be decided on general principles. Nothing is more weak and childish than to reason in respect to it, from some frightful supposition of an interested or frightened imagination. It is not the supposition of such extreme cases, that is to furnish the proper rule of judgment in the matter, even if all the frightful things which are imagined were to be realized as the actual result, and much less when they are only anticipated and conjectured evils.

And farther, it ought to be understood, that in applying the remedy, whatever it be, most men would have sense enough not to apply it to the worst cases first. And so, in this case in applying the doctrine of immediate emancipation, we do not intend to apply it to the worst cases first. We purpose to go first to that slave-holder whose mind is most open to conviction, and in whose case there are fewest obstacles to emancipation—fewest difficulties and fewest dangers, and ply his conscience with the doctrine, and when we have succeeded with him, we purpose to go to another, and ply his conscience, and add to all our other motives the example of his neighbor, and so on. And if in the end, we find some extreme cases that do not admit the possibility of remedy, without the direful results anticipated, all we can do is to meet them, and let the individual die in his sin, rather than abandon general principles. Our business is with the public, and if, therefore, the scheme of remedy that is best for the public as a whole operates hardly here and there on the individual, it is indeed to be regretted, but nevertheless we must abide by general principles. It is better that one member perish than that the whole body be cast into hell.

I remark again 2. *That the remedy, whatever it be, must respect the rights and interests of the injured, in preference to those of the injurers.* This is demanded on every principle of justice and humanity. If the case in respect to slavery is a desperate one, so that there is no alternative but that the rights and interests of one or the other must be sacrificed, then I hesitate not to affirm that those of the master must yield to those of the slave. If there be no remedy in the case, save one that shall compromit, in whole or in part, the interests and rights of one or the other, then it is a clear case that, that party should suffer which is in the wrong. The remedy, whatever it be, must aim primarily and mainly at the reparation of the injuries inflicted on the injured. Every other consideration and object must bend and be subordinate to this.

Nor will it answer for the slaveholder to say in reply, that the state of society in which he finds himself is not one of his own choosing; that the evil of slaveholding is entailed on him, and is his misfortune and not his crime. If it be so, he is bound to bear it *as his*; and it is only adding insult to injury to attempt to throw it off from himself upon his poor slave. The slave's own cup is full enough of bitterness. He has as much misfortune of his own as he can well bear. The master has no right to add his to it. If it be his calamity, he must meet it as his, and not screen himself, and redeem his misfortunes at the expense of his already too much injured slave; and especially must this be so, when instead of calamity merely, slavery is the master's crime.

This is said on the supposition that the rights and interests of one or the other *must* be sacrificed. It is believed, however, that there is no necessity for this; that if the master will but do his duty voluntarily to his slaves, it will be for the best good both of him and them. Emancipation will be for the interest of both. I make the above remarks, therefore, not because I suppose that the real rights and interests of either must be sacrificed, but for the purpose of guiding you to a remedy of the proper *moral character*, as well as adequate to meet the exigencies of the case. It will not do to remedy oppression *by* oppression. Such remedy is no remedy. It is only adding insult to injury. And yet such, to all intents and purposes, is every scheme of remedy which goes on the principle of consulting the assumed rights and imagined interests of the master, in preference to the real rights and interests of the slave. If it be eagle-eyed and trumpet-tongued in behalf of the master—talking loudly of his 'chartered' 'sacred' rights, &c., while at the same time it is well nigh blind and dumb in respect to the sacred, the 'inalienable-rights' of the slave, it has the marks of oppression about it. It exalts assumed rights above real— usurpation above justice. Whatever its professions, therefore, and however well-meant on the part of many of its abettors, it is still a scheme which takes sides with the oppressor against the oppressed, and sets up his imaginary claims as paramount to those which God and nature give. It puts its foot along with the oppressor's, on the neck of the oppressed, and cannot therefore be either an equitable or efficient scheme of remedy. Under the government of a righteous God, oppression can never be remedied by oppression.

But the main question returns—what is the remedy for slavery? And the plain answer is, *complete and universal emancipation.* The question, however, commonly has a more limited signification. All are agreed that the only remedy for slavery is its abolition. The question of remedy, therefore, has reference to the *means* of remedy, rather than to the thing itself. So that the practical and more important form of the question is this—*how, by what means, is complete and universal emancipation to be effected?* I answer,

1st. *Not by any schemes of amelioration.* All such schemes are futile, and worse than futile, so far as emancipation is concerned. They do not even aim at it. Their object is amelioration simply, and not remedy. They go on the assumption that slaveholding is a necessary evil, and that the best, and all indeed, that can be done in the case, is to modify and meliorate and soften some of its harsher features. They admit and act in respect to it, on the old maxim that 'what cannot be cured must be endured'; and they aim, therefore, not at its cure, but simply at making its endurance as tolerable as may be. Remedy then is out of question on any such scheme. Indeed, as I have before said, such schemes, if successful at all, are on the whole an obstacle in the way of the only real remedy, emancipation. They cover up the hideousness of slavery. They hide its dark features, and thus put the moral sense of the community asleep, and leave the slave, comparatively unpitied, to drink still oppression's bitter cup.

Again 2. *Slavery cannot be remedied by any schemes of gradual emancipation.* And, for the better understanding of the matter, it is in point here, to ask the advocate of gradual emancipation, what he means by it; and, since we are practical men, when and how he is going to make his schemes work out the desired result? What, then, does he mean. . . .

Will you tell us, when? Is it one, ten, fifty, a hundred, or two hundred years hence? Is it before or after you are dead?—before or after the present generation of slaves are dead?—before or after slavery has severed the Union, and brought down upon us the judgments of an insulted and sin-avenging God? 'Vengeance is mine, I will repay, saith the Lord.' Do then tell us when you intend to take the ground of immediate emancipation? And besides, admitting that you have gotten over all other difficulties in the way of instruction, &c. how will you contrive to keep these instructed ones quiet? When most stupid and brutish, they have, as you say, so much of sense, that they feel their wrongs most keenly, and so much of spirit, that they pant for the opportunity to avenge them. How then will you keep them quiet, as the work of instruction goes on? Will they feel their wrongs less keenly as their minds become more enlightened, and they are thus enabled to understand and appreciate them, in all their length and breadth, and height and depth? What is fact? Do the most enlightened slaves feel their wrongs less keenly, or breathe less of the spirit of revenge than others? How then are you going to keep them quiet?

But suppose you succeed in this, and the time does at last come for you to take the ground of immediate emancipation, how are *you* going to work out the desired result? How are you going to make your gradualism of theory and practice slide off into immediatism? Will you take your stand alone? Ten to one they will call you a 'fanatic' or an 'incendiary' if you do. Will you wait, then, until you can go with the multitude? Many men have many minds, and though you may think that every thing is ripe for immediate action, others may take the liberty to differ from you, just as you now take the liberty to differ from us; and how then are you going to make the multitude think with you, and take the same stand with you? or rather, lead the way for you? And, these difficulties removed, how will you contrive to get the master's consent? How will you show him that the condition of his instructed, well-fed and well-clothed slaves, is not infinitely better than it would be, if they were free; and that he is not therefore bound, on the principles of benevolence, to retain them in that happy servitude? And, difficulties of this character being overcome, how are you going to manage these instructed slaves when you set them free? Will instruction make them all christians, and cause them to return good for evil? Or will it, in the vast majority of cases, only kindle the spirit of revenge to deeper indignation, and arm it to greater mischief? And if, as you say, so keen is the sense of injury, and so rife the spirit of revenge among them now, when most senseless and stupid, that the announcement of freedom would be but the watchword of insurrection and blood, what are you to do when they have become instructed? Will not the sense of injury then be keener, and the spirit of revenge fiercer? As you make proclamation of freedom, will not these oppressed, but instructed ones, who have seen their wrongs more clearly and felt them more keenly than while in ignorance, turn upon their masters, and, with vengeance in their eye, demand why they did not give them their freedom before? In a word, how will you avoid the evils of immediate and universal emancipation at that time? While you have been getting rid of some difficulties, will not others have risen up? How will you guard against, and how dispose of them?

But without waiting for an answer to these inquiries, I will proceed with my remarks. It should be recollected here, that different schemes of emancipation take their names from the different *doctrines* on which they are based, rather than from their actual operation. Thus the scheme of Immediate Emancipation is built upon the doctrine, that *immediate emancipation is the duty of the master and the right of the slave*, and takes its name accordingly. All schemes of Gradual Emancipation are built upon the doctrine, *that gradual emancipation is the duty of the master and the right of the slave*, and take their name accordingly. Now the actual operation of the doctrine of immediate emancipation may be gradual on the community, taken as a community—just as is the doctrine of immediate repentance. Indeed, the doctrine of immediate emancipation is nothing more or less than that of immediate repentance, applied to this particular sin; and therefore in this case, as in others, its actual operation on the community as such, may be gradual. It may in point of fact become the power of God to the actual repentance of one here and another there, and not of the whole community at once. And if any are disposed to rate out at this, that after all it is nothing but a scheme of gradual emancipation, then I have only to say *first*, if this be so, that there is no such thing as immediate repentance in respect to any sin, and the doctrine that teaches it is false; and *second*, that if this scheme be gradual, then schemes that are built on the doctrine of gradual emancipation, are not schemes of emancipation at all, but rather schemes of perpetual and everlasting servitude; and *third*, that there are none so blind as those who will not see.

The distinction I have made is a most obvious one. The veriest child can see and understand it. On the one scheme, I come to the conscience of the community as a community, and of the individual as an individual, with the pressure of immediate duty—duty now—duty on the spot; and if, in point of fact, it be only here and there one at a time who yields to that pressure and repents—what then? Am I to be cashiered as a gradualist, and my scheme of repentance as mere gradualism? Not by men of sense and candor.

My remark then is this, that slavery can never be remedied by any schemes of gradual emancipation—i.e. by any schemes which are built, and which act on the principle that gradual emancipation is the duty of the master and the right of the slave. And the plain reason is, the *principle of reform*, with which they start and on which they proceed, is a wrong principle. It does not teach the *'vital power'* of the mischief. This is clear; for in the first place, the doctrine on which these schemes are built is *a false doctrine.* It expressly asserts that present emancipation is not duty, and therefore virtually asserts that present slaveholding is duty and is not therefore sin. It asserts this to day. The morrow comes, and it asserts the same to-morrow. The next day comes, and it still asserts the same. Weeks, months, years roll on, and still the doctrine is evermore the same—present emancipation is not duty and present slaveholding is not sin. Duty and guilt are always crowded into the morrow, and thus to all intents and purposes crowded out of existence. And now I affirm that the doctrine which does this is a false doctrine. It admits, perhaps, that there is guilt somewhere, but it always screens the culprit. It cannot therefore be true.

And farther, it is a *wicked doctrine*, and all schemes built upon it are therefore wicked. It is so, because it respects the assumed rights and imagined interests of the master, in preference to the real rights and interests of the slave. If either party is to be favored in the work of remedy in preference to the other, most obviously it should be the injured. But the doctrine of gradual emancipation, and all schemes built upon it go on the assumption that the rights and interests of the injurer are to be consulted first. They take the ground, therefore, that the rights and interests of the slave are of secondary importance, and that the rights and interests of the master, though usurped and imaginary, are to be the *primary* standard of decision, in respect to the time when and the mode in which the wrested and trampled rights of the slave are to be restored. Now I maintain that such doctrine and such schemes are *wicked.* They do not lift a finger in the way of breaking the rod of the oppressor. On the contrary, they take sides with him against the oppressed. They justify him in the present retention of his usurped authority and power. They even give his continued oppression the sanction of their authority. They license his present retention of the wages of iniquity, and authorize its continuance, until such time as he, himself being judge, can give them up without inconvenience; and thereby, they frame an excuse behind which, if disposed, he may entrench himself forever.

This leads me therefore to say, that the doctrine in question is an *inefficient doctrine.* How can it be otherwise? False and wicked, what efficacy can it have in the work of remedying falsehood and wickedness? It throws the charge of guilt back upon the past, or on upon the future, and brings in a plea of innocence for the present. How then can it awaken conviction of guilt—the indispensible prerequisite to all genuine repentance and real reformation? It pushes emancipation, too, into the distant future, and talks of it as duty at some time and in some way; but it always talks of doing duty to-morrow, and doing it gradually even then. But what child does not know, that to-morrow never comes—that the duty of the morrow is never the duty of to-day?

But this is not the worst; this doctrine gives up the whole ground of debate between freedom and slavery, and virtually takes the side of slavery. For it admits the principle, that in some cases it is lawful to hold man as property, leaving it to the slaveholder to decide whether his be such a case or not; or rather, deciding for him, that it is. It yields therefore the whole ground in debate. It admits the very principle out of which all slaveholding has grown; by which it is perpetuated on which the slaveholder, in his present practice, acts; under which he ever finds an apology for his sin, and for which, therefore, as the fundamental principle and only safeguard of continued slaveholding he warmly contends. What power on the conscience, what influence on the life, then, can such a doctrine have? Can you change a man's opinions and practice on a subject, so long as you yield him the main and fundamental principle in debate? Can you make the slaveholder quit his slaveholding, so long as you admit to him, that in some cases, himself being judge, it is right for him to practice it? As soon might you think to stop the slave-traffic, and yet admit to the slave-trader that in some cases, himself being judge in the case, it is perfectly right to carry it on. He would be very sure not to find a case in which it would be wrong for him to do it, whatever might be true of others. You never would find him condemning himself as a pirate. He would understand the law of self-preservation, if not the law of interest, too well for that. Such doctrine would never reach the case. It would be the extreme of impotency....

3. *That the only true and effectual scheme of remedy, is that of Immediate Emancipation.* This scheme, as I have said, is so named, because it is built and acts on the doctrine, that immediate emancipation is the duty of the master, and the right of the slave. And I maintain, it is the only true and efficient means of remedy. It is so,

(1). Because it *starts right in theory.* Its doctrine is the *true doctrine.* It takes the ground that slaveholding is, in all cases, wicked; and this, as I have shown, is the true ground. The scheme thus entrenches itself in the omnipotence of truth, and cannot but be an efficient one.

And besides, whether true or not, the doctrine at *the outset, calls in question the starting point and fundamental principle of all slavery.* That principle, as I have shown, is the principle, admitted in theory and acted on in practice, that in *some* cases, at discretion, it is lawful to hold man as property. From this admitted in theory, as the *starting point* has originated, first the demand and market for slaves, then the traffic, and then the system of slavery. Slaveholding, traffic, market, all are but parts of the same system of iniquity and blood. They all originated from, and are all perpetuated by the one principle, admitted in theory, and acted on in practice, that in *some* cases at discretion, it is lawful to hold man as property. This one principle, then is the originating and the sustaining principle of all slavery. This once denied and abandoned as a principle of action, and all slaveholding would be at an end. Now the doctrine of immediate emancipation, and therefore the scheme built upon it, *begins* its operations here. It calls this principle in question at the outset, and pronounces it false and wicked. It thus lays the axe at the root of the tree. It admits not as valid, either the fundamental principle of slavery, or the objections urged in apology for it. It denies the whole, and pronounces the whole matter of slaveholding wicked, both in theory and practice. Slaveholding and all its connected sins began by *starting wrong in theory—* on a wrong and wicked principle of action; and its iniquities are perpetuated by continued action on that principle. And now the doctrine of immediate emancipation proposes that the remedy shall begin at the same spot—viz. *by starting right in* theory—i.e. with the denial and abandonment of that wrong principle of action, out of which all slaveholding has grown. Of course, true or not, if this doctrine prevails, slavery is demolished. Its efficacy on slavery must of necessity be radical and mighty.

And more, this scheme of immediate emancipation starts right in theory in another respect—viz. *it assails slavery in its true character, as a moral, rather than a physical evil.* All moral evils, it is true, have more or less of physical evil connected with them, and growing, as a necessary consequence, out of them. Intemperance, for example, carries most frightful physical evils in its train, and these taken by themselves may be spoken of as such; and intemperance, when you speak only with reference to these, may very properly be called it an evil, &c. But it were wide of the truth to call it an evil merely, when you speak of it in reference to its *moral character.* When you talk of character, it were treachery to truth, to call it aught less than sin. Its true and real character is that of a moral evil—a sin. The same is true of slavery. There are, it is true, many physical evils connected with and growing out of it, and these may be spoken of, separately, as physical evils. But to speak of slavery, taken as a whole, as *an* EVIL, meaning by it a mere physical evil, or at best, nothing more than a physical moral evil; to speak of it as a calamity, an unfortunate system, &c., is to talk utter nonsense. It is to misrepresent its character. Slavery, in its true and real character in the sight of God, is a moral evil—a sin—a crime, and not a mere undefined evil, or calamity, or misfortune. And every man who is in any way implicated in the matter, is implicated in a sin, and not merely in a misfortune or calamity. If, therefore, this sin is ever remedied, it must be assailed and remedied in this, *its true character.* To assail it in any other is certain defeat. . . .

It is as a moral evil—a sin then, that this matter is to be assailed, and remedied, if remedied at all. To talk about it, and operate on it as a mere physical evil, or if moral, as moral only to generations past, is utter folly. You can never reach the difficulty in this way. It is a moral evil, and must therefore be so regarded and acted on, if you would act to the purpose. Removal, colonization—what is it but a mere physical operation? What, but a mere *carting off* of slavery? . . .

No—no—you can never operate on mind, to move it to action, by the law of physics, or by those moral influences, which may be imagined to cluster around, and be incidental to physical processes and operations. To think of remedying slavery thus, is absurd. Do your utmost, and the spirit of slavery, its fundamental principles, yet live. If you would act to purpose, you must assail it in its true character—as a moral evil, for the existence of which, moral agents are responsible and guilty.

Now it is in this character, especially, that the scheme of immediate emancipation assails it. The fundamental doctrine of this scheme is, that slaveholding is wicked. As certain, then, as it is, that truth is power, so certain is it that this doctrine, laying the axe as it does at the root of the tree, will sooner or later become mighty, through God, to the pulling down of this strong hold.

There is every reason, then, for supposing that the scheme in question is the only efficient one. *It starts right in theory.* Its doctrine is just what it needs to be, in order to make it efficient. It is the true doctrine. It calls the fundamental principle of slavery in question at the outset, and pronounces it wrong and wicked; and finally, it assails the matter in its true character—as a sin, and not as a calamity or evil merely. No theory could be better fitted to secure its end, and therefore, the scheme that is built upon it, cannot but be of mighty efficacy.

(2). This scheme is the only true and effectual one, because *it starts right in practice.* Right theory generally leads to right practice. It is so in this case. Other schemes of emancipation content themselves with lopping off the branches, in the hope that in this way the tree will ultimately die. And perhaps it would, but for the fact, that the branches grow faster than they are, or can be cut off. This scheme, however, aims its blows at the root. It first corrects the wrong and wicked *theory*, out of which all slaveholding in practice *has* grown, and by which it is perpetuated. It then proceeds to apply its principles to the right spot—viz. *that practice itself.* Now this is beginning in the application of its principles just where it should begin. It assails the practice first and directly; and does it on the principle, that all indirect attacks are fruitless. What! abolish slavery indirectly, by a mere incidental influence, or rather by no influence, save just letting it alone to its own 'calm and dispassionate reflections'!! Leviathan is not so tamed. There never was a grander mistake than has been made on this subject. Philanthropists in England and America once thought that if they could succeed in putting a stop to the Foreign slave trade, slavery would ultimately die, of its own accord. And so they wasted their energies in the tedious, though at length successful efforts for its abolition. The civilized world, with one consent, pronounced the traffic crime, and forbade it under the severest penalties. And what was the result? Did slavery die? Was the monster starved, for want of new supplies? Nay, were his supplies diminished a whit? The truth is, they went to work the wrong way. They began at the wrong place. It has been so proved by the actual experiment. The whole matter thus far is a comparative failure. . . .

In the remedy of all such prevailing sins, you begin where the sins themselves begin. You must dry up the fountain, or you can never dry up the stream. You must shut up the market, or you can never cut off supply. Abolish slavery, by abolishing the traffic in slaves! Shut up the market by cutting off supplies! Yes, truly, if it *could* be done. But it cannot. Cover the ocean with your fleets, and the shores of Africa with your colonies, if you will, but you cannot stop that traffic. So long as the market exists, and cries 'give,' 'give,' it will be supplied. The traffic will go on. You cannot prevent it. . . .

Now the scheme of immediate emancipation does this. It begins with the market. It takes the ground that all slaveholding is wicked, and demands therefore that it cease, it plies the conscience with the doctrine of immediate duty, and rests not until the master has yielded his assent. In this way it abolishes the practice of holding slaves, and of course shuts up the market, annihilates the traffic, and puts an end to the whole system of slavery, and its connected iniquities and woes. I say, then, that the scheme of immediate emancipation is the only true and efficient scheme of remedy for slavery. It is the only scheme that starts right in theory, and in practice too. Let it once become the prevalent scheme, let its doctrine once become the prevalent doctrine in our land, and slaveholding, and with it, the slave-traffic is abolished forever. The rod of the oppressor is broken. The cry of violence ceases. The oppressed go free. The shouts of jubilee are heard. The judgments of heaven are turned back, and God, in mercy, smiles on us again. . . .

. . . Let the pulpit and the press speak out with all their power, and the years will not be many before jubilee will be proclaimed throughout our land, and the world be permitted, in millions of slaves emancipated, to see a living witness to the power and efficacy of the scheme of IMMEDIATE EMANCIPATION.

But you will say, perhaps, 'all this *sounds* very well; but after all, it is a most absurd and Quixotic scheme—"the wildness of fanaticism" itself. What! turn two millions of slaves out upon the community at once'!

By no means. Nothing is farther from our designs and wishes. We would not turn them adrift on society, if we could. So far from it, we are opposed to such a measure. We insist, even, that the master has no right thus to set them afloat on society, unlooked after and uncared for. He may not add insult to injury in this way, any more than by retaining them in bondage, or giving them their freedom on condition of expatriation.

'Well, then, what would you do? What does your immediate emancipation mean?'

It means simply and only an immediate emancipation from slavery, not from all its consequences. It is simply, that the slaves be at once delivered from the control of arbitrary and irresponsible power, and, like other men, put under the control of equitable laws, equitably administered. Slavery, as I have shown, is the principle that man, in some cases, at his own discretion, may hold his fellow man as property. This, adopted as a *practical principle*, is slavery. Rejected as a *practical principle*, is slavery rejected. Immediate Emancipation, then, means that slaveholders, as individuals, and as a community, should at once give up this as a principle of action, and so doing, give up all that treatment which is based upon it, and thus put their slaves on the footing of men, and under the control of motive and laws. It is, for example, that England should at once yield the *principle* of taxing us at pleasure, with out our consent; and in this *one* act, yield of course, all the treatment growing out of; and based upon that principle.

Or more specifically, immediate emancipation means,

1. That the slaveholder, so far as he is concerned, should cease at once to hold or employ human beings as property.

2. That he should put them at once, in his regard and treatment of them, on the footing of men, possessing the inalienable rights of man.

3. That instead of turning them adrift, on society, uncared for, he should offer to employ them as free hired laborers, giving them, however, liberty of choice whether to remain in his service or not.

4. That from this *starting point—this emancipation from slavery itself*, he should at once *begin* to make amends for the past, by entering heartily on the work of qualifying them for, and elevating them to all the privileges and blessings of freedom and religion;—thus doing what he can to emancipate them from their ignorance, degradation, &c.—in other words, from the *consequences* of slavery, as well as from the thing itself.

Thus much in respect to the individual. In respect to the community as such, the scheme means,

1. That, in its collective capacity, it should yield the principle of property in man, and thus cease to recognize any human being as the property of another.

2. That, by wise and equitable enactments, suited to the various circumstances of the various classes of its members, it should recognize them, all alike, as men—as subjects of equal law, under its, and only its control, to be deprived of 'life, liberty and the pursuit of happiness,' on no account but that of crime, and then, by due and equitable process of law.

And farther, in respect to those slaves, who might be disposed to leave their master's service, and become idle vagrants in society, the scheme means,

1. That they should come under the control vagrant laws—just as white vagrants do.

2. That, if they commit crimes, they should be tried and condemned, like other vagrants, by due process of law.

And finally, in respect to non-slaveholders, the scheme means,

1. That they, acting as individuals, should *yield the principle of slavery*, and so doing, yield all that supineness and inaction on the subject, which grows out of its virtual, if not professed admission.

2. That they should adopt its opposite as *their* principle of action, and so doing, *begin* at once, in *every* lawful and practicable way, to enlighten the public mind, to change the tone of public sentiment, to organize and concentrate its energies, and, in this and other ways, do what they can to convince slaveholders of their duty, and persuade them to do it. In a word, in respect to all the parties concerned, the scheme means, *a yielding up of the* PRINCIPLE *of slavery as a practical principle—a basis of action, and the adoption of its opposite.* This one act is emancipation from *slavery*. All that follows is the carrying out of the new principle of action, and is to emancipation just what sanctification is to conversion; or just what a subsequent sober life, the

recovery of health, reputation, property, &c., are to the adoption, as a basis of action, of the principle of entire abstinence from ardent spirit. . . .

The evil to be remedied is a moral evil, and we propose therefore to remedy it as such. In the first place, then, we disclaim all physical force, and all unconstitutional legal interposition.

We disclaim all trickery, either in doctrines or measures. We have no idea of playing the hypocrite. We would not, if we could, frame a set of doctrines or adopt a system of measures, which should say one thing here and another there, or which should profess one thing, viz. to let slavery alone, and yet at the same time aim to overthrow it. We are for being frank, open, plain-hearted. We mean to think out, and speak out our opinions and designs. If we really think the present slaveholder guilty, we mean to tell him so frankly, and not lull him to sleep, and lead him to perdition by the soothing lullaby of entailment, present innocence and future repentance. And if our *real* design is the overthrow of slavery, we mean to avow it and, from what we know of our Southern friends, we believe they will like us the better for our frankness. We have no idea of catching the slaveholder asleep on this subject, and, by honied words and smooth speeches, tricking him out of his slaves, before he knows it. He will not let them slip through his fingers so easily. This is a case that demands plain dealing. Nothing else will answer. And, therefore, we intend frankly to avow our design; and then, in order to accomplish it, we mean,

To preach the truth, the whole truth, on the subject. The grand obstacle in the way is, the *will* of the slaveholder. This being changed, there would of necessity be a change in all those laws and other obstacles which have grown out of it; and this will, if changed at all, is to be changed by 'light and love' on this subject, as well as on others. So, by God's blessing, we intend to change it; and therefore, instead of concealing our light, and showing out our love in honied words and smooth speeches, we intend to go on the principle that 'faithful are the *wounds* of a friend,' and believing that 'open rebuke is better than secret love,' speak out clearly and distinctly, and let in on the slave-holder's conscience the concentrated light and authority of the pulpit and the press. In this way we hope to reach him, and at the same time organize, and concentrate a public sentiment on the subject, that shall strike off every chain, break every yoke, and sweep away, in its onward and resistless progress, every vestige of slavery. Such things have been done in other cases, and we trust they can be done in this.

And now do you say, that this is not telling how?—that here is no plan? It is the how, and the plan of Jesus Christ, in respect to all sin—slavery not excepted. It is the plan on which he has been acting, and is now acting, in conjunction with his people, for the conversion of the world. It is simply the application of his plan for the abolition of every sin to the abolition of a particular one. How does Christ propose to change the will of the world and convert it from all sin to himself? Not by magic—not by miracle; but by the humble, yet mighty instrumentality of his people and his ministers, living out, speaking out, printing out, and preaching out the *truth*—the one great truth, to which all others are subservient, that 'God now commandeth all men, every where, to repent.' This, is the grand weapon in the warfare, and, through God, it is mighty to the pulling down of strong holds, and will yet bring the world into captivity to Christ. We propose to try it in the present case, and we doubt not its efficacy will be such as to show that its temper is etherial.

And now, do you say still that this is all talk—that it does not go into the detail of the plan at all? Let us come then to the detail? We propose,

1. A national Society, whose special business it shall be to superintend this great movement, to collect facts, print tracts and send them abroad upon the winds, to enlist the press and the pulpit, to employ agents and send them abroad to confer with influential individuals, address popular assemblies, assemblies of clergymen, firm auxiliaries, &c.; in a word, to throw out an influence, steady, strong and increasing on the subject, until every section of the land shall be pervaded with it, and the people with one consent, shall rise and say to the oppressed, 'Go free.'

And in carrying this operation into effect, we propose—

2. To begin where the influence of slavery is least felt, and there are, therefore, fewest obstacles to success. Of course, we shall begin with Northern ministers and Northern men, and among these, with those who are not committed on the side of slavery, but whose minds are most open to conviction. And by the time we get these right, we shall expect to find that other minds have become open to conviction, and long before the work is thoroughly done up at the North, if we mistake not, the leaven will have begun to work at the South. Minds there will be open to conviction. We shall then go there, and first address ourselves to the ministers of the gospel, then to other good men, then to the community generally, and among others, to those broken-hearted mothers and deserted wives, who are doomed to weep (day and night over sons and husbands that have fallen victims to the shameless licentiousness, which slavery every where begets. In this way we expect to proceed, and what is more *succeed*. . . .

III

Moral Suasion and Politics

6

"An Address to the Abolitionists of Massachusetts, on the Subject of Political Action" (1838)

Massachusetts Anti-Slavery Society

By the late 1830s, moral suasion had succeeded in creating a critical mass—albeit still relatively small—of antislavery voters who were anxious to take their cause to the polls and to engage more actively in political agitation. In the following selection, Francis Jackson and Amos A. Phelps, writing for the board of managers of the Massachusetts Anti-Slavery Society, lay out the political actions that abolitionists might employ on behalf of the slave. The general strategy was to work within the two-party system, using their influence to shape party platforms, influence the nomination process, and serve as a balance of power between Whigs and Democrats. Acceptable tactics included petitioning legislatures, questioning candidates, and voting for antislavery politicians. If no candidate were a friend to the slave, abolitionists were encouraged to "scatter" their votes by writing in the names of abolitionists.

To the Abolitionists of Massachusetts—

The Board of Managers of the Massachusetts Anti-Slavery Society, desire to offer you a few suggestions, on the course recommended to you by duty and a wise policy, in relation to the exercise of your political privileges.

The uncompromising character of the early adherents to our cause, compelled the respect of the conscientious and reflecting part of the community. They stood firm, announcing the most thorough principles, not yielding one jot to the most plausible or popular prejudices. Men at first were startled by the boldness of their position, but they had at length the satisfaction of seeing public sentiment slowly turn in their favor. The mighty re-action is felt, and we are now going forward with wind and tide. The grandeur of the principles developed,—the constancy with which they were maintained, through odium and danger,—the magnitude of the interests contended for,—these things appealed to every man in the land, who had a spark of heroism or heavenly enthusiasm in his nature. Our cause has gathered into its ranks in the short space of seven years, its hundreds of thousands; and numbers, among its friends, the most fearless, and God-devoted spirits in the land.

We mention these things, not as an idle boast, but that you may lay to heart the responsibilities, that grow out of your present position. Your duty, as citizens of the State, more than ever demands your serious attention and thought. We pray you to consider what we shall say to you on this subject.

There are those who disapprove of every form of political action, on the part of abolitionists. They contend that our cause should be presented exclusively under its religious and philanthropic aspect; that it will be degraded and enfeebled at the North, by connecting it with politics,—while, at the South, our political efforts will rouse a more united and determined resistance to our objects.

We cannot yield to this reasoning. It proceeds, we think, upon a narrow view of the subject. Politics, rightly considered, is a branch of morals, and cannot be deserted innocently. Our moral convictions must follow us to the ballot-box. They are not less imperative on us as citizens, than as members of the church, or fathers of families. In each, we have nothing to do, but to carry out our highest idea, simply and fearlessly. If the public mind is misled or vitiated on the subject of politics,—if politics has come to be considered as a game played by the desperate and unprincipled for power or emolument, it must not therefore be abandoned to them. The worldly and corrupt would like nothing better, than that the good should retire, in fear or disgust, from this wide sphere of action. It seems to be our mission to substitute, in the minds of men, a new set of associations with the subject of politics. We believe that the tendency of the abolition efforts has, visibly, been to infuse more comprehensive principles into political bodies, and suggest to them purer motives of action, than have prevailed heretofore. Look at the dignified tone of the Reports and Resolves on Slavery and the Right of Petition, in several of the State Legislatures. Mark the high religious and moral stand assumed by Adams, Slade, Morris and others, in Congress. It is worth noting that the abolitionists form the only great party, in our age, who, aiming at a wide social reform, and operating on and through social institutions, yet rest their efforts and their hopes professedly on religious ground;—on faith in God, and faith in the God-like in man. That slavery is a sin against God, has been our rallying-cry from the beginning; heard not merely from the pulpit, but in the courts of justice, the popular assembly, and the halls of government. Our strength lies, and we well know it, in the religious sentiment of men, recognizing a Christian brother in the crushed slave, and at once stimulating, emboldening and sanctifying the efforts for his deliverance.

To think of purposely keeping such a question—a question of essentially moral and religious character, but having important public bearings—out of politics, is like the view some persons have, that religion belongs to the temple and the Sabbath, but is out of place in week-day life. Religion runs the risk of being sadly profaned, adulterated, caricatured, counterfeited, in encountering or mixing with the common business or amusements of men; but we nevertheless press it in among them. This is, after all, but a question of time. The subject of slavery must, obviously, sooner or later, enter deeply, into general politics. Slavery is itself the creature of law, that is of political action. It can only be finally destroyed, by the same power that gave it being.

We, however, value political action, chiefly as a means of agitating the subject. The great support of slavery,—without which it could not stand in the United States, two years,—is a corrupt public sentiment, among those who are not slaveholders. The current doctrine of the North is, that slavery is, indeed, an evil, and if southern society were to be reconstructed, slavery should, by no means, be introduced as an element; but that *in present circumstances, and with a view to probable consequences*, it cannot reasonably be expected of slaveholders to give up their slaves. This is what we suppose to be meant, by people's being opposed, to slavery *'in the abstract.'*

Now, our first object is to replace these views, by an earnest conviction, embracing the heart and understanding of every man, woman and child we can reach, that duty and interest do now require of every slaveholder, the immediate emancipation of his slaves. We would make the public sentiment of the North a tonic, instead of an opiate to southern conscience; we would unite and concentrate it, until it shall tell, in a manner perfectly irresistible upon the sense of right, the pride of social standing and character, even upon the interest of the slaveholder; until it shall help to make real to his mind, and he shall feel, in the air around him, the guilt, the danger, the deep disgrace, the ruinous impolicy of the relation he sustains. We believe this course to be enjoined by Christianity, free from all constitutional objections, and consecrated by the example of our elder abolitionists, Franklin, Jay, Rush, and other revered founders of the Republic. Such have, indeed, ever been the appointed means for the removal of great social abuses. These means will not lack their accustomed power, in a country whose institutions are so emphatically the exponents of the popular will.

Another objection originating in a less friendly spirit, but resting on political grounds, is gravely put forth. We are told that our feeling for our fellow man (at least if he be colored,) must be defined by geographical lines; that we have no right to plead for an oppressed brother if he stands outside of our own political enclosure. To this is added the certainly novel theory, that it is the nature of sin to reform itself and that the oppression of the slaveholder would soon cease, if we would only withdraw all open sympathy from the injured, to bestow it on the oppressor. However absurd and revolting these sophisms may appear to you, they are reiterated with great confidence and frequency. To state them distinctly seems all that is necessary to expose them to the contempt they merit.

All we need for the overthrow of slavery is to gain the ear of the people. This is done by agitation; and never is agitation so thorough and effectual, as when it begins in the halls of legislation. We laugh to scorn the pomp and circumstance with which Mr. Calhoun, or Mr. Clay, or some other great slaveholding statesman, annually proclaims a final victory over fanaticism. Do they not see that our very defeats are triumphs to us? Have they yet to learn that revolutions never roll backwards? That our opposers are but erecting paper-ramparts, against the surges of an inswelling Atlantic? That their resolutions are but words?

That a breath unmakes them, as a breath has made? They are only doing our work. The country has learned more of the dangerous tendencies of slavery, and of the desperate character and designs of its supporters, by the discussions in Congress, than we could have instilled directly for years. Again, in the mere process of signing a petition,—the simplest form of political action,—strength and clearness are added to the convictions of thousands. So much force and definiteness do our principles and feelings acquire, by expression; so much moral vigor does a man gain, by openly taking his side.

We cannot be justified in abandoning any wide field of action, be it moral, social, religious or political. There can be no vantage ground for the wrong side. The slavery question cannot, and ought not, we think, to be kept wholly disjoined from politics. It should not be made a mere political question, but the religious and moral sense of the people must speak out, on the subject, with precision and authority, to their political representatives.

Unquestionably that voice is to go forth, commanding the use of all moral, lawful and constitutional means to overthrow slavery. We believe the question of abolition is one, perhaps the only one, on which the North can be brought to unite. Our cause is, we think, destined to increase so rapidly, as to threaten political extinction to every public man here, who arrays himself against it. Instructions will go forth from the constituent bodies, that will command the obedience of northern representatives in Congress. When this is done, slavery must cease in the metropolis of the nation, and slavery in the States cannot long survive. We doubt not, before five years are gone, it will be the South, instead of the North, that will be disunited and vacillating. It does not belong to the character of their cause, or of the age and country we live in, that the South can long keep their ranks unbroken. Even now, there is no real unity of interest or opinion, between the farming and planting slave States.

Political action doubtless brings temptations and hazards; but so does any successful action. Success is itself dangerous. What then? shall we not aim at success? Shall a man seclude himself from the world, lest the world prove too strong for his virtue? As practical men we cannot proceed on these scruples. We cannot consent to forego the power to do good, from the apprehension that its possession may tempt us to use it for evil.

Is it then our purpose to recommend to abolitionists the formation of a distinct political party? So far from this, we think such a policy would be in the highest degree dangerous, if not fatal to the efficiency of our organization.— Our most intelligent friends, throughout the country, deprecate our assuming the character of a third political party. Such a course would be opposed to the well settled policy and wise example of the English abolitionists, who have always kept the political aspect of their cause subordinate to the religious. Remember that abolition was carried in England, mainly as a religious question.

If we were a political party, the struggle for places of power and emolument would render our motives suspected, even if it did not prove too strong a temptation to our integrity.

Make our cause mainly political, and it would be at once excluded from nearly every pulpit in the land.

If we were a distinct party, every member of it must vote for its candidates, however he might disagree with them on other important points of public policy. This would involve two great evils. The sacrifice thus demanded, being greater than we can reasonably expect most men to make, accessions to our party would be greatly retarded;—and, what is a more serious difficulty, divisions would inevitably arise among ourselves, growing out of the struggles of different sections of our own party, to secure, the nomination of candidates of their peculiar sentiments. Whig abolitionists would ask for a whig candidate: the democrats of our party would insist on our nominating a democrat.

Experience seems to show, that under a free government, there cannot be at one time, more than two powerful political parties. The parties that now divide the country are active, zealous and strong. Years must elapse, if we should organize politically, before we could be any thing but an uninfluential minority.

Our position, as a small minority party in politics would be hazardous and perplexing. There is danger that low considerations of expediency would intrude upon our sense of eternal right.

Political adventurers, loud in their professions, unscrupulous in their means, would attach themselves to us. Disappointed men who have been disowned by other parties, would come among us to use us as tools for their personal advancement, to disgrace us by their inconsistency, to lower our hitherto high standard of principle, and perhaps sacrifice us in the day of trial.

Belonging, as we now do, to the various political parties, we can readily work our principles in, among them. Our present political ties and sympathies give us a strong hold over political associates. We should lose all this mode of influence, by withdrawing from them. Our withdrawal would be held equivalent to a declaration of war.

A new political organization would have, of course, the combined hostility of the old parties. It is now the interest of each to conciliate us, for the sake of our votes. Were those votes pledged to our own candidates, the other parties would have a common interest in crushing us.

To form a political party, on anti-slavery grounds, would involve a needless abandonment of our other political preferences, and therefore would imply, not merely that abolition is the *first*, but that it is the only public object, in which abolitionists feel interested. This is not true, and to produce such a state of feeling is as undesirable, as it would be impracticable.

To conclude this part of the subject, our true policy is not to turn party politicians, but in politics as elsewhere to stand firm by our principles, and let the politicians come to us.

Of each of the three forms of political action, petitioning, the interrogating of candidates for office, and suffrage, we have a few words to address to you.

We pray you not to weary in the work of petitioning the national and state legislatures. It is the anti-slavery petitions, mainly, that have unlocked the lips of our legislatures, on the subject of abolition, and slowly compelled the newspaper-press to recognize, and unwillingly to aid, our movements. The agitation, caused by the rejection of our petitions, has spread into every village. This simple mode of action marks our growing strength; indicates, definitely the people's will; enlightens our adversaries with the knowledge of our numbers; and is felt, by our representatives, as a great support in the discharge of their duty. Depend upon it, the time has come when the members of Congress, from this State, feel relieved, under their great responsibility, by their constituents holding a decided—aye, even a peremptory tone, on the subject of slavery.

We hope women will pour in their petitions to Congress, at its next session, in redoubled numbers. Let them thank God, and take new courage, for they have done great good. We feel deeply the value of the earnest labours of women, in our cause. All admit slavery is to be overthrown by a reformed public opinion; but public opinion is not composed of the opinion of either sex exclusively. In every christian and civilized community, self-devoted, intelligent women are among the most important sources of moral and religious influence. Grievously do they err, who deem lightly of the fact, that in the moral strife between freedom and slavery, the women of the North are with the abolitionists.

Your representatives in the next State Legislature, and for the Congress of 1839, are to be chosen the coming autumn. They should be seasonably interrogated, as to their opinions on the most important matters connected with our cause, on which they may probably be called to act. After some consideration, the Board have concluded to recommend, that the interrogatories to candidates be limited, for the present year, to the two following subjects:— The immediate abolition of Slavery in the District of Columbia; and the admission of new States into the union whose Constitutions tolerate slavery.

Our Legislature at its last session, resolved 'that Congress ought to take measures for the abolition of slavery, in the District.' This vague language can satisfy no one. *When* ought Congress to take these 'measures'?—what are the 'measures' that Congress ought to take? and how long a time are these 'measures' to occupy, before the slave is to be free? Remember, that the Senate and the House both refused to assert that Congress ought to immediately abolish slavery in the District, though this proposition was moved as an amendment. The resolution of the Legislature, as passed, would be accorded to, even by some slaveholders. It may mean apprenticeship,—it may import colonization. This State owes it to herself to speak out distinctly, that none may misunderstand or gainsay. She will be shorn of a portion of her moral power, till this is done.

The application of Florida, to be admitted as a slaveholding member of the Union is to be acted on, at no distant day—probably at the next session of Congress. You ought, therefore, to see to it that remonstrances against its admission as a slaveholding State, are presented early in the session. Our northern statesmen should be seasonably taught, that they must not in future misrepresent and betray the rights and principles of New England, as was done in the recent admission of Arkansas.

We request the officers of County Societies, within their respective limits, to see that the candidates for Congress and for the State Senate and House of Representatives are duly interrogated and their answers published in the local newspapers.

The questions should, of course, be in writing; and it seems better that they should be written and signed, not by the officers of societies *as such*, but, as far as practicable by individual electors, political friends of the candidate interrogated. It is not advisable to ask any pledge from the candidate, but simply to inquire his present opinions. The questions to the State candidate may be, substantially, thus:

'Are you in favor of the passage of a resolution, by the State Legislature, declaring that Congress ought immediately to abolish slavery, in the District of Columbia?'

'Are you in favor of the passage of a resolution, declaring that no new State ought to be admitted into the Union, whose Constitution tolerates slavery?'

The questions to candidates for Congress should run thus:

'Are you in favor of the passage of an act of Congress for the immediate abolition of slavery, in the District of Columbia?'

'Are you opposed to the admission of any new State into the Union, whose Constitution tolerates slavery?'

A large school in politics, both in Great Britain and America, deny the right of instruction; principally on the ground, that if carried out, it would destroy the deliberative character of the representative body, and convert it into a mere instrument to register the edicts of the people. The practice, of exacting pledges from candidates, may be considered liable to similar objections. It is, however, sufficient to advert to the fact, that the presidential electors of all parties are uniformly chosen under an express pledge to vote for particular candidates, in order to shew, that no party has, in practice, scrupled to pledge its candidates. But in order to avoid any doubt or cavil on this point, we think it best to confine your inquiries, as we have already intimated, to the mere opinion for the time being, of the candidate. This you have a right to know; as without such knowledge it may often happen, that you cannot exercise intelligently your right of suffrage. It may be said, that a simple expression of opinion would, under the circumstances, be equivalent to a pledge. We deny that such is the fact, or that the thing is so understood. A pledge binds in all events. A previous expression of present opinion is not incompatible with keeping the mind still open to conviction, on listening to the opposing arguments. It is true, that a representative who should vote contrary to his previous professions, would find it necessary, before the next election, to satisfy his constituents that he came honestly by his new opinions; but this is certainly a very wholesome obligation, and one from which no honest man would desire exemption.

If it be objected, that these interrogatories may tempt candidates to belie their consciences for the sake of gaining votes, we reply, that to men of this easy virtue the whole action of society is full of temptation, but it cannot be suspended for their sakes. If the further objection be urged, that there is an indecorum in submitting to be thus questioned on the eve of an election, it is enough to reply, first, that as candidates are not usually nominated until the eve of an election, inquiries can be made at no other time; and, secondly, that inquiries of this nature, as they clearly imply confidence and not distrust, must be regarded rather as complimentary, than as derogatory to the candidate. We address him as an honest, straight-forward citizen, and no man of genuine dignity of character will feel himself degraded, either in public or private life, by giving a plain answer to a plain question, where the inquirer has a right to the information asked. As to the fear of indecorum, like most overstrained modesty, it will be usually found symptomatic of conscious corruption within. Suppose you were about to engage a commander for your ship, a superintendent of your farm, an agent for your factory, and were to inquire his views as to the principles or details of the employment he was to undertake. Would you endure his insolence if he were to reply, 'I consider it undignified and improper to satisfy you on these points. You are at liberty to gain what information you can of my history and reputation, and then to infer what are my views on the matter in question?' You would think, and probably but too justly, that he meant to cheat you. Will you bear such language from your political servants? No public man in this country is strong enough to sustain himself long, in this mode of defying the popular will. No party can do it. The right of the electors, to call for a frank disclosure of the opinions of candidates, on all subjects which may come within the scope of their official duties, has been expressly admitted by Martin Van Buren, Henry Clay, William H. Harrison, William Wirt, Edward Everett, and Marcus Morton, and by a host of other eminent statesmen. It is too late to question its validity. No man of plain integrity would shrink from the ordeal. The practice is eminently republican and useful. It is calculated to promote political honesty and open dealing, and to put an end to that double-faced and non-committal policy, by which politicians, of inferior abilities and low arts, sometimes crawl into power.

Your duties as voters are mainly negative. *Vote for no man, however estimable from general character and acquirements, who is not prepared to give a prompt, explicit, and satisfactory answer on the topics we have mentioned.* Be uncompromising on points of principle. Have no respect to persons. It is the secret of your strength, hitherto. Shew by your firmness, whether your heart is in your cause. Let not the fervor of political zeal, or the warmth of personal attachment, lead you to forfeit your character for resolution and consistency. Whoso loves father, or brother, or friend better than the truth, is not worthy of it.

We pray you to take no part, *as abolitionists*, in the nomination of candidates. Do not even vote, *by concert*, for candidates already in nomination. Let the act of voting be an individual act, but performed, by each voter, under a deep sense of responsibility. We are aware, that in many towns and districts, where you have considerable numerical strength, and where the answers of the regular political candidates may not be satisfactory, the temptation will be strong, to unite your forces upon a candidate of your own. We entreat you not to do this. Your example will be a dangerous one. On the other hand, do not stay away from the polls. Go, rather; and scatter your votes. This is the true way to make yourselves felt. Every scattering vote you cast, counts against the candidates of the parties; and will serve as an effectual admonition to them, to nominate the next time, men whom you can conscientiously support.

The candidates presented to your choice will, of course, be nominated either by the whigs or democrats. The most prominent individual of the whig party, and probably their next candidate for the presidency, is a slave holder, president of that stupendous imposture the Colonization Society, author of the fatal Missouri 'compromise,' and of the slavish resolutions against the abolitionists, lately passed by the Senate of the United States. On the other hand, the leader of the democratic party, 'the northern president with southern principles,' has deeply insulted this nation, by avowing his determination to veto any bill for the abolition of slavery in the District of Columbia, which may be passed by a majority of the people, in opposition to the wishes of the slave States.

No consistent abolitionist can vote for either of these individuals. It does not however follow, that he cannot vote for candidates for State offices or for Congress, who may be their friends and supporters. If the candidate before you be honest, capable, and true to your principles, we think you may fairly vote for him, without considering too curiously, whether his success might not have an indirect bearing on the interests of Mr. Clay or Mr. Van Buren. It is a golden maxim, 'Do the duty that lies nearest thee.' Vote for each man by himself, and on his own merits. If you attempt to make your rule more complicated, so as to include distant contingencies and consequences, it will be found perplexing and impracticable.

The independent course in politics, which we have recommended, supposes great prudence, disinterestedness, energy of purpose, and self-control, in those who are to adopt it. May you justify our confidence in you. Do your duty. Come out, in your strength, to the polls. Refuse to support any public man who trims, or equivocates, or conceals his opinions Beware of half way abolitionists; and of men, who are abolitionists but once a year. Prove that you do not require the machinery of party discipline, to vote strictly according to your professed principles. Do this, and you will rapidly acquire a deserved influence. 'Such a party,' as, Mr. Webster justly said, in speaking of the abolitionists, 'will assuredly cause itself to be respected.' Within the next two years, the friends of freedom might hold the balance of power, in every free State in the Union; and no man could ascend the presidential seat, against their will.

Our cause demands of us entire disinterestedness. We are not to desire power, for power's sake. Our prayers, and toil, and tears are not our own, but the slave's. We need circumspection. The attacks, that were formerly made on our principles and measures, are now turned upon our motives and personal characters. The corrupt and bitter portion of the newspaper press are beginning to discover, that the facts and arguments, in favor of our great doctrine of immediate emancipation, are irresistible, and are carrying conviction to almost every well informed and reflecting mind; and they are now trying to distort our motives, and blacken our reputations. This is making a false issue, but let it not too much disturb us. The true question for the public evidently is, Do we speak the truth? The inquiry, whether we are actuated by a right spirit, is, in reality, of very little comparative importance. The principle is all; the men nothing. Let God be true, and every man a liar.

Beware of forming alliances with any party. Enter into no stipulations in advance, for the disposition of a single vote. The party, or the press, or the politician that courts you most warmly to-day, will perhaps shew most malignance and treachery toward you, to-morrow. We have reason to be grateful to Heaven that, thus far, we have so little to thank either of the great parties for. The leading presses on both sides, have done their best to outrage and insult us. There has been an eager competition between them, to purchase southern votes, by sacrificing the rights, and aspersing the character of the abolitionists. Even now, though it is seen by all persons of common sagacity, and is even generally admitted in private conversation, that our ultimate success is certain, the same treatment is, to a considerable extent continued. The class of trading politicians take no far-sighted views even for themselves, still less for their party,—least of all, for their country. They cannot wait for the slow returns of an honest and liberal policy. Their object is to meet the exigency of the moment, to carry the present point; like prodigals lavishing the resources of the future upon the passing hour; like gamblers trusting to chance or trick, to extricate them from the embarrassments they are aware must, by and bye, come.

This competition for southern votes, has saved us from the too dangerous friendship of either of the political parties. The President of the United States, had, (in his first message to Congress,) avowed himself the suppliant tool of the southern slaveholders, when the Whig merchants of New York, determined not to be outbid, took occasion, in their address to the nation, to assure their southern brethren, that they were men, who 'thought the *possession* of property [not *its honest acquisition*] was evidence of merit!' and that persons of such sentiments, would be the last to disturb 'the peculiar property' of the south.

By counteracting forces like these, have we been providentially preserved from being absorbed by either of the political parties. With the fundamental principles of those parties, when properly understood, abolitionism has strong affinities. The idea of the whig party in this country is order, the supremacy of law, the sacredness of the person, the inviolability of property. Who has a stronger interest in these things than we? Who have suffered more than we, from anarchy and misrule? Who have pleaded more earnestly, for the right of every man to that which he produces by his own labor;—a right which is at the foundation of all property ?—On the other hand, the great Democratic idea is Liberty, Reform, Progress, Equal Rights;—and are not these our very breath of life?

We are far from asserting, that these noble principles are actually embodied, in the leaders of either of our political parties. So far from this, the principles are in danger of being themselves brought into disgrace, by the selfish and inconsistent men, who pretend to represent them. Still, while these principles are, however imperfectly, represented in the struggle of the adverse parties, it is natural and right, that individual abolitionists should range themselves, in these struggles, according as their political theories may incline them to take one or the other set of views. This must, however, be done in strict subordination to the interests of that hallowed cause, to which we have pledged our character and influence. Be assured, that not one man, in the very first ranks of the political parties, has any sincere attachment to your principles. Therefore, as you have little to hope for the abolition cause, from the sincere good will of the parties, as such, do not be driven to act with the one, or renounce the other, merely because, for some temporary purpose, the one side or the other happens, to-day, to treat you with unaccustomed consideration, or to heap upon you peculiar outrage and abuse. Circumstances may, for a while, induce the presses, of one or the other party, to conciliate you; but, depend upon it, there is, at bottom, but very little to choose between them. There is certainly, no reason, thus far, why you should as a body, ally yourselves exclusively with either, but many and urgent reasons against it.

There is much, in the aspect of the times, to cheer us, in our political efforts. The danger of the admission of Texas is, probably, past. Thanks to the abolitionists, the free States have been roused to the disgrace and ruin of becoming a partner in the crimes of that bloody and slave-trading Republic. Slavery in the United States, and slavery in Texas, will not be suffered to double their strength, by union. The gag resolution in Congress, has received its death blow, from the intrepid, illustrious and venerable Adams. The subject of slavery will henceforth be an open one, in that body. Within three years, we shall probably have a favorable report on slavery in the District, and in less than five, we have little doubt of witnessing its peaceful abolition.

Slavery once abolished in the District, what a vast accession of moral power is gained, both in the process, and from the result! Friends animated,—oppressors disheartened,—all consciences awakened! It is a gain to the cause of virtue every where. The spiritual atmosphere is purified. Each man draws freer breath into his soul. The Lord is seen indeed to reign. The testimony of the nation is thenceforth added to the general reprobation of slavery, and will help to shame it out of existence. Another illustrious proof is given, of the possibility of the highest public virtue.

Instead of calling on you to descend from these heights, from a fear that the elevation may make you giddy, we say to you, your only danger is in looking down. Keep your aims ever upwards, and there is no fear that your footing will not be firm.

FRANCIS JACKSON, *President.*
AMOS A. PHELPS, *Secretary.*

7

"A Letter on the Political Obligation of Abolitionists, with a Reply by William Lloyd Garrison" (1839)

James G. Birney

James G. Birney (1792–1857) was the son of a wealthy Kentucky slaveholder and the proprietor of his own plantation in Alabama. By the late 1820s he came to favor gradual emancipation and colonization, and in 1834 he converted to immediate abolitionism and freed his slaves. He served as an agent for the American Anti-Slavery Society and then as its vice-president. In 1835, he left the South and moved to Cincinnati and then to New York. Birney was a staunch anti-Garrisonian and was a leader in the failed attempt to force the radicals out of the national Anti-Slavery Society. Birney was also one of the leading advocates for greater abolitionist involvement in politics, and he was eventually appointed as the presidential nominee of the Liberty Party in 1840 and 1844.

The debate that follows between Birney and Garrison represents one of the dramatic turning points in the abolitionist movement. At its core, their exchange came down to one question: Are members of the American Anti-Slavery Society obligated by the society's constitution to vote for antislavery candidates? Birney answered yes, Garrison answered no. Birney's "A Letter on the Political Obligation of Abolitionists" presents a trenchant critique of Garrisonian political abstinence. Birney argued that the politicization of slavery could only be cured by the de-politicization of slavery, which meant that abolitionists would have to organize politically in order to defeat a politically organized Slave Power. Birney contended that abolitionists had a moral obligation to use all means at their disposal to defeat slavery, including direct political action. Standing in the way, though, was Garrison and his refusal to sanction direct political action. Garrison, in response, charged Birney with abandoning and polluting the only true method of abolishing slavery—namely, moral suasion. Garrison believed his views to be entirely consistent with membership in the American Anti-Slavery Society, and he supported the idea

> that the society be open to any person who advocated immediate emancipation regardless of the particular tactics they supported to bring about emancipation.

Of the Constitution of the American A.S. Society as Connected With the 'No-Government' Question

The OBJECT of the American Society was—*the entire abolition of slavery in the U.S.* The MEANS for effecting it were,—

1. The admission, that each State in which it exists has, by the Constitution of the U.S. the exclusive right to *legislate* in regard to its abolition in said State.

2. To convince our fellow citizens, by arguments addressed to their understandings and consciences, that slaveholding is a heinous crime in the sight of God, and, that the duty, safety, and best interests of all concerned, require its immediate abandonment, without expatriation.

3. In a constitutional way to influence Congress to put an end to the domestic slave trade—and

4. To abolish slavery in all those portions of our common country which come under its control—especially in the District of Columbia; and lastly,

5. To prevent the extension of slavery to any State that might hereafter be admitted to the Union.

By the 4th article of the Constitution, any person may become a member who consents to the principles of the constitution—who contributes to the funds of the Society, and is not a slaveholder.

The first question which presents itself is—what are *'the* principles' of the constitution? The answer is—they are embodied in the OBJECT and MEANS above enumerated.

The next question is—what is it to 'consent'—or, rather, *not* to consent to these principles? If any one maintain, that the abolition of slavery in the United States ought not to be entire—or that each State in which slavery exists has *not* the exclusive right, by the constitution of the U.S. to legislate in regard to its abolition in said State—or that arguments, of whatever value, ought *not* to be addressed to the understandings and consciences of our fellow citizens, to prove that slaveholding is a heinous crime—or, that the immediate abandonment of slavery is *not* the duty of the slaveholder, nor promotive of the best interests of all concerned—or that it ought not to take place *without expatriation*—or, if he maintain that, any and every effort in a constitutional way ought *not* to be made to influence Congress to put an end to the domestic slave trade—to abolish slavery in all those portions of our common country which come under its control, especially in the District of

Columbia—or, to prevent the extension of it to any State which may, hereafter, be admitted to the Union:—such an one (even admitting his object to be better, and his means more effective than any which have been adopted by the American Society) cannot he said to 'consent' to the principles of the Constitution.

ALL the action required by the constitution is MORAL. Arguments addressed to the understandings and consciences of members of Congress are as much *moral*, as when addressed to our fellow-citizens generally. But the framers of the constitution were not content, it would seem, to leave a *particular species* of this action undistinguished in the mass—to be apprehended or not (as it might happen) under the general expressions, 'aim to convince'— 'arguments addressed to *the* understanding,' &c. So important did they deem it, and so anxious were they to remove all doubt of what they intended, that they separated it from the mass, by declaring, 'the society will also endeavor, in a constitutional way, to influence Congress to put an end to the domestic slave trade,' &c.

It is not unworthy of remark, that whilst our fellow citizens, generally, were to be *'addressed'*—Congress were to be *influenced.* Not that members of Congress were not included in the words '*all* our fellow citizens,' to whom arguments were to be addressed; but, because certain of our fellow citizens were members of Congress and possessed, in virtue thereof, extraordinary power, with *them* the society were to use *additional* means. They were *'also* to endeavor, in a constitutional way, to *influence* Congress,' &c., that is, by such considerations as are usually found to have a *peculiar* influence on men enjoying *peculiar* stations at the will of the people. They were to be asked to do, only what, in their public character, they were *authorized* to do—what it was *right* for them to do; if their action was not responsive to our petitions, they were to be *influenced* by the fear of incurring the displeasure of their constituents; consequently, of being removed from their places, that others might occupy them;—the only 'constitutional way' of doing which was, by the use of the Elective Franchise.

This action on Congress has been called, by way of distinction, *'political.'* For several years after the organization of the American Society, our numbers were too few to attempt it. It was therefore, generally, deprecated as inexpedient. Notwithstanding, however, on one occasion, if no more, the very next year after the institution of the Society, when the moral propriety of abolitionists carrying out their principles at the ballot box was denied by some, it was strenuously upheld by the editor of the Liberator, who had aided in forming the constitution—he himself setting the example of voting for a professed abolitionist, and encouraging others to do the same,—taking the ground, that, although the votes of all the abolitionists in Boston (where the election referred to took place) would not have been sufficient to elect the anti-slavery candidate on that occasion, the course recommended would, *if persisted in*, facilitate his election at some future period. (See Liberator, Dec. 1834.)

The constitutions of none of the State societies (and they are all auxiliaries to the American) contain anything repugnant to political action. That of the Massachusetts society declares in Art. 2, 'The objects of the society shall be, to endeavor, *by* all means, sanctioned by *law*, humanity and religion,' &c.

The Declaration of Sentiments, published simultaneously with the constitution by those who had subscribed the latter, contains the following passage.

'We also maintain, that there are at the present time, the highest obligations resting upon the PEOPLE of the free States, to remove slavery by moral and political action, as prescribed in the Constitution of the U.S.'

After mentioning the pledge of the free States to put down servile insurrection—the danger, expense, and political inequalities produced by slavery, it proceeds to the conclusion that, 'IT MUST BE BROKEN UP.' How it was to be broken up, except by means of the Elective Franchise, does not appear. The Declaration of Sentiments, although possessing no *obligatory* force, is the highest evidence that can be had, apart from the constitution, of what was intended by the *body* of the abolitionists in that instrument.

It is not recollected, that any amount of opposition worthy to be mentioned was made to political action as inculcated (according to the foregoing interpretation) in the constitution—in the Declaration of Sentiments—in the State Societies' constitutions—and in the Editorials of the Liberator—till after political action was, in consequence of the increase of our numbers, decided upon. Within the last twelve or eighteen months, it is believed— after efforts, some successful, some not, had been begun to affect the elections—and whilst the most indefatigable exertions were being made by many of our influential, intelligent and liberal friends to convince the great body of the abolitionists of the necessity—the indispensable necessity—of breaking away from their old *'parties,'* and uniting together in the use of the elective franchise for the advancement of the cause of human freedom in which we were engaged;—at this very time, and mainly, too, in that part of the country where, *political action* had been most successful, and whence, from its promise of soon being wholly triumphant, great encouragement was derived by abolitionists everywhere, a Sect has arisen in our midst, whose members regard it as of religious obligation, IN NO CASE, *to exercise the elective franchise.* This persuasion is part and parcel of the tenet which it is believed they have embraced,—that as Christians have the precepts of the Gospel to direct, and the Spirit of God to guide them, all Human Governments, as necessarily, including the idea of *force* to secure obedience, are not only superfluous, but unlawful encroachments on the Divine government, as ascertained from the sources above mentioned. Therefore, they refuse to do any thing voluntarily, by which they would be considered as acknowledging the lawful existence of human governments. Denying to Civil government the right to use force, they easily deduce, that family governments have no such right. Thus, they would withhold from parents any power of personal chastisement or restraint for the correction of their children. They carry out to the full extent the 'non-resistance' theory. To the first ruffian who would demand our purse, or oust us from our houses, they are to be unconditionally surrendered unless *moral suasion* be found sufficient to induce him to decline from his purpose. Our wives, our daughters, our sisters—our mothers we are to see set upon by the most brutal, without any effort on our part, except argument to defend them—and even they, themselves, are forbidden to use in defence of their purity such powers as God has endowed them with for its protection, if resistance should be attended with injury or destruction to the assailant. In short, the 'No-Government' doctrines, as they are believed now to be embraced, seem to strike at the root of the social structure; and tend—so far as I am able to judge of their tendency,—to throw society into entire confusion, and to renew, under the sanction of religion, scenes of anarchy and license that have generally heretofore been the offspring of the rankest infidelity and irreligion.

It is but justice to say—judging from the moral deportment of the adherents of the 'No-Government' scheme—that so far from admitting, what I have supposed to be, its legitimate consequences, they would wholly deny and repudiate them.

These Sectaries have not as yet separated themselves from the American society. Far from it. They insist that their views are altogether harmonious with what is required for membership by the constitution. So confident do they seem in this, that they say, any interpretation of that instrument which would prove them unqualified for membership—and, therefore, throw on them the duty of retiring from the society—ought not to be tolerated as sound for a moment; they assert that such an interpretation of the constitution cannot be maintained by the American society without dashing the whole antislavery organization into fragments, and that it is not warranted by any thing in the letter or spirit of the constitution.

As this seems to be mere assertion—no fact being stated which can be denied, and no argument advanced in support of it which can be combatted—it admits of no other answer than this;—that, respect for the American society induces the belief that it will construe the constitution according to the generally received principles of construction, and not obediently to the mandate or the menace of any particular portion of its members.

Again—it is said there is nothing in the *history* of the abolition reformation to warrant my interpretation of the constitution. The proof adduced is—that many good men have united with the American society or its auxiliaries, and remain members, who are, in principle, opposed to using the elective franchise on any occasion. The conclusion from these premises to which the new constructionists come, is that the constitution is *consistent* with this state of things. But, if it prove any thing logically, it is, that if Sectaries be not expelled from an institution, and are content themselves to remain in it, therefore the rules of the institution consist with their heresy: which is absurd.

A simple statement, however, will correct whatever wrong impression may have been made on the minds of the candid as to this part of the subject: The American society have no *Board of Inspection* appointed to scrutinize the qualification of persons proposing themselves for membership. They publish their constitution—submit it to all—leaving it to the integrity of every one to decide for himself, whether he possesses the qualifications it requires or not.

Neither have they committed to any portion of their body the power of *expelling* such as enter the Society without the proper qualifications, or who disqualify themselves after entering. As no benefit of a selfish character is known to follow, on uniting with the Society, it is presumed that every one *honestly* considers himself qualified for membership at the time of uniting. If, after uniting, he should find that he had become disqualified, as several have, by materially changing their opinions, the same integrity and self-respect which would have restrained him under such circumstances from *joining* the Society, ought, it is thought, to persuade him to retire from it.

But the No-Government men exclaim against this suggestion, as illiberal and bigoted. But where is the illiberality of attributing to men opinions which they cherish—acts which they are doing—and if those be found inconsistent with the terms of a particular association, of saying so? Is any one harmed by it, if he be not thereby prevented from acting according to his own views, and associating with others who agree with him? Would a Christian think himself illiberally dealt by, if, on making application to be admitted to membership in a particular church, he should frankly make known his religious views, and he as frankly told by the proper authorities that they differed essentially from those which *that* church had considered and settled as right for itself—as the most proper for carrying forward the cause of Christianity—that, therefore, he was unqualified to be connected with it;—but, that, there were other churches with which his opinions coincided, who would be glad to receive him—or, if there were none such, that still he was at full liberty to become the founder of a new religious order—or if this was not to his taste, that he might worship *alone* with none to molest, or make him afraid? Would such an one have any ground of complaint? Surely, none. Nor does this view at all conflict with the right possessed by every one, already a member of a religious or other association, to attempt so to change its movements as to make it more effective for the object proposed. But as associations generally make provision for such changes, they ought-to be attempted according to the prescribed form (where they are sufficient for the purpose) and not by straining or distorting the principles of the organization, so as to make them cover cases to which all concerned know, they were never intended to apply. If this be the right course of procedure in such circumstances, and my interpretation of the constitution be correct, it would seem to be the most honorable, amicable, and respectful course for the No-Government men to move directly for an alteration of the constitution. To this, I think, no one would take exception.

But to this it may be replied—where is the necessity of a change of the constitution, when both the No-Government men and the Government men can act under it according to the dictates of their consciences respectively? But is this really so? Is the difference between those who seek to abolish any and every government of human institution, and those who prefer *any* government to a state of things in which every one may do what seemeth good in his own eyes—is the difference between them, I say, so small, that they can act harmoniously under the same organization? When in obedience to the principles of the society, I go to the polls, and there call on my neighbors to unite with me in electing to Congress, men who are in favor of Human Rights, I am met by a No-Government abolitionist inculcating on them the doctrine, that Congress have *no rightful authority* to act at all in the premises—how can we proceed together? When I am animating my fellow-citizens to aid me in infusing into the government salutary influences which shall put an end to all oppression— my No-Government brother cries out at the top of his lungs, *all* governments are of the Devil (!) where is our harmony? Our efficiency? We are in the condition of two physicians called in to the same patient—one of whom should be intent on applying the proper remedies for expelling the disease from the body and thus restoring and purifying its functions; the other, equally intent on utterly destroying body, members, functions and all. Could they be agreed, and could they walk together? It seems to me not. And simply because their aim, their objects are radically and essentially different. So with the No-Government and the Pro-Government abolitionists. One party is for sustaining and purifying governments, and bringing them to a perfect conformity with the principles of the Divine government—the other for destroying *all* government.

'*But, although the No-Government Abolitionists refuse themselves to vote, they do not object to petitioning Congress.*'—True—and so far so good. If this seem an absurdity to others, it may not to them. They may have some method of accommodating their principles to such a proceeding, of which others are ignorant. And even if there be a substantial inconsistency in refusing, from religious considerations, to have any hand in *electing* members of Congress—and afterward, when they are elected by *others*, using them *as* members of Congress, and *only*, as such, it is nothing more than what often happens to good men who embrace absurd dogmas to which their practical humanity and common sense cannot be brought entirely to submit.

'*But do they not also inculcate on all such as believe they can* CONSCIENTIOUSLY *use the elective franchise, to vote for the slave?*' It is said they do. And yet it is also said to be a difficult thing, of late, to secure the passage of resolutions embodying even this diluted principle, in the abolition meetings where the No-Government men have the ascendancy of numbers. But admitting that they do ask those who can conscientiously vote, to vote for the slave, it does not touch the question whether *they* as members of the society are not themselves bound to vote. If it be the duty of one, it is the duty of all. Beside, what influence can he who, refusing, on religious grounds, himself to vote, have on others who do vote—when the very *act of* voting, irrespective of the particular person voted for, is felt by him to be an unrighteous and irreligious one? The attempt to exercise influence, under such circumstances, would seem, at least, as much out of place, if not, as philosophically absurd, as for the Celestial angels to direct their 'fallen' brethren how best they might make their *sinful* movements declare the glory of God and advance the cause of universal benevolence.

'*But would you trample on the conscientious scruples of the No-Government abolitionists, by requiring them to vote?*' By no means. There is no power to do so—nor would I if I could. But *Right* is to be respected as well as conscience—consciences are to be moulded by right, and not right by the consciences of men. If the Constitution of the American Society requires of those who subscribe to it, to use the elective franchise, for the abolition of slavery, and men join the Society knowing this, they are *justly* bound to vote. From this no man's conscience can exempt him any more than it can exempt him from the obligation of paying an amount of money which he owes his neighbor for value received. If a rule established by an association having the right to establish it, may be nullified by one man's conscience, so it may by another. Thus it ceases to be a rule altogether. If this may be done, with regard to one rule, so it may with regard to another. Then we have a society without *any rule* for its government. In this way the society itself is nullified.

But there is no need of violating any one's conscientious scruples. If the No-Government men do verily believe that there rests on them the religious duty of directing their efforts to the annihilation (peaceable, of course,) of all existing Governments, and that the abolition of slavery, by the use of the elective franchise, is inconsistent with it, they are certainly bound by their own rules as honest men to renounce the latter. But in doing so, they should remember, that they have ceased to 'consent' to one of the 'principles' of the Constitution, and are virtually no longer entitled to membership. In such a case it would seem that the duty of withdrawing from the Society was altogether plain. *Justice* to those with whom they associated, and to the slave, requires it;—*self-respect* requires *it—the No-Government enterprise*, which they have nearest at heart, requires it. For what can be more unjust to those who originally associated for the reasonable and single purpose of abolishing slavery, than the attempt to compel them into a crusade for abolishing Government? What more unjust to the suffering slave, than to tie on to his magnificent cause a project that is hopeless, because cast out by the common sense of the nations of the world?* What more prejudicial to the scheme of annihilating human government, than to remain associated with those who are striving to purify, invigorate and immortalize their own?

For my part I can see no good reason why the No-Government party should *wish* to remain in the Anti-Slavery Association, seeing it must be productive of endless dissentions;—especially, when, by withdrawing and forming on a platform of their own, they could conduct their enterprise vigorously and harmoniously, and permit the abolitionists, who are the advocates of the elective franchise, to do the same with theirs.

I am prompted to publish the foregoing remarks by no personal ill-will to any of those who are counted as teachers or disciples of the No-Government doctrines. I have no ground for ill-will. On the contrary, I know of nothing which would authorize me to say, speaking of them in the mass, that they *intend* anything but good; whilst for several of them I cherish particular sentiments of regard. But it is high time that something was done to bring this subject directly before the great body of the abolitionists, in order that they may believe their cause from an incubus that has so mightily oppressed it in some parts of the country during the last year. It is in vain to think of succeeding in emancipation without the co-operation of the great mass of the intelligent mind of the nation. This can be attracted, *only* by the reasonableness, the *religion*, of our enterprise. To multiply causes of repulsion is but to drive it from us, and ensure our own defeat—to consign the slave to perdurable chains—our country to imperishable disgrace.

JAMES G. BIRNEY

---

* The 'No-Government' theory is but a new growth of one of the *fungi* which sprung up in the early period of the Reformation, when the minds of men were heated by the new ideas presented to them. It soon led to the most horrible excesses. Against it Luther spoke and wrote, and even invoked the civil authority—but all availed nothing. It ran its career through such scenes of lust and blood, that humanity could not but rejoice at its extinction. (See Robertson's Chas. 5.)

Reply to James G. Birney

To the Editor of the Emancipator,

DEAR SIR,—In the Emancipator of the 2d Inst., appeared an elaborate essay from the pen of JAMES G. BIRNEY, giving his 'View of the Constitution of the American Anti-Slavery Society, as connected with the NO-GOVERNMENT question.' I read that essay with grief and amazement, and intended to make an immediate reply to it; but various engagements have prevented the completion of my design up to the present hour. This rejoinder, however, will not come at an unsuitable period.

Mr. Birney's Positions

I will first briefly recapitulate the leading position, assumed by Mr. Birney, in his extraordinary exposition of the Anti-Slavery Constitution. He declares—

1. That, by the terms of the Constitution—its letter and spirit—every person who subscribes to it, and joins the Society, is under a religious obligation to go to the polls, and use the elective franchise for the abolition of slavery.

2. That, consequently, those members of the Society, who, from conscientious scruples, refrain from voting at all, on any question, 'have ceased to consent to one of the principles of the Constitution, and are virtually no longer entitled to membership.'

3. That it is the duty of all such to withdraw from the Society, on the ground of 'justice,' 'integrity,' and 'self-respect.'

4. That it must be 'productive of endless dissentions' for them to remain in the Society.

5. That they have attempted 'to compel' the great body of abolitionists 'into a crusade for abolishing government,' and have tied, to the 'magnificent cause' of the slave 'a project that is hopeless, because cast out by the common sense of the nations of the world.'

6. That they are, virtually, apostates from the anti-slavery enterprise—pretenders, whose professions and practices are utterly at variance—intruders into a Society, from which, indeed, there is no power to expel them, but which they no longer sustain—heretics, who have departed from the faith once delivered to abolitionists.

7. That, in his opinion, their doctrines 'strike at the root of the social structure, and tend to throw society into entire confusion, and to renew, under the sanction of religion, scenes of anarchy and license, that have generally heretofore been the offspring of the rankest infidelity and irreligion.'

8. That, while others are 'for sustaining and purifying governments, and

bringing them to a perfect conformity with the principles of the Divine government, they are for destroying *all* government.'

9. That their theory 'is but a new growth of one of the *fungi*, which sprung up in the early period of the Reformation—which soon led to the most horrible excesses—which run its career through such scenes of lust and blood, that Humanity could not but rejoice at its extinction.

As an abolitionist—a member of the National Anti-Slavery Convention in 1833—a signer of the Declaration of Sentiments—a framer, member, and manager of the Parent Society—I positively affirm, and shall undertake to prove, that the first six of the above specifications are utterly groundless.

As an advocate of 'peace on earth, and good will among men'—a supporter of government—a disciple of Christ—I as emphatically declare, that the remaining allegations are truthless, slanderous, cruel—caricatures of the pacific precepts of the gospel—phantasms of a disordered imagination—satires upon the obligations of Christianity—libels upon the character and conduct of the Prince of Peace—unsupported by any show of reasoning, any appeal to the scriptures, any presentation of evidence. . . .

The Political Argument

I proceed to show, that the premises laid down by Mr. Birney, in respect to the political duties enjoined by the Anti-Slavery Constitution, are unsound; and, therefore, that his conclusions are all false.

The clause in the Constitution, upon which Mr. Birney relies to sustain his position, is that which declares, that 'the Society will endeavor, in a constitutional way, to *influence* Congress to put an end to the domestic slave trade,' &c. Commenting upon this language, he says—'It is not unworthy of remark, that whilst our fellow-citizens, generally, were to be *addressed*, Congress were to be *influenced*.' This philological distinction he seems to think so important, as to settle the question respecting the duty of every member of the Society to use the elective franchise!

Is it possible that Mr. Birney ventures to erect his political superstructure upon so slender a foundation? Why, a mere *grain* of logic will be ponderous enough to dash it to the earth! 'Congress were to be *influenced*'—very good! My reply, then, to his labored argument, occupying more than two columns, shall be compressed into a short syllogism:

To 'endeavor to influence Congress' is required by the Anti-Slavery Constitution.

But Congress can be influenced, independent of political action at the polls.

Therefore, such action is not required by the Constitution.

The first proposition needs no proof, being admitted.

The second is thus shown to be true:

Congress can be influenced by petitions, remonstrances, facts and arguments.

But these are wholly distinct from political action at the polls.

Therefore, Congress can be influenced, independent of such action.

The third follows from the other two. And hence, to arraign any man in the anti-slavery ranks, for refraining from going to the polls on account of religious scruples, or to assume that those who belong to the Anti-Slavery Society are bound to use the elective franchise, is to enforce a test of membership not required by the Constitution.

Again:

Abolitionists, by belonging to the Anti-Slavery Society, are pledged only to what is required in the Constitution.

The use of the elective franchise is not so required.

Therefore, they are not pledged, individually or collectively, to use the elective franchise.

Again.

Congress can be influenced, though it cannot be created, without a resort to the ballot-box.

But abolitionists are bound by their Constitution to influence, not to create or assist in creating Congress.

Therefore, they are not bound to resort to the ballot-box.

Again:

It is only to *creation*, but not to the exercise of an *influence*, that power is necessary.

But the Anti-Slavery Society is pledged 'to endeavor to *influence*,' not to *create*.

Therefore, the possession and exercise of the *creative power* are not requisite to membership in that Society.

Reasoning from Mr. Birney's own premises, I ask of every candid person, whether each of these syllogisms is not strictly legitimate and conclusive? Congress were, to be influenced, he says. Granted! But, I repeat—to *influence* AN EXISTING BODY, is one thing: to be a participant in *creating* SUCH A BODY, is another and a very different thing. Power is essential to creation; but the feeblest soul in the universe may 'influence' the most powerful body. . . . Mr. Birney concedes, that 'the [nicknamed] no-government abolitionists do not object to petitioning Congress.' Then they exactly and fully comply with the terms of the Anti-Slavery Constitution! For what are the thousands of petitions annually presented to that body, but to 'influence' it to cease upholding slavery in the District of Columbia ?—Is it not surprising, therefore,—nay, is it not presumptuous in my brother,—that he should urge upon those who are thus faithful in discharging their anti-slavery obligations, to 'retire from the Society,' as persons disqualified from being members of it?

Moral Action

Mr. Birney also concedes, that 'ALL the action required by the Constitution is MORAL.' But moral action is a duty enjoined upon all men by the great Lawgiver, to be employed at all times, and under all circumstances; and there is no difference of opinion among abolitionists, as to the propriety and necessity of using it for the overthrow of slavery. Political action, or the use of the elective franchise, is a privilege granted, in this country, by a majority of the people—purchased with money, or obtained by a term of residence, or by naturalization—sometimes conceded to the many, sometimes monopolized by the few—and treated, on all hands, throughout the civilized world, as something entirely distinct from obedience to God; so that in determining a man's character, it is never asked, 'Does he believe in the duty of political action?' any more than an enquiry is made as to his comparative height or bulk. It is *not* dependant upon the will of man, whether I may love the Lord my God with all my heart, and my neighbor as myself; but it *is*, whether I may be an elector. If, then, as Mr. Birney truly affirms, *'all* the action required by the Constitution is *moral*,' it is a complete refutation of his political doctrines;—he has signally answered his own reasoning. . . .

The Anti-Slavery Constitution

In this controversy, I adhere strictly to the Constitution of the Parent Society, because it is a question affecting the right of membership, of loyalty to the cause of the slave, of rectitude of conduct that is under consideration. . . .

I throw Mr. Birney's argument into the following shape:

The Constitution requires of those who subscribe to it, the exercise of the elective franchise:

Those who are disqualified by law, or through conscientious scruples, from voting at the polls, are not entitled to be members:

But women, minors, aliens, Covenanters, Non-Resistants, many of the Society of Friends, some of the signers of the Anti-Slavery Declaration of Sentiments, and also of the framers of the American A.S. Constitution, and other persons, are thus disqualified.

Therefore, all such persons, if now members of the Parent Society, are required by 'justice to those with whom they are associated, and to the slave,' and also by their 'integrity' and 'self respect,' to withdraw from the Society; and thus 'relieve the abolition cause from an incubus, that has so mightily oppressed it'!!

In other words, the American Anti-Slavery Society ought and was designed to be, a thoroughly POLITICAL ORGANIZATION!

I think I do no injustice to the sentiments of Mr. Birney. If he does not mean all this, he has written to no purpose. Ever since I began my labors in the anti-slavery cause, I have rejoiced in believing, that all persons who hold and inculcate the doctrine, that Slave-holding is under all circumstances a crime against God and man, and ought to he immediately abandoned,—of whatever party or denomination, tribe or nation, complexion or sex,—might be members of the Anti-Slavery Society; but, it seems, I have been cherishing a delusion, if Mr. B's 'View' be correct. Who, now, has been guilty of 'straining or distorting the principles of the organization, so as to make them applicable to cases, to which all concerned know they were never intended to apply,' if it be not himself? It is marvelous, truly, after passing wholesale condemnation upon myself, and some of the choicest abolition spirits in the land, and 'logically'(?) proving that for us any longer to remain in the Society would be *contra bonos mores*,—evincive of a lack of integrity, self-respect, and a sense of justice to those with whom we are now improperly associated—he should acknowledge that.

'The American Society have no *Board of Inspection* appointed to scrutinize the qualification of persons proposing themselves for membership. They publish their constitution—submit it to all—leaving it to the integrity of every one to decide for himself, whether he possesses the qualifications it requires, or not.'

So I have always thought; and therefore I marvel the more, that my friend should resolve himself into such a 'Board of Inspection,' and venture to occupy ground which the Parent Society has never felt authorized to assume!

Non-Resistants Will Not Leave the Society!

But what is to be done? Pass ten thousand resolutions in anti-slavery meetings, that political action is a religious duty, and still they would all avail nothing—so long as Mordecai the Jew is seen sitting at the king's gate. 'These sectaries,' the 'no-government' abolitionists, 'insist that their views are altogether harmonious with what is required for membership by the constitution,'—and 'it is presumed that every one *honestly* considers himself qualified for membership at the time of uniting,' and just so long as he consents to remain in the society. Hence, not one of them is disposed to withdraw from the present anti-slavery organization; for they appreciate it too highly to make a disturbance, and secede, merely because their brethren entertain different views of the gospel of peace from their own. They believe that 'both the no-government and the government men can act under the constitution, according to the dictates of their consciences respectively.' 'But is this really so?' Mr. Birney asks, with an air of incredulity. I answer—*it is really so:* so it has been for years, and so it may be till the jubilee come, if we truly 'remember them that are in bonds as bound with them,' and do not attempt to make out individual views of religion or politics—of the Church or the State—the standard by which to measure the whole body. We are all perfectly agreed as to the sin of slaveholding, the duty of immediate emancipation and the obligation which every abolitionist virtually takes to *carry out his principles* wherever he can act conscientiously, whether in the church or out of it, at the ballot-box or elsewhere. Why, then, in the name of humanity and of brotherly love, should we fall out by the way, and insist upon a separation, because we are not all united in opinion on political or theological points? Before I can be guilty of such unnatural conduct, I am sure that my right hand will forget its cunning, and my tongue cleave to the roof of my month. In the sacred cause of emancipation, I have known no man after the flesh, and been no respecter of persons, of creeds, or sects, or parties. I have given the right hand of fellowship to all who believe in the duty of immediately letting my fettered countrymen go free and have refused to associate with none on account of a disagreement of views on other subjects. . . .

On Trial as Abolitionists

Commenting on the fact, that 'the no-government (!) abolitionists do not object to petitioning Congress,' Mr Birney remarks, in a strain of sarcasm— 'So far, so good. If this seems an absurdity to others, it may not to them. They may have some method of accommodating their principles to such a proceeding, of which others are ignorant. . . . It is nothing more than what often happens to good men who embrace absurd dogmas, to which their practical humanity and common sense cannot be brought entirely to submit.' I dismiss this fling by saying, that, allowing it to be merited—what then? True, it may serve to convict non-resisting abolitionists of glaring inconsistency, as *non-resistants*; but it as conclusively shows that, *as abolitionists*, they faithfully abide by the A.S. Constitution, in thus endeavoring to 'influence Congress.' And it must be kept in mind, that they are now on trial AS ABOLITIONISTS not AS NON-RESISTANTS.

Political Inconsistency

Consistency is said to be a jewel. Mr. Birney gives us a rare specimen of it, on the part of the 'pro-government abolitionists.' He tells us in one breath, that, from the moment they endorsed the A.S. Constitution, they were as sacredly bound to use their elective franchise for the benefit of the slave, as to inculcate the duty of immediate emancipation. In the next breath, he makes the astounding confession—'For SEVERAL YEARS after the organization of the American Society, our numbers were *too few* to attempt political action [i.e. too few to perform an imperative duty!] It was, therefore, *generally* DEPRECATED AS INEXPEDIENT.' How many abolitionists are necessary to make political action a duty, we are not told. It is, certainly, a novel criterion, by which to determine the guilt or innocence of a body of men, pledged to do a certain act, the performance of which, for a series of years, they deprecate as inexpedient! I thought it was the creed of a genuine abolitionist to do right *now*, let who will delay. But, according to Mr. Birney, these 'pro-government abolitionists' have for a long time 'stepped out of the cause, into the work of producing an abstract religion, a sort of quintessence of humanity, which *they bottle up as they go along*, to be used WHEN there *is enough of it to flood the land.'** If, then, the 'no-government abolitionists' have acted inconsistently *in petitioning Congress*; 'what shall be said of the conduct of our 'pro-government' brethren, in neglecting for years to vote at the polls against slavery?

The True Abolition Platform

The ballot-box is the final abolition argument, says Mr. Birney. 'THE BALLOT-BOX IS NOT AN ABOLITION ARGUMENT,'** says Elizur Wright, Jr. The witnesses are both 'pro-government' men, and yet they do not agree in this matter.

Again:

Abolitionists have but one work: it is *not to put any body into office, or out of it*, but TO SET RIGHT THOSE WHO MAKE OFFICERS. It is not an action *upon church or State*, but UPON THE MATERIALS OF BOTH. Success will certainly develope itself, both through those who make human laws, and those who interpret the divine. But it would seem the natural order, that it should show itself first through the latter. The interpreters of divine law are, in fact, the chief sinners. The have given license, *ad libitum*, to man stealing; and it cannot be expected hat the statutes of a State should be better than its religion.***

---

* Fourth Annual Report of the Parent Society.
** Quarterly A.S. Magazine for January, 1837.
*** Idem.

Again:
The great end at which we aim is to subvert the relation of master and slave—*not by machinery*, POLITICAL OR ECCLESIASTICAL, but by establishing in the hearts of men a deep and wide-spreading conviction of *the brotherhood of the human race*; that God hath indeed made of one blood all nations of men for to dwell on all the face of the earth; that all men who mean to obey the divine appointment, and honestly get their bread by their labor, have a common interest in sustaining the principle, that the laborer is worthy of his hire.*

This is a correct representation of the ground-work of abolitionism. The Anti-Slavery Society is not an organization to determine the question, whether Church or State, as now constituted, is, *per se*, right or wrong—but, simply, to 'influence' both by 'the foolishness of preaching' the doctrine, that slaveholding is man-stealing. Its *principles* are immutable, and purely religious; its *measures*, 'such only as the opposition of moral purity to moral corruption—the destruction of error by the potency of truth—the overthrow of prejudice by the power of love—and the abolition of slavery by the spirit of repentance.' . . .

A False Accusation

'What can be more unjust,' Mr. Birney asks, 'to those who originally associated for the reasonable and single purpose of abolishing slavery, than the attempt to compel them into a crusade for abolishing government? What more unjust to the suffering slave, than to tie on to his magnificent cause a project that is hopeless, because cast out by the common sense (!) of the nations of the world?' To these interrogations I answer—that, whoever charges me, or any of my brethren of the Non-Resistance Society, with having at any time introduced our peculiar views of government into the meetings of abolitionists, or attempted to make us of the Anti-Slavery Society to give them currency, bears false witness. The charge is utterly untrue. Our accusers are the real transgressors. They have not scrupled, as abolitionists, in the official organs of the anti-slavery cause, in the capacity of abolition lecturers, in the meetings of abolition societies, to make war upon the pacific views of a portion of their brethren—views which these brethren carefully avoided promulgating as connected with the objects of the A.S. Society. Among those who have thus unfairly made use of their abolition standing and influence, in an official manner, to carry on their belligerous crusade against the friends of

---

*Fourth Ann. Report of the Parent Society.

non-resistance, James G. Birney, Henry B. Stanton, Elizur Wright, Jr., Amos A. Phelps, and Orange Scott, may be included. I never expected to receive such treatment from these brethren:—their conduct fills me with surprise and grief. To accuse me, and those who agree with me in respect to political action, with designing and striving to 'tie on' to the abolition cause THAT OF NON-RESISTANCE, so that the latter may obtain an adventitious support, is plainly to declare us devoid of all honesty, and to represent us as false and treacherous men. If we have indeed fallen so low in the estimation of our 'pro-government' associates, then not only should they desire no longer to be with us in the anti-slavery organization, but they should shun our company on ordinary occasions. If what they allege against us be true, then we are as unprincipled as the slaveholders are oppressive. But we deny the allegation, and demand the proof. We are very certain that we are 'more sinned against than sinning.' As men, as citizens, as Christians, we confess that we have advocated the heaven-originated cause of Non-Resistance, and shall continue to do so, until we are convicted of error; *but not as abolitionists.* 'The head and front of our offending hath this extent—no more.'

The Non-Resistance Theory Embodied in the Anti-Slavery Constitution and Declaration of Sentiments

Mr. Birney sums up his accusations against us as follows:

'They carry out, to the full extent, the non-resistance theory. To the first ruffian who would demand our purse, or oust us from our houses, they are to be unconditionally surrendered, unless *moral suasion* be found sufficient to induce him to decline from his purpose. Our wives, our daughters, our sisters, our mothers, we are to see set upon by the most brutal, without any effort, on our part, except argument, to defend them; and even they, themselves, are forbidden to use in defence of their purity, such powers as God has endowed them with for its protection, if resistance should be attended with injury or destruction to the assailant.'

I shall not attempt to vindicate the principles of Non-Resistance, in this already too protracted reply. What I wish to remark is, that all that Mr. Birney alleges against us, in the paragraph just quoted, he and the great body of abolitionists have repeatedly enjoined upon the slave population, of this country—i.e. *in no case to resist evil.* The solemn and affecting language of the Anti Slavery Declaration of Sentiments, (which, according to Mr. Birney, 'although possessing no *obligatory* force, is the highest evidence that can be had, apart from the Constitution, of what was intended by the *body* of the abolitionists in that instrument,') is to this effect:

'Their [our revolutionary fathers'] principles led them to wage war against

their opponents, and to spill human blood like water, in order to be free. *Ours* FORBID THE DOING OF EVIL THAT GOOD MAY COME, and lead *us* to reject, and to entreat the *oppressed* to reject the use of *all carnal weapons* for deliverance from bondage—relying *solely* upon those which are *spiritual*, and mighty through God to the pulling down of strong holds.'

Here is strong and emphatic condemnation of the conduct of those who achieved the independence of this country, in forcibly resisting their oppressors; here is a solemn declaration, that, such are the 'PRINCIPLES' of the signers of that instrument, they cannot defend themselves by a resort to physical force, in any case; and here the slaves are entreated to see their 'wives, daughters, sisters, mothers,' set upon by the most brutal, without any effort, on their part, to defend them, except by 'moral suasion'—and to unconditionally surrender themselves to the first slaveholding ruffian, who may be disposed to plunder them—because they may not do evil, that good may come—i.e. may not seek to deliver themselves, from the most horrible fate, by the use of 'such powers as God has endowed them with for their protection, if resistance should be attended with injury or destruction to the assailants'!! The cases are precisely analogous. Now, is it not one article in the creed of abolitionists, that the rights of a black man are equal to those of a white one—and that what may be justified in one, may be done by the other, under similar circumstances? Here, then, are the doctrines of non-resistance in a nut-shell!

Again: The last clause of the second article of the Constitution of the American Anti-Slavery Society is in these words:

'But this Society will *never*, IN ANY WAY, countenance the oppressed in vindicating their rights by a resort to physical force.'

This is tantamount to what is laid down as a *moral duty* in the DECLARATION. It is non-resistance to the most brutal tyrants that ever preyed upon the human race. Yet some of the very men, who have subscribed to that Constitution, are the most violent in their detestation of the non-resistance doctrines, and say that they 'hate them with a perfect hatred'!! Yes, those who have solemnly promised, before heaven and earth, that they will 'NEVER, *in any way* countenance the oppressed in vindicating their rights by a resort to physical force,' now scout the doctrine of passive submission as most absurd and wicked, and are full of the spirit of war! *'Never* countenance'—it is not, therefore; because it would be *inexpedient* to do so, to-day, next week, or peradventure next year—but because it would be *always* contrary to the will of God, to the spirit of the Gospel, and the example of Christ! 'Whatsoever ye would that men should do to you, do ye even so to them'—*negroes though they be*. *'Never*, in ANY WAY, countenance the oppressed'—mark that! How can Messrs. Birney, Phelps, Scott, &c. more directly encourage the slaves to rise against their masters, than by avowing, as they do, that self-defence against brutal assailants, by the use of carnal weapons—clubs, swords and pistols—is not only right, but a sacred duty? Non-resistants are the only persons in the land, and especially in the anti-slavery organization, who do not, 'in any way,' either in theory or practice, by precept or example, 'countenance the oppressed in vindicating their rights by a resort to physical force!' Yet, because they follow the letter and spirit of the anti-slavery constitution, in this particular, they are compared to the bloody-minded Anabaptists, and represented as being disqualified to act as members of the Parent Society!

Inconsistency of Abolitionists

If it be said, in reply, that those who endorsed the pacific views of the Declaration of Sentiments and A.S. Constitution, did not mean to be understood as sanctioning the principles of non-resistance, as applied to all classes and descriptions of men, I answer—

1. Whatever they may have meant, it is certain that a fair interpretation of their language commits them in favor of the doctrine of universal non-resistance, as a religious duty, binding upon every individual suffering unjustly, whether white or black.

2. If they do not mean what their language obviously implies, why do they not alter the phraseology of the Constitution?

3. It is certain that to reject the use of all carnal weapons, even in cases of extreme peril and suffering, and to rely solely upon those which are spiritual, for succor and deliverance, is to declare ourselves non resistants in principle.

4. Up to the hour that Lovejoy fell, abolitionists made high pretensions to the character of 'ultra peace men'—they did not resist evil—they took up no weapons in self-defence but those of prayer, and the sword of the spirit, though cruelly treated by their enemies; and how united, invincible, victorious, they were at every onset! How, in their weakness, the omnipotence of God was made manifest, to the utter discomfiture of the enemies of emancipation! Since that time, so radical has been the change effected in the views and feelings of abolitionists, on this subject, that the following resolution, (drawn up by John G. Whittier) was rejected at the annual meeting of the Parent Society in 1838, by a vote of 19 in the affirmative, and 44 in the negative!!

Resolved, That we earnestly desire, that the agents and members of this Society, while engaged in advocating the pure and *pacific* principles of emancipation, may continue patient under their manifold provocations, forgiving their enemies, not relying upon physical strength for their defence against the violence of others; but, by their patient endurance of evil, evince the spirit of their Master, whose mission was one of 'peace on earth, and good will to men.'

It was a body of 'ultra peace men,' who could vote down that harmless resolution! Alas! 'how has the gold become dim, and the most fine gold changed!'

Let me not be misunderstood. I do not mean to affirm, that either the signers of the Declaration, or the members of the Parent Society, really intended, at any time, to take the ground now occupied by those who are technically called 'non-resistants,' or 'no-government men.' That they laid down and sanctioned all the principles of non-resistance, cannot be denied; but I do not believe that, as a body, they understood how far they had, in fact, committed themselves. They were agreed that the starved, lacerated, down trodden slaves had no right to fight for liberty; but they did not exactly mean that they themselves were not to use carnal weapons, when *their* 'wives, daughters, sisters, mothers,' and their own sacred persons, should be put in jeopardy by 'the most brutal'! They did not perceive that, in stripping those who are the most terribly abused and outraged, of all right to lift a finger in self-defence, they also deprived themselves, and all others, of such right! They did not understand that the rule was to work both ways! All this I readily admit. What I mean to say is, that, by a strict and fair construction of the instruments above alluded to, *non-resistance is more explicitly enjoined upon abolitionists, than the duty of using the elective franchise.* I cannot, therefore, think highly of the fair-mindedness of Mr. Birney, in that, while he attempts to prove that abolitionists are bound to go to the polls, by torturing the words, 'will endeavor to influence Congress,' &c. into such an obligation, he says not one word about the pacific principles embodied in the Constitution and Declaration, while attacking non-resisting abolitionists.

Abolition at the Ballot-Box

Once more, I beg not to be misapprehended. I have always expected, I still expect, to see abolition at the ballot-box, renovating the political action of the country—dispelling the sorcery influences of party—breaking asunder the fetters of political servitude—stirring up the torpid consciences of voters—substituting anti-slavery for pro-slavery representatives in every legislative assembly—modifying and rescinding all laws which sanction slavery. But this political reformation is to be effected solely by a change in the moral vision of the people;—not by attempting to prove, that it is the duty of every abolitionist to be a voter, but that it is the duty of every voter to be an abolitionist. By converting electors to the doctrine, that slavery ought to be immediately abolished, a rectified political action is the natural consequence; for where this doctrine is received into the soul, the soul-carrier may be trusted any where, that he will not betray the cause of bleeding humanity. As to the height and depth, the length and breadth of CHRISTIANITY, it is not the province of abolition to decide; but only to settle one point—to wit, that slaveholding is a crime under all circumstances, leaving those who believe in the doctrine to carry out their principles, with all fidelity, in whatever sphere they may be called upon to act, but not authoritatively determining whether they are bound to be members of the church, or voters at the polls. It has never been a difficult matter to induce men to go to the ballot-box; but the grand difficulty ever has been, and still is, to persuade them to carry a good conscience thither, and act as free moral agents, not as the tools of party.

Effects of Non-Resistance upon Political Action

I go still further. I not only expect to see abolition at the polls, but I feel as sure as that day will follow night, that the political action of this country will be purified and renovated, in exact proportion to the prevalence of the great conservative doctrines of non-resistance! This may seem, to many, absurd, paradoxical, impossible; but it is strictly natural, rational, philosophical....

That non-resistance will essentially aid, instead of injuring the anti-slavery cause, politically and morally, is proved to a demonstration.

In the first place, no person can be a non-resistant, without being a whole-hearted abolitionist—(the greater includes the less, always)—though a man may be an abolitionist, and yet not a non-resistant.

Secondly, the principles of non resistance have taken root more deeply, and spread more widely, in Massachusetts, than in any other State. All who embrace them are abolitionists. What State can compare with her for devotion to the cause of the slave,—for abolition integrity, activity, intrepidity,—in liberal contributions and self-sacrificing efforts to redeem the captives in our midst—in vigorous political action at the polls? To what State are the eyes of the South turned with so much anxiety and alarm, as to Massachusetts? Is she not regarded, every where, as the leader of the States in this great struggle?

Thirdly, the principles of non-resistance have been discussed in the columns of the Liberator, with more or less freedom, for the last three or four years. What has *made* the abolitionism of Massachusetts, (I do not say this boastingly, but as a historical fact, pertinent to the present argument,) but the Liberator? I appeal to Henry B. Stanton, and to every other agent who has lectured in or out of Massachusetts, whether, as a general rule, those who take the Liberator are not the very salt of the anti-slavery enterprise—the most uncompromising, clear sighted, active, generous, among abolitionists—the most faithful to their principles, the most to be relied on at the polls? If this be not so, then these agents have testified falsely. Again and again have they declared, that, in going into a new field of labor, or even into an old one, almost their first inquiry has been—'Who takes the Liberator?'—because they felt sure of finding a genuine abolitionist, whether the subscriber proved to be a man or *woman.*

I repent it, as the stirring conviction of my heart, and the logical deduction of my understanding, that Non-Resistance is destined to pour new life-blood into the veins of Abolition—to give it extraordinary vigor—to clothe it with a new beauty—to inspire it with holier feelings—to preserve it from corruption—though not necessarily connected with it. . . .

8

"Talk About Political Party" (1842)

Lydia Maria Child

The debate between Birney and Garrison did not end the controversy over the role that abolitionists should or should not play in politics. Lydia Maria Child's contribution to this debate is significant for two reasons. First, because it is an exceptionally clear statement of the Garrisonian position for the superiority of moral suasion to direct political action. Second, because it was rare throughout the whole history of the abolitionist movement for women to take up political questions. Prohibited from voting and participating in political action, the most prominent female abolitionists naturally gravitated to Garrison's circle where they were welcomed as full members of, and active participants in, the movement for immediate emancipation.

A. I wish you would explain to me the position of the American Society with regard to political action.

B. In good truth, I am weary of explaining what appears to my own mind so perfectly clear, that I cannot easily imagine how it can seem obscure to any one. The American Society stands on precisely the same principles that it did the first year of its formation. Its object was to change public opinion on the subject of slavery, by the persevering utterance of truth. This change they expected would show itself in a thousand different forms;—such as conflict and separation in churches; new arrangements in colleges and schools; new customs in stages and cars; and new modifications of policy in the political parties of the day. The business of anti-slavery was, and is, to purify the *fountain*, whence all these streams flow; if it turns aside to take charge of any *one* of the streams, however important, it is obvious enough that the whole work must retrograde; for, if the fountain be not kept pure, no one of the streams will flow with clear water. But just so sure as the fountain is taken proper care of, the character of all the streams *must* be influenced thereby. We might form ourselves into a railroad society, to furnish cars with the same conveniences for all complexions; but we feel that we are doing a far more effectual work, so to change popular opinion, that there will be no *need* of a separate train of cars. We might expend all our funds and energies in establishing abolition colleges; but we feel sure, that we have the power in our hands to abolitionize *all* colleges. With this reliance on the might of moral influence, the American Society started; and her faith in it is undiminished. Many have faltered by the way, on account of sectarian attachments, or an honest fear of being implicated in the advancement of other things which they did not approve, or from impatience to do up the arduous work by a quicker method. Some of these have misunderstood us, others have intentionally misrepresented; but through all forms of mistake and calumny, the American Society stands on precisely the same basis it did at the outset.

A. I cannot myself tell in what particular it has changed; but I know it is very common to hear people say, that they have no choice except between Non-resistance and Liberty party.

B. As it is a very common *ruse* for whigs and democrats to stigmatize each other as abolitionists, for the purpose of exciting popular odium, so is it a common devise of the third party to stigmatize all abolitionists, who do not co-operate with them, as non-resistants. Political trickery is alike in its character, under all forms. If "Liberty party" writers and editors are not aware of the fact that the American Society no more endorses non-resistance, than it does baptism, or Unitarianism, or Calvinism, or homeopathy, it certainly is not for the want of means of information. Probably not ten in a thousand of the American Society are non-resistants; but when it was demanded by some that these ten *should* vote, or else be turned out of the society, a very large number arrayed themselves against it; because such a proceeding would violate the very principles of freedom, on which our platform rests. Had any one proposed that abolitionists should *not* be allowed to vote, a majority would have stood equally strong to protect freedom on *that* side. Had the Quaker demanded that those should be turned out of the society who endeavored to advance the cause by stated prayer, every liberal mind would have resisted the test, as a violation of freedom; and if the Calvinist had made an opposite demand, the feeling would have been the same.

A. But you advise people not to vote for pro-slavery candidates, and not to join the liberty party; if this isn't non-resistance in practice, I don't know what is.

B. The difficulty in your mind arises, I think, from want of faith in the efficiency of moral influence. You cannot see that you act on politics *at all*, unless you join the caucus, and assist in electioneering for certain individuals; whereas you may, in point of fact, refuse co-operation, and thereby exert a tenfold influence on the destiny of parties. In Massachusetts, for instance, before the formation of a distinct abolition political party, both parties were afraid of the abolitionists; both wanted their votes; and therefore members of both parties in the legislature were disposed to grant their requests. All, who take note of such things, can remember how the legislature seemed to be abolitionized, as it were, by miracle. "The anti-slavery folks are coming strong this session," said a member to a leading democrat; "they want a hearing on five or six subjects, at least." "Give 'em *all* they ask?" replied the leader; "we can't afford to offend them." When a similar remark was made to a whig leader, the same session, his answer was, "Concede everything; it wont do to throw them into the arms of the democrats." Now, there is a third party in Massachusetts, the two great parties have much less motive to please the abolitionists. Last year, the legislature of that State seemed to have gone back on anti-slavery, as fast as it once went forward. In Vermont, the system of refusing co-operation produced the effect of inducing both whigs and democrats to put up an abolition candidate, in order to secure abolition votes; neither party was willing to give its opponent the advantage that might be gained by pleasing this troublesome class. Had we never turned aside from this plan, I believe the political influence of anti-slavery would have been an hundred fold greater than it now is.

A. But after all, these legislators that you speak of, were not made genuine abolitionists, or else they would not slip back so easily. I want to see the Statehouse filled with true anti-slavery men.

B. Those men, let me tell you, did the *work* of sound anti-slavery; and *in* doing it, got imbued more or less with anti-slavery sentiment, in spite of themselves. The machinery of a third political party may send into Congress, or the halls of State legislation, a few individuals, who are anti-slavery to the back-bone. But could *one* Alvan Stuart do as much for our cause in Congress, as *twenty* of Joshua R. Giddings? Fifty men who have a strong motive for obliging the abolitionists, could surely *do* more for our cause, in such a position, than merely two or three radical abolitionists. I too want to see *all* our legislators anti-slavery; but when that time comes, there will most obviously be no *need* of a distinct abolition party; and in order to bring about that time, we must diligently exert *moral influence* to sway *all* parties; so we move round in a circle, and come back to where we started from. As for purity of *motive*, in those who aid anti-slavery politically, do you think the "Liberty party" runs the chance of more thorough and disinterested recruits? Look around you, in every part of the country, and see how many belong to that party, who were never before heard of as abolitionists! how many, that up to the date of their joining, even opposed abolition! In one county, you see democrats joining with liberty party, pro tem. to defeat the election of a whig, which they could not accomplish by their own unaided strength; in another county, you will see a transient accession of whigs to defeat a democratic candidate. Are these elements any purer to work with, or any more to be relied on, than the legislators of Massachusetts, who were willing to give the abolitionists everything they asked? I never doubted that large numbers of the third party were influenced by perfectly honest motives, and were sincere abolitionists; but I do say, that by the natural laws of attraction, their party will draw around them the selfish and the ambitious; and this they will find to their cost, much as they may scorn the prediction now.

A. But if party machinery does as much mischief to moral influence as you think, how can you work with whigs or democrats? You talked just now of making them *both* set up candidates that would be afraid to go wrong on this question.

B. By adhering closely to moral influence, we work *through* both parties, but not *with* them. They do *our* work; we do not *their's*. We are simply the atmosphere that makes the quicksilver rise or fall.

A. But you say by your plan, men will eventually have more freedom to vote as conscience dictates on other subjects, without being false to anti-slavery principles. If politics are so polluting as non-resistants suppose, how can they do this?

B. Into the question of non-resistance, I do not enter; not from disrespect, or to avoid odium; but simply because it does not belong to the anti-slavery enterprise. Long and long before non-resistants were heard of, religious men, of all denominations, took note of the polluting tendency of political partisanship. Thus John Newton says: "From poison and politics, good Lord deliver us. The *crooked* things I would leave to Him who alone can make them straight. Politics is a pit, which will swallow up the life and spirit, if not the form of religion." My own observation abundantly confirms the truth of this. I decide for no man, whether he ought to vote, or not; that lies between his own conscience and his God. An overwhelming majority of the American Society consider it both a privilege and a duty. It is obvious enough that the debasing tendency of caucusing, and party management, and party strife, need not reach the quiet citizen, who simply deposits his vote for what he deems good men and measures.

A. But if you believe many liberty party men to be honest and sincere, why need you quarrel with them [?]

B. I do not quarrel with them; and most earnestly do I wish they could understand me as speaking my own convictions, without any admixture of partisan jealousy, or personal unkindness. I believe that the tendency of their scheme is to weaken our cause; I believe it has greatly retarded its progress, and will retard it more; I believe that it is of vast importance to keep alive the old-fashioned anti-slavery, whose work it was to purify the *fountain* of public opinion, and thence affect the streams, political and ecclesiastical. Therefore I deem it absolutely necessary to warn our agents, and others, against *admixture* with this policy. I do not ask them to make war; I only beseech them to keep clear of it.

A. I think you must admit that the South dread anti-slavery at the *ballot-box*, more than anywhere else?

B. Again you return to your idea that the ballot-box cannot be affected, except by a distinct abolition *party.* I never doubted that political action would be a powerful engine for the overthrow of slavery. The only question between you and the American Society seems to be, whether the speediest and most extensive political effect would be produced by the *old* scheme of holding the balance between the two parties, or the new scheme of forming a distinct party. I apprehend what the slaveholders would like least of all things, would be to see *both* the great political parties consider it for their interest to nominate abolitionists; and this *would* be the case if anti-slavery voters would only be consistent and firm.

A. Ah, there is the pinch! They will *not* be consistent and firm. Under the old scheme, they were always coaxed aside to their favorite party banners; one voting for Harrison, and another for Van Buren.

B. And by what superior magic does the "liberty party" expect to keep its allies more closely rallied around *her*, in time of tempting emergency? Will the two-thirds abolitionized democrat, who has joined them to defeat a whig, stand by them when his vote is greatly needed to secure a triumph to his own party, at the polls? Will the half-abolitionized whig, who has been drawn into their ranks, pass safe through the fire of a similar temptation? I trow not.

Men of strong party predilections, favorably inclined to anti-slavery, might be induced to act openly in its favor, if they had the two-fold object of obeying their own consciences, and of gaining all the strength of the abolition voters who were inclined to the same party. But when a distinct abolition party is formed, this stimulus is taken away. In acting with such a party, a man must not only take upon himself the unpopularity of abolition, but must relinquish action upon all other subjects which may seem to him important; such as national bank, tariff, &c. Politicians may be induced to do this for a while; but it is not according to human nature that it should last.—Should the "liberty party" obtain sufficient power to sway the legislation of State or nation, that moment one man will demand action for the tariff, and another against the tariff; they will split, and be swallowed by the great parties from which they seceded; of course, their strength, as a party, will be broken the very moment it could be brought to act.

A. Perhaps legislators would be conscientious enough to sacrifice all minor considerations to anti-slavery.

B. Then their constituents would say their interests on *other* subjects had not been attended to; and they would not vote for them again. A democratic district would not re-elect a man who sustained a national bank, because a majority of the abolition party chose to do it; they could not do so with a clear conscience; and so, vice versa. In the nature of things, abolition cannot be the whole of Church and State; but it can be a moral atmosphere modifying the whole. This difficulty is seen at the outset, in the attempt to form a *church* on anti-slavery grounds. It proposes to include only *evangelical* sects; for the simple reason that these could not conscientiously co-operate with Unitarians, Quakers, Universalists, &c. If they can compromise on minor matters, such as baptism, church discipline, &c. so as to remain united for any considerable length of time, they will work wonders. But in the meantime, an influence is needed to move both orthodox and liberal sects, on this plain question of humanity and justice. Again we have gone round the circle, and come back to *moral influence*, as the legitimate work of anti-slavery.

A. But while people are working for liberty party, they are at the same time exerting moral influence.

B. With sadly diminished power, let me assure you—Their motives are distrusted; suspicion enters the mind, that they may care more for offices than for truth; and they themselves gradually get accustomed to trust more to party machinery, than they do to the potency of truth. The advocates of "liberty party" show a most glaring want of faith in moral influence. Some of them, who used to talk and write as if it could regenerate the world, now speak of it with contumely and scorn.

A. But since the liberty party *is* started, if they set up candidates who are good men and thorough abolitionists, ought we not to vote for them?

B. I believe that is the bait that has hooked half their numbers. Men who consider the third party a hindrance to the cause, yet co-operate with it, because it is started, and its existence cannot be helped. The consequences of this are more important than appears on the surface. One of these elements *destroys the other. Moral* influence dies under *party* action. If you do not see this now, you will see it. Many honest minds will try the experiment, with perfect sincerity of purpose; they will gradually become disgusted with the management and crooked devices, that always spring up in political encounters, and which are sure to increase in proportion as a party gains power; they will lose their confidence in men, if not in principles; they will cease to attend anti-slavery meetings, and will feel disheartened in their efforts for the cause. To some extent, this is already the case. I hope those who think of voting for a "liberty-party" candidate, because they believe him to be a good man, will reflect well whether the limited good they may effect thereby, will not be overbalanced by the harm they will inevitably do in sustaining a fallacious and mischievous scheme.

A. But what am I to do if they really become powerful enough to choose their own candidates, and men of whom I approve?

B. Wait till that time comes, and decide your duty then.—L.M.C.

IV

The Liberty Party

9

"Lecture Showing the Necessity for a Liberty Party, and Setting Forth Its Principles, Measures, and Object" (1844)

Arnold Buffum

Arnold Buffum (1782–1859) was a New England Quaker, hatmaker and inventor, first President of the New England Anti-Slavery Society and a founding member of the American Anti-Slavery Society, and a lecturing agent and editor for the abolitionist cause.

Early on, Buffum rejected Garrison's and Phillips's radical "non-resistance" principles and became a vocal supporter of abolitionist political action. Eventually, he would support the Liberty, Free-Soil and Republican parties. In the selection that follows, Buffum catalogues the advantages and elucidates the principles of the Liberty Party.

Having been a careful observer of the proceedings of the National Government for half a century—having witnessed its devotion for upwards of forty years to the Slaveholding interest, I have been led to look carefully over the acts of national legislation, and to examine minutely the operation and bearing of the measures which have been adopted, and I can arrive at no other conclusion, than that for the last *forty years*, every act of a national character, has originated with the Slaveholders, and has been adopted in a spirit of devotion to their interests, and of hostility to every other interest in our country. Thus OUR *national Government* has already been made, like the governments of Europe, an engine for building up an ARISTOCRACY in OUR country, which when once completely organized, will rob, not only the slaves on their own plantations, but also nine-tenths of the American people of *their* rights, and reduce *them* to the same wretched condition, which is now witnessed among the laboring population in Europe.

Notwithstanding the representation of the *property* of Slaveholders in the national government, we in the non-Slave-holding States, having nearly three-fourths of the popular vote of the nation, have a majority of 47 members in Congress, and the same majority in the Presidential Electoral Colleges: So that, were it not for the dough-faced servility of a portion of the representatives of freemen, in the Presidential election and in Congress, we might even now, have *our* rights protected, *our* welfare promoted, and all *our* elements of prosperity and sources of wealth successfully developed.

The remedy which we need, for the difficulties we now suffer, is to be found in the election of a President and members of Congress, who will *not* basely bow themselves down to the moloch of Slavery, but who will impartially administer the government on its true and original principles, for the promotion of the general welfare, and equally for the benefit of all who are subject to its power. The election of such men, is entirely within the power of the non-slaveholders of the country; and such men will be elected, just so soon as the non-slaveholders shall have been effectually aroused, to investigate and understand the arts of designing demagogues, who have heretofore but too successfully deceived the majority, into the support of Slave holding Aristocrats, or the sycophantic tools of the Slave power.

Within the last 42 years, Slaveholders have filled the Presidential office 34 years, and non-Slaveholders only 8 years. The office of Chief Justice of the Supreme Court, Speaker of the House of Representatives, President pro tem. of the Senate, Secretary of State, and most of the other departments of the Government, have been equally occupied and controlled by men, who from the nature of their *"peculiar in*[s]*titutions,"* are inevitably hostile to a laboring community of freemen.

Some of the measures which the Government has adopted, intended for the promotion of the Slave interest, have, by the ingenuity and enterprize of freemen, been so appropriated as to become productive of general benefit to the whole community, and to promote the prosperity and welfare of all; but when it has become evident, that an adherence to the existing order of things, would be productive of such *favorable* results, the policy has been changed, and measures which were operating thus beneficially, have been abolished; so that we have in the end been made deeply to suffer, in consequence of having conformed our business arrangements, to the operation of the acts of the Government.

When the Slaveholders have desired any measure of foreign or domestic policy, calculated to strengthen their power in controlling the action of the Government, or to promote their individual prosper[i]ty, they have always come up to the executive or legislative department of the Government, with an authoritative demand for compliance with their interests or wishes, and they have in no case been finally defeated. Every law has been passed, every measure adopted, at whatever sacrifice of all other interests it might require, which the Slaveholders have demanded for their benefit. On the other hand, the interests of non-Slaveholders, have as invariably been unheeded; or what is still worse, the action of the Government has in many important cases, been *hostile* to the non-Slaveholding interest, without the anticipation of *benefit* to any body. No Measure of a general character, tending to *our* benefit, has been permitted to stand any longer than was *necessary* to answer some sinister purpose of the Slaveholders, or to operate upon our concerns, as the bait operates upon the fox, who is thereby beguiled into the well-concealed trap, which is then sprung upon him, whereby his foe is enabled to rob him of his skin. Such precisely has been the operation of our tariff laws, by which the citizens of the non-Slaveholding States, were induced to invest a hundred million dollars in manufacturing establishments, all to be swept away, by the springing of the Calhoun and Clay compromise trap upon them in 1833. Such too was the operation of two United States Bank charters, each running 20 years; just long enough for the people to conform their business arrangements to the operations of *"the Great Regulator";* when by the demand of the Slaveholders, they were both forced to go *down,* that they might carry down with them the general prosperity of the people.

To these statements and charges, bold and sweeping as they are, I challenge an answer. If there is any politician, Whig, Democrat, or Tyler man, who can name *an instance* in which the Slaveholders have failed of obtaining a compliance with their interest and wishes, or in which any measure has been *adopted, carried out, and persevered in,* for the advancement of any of the other great interests of the country, I hope that through some medium, they will let the public know what it is. I call not for private contradictions of my statements; my allegations are publicly made, and the challenge for an answer is a public one; let the refutation be as public as are my charges, and then I will conclude, that the respondant has some confidence that he will be able to maintain his ground. I call not for mere declamation, or common party slang; but I call for facts, and I challenge the world to name the facts, in contradiction of the statements herein contained.

I call upon the leaders of the two great political parties, which have ruled the nation for the last forty years, to let the *people* know what *benefits they have derived* from the action of the Government, to support which, we have paid more than five hundred millions of dollars in taxes, of the earnings of the laboring people. For let the revenue of the Government be collected in what manner it may, whether by direct taxation, or indirectly, by the laying of duties on articles of consumption, the whole amount must be supplied by the productive industry of the country.

If any measures have been adopted by the Government, which were intended by *any portion* of those who voted for them, to promote the prosperity of the non-Slaveholders of the country, such measures have been suffered to remain in operation, *only* long enough to induce a change in individual pursuits in conformity to the encouragement thus held out by the Government, and then, they have been prostrated at the demand of the dealers in human flesh, and those who had trusted to the faith of the Government, have been prostrated with them.

The Slaveholders in all the States of our Union give but about two hundred and fifty thousand votes in popular elections; while the non-Slaveholders give more than two millions, being more than eight times as many as are given by the Slaveholders. Hence it is evident, that when the *true issue,* of *Slavery,* or *Liberty,* shall constitute the division line of political parties in our country, the *aristocratical* power will be entirely prostrated in the National Government, and the traffickers in human flesh will be left to rely on State legislation alone, for the protection of their *"peculiar institution."* Then a President and a Congress will be elected, who will be neither Slave-*holders,* nor the sycophantic tools of *Slaveholders.* Our Government will then mark out and establish a systematic and permanent policy, and will conduct the affairs of the nation, in accordance with (not "the wishes of Slaveholders," but) the interests of freemen, and with the principles of the Declaration of Independence; giving stability and permanency to that cause, in which our forefathers embarked, when they declared it to be a self-evident truth, that all men are created equal, and endowed by their Creator with an unalienable right to be free, and to pursue their own happiness. The principles of a true democracy will then be practically applied in the administration of the Government; the rights of the people will then be maintained, and their welfare and prosperity will be so promoted, that the spirit of aristocracy will stand abashed, in despair of obtaining a royal diadem, or of effecting by any means the subjugation of the people. Then indeed will our institutions and our prosperity hold out to an admiring world, an irresistible invitation to demolish their thrones, dash their crowns in pieces, and build upon their ruins a temple of freedom, to guard the rights, and promote the happiness and welfare of the people.

Our whole object as a political party is, the inculcation and practical application of the great principles of human rights, derived from the charter given forth by the SUPREME LAW GIVER of the universe, when He created man in his own image, and gave to man universally the right to exercise dominion over all inferior beings in this world. We believe, that it is only by the faithful maintenance of these principles that any people can long retain their liberty, and enjoy the rights and privileges mercifully dispensed to *all,* by the common PARENT of us *all.* The practical application of these principles will put an end to all tyranny and oppression throughout the world, and secure to every human being the perfect enjoyment of the right to pursue his own happiness; restricted only by the divine prohibition of authority to trespass upon the happiness of others. . . .

... The American LIBERTY PARTY, is not, (as it is often denominated by our opponents) a *third* party. We are the true original American party, seeking to carry out the principles of our forefathers, as set forth in the declaration of Independence. These principles have for a long time been lost sight of, in the fog of the two great parties, which are contending with each other for the mastery, *not* for the promotion of the cause of liberty, but for the establishment of a domineering Oligarchy, and for the perpetuation of the old monarchical and aristocratical doctrine, that the well born and the rich have a right to tyranize over the poor, and to appropriate to themselves the product of their labor.

... Some of our opponents, probably through ignorance, have represented it to be our intention *forcibly* to emancipate the slaves in the Southern States; we intend no such thing. We complain, that by the action of the national Government, and also of the governments of many of the non-slaveholding States in *support* of Slavery, we are made participants in the crime of robbing men of their natural rights—we wish to absolve ourselves from such crime.

By the voluntary act of Virginia and Maryland, in ceding to Congress the District of Columbia, the institution of Slavery in that portion of those States, standing as it did *only* on State authority, would have fal[l]en to the ground, had not our *Northern* members of Congress yielded themselves as props for its continued support; and all we ask of them in regard to Slavery in that district—in Florida, and on the high seas, is, that they get out from under it, and let it fall of its own weight, as it assuredly must, when the national government no longer stands its god father and supporter.

In relation to Slavery in the States, politically we claim no right to interfere. So long as the people of the South may choose to hold a portion of their children in bondage, and traffic in them as they do in brute animals, they must do it; but we are not willing that men who plunder their *own* children of their rights, should rule over *our* children; we will not therefore support any Slaveholder for office in the government—besides, regarding Slavery as the most grievous wrong that was ever inflicted by one man upon another, and as a palpable violation of the laws of God; and knowing that its existence in our country, has a powerful tendency to stifle every feeling of humanity—to annihilate every principle of justice—to drive morality from our land, and to build up a lordly aristocracy, which if unresisted would eventually establish itself in power, to the entire subversion of the liberties of the nation, we can but feel, that it is an object which should claim the untiring devotion of every patriot or philanthropist, to promote the speedy and entire abolition of the system. We should therefore be *criminal,* were we to neglect the use of all *legitimate* means for accomplishing this great object.

Slavery is a dark institution—it cannot stand before the light of truth; this the Slaveholders well know, and enact laws prohibiting the education of the oppressed. We believe however, that although they may keep the minds of their enslaved children, in a state of mental and moral darkness and degradation, the system cannot stand before that full blaze of intellectual and moral light, which is now being disseminated *among the free.*

The abolition of Slavery in our country, will be but an incidental result of the establishment of our principles; the practical adoption of which, in the administration of the government, is as necessary for the security of *our* rights, and the rights of *our* posterity, as for the security of the rights of the oppressed in the Southern States.

Such, fellow-citizens, are the principles, such the aim, of the Liberty men in our country. Against these principles, and this aim, are arrayed in unholy combination, the aristocratic enslavers of men, and through their influence, the existing administrations of the National and State Governments. These are sustained in their opposition, First, by the drunken mobocrats, whose arguments consist of rotten eggs, tar, feathers, and brick-bats. Secondly, by a majority of the Clergy and the Church; these have *no* arguments, but "stopping their ears against the poor,"—("Whoso stoppeth his ears at the cry of the poor, he also shall cry himself, but shall not be heard"—*Proverbs,* xxi: 13) and on secretly circulating *slanderous falsehoods* against the prominent advocates of our cause!!! Thirdly, and strange to tell, by a small party of Abolitionists; they rely on either ignorant or intentional misrepresentations of our principles, motives and measures.

If any class of the above named opposers, are honest in their opposition, we invite them to meet us in the field of reason, argument and truth, and to debate with us the questions which divide us. We have in our ranks many, in various parts of the country, who hold themselves in readiness to discuss these questions, either orally or through the medium of the press. We ask for *open* opponents—such *as are not ashamed to subscribe their names* to their arguments that posterity may know that in *this* age of the world, they stood forth in opposition to the holy cause of liberty and human rights, as advocated by us. Let them show to the world, if they can, that our principles are unsound—that our measures are unwise—that our facts are unreal, or that the object which we seek, is unworthy of the efforts which it will cost. If they can successfully do this, then we must fall; but should they fail in the attempt, or should the conviction that we are right in all our propositions, prevent them from making the attempt, then let them, if they choose, continue as heretofore, to rely upon mobocracy and slander, and let the intelligence and the moral sense of the world decide, on which side lies the truth, and the best interests of mankind. Let every Patriot, every Philanthropist, every well-wisher to the happiness of our race, frown indignantly upon all attempts to stifle a discussion which has for its object the regeneration of the public sentiment of the world, and the abrogation of *all* the abuses which keep the mass of mankind in poverty, and tend to perpetuate among them, ignorance, degradation and vice. Let *all honest* men, unite in proclaiming the inviolability of human rights; and the spirit of despotism shall soon be driven from the world—man every where shall assume his true position, and standing in his native dignity, "redeemed, regenerated, and disenthralled," shall rejoice in the assurance, that his posterity to the latest generation, shall inherit and enjoy the blessing of RATIONAL LIBERTY.

10
"Address of the Macedon Convention" (1847)

William Goodell

William Goodell (1792–1878) was a leading abolitionist organizer, editor, publicist, and intellectual from upstate New York. He published and edited two of the most important abolitionist newspapers, The Emancipator *and the* Friend of Man, *and he helped to found the Liberty Party and later the Liberty League. He was also one of the earliest abolitionist theoreticians to argue that the Constitution authorized Congress to do away with slavery. Among his principal abolitionist works are* Views Upon American Constitutional Law, in its Bearing Upon American Slavery *(1844),* Slavery and Anti-Slavery: A History of the Great Struggle in Both Hemispheres *(1852), and the* American Slave Code, in Theory and Practice *(1853).*

In the selection that follows, Goodell makes the case that the time has come for the Liberty Party to drop its single-issue platform and to adopt a multi-planked platform to address a whole range of economic, political, and social issues. In addition to immediate abolition, Goodell argues that the Liberty Party should adopt a position on issues such as tariff reform, land monopolies, liquor traffic, war, and secret societies.

Introduction

We take the liberty to address you in respect to the objects we have in view, in convening together and nominating candidates for President and Vice-President of the United Slates. Those objects are not *partizan* in the ordinary acceptation of that term. We have no interests to promote distinct from the interests of each and all of our fellow-citizens. We espouse no other principles of government than those which our entire nation has declared to be self-evident. We only ask that the rights of all shall be equally and impartially protected—that the fundamental and acknowledged principles of civil government shall be, at all times, on all occasions, every where, and in every direction, applied and carried out into consistent and undeviating practice. If there are some who solicit your aid in protecting the rights of the *white* man—and if there are others who ask you to assist them in protecting the rights of the *colored* man, we agree with them both, and we differ from them both, in desiring you to co-operate with us in securing the equal protection of the rights of ALL men. If there are some who wish to enlist you in a political contest against one form of injustice and oppression—if there are others who would have you combine against another form of injustice and of oppression, or another, or yet another, we agree with them all, and we differ from them, all, in asking you to assist us in securing an administration of government that shall protect all its subjects alike, from all forms of injustice and oppression, so far as civil government can apply the remedy, in the appropriate exercise of its characteristic powers. . . .

Civil Government we understand to be that degree and description of authoritative control which the Common Father of all men has committed to society, to be exercised, in accordance with equity and justice, over each one of its members, for the protection of all and of each, in the safe possession and full enjoyment and use of all their original and heaven-conferred rights unimpaired; forbidding nothing but the infringement of those rights, and requiring and enforcing nothing but what is requisite for their protection and enjoyment.

Assuming, as it does, the essential equality of all, and being committed to all, it imposes equal restraints upon all, and affords equal and impartial protection for all. It recognizes no caste. It knows no distinction of birth, property, nativity, avocation, condition or color. It punishes nothing but crime. It infringes no original, natural rights. It permits no such infringement. It recognizes no man's right to infringe the equal rights of his neighbor. It creates and allows no monopolies. It confers no exclusive privileges. It has no power to frame a valid and binding law that violates any original right, or conflicts with natural equity and justice. And all its courts, magistrates and jurors are bound to consider all legislative enactments or judicial precedents or usages, which are contrary to natural justice, null and void. We hold slavery to be illegal and unconstitutional, and that the Federal Government is bound to secure its abolition by the guaranty, to every State in this Union, of a republican form of government. If the South demurs, let her, peacefully, withdraw from the Union. We demand, for the injured aborigines of this country, the same protection, mercy and justice that we demand for the injured slave. *We* go for the repeal of all tariffs, whether for protection or revenue, the support of the government by direct taxes, the consequent diminution of the revenue, the retrenchment of expenses, the reduction of salaries, the abolition of unnecessary offices, and of the whole naval and military establishment, the prompt abandonment of the present wicked war with Mexico, the restoration of her conquered territory, including Texas, and ample remuneration for the wrongs we have inflicted upon her. Along with the abolition of all other monopolies, we would restrict within reasonable bounds, the extent to which individuals, corporations, or the government, should hold properly in land, providing an opportunity for all to become possessors of the soil, and thus enjoy (without its being contested) the original right of every human being to occupy a portion of the earth's surface, and breathe its free air. To this end, we would also have the public lands thrown open to actual settlers, free of cost, and every man's homestead held inalienable, except with his own consent, not being liable to seizure and sale for debt.

We would abolish the Post Office monopoly, allowing citizens to exercise the original right of transporting letters and newspapers, as well as other freight. If the government cannot compete with them, let it discontinue the business, or if it chooses to run mails at the public expense, let all who use the mail pay equally at a cheap rate, for its use, without privilege of franking.

We would confer office on no slaveholders or members of pro-slavery bodies, political or ecclesiastical—on no venders of strong drink or advocates for the license of that traffic—on no members of secret societies—and on no persons known to be immoral, unjust, dishonest, or (by position or principle) in a state of hostility to the essential elements and conditions of civil, political and religious freedom.

Application of Principles a Duty

It is now nearly two years since this general outline of political principles and measures was definitely proposed by some of us, as a basis of associated political action, believing as we then did and still do, that the Liberty party, to which we belonged, was not only pledged to those general principles, but was also pledged, by its own original and oft-repeated promises, to apply those principles to all public questions, as the appropriate occasions should arise for their application. During the period that has intervened, although strong exceptions have been taken, and determined opposition manifested, to the course we had proposed, we have found no antagonists who have been willing to join issue with us on the *moral* question involved, whether the action proposed is, or is not, in accordance with the *right and the true in the abstract*. No one offers to show us, and few, if any, are prepared to affirm, that our principles and our measures are not RIGHT, EQUITABLE and JUST. Our principles are the professed creed of the nation. They are loudly insisted on by Abolitionists in general, and by Liberty party men in particular. And not the first man among them has attempted to prove that the measures we propose are not legitimate deductions from those principles; that our application of them is not appropriate and proper, or that there is not occasion, in consequence of existing wrongs, that a remedy should be applied. It is almost universally admitted by them, as well as by a large portion of the community in general, that the wrongs we have enumerated are evils, and that it is desirable that they should be removed. Abolitionists in general, and Liberty party men in particular, have been accustomed to maintain, moreover, that it is always safe to do right, and safe as well as obligatory to do right at the present time—that it is morally wrong to defer doing right,—and that it is holding the truth in unrighteousness to acknowledge a truth in the abstract, and yet decline, on prudential considerations, reducing that truth to practice. On this ground it is, that Abolitionists persist in applying the epithet pro-slavery to that portion of the community, who, while they acknowledge the moral wrong of slavery, excuse themselves as on the ground of expediency, from reducing their convictions to practice, in the bestowment of their votes.

We cannot perceive why we are not bound to reason in the same manner and to act in accordance with the same considerations in respect to all other moral evils within the admitted sphere and province of political action. Admitting that chattel slavery is the greatest moral and political evil upheld and sanctioned by the government, (though the moral and political evils of intemperance are scarcely less,) we cannot feel ourselves, as moral and accountable beings, at liberty to undertake the mensuration and guaging of the moral and political evils upheld by the government, with a view of ascertaining which is greatest, and thus determining which moral evil we will select as our antagonist, and which we will enter into a truce with, at present, and virtually support, by not making opposition to it a test, in the bestowment of our votes. If those who wish to oppose, at the ballot-box, the licensing of the sale of intoxicating liquors, or the enactment of certain unjust and wicked laws which oppress the poor white man, may not for such objects, without moral wrong, and without becoming justly obnoxious to the charge of being pro-slavery, hold in abeyance their anti-slavery convictions and sympathies, bestowing their votes on pro-slavery lawmakers, for the sake of preventing rum licenses and the enactment of unjust laws for oppressing poor white men, then we cannot see how, without, moral wrong, we can hold in abeyance our temperance principles, or our convictions of the moral wrongfulness of corn laws, cloth laws, and other legislative devices for grinding the face of the poor, in order to bestow our votes on the opposers of chattel enslavement. Nor do we see the necessity, or the good policy of so doing. The most trustworthy opponents of chattel enslavement—indeed the only really trustworthy ones—are those whose opposition is founded on fixed moral principle, and impelled by simple-hearted benevolence and good will to mankind—men who are opposed to chattel enslavement, because it is morally wrong and inhuman, who are therefore opposed to rum-licenses, and to all other wicked and unjust acts of legislation, because they too are morally wrong and inhuman—men who will not stifle, nor compromise, nor hold in abeyance their moral convictions, either in the one case or in the other. To do otherwise would be choosing between the least of two moral evils, consenting to the one, but opposing the other, which we hold to be morally wrong whether we select one or the other of the moral evils for our antagonist.

To co-operate with a political party that refuses to array itself against any of the wicked and unjust acts of the government except chattel slavery, would be choosing the least of two moral evils. And we can perceive nothing more sagacious or more Christian like, in this process of choosing the least of two moral evils, than in the similar process of those whose political action, in their own apprehension, might be directed to the removal of all unjust and wicked legislation, except the legalizing of slavery. On the one hand, it might be pleaded that slavery is only one evil, and impossible, at present to be removed, so long as other similar and numerous evils are left to support it, while these are not too inveterate to be removed in detail, in the first place, thus preparing the way for the accomplishing of the more difficult task afterwards. On the other hand it might be pleaded, as indeed it is, that slavery is the greatest evil, the promoter, if not the source of all the rest; that it is the dictate of wisdom to unite our energies against this in the first place, and leave the rest to be attended to afterwards. It concerns us not to say which of these rival methods is marked with the greatest degree of falsehood and error. In neither of them can we discover the marks of true wisdom. Both methods we reject as contrary to true philosophy, sound morals, and practical good sense. The proclamation of neutrality in respect to one or more moral evils, amounting to a truce with them, and a co-operation with their supporters, is but a lame preparation for an onset with another moral evil, admitting it to be the parent and chief support of all the others. Such a Policy resembles too closely—nay, is it not in substance, a proposition to enter into an alliance, offensive and defensive, with ALL the lesser devils of the pit, in the hope of decoying them into a successful campaign against the Prince and Father of them all? The friends of temperance were thus seduced, for a time, to hold a truce with the lesser demons of inebriation, the wine, the beer, and the cider, while they concentrated their energies against the Giant Fiend, Distilled Spirit. The result proved that a truce with the subalterns and privates of the army of intemperance was a truce with the Commander-in-Chief of that army himself, and the World's history fails to furnish us with any other instance of better success in the attempt to cast out the Prince of the Devils by a truce or co-operation with his legions.

Law of Free Trade and Inalienable Homestead, a Moral Law

It is an easy and cheap mode of argument to assume, as is sometimes done, the main point in debate, or rather, to assume as true, what is commonly admitted, in reality, on both sides, to be false. It is easy to represent, and take for granted, that whereas the slave question is a great MORAL question, all the other great questions before the nation, are mere questions of policy, involving no moral principles at all. On the ground of this assumption, it is easy to represent those who occupy the position we have chosen, as lowering down or throwing into the shade, a great moral question, for the sake of settling mere questions of finance, of profit and loss, of pecuniary advantage or disadvantage. The questions of free trade, of monopolies, of the public lands, &c., are treated as being of this character. But there is no solid ground for this representation. It stands contradicted by the almost universal sentiment that the law of free trade is an original law of nature, and consequently, a law of God, founded on the original and inalienable right of every man to the products of his own labor, including the right to dispose of the same, wherever he can find a brother man to become the free purchaser. All writers of any note on moral and political science and on political economy, who have treated of the subject, have assumed this as an axiom. Not a work of the kind can be found in our Colleges and Seminaries, in which the point is not conceded or assumed. It is as self-evident as the right of self-ownership, of which it is an essential part. And the intelligent advocates of commercial restrictions always concede this truth, and admit that free trade is right "in the abstract." Their pleas for international tariffs are all founded on the supposed pecuniary advantages to the country, or to particular portions of its citizens under existing circumstances, to be derived from certain departures from this law of nature and of God, this law of original and "abstract right," especially while other nations persist in departing from it, in a word, the plea for human chattelhood and for restrictions on the right of human beings to the free interchange of their products (an essential feature of self-ownership) rest on the same basis, viz: the utility of impairing man's essential humanity, or crippling its exercise; the utility of counteracting the original and heaven-established laws of man's social existence and moral freedom, under the present circumstances of the case.

If laws sustaining the claim of human chattelhood are sinful, because they violate the original law of man's nature; then laws restricting the free interchange of the lawful products of human industry are likewise sinful for the same reason.

Similar remarks might be made concerning man's right to occupy a portion of the earth's surface, and the consequent unrighteousness of the legislation and the arrangements by which that original and fundamental law of nature and of nature's God, is contemptuously set aside. To talk of man's inalienable right of self-ownership, without the right to the products of his own skill and industry—to talk of his right to those products without the right to exchange or sell them, wherever he can find the best market—to talk of a man's right to SELF-OWNERSHIP without a right to an inch of the earth's soil, without a right to be in the world where he was born, is to talk self-contradiction and nonsense; for the right of self-ownership includes or implies the right of existence, of soil, and of free intercourse. Whoever succeeds in proving that the legal sanction of an unlimited land monopoly, and that commercial restrictions, are morally right, will have done more than the slaveholders and their apologists have ever yet been able to do, towards proving that chattel enslavement is not essentially and inherently wicked. That man's claim to the right of self-ownership must be in a sad predicament, who has neither a right to be nor to do—to exercise his faculties or to occupy space! The principle of illimitable land ownership, if admitted, covers the one predicament—the principle of commercial restrictions the other. If one white man, or if fifty, or if two hundred, may own all the soil of the slave States, what becomes of the colored man's right to freedom in the land of his birth, for which Abolitionists have so long contended? And if, in addition to this, the government may restrict commercial intercourse by a tariff, (if it has this right, it has it, at discretion and without bounds,) then it may prohibit, and not merely cripple, the commercial intercourse of the laboring population with the rest of the world, and render labor unavailing for its great ends. The mockery of a nominal self-ownership is all that then stands between them and their re-enslavement, in case they had been previously enfranchised. . . .

Inefficiency of Voluntary, or "One Idea" Societies

It may be admitted that *voluntary societies*, selecting one distinct object, have been productive of some benefits. We do not allege that it is morally wrong to organize such societies, for the man that co-operates with one of them for the promotion of one good object, may at the same time, co-operate with another of them for another, and thus discharge in one, the obligations not discharged in the other. In supporting one of these societies, while its affairs are properly conducted, we do not necessarily neglect, much less oppose, any other good object. The case differs when, in attempting the promotion of one good object, a society loses sight of those moral affinities that bind together all good enterprises, and violates one class of obligations for the sake of discharging another. Thus a society that sanctions caste, in order to circulate Bibles, or that lends its sanction to slavery, in order to extend missions—or that thinks to convert the world without opposing all the world's vices—or that, in attempting to oppose licentiousness, is careful to take no notice of its strongest and deepest and most wide-spread entrenchments,—such societies, very evidently, while thus conducted, not only become the opponents of other good objects, but fail of fidelity to their own special trusts. An abolitionist that should content himself with that one department of benevolent or reformatory effort—an Anti-Slavery Society that should violate one class of moral obligations, in order to discharge another class that should lead its members into a truce with other vices, and especially with other forms of oppression, as a means of abolishing chattel slavery, would become equally reprehensible, and undeserving of the public confidence.

We call attention to these plain considerations, in order to meet an objection against the course we propose, founded on the supposed teachings of experience in the use of our modern voluntary associations. We are admonished to take them as our models, and are particularly referred to the supposed secret of their efficiency, in the strictness with which they have confined themselves exclusively to one definite and distinct object; and because the Temperance Societies have done good by confining their attention to one distinct thing, we are told that a political party, to be efficient, must pursue a similar course.

To this argument we answer, in the first place, that the experiment of these voluntary associations falls far short of justifying the conclusion that they have always been conducted in the best manner, and that their success would not have been greater, had they taken more comprehensive views of the evils they undertook to remove. The Temperance enterprise, as already noticed, has suffered severely from the attempt to limit attention and effort within narrower bounds than the case demanded. The Missionary Society, too, in the same manner, has made still worse shipwreck, by too limited and technical a definition of its object. Scarcely a voluntary association can be mentioned, that has not fallen more or less into the same error, the present effect of which is sufficiently visible *in* their mutual rivalries and recriminations, and still more, in their all coming to a dead stand. The most experienced and observing men connected with those enterprises, to a great extent, are coming to look upon them as having passed their meridian, at least in their present shape, and partly because each one of them finds its wheels blocked by obstacles which the original plan of the society does not permit it to touch or to remove, and any thing like cooperation or mutual assistance, is, of course, out of the question, for the same reason. The Bible Society cannot assist the Abolitionists in giving Bibles to the slaves, because the Bible Society cannot go beyond its "one idea," as it would do, should it commit itself on the slave question. The Moral Reform Society, for the same reason, must make little or no allusion to the system of southern prostitution. The Temperance Society can have nothing to say of the theatres, gambling houses, and brothels, and licentious fashionable literature, that lead so many thousands to intemperance. And the Anti-Slavery Society can say nothing of any of the numerous systems of despotism and oppression by which the slave system is supported, and which it wields at pleasure, because each one of these falls short of "chattel" enslavement, and is not embraced in its "one idea." . . .

But we have a still further answer to the argument thus urged upon us. . . . So the "one idea" of abolishing chattel slavery may suffice for the Anti-Slavery Society, but we must beg to be excused from admitting the inference that all the functions of civil government are exercised, and all its obligations discharged, by the simple abolition of chattel slavery, without the redress of any of its other abuses, the repeal of any other of its own unjust acts, the repression of any other species of crime. Because its penal code should prohibit and punish man-stealing, it does not follow that it should prohibit and punish nothing else. And just as broad and comprehensive as are the functions and duties of civil government, just so broad and comprehensive are the duties of free citizens and voters in their participation in the acts of the government. And just so broad and comprehensive, likewise, are the duties of any political association of voters and citizens uniting together in the nomination and support of all the officers by whom the government is to be administered. . . .

Morality of "One Ideaism"

It is appalling to witness the inroads made upon the consciences and moral sensibilities of men, by the operation of the "one idea" theory, as it is commonly understood and applied. . . .

If it be said that the duties inappropriate to one, or another, or to each and to all of these associations, may nevertheless be discharged by us, as individuals, in addition to the duties we discharge in our several associations; we answer, that this remark cannot be true in respect to the political party we support, if that party proposes any thing short of the discharge of all our political obligations. We might indeed discharge many (though not all) of our duties concerning intemperance in our co-operation with a Temperance Society, provided its basis were sufficiently broad for the purpose. We might then, perhaps, step into the Anti-Slavery Society and do up a part, though not the whole, of our anti-slavery work, there. But we *cannot* co-operate with an anti-slavery political party confined to the one object of abolishing chattel slavery, and reserve to ourselves the *possibility* of discharging, in any other manner, the rest of our important and heaven-imposed political duties. We have only one vote to bestow, and can belong to only one political party. Having deposited our vote for the anti-slavery candidate, there is not, and cannot be, another political party into which we may step and deposit our vote for the temperance candidate; and another into which we may enter and vote against the iniquities and oppressions of a combined revenue and protective tariff, and so on. And even if we could, we might only be voting for a tariff in the one party, and against it in the other; for slavery in the one party and against it in the other; for temperance in the one party and intemperance in the other; thus dividing ourselves against ourselves, and nullifying our own votes. When we vote for a man to hold a civil office, we have to vote for the whole man, so far at least as his general character and public acts are concerned. In voting for a pro-slavery man we cast a pro-slavery vote, though our object in voting may be something else; and in voting for a tariff *man*, we vote for a tariff though our object be something else. If slavery and if tariffs are morally wrong, we can do neither of these things without committing an immoral act. That portion of the Liberty party in the State of New-York, who insist that the Liberty party is not, and must not become, a party for other purposes than the simple abolition of chattel *slavery*, have been compelled, by their own sense of their political responsibilities, on other subjects, to step occasionally out of the Liberty party and vote for the pro-slavery candidates of the pro-slavery parties, in reference to those other objects. Thus in attempting to discharge one political obligation, they have violated another. With all their devotion to the "one idea" of abolishing chattel slavery, and in the very moment of repudiating the solicitude of Abolitionists for "other and minor objects," they have actually been driven into the position of casting pro-slavery votes, for the accomplishment of those "other and minor objects." So that fidelity to the cause of the slave is found to require an anti-slavery political party that will provide for the discharge of *all* our political obligations.

A Political Party—Its Obligations

Let not our position be misunderstood—or mis-stated, as it has been. We do not say that our political party must provide for, or furnish an arena, for the discharge of all our moral duties. We only say that it must cover the ground of all of them that are appropriately political. This is only saying that all our political duties must be discharged—We do not look to a political party, nor to political action, nor to civil government, to remove all moral and social evils. Far from it. We only look to them to do their proper work, along with other appropriate moral influences, for securing to all men, their original and essential rights. The field, tho' not without well-defined limits, is too broad for any one single political measure—any one legislative enactment. The most strenuous advocate for the narrow construction of our "one idea" would hardly venture to affirm, in so many words, that all the moral obligations resting upon our government could be discharged and fulfilled by the simple enactment of a statute abolishing chattel slavery—But if the moral responsibilities of the government extend further than that limit, how can it be made to appear that the moral responsibilities of those who vote and who nominate the officers of the government do not extend farther?

Will it be said (it has been said) that a political party and an administration abolishing chattel slavery may be trusted, without further inquiry, to execute justice in all other respects? As well might it be affirmed that a man guiltless of burglary might therefore be safely entrusted with the reins of the government—that because a man had never robbed on the highway, he was therefore upright enough for a judge, that whoever assists in rescuing a child from the flames, or a drowning man from the river, is entitled to implicit confidence as an arbiter between man and man! Let "practical men" inquire after the facts. The British Government that abolished chattel slavery in the West Indies is starving the people of Ireland, is crushing the operatives of Birmingham, is enforcing upon dissenters in England the payment of church tithes, is excluding large masses of the people from the sight of suffrage, is building up a bloated aristocracy, is grinding the faces of the poor, is consenting to the oppression, by tariffs, of the lately emancipated West India negroes, is lending its aid to the importation of East India coolies to compete with them, and reduce still lower their wages, entailing hopeless destitution upon both negroes and coolies, thus reviving, though without chattelhood, the closest possible resemblance to the slave trade

If the opponents of chattel slavery in America are more comprehensive in their views of human rights, let it be shown by their promptly coming up to the position to which we invite them! If they are opposed to all other oppression as well as the oppression of human chattelhood, and if they are ready to act against both the one and the other, let them say so, and show their sincerity by their deeds. But if they *refuse* to do this when invited to do it—if they persist in claiming the privilege of bestowing their votes for the known supporters of the tariff, monopolies, and class legislations, that are grinding the faces of the poor in our midst, for the emolument of the rich, let them cease urging the claim that the simple fact of opposition to chattel enslavement is proof positive that they may be safely entrusted with the protection of human rights. The merit of mere opposition to chattel slavery is becoming cheaper than it has been, and will be much cheaper still. The time hastens when, (by the elevation of a higher moral standard in politics than had before been attempted,) politicians of all parties, the most sordid and selfish, will be forced to come up, at least, as high as the level furnished by the Anti-Slavery Societies. This they will be glad to do, as a cover to their delinquencies in other respects. But the covering will become too narrow to hide them, and then, the mere merit of being anti-slavery, will avail a political party about as much as would, at the present time, the boast of legislation against sheep-stealing, or the glory of selecting candidates unsuspected of robbing hen-roosts. Those who rightly estimate and properly *feel* the inexpressible meanness and moral turpitude of baby-stealing, should be the last to claim for themselves and associates, any high degrees of humanity, moral discernment, regard to human rights, or competency to the task of defining and protecting them, on the mere ground of their readiness to treat baby stealing as a penal offence—their capacity to distinguish a man from a beast! High time were it for American citizens and their political parties to set up a higher standard of political trustworthiness than that which the oppressive British Government may claim.

When called upon to define the "one idea" to which we would render homage, we say that the great, all-comprehensive idea, with us, is the idea of pursuing, steadfastly and undeviatingly, wherever they are revealed to us, the TRUE and the RIGHT. In the department of Civil Government and of political responsibility, it takes the form of "The Protection of Human Rights." This one idea we would honor by the prompt, impartial, and uniform application of it, to all classes of men, and the redress of all the wrongs of which Civil Government may take cognizance. With MORAL PRINCIPLE for our foundation and our polar star, we hope to shape our measures in accordance with them, desiring no other policy than adherence to the right. . . .

Time for Definitive Action

To those who profess a full agreement with our views, but who think the time for definitive action, in the present shape, has not yet arrived, we have a word further to say. If our principles are sound—if our measures growing out of them, be just, when, if not now, is the time for reducing them to practice? Half the nation, perhaps, would admit them to be right "in the abstract." Is it not holding the truth in unrighteousness to do as they do? And how much should we differ from them, if we longer deferred? Have we not given due notice two years ago, of our convictions and intentions? Have we not done what we could while in that position, to disseminate our views? Is not the time long enough to reflect—to re-examine—to invite a discussion of our proposed measures—to *see* if any good reasons could be produced against them—to ask our associates to go along with us? If we longer deferred, how could we be true to our professions? To go into a Presidential nomination with those a majority of whom we knew were not prepared to take the only course that could satisfy our consciences, would be to give up our principles, to smother our convictions, to do violence to our sense of the right. Could we have gained access, with our views, to the entire Liberty party, through their presses, our position might have been different, but the discussion, to any extent, has not appeared in them. So far from being precipitate, we have erred in being too tardy. Considerable numbers, in other States, who early espoused our views, have inferred, from our long waiting, that we had waived our scruples, and given up our measures. To defer longer would be to justify such conclusions. The present state of all the parties, the Liberty party in particular, indicates a crisis admitting of no further delay. We have not moved without good counsel. The deliberate and truly sagacious, and ever trusty statesman, James G. Birney, was among the first, if not the very first, to suggest the necessity of this present Convention, at this crisis.

Whether few or many will go with us at present, we do not stop to inquire. Very few were ready to go into a Liberty party when the movement first commenced. We know that large and increasing numbers sympathise more or less with us, and are waiting for us to move. It will be found to be no local sentiment, and no temporary one. We have learned to estimate the value of political parties less by their numbers, than by the purity of their intentions, the nobility of their objects, the soundness of their principles, the comprehensiveness yet discrimination of their views, the deliberative wisdom and righteousness of their measures, the inflexibility of their purpose, and the integrity of their action. Give us these, and we are content. Give us seven thousand men in this great nation, who will hold up, by their votes and their teachings, the great fundamental principles and objects of civil government, as God and nature have established them, and we are fully persuaded that it will be the most powerful political party in the nation or in the world. It will be a great teacher of the long neglected but vitally important sciences of civil government, of political morality, of political economy. The growth of such a party might not be rapid, but it would be sound. It would insensibly mould other parties into an approximation towards its standard, not simply nor chiefly by the base motives of fear and rivalry, but more by the nobler force of conscious conviction. If it never elected a candidate (and how many has the Liberty party elected?) its control over the other parties might abolish slavery and other monopolies. If the Liberty party has done any thing (and who doubts it?) it has been chiefly in this way. When "Wilmot provisos," and similar indications marked the approach of the community at large to the Liberty party's actual standard, the true wisdom of that party and its leaders would have been—instead of half inviting a compromise, dividing the difference between them—to have elevated and more clearly defined its own standard, in accordance with its professed principles—its early promises, and the standard of IMMUTABLE right. Had she manifested the disposition to do this, this present convention would not have been needed. As it is, whatever the Liberty party may do, we must assume the responsibility for ourselves and for those who may cooperate with us, of erecting that standard. Excelsior (higher—still higher) is our motto. We beckon not only the Liberty party, but the "Wilmot proviso" men, and all other seekers after truth, to come up and stand with us on a higher, a broader, a firmer foundation.

Conclusion

Fellow-Citizens of the United States—Especially of the Non-Slaveholding States:—We have shaped the preceding argument and appeal more directly for our coadjutors, hitherto, in the Liberty party, but we design it, substantially, for you all. We have no interest distinct from yours—and, as already expressed, we seek no other political object than the equal protection of the equal rights of all. The greater part of you, hitherto, have not co-operated in the measures we have employed, for the removal of American slavery. But you, as well as we, have been gaining important information within the last fourteen years. You have disputed—and on various grounds—the wisdom of our anti-slavery measures. We claim not to have been infallible. This document shows that we are not averse to making improvement upon our plans of operation, when we can discover good reason for so doing. So many measures for abolishing slavery have been suggested, that some of them ought to succeed. We offer you, in some particulars, a new platform, to-day. We do not lower down any of our anti-slavery demands. We repeat them still more distinctly, and call for still stronger measures. We began with asking Congress to abolish slavery in the District of Columbia. We now demand its abolition throughout the United States, in conformity with the constitutional guaranty of a republican government to every State in this Union! The demands of Abolitionists rise higher and higher, and must be trumpeted louder and louder, till the nuisance is abated. Of the abominations and cruelties of the system—of its daring impieties—of its encroachments upon republican liberty—of its heavy exactions upon the free States—of its foul blot on our national character—of its arrogant and insatiable demands—we cannot stop to speak on the present occasion, nor is it needful. The community at large are coming to understand all this, now, better than Abolitionists themselves did, when they commenced agitating the subject. The North is brought to a position of reflection and deliberation. To tell you that your liberties are not safe while the slave system continues, is to tell you what most of you already know. We have a right to take it for granted that you have pondered these things. Let us inquire of you, then, whether you are not ready to act, in some way—and if so, whether the plan we propose is not the right and the feasible one.

While we do not lower down, but elevate our standard of anti-slavery political action, as hitherto urged by the Liberty party, we take the additional and important step of defining our position, (in strict accordance with our principles) on all the prominent political questions of the day. We offer you a connected and consistent system of political economy—of political action. Though we have said that we will not wait for numbers—that we value numbers less than truth and integrity—that a small party adhering to the whole truth, is more powerful for good than a great party, affirming but half the truth, or listening to unrighteous compromise—we nevertheless earnestly solicit the co-operation of all men, in that which we firmly believe to be in accordance with the right and the true. And we cherish strong hopes that when our principles and measures come to be understood, we shalt become a party, strong in numbers as well as strong in the truth. Why should it not be so? Are we not in the midst of a republican people? Or have we mistaken the republican and progressive tendencies of the age?

We count it no arrogance to say, then, that we offer to you the privilege of co-operation in the only true, thorough, consistent, whole souled and even footed democratic party in the country, or in the world—the only party distinctly and definitely proposing, as a practical reality, the equal and impartial protection of the equal rights of all men—the opponent of all oppression, the vindicator of all the wronged:—the only party that is opposed to all the monopolies, class legislations and aristocracies now existing or that may exist.

In asking you to assist us in vindicating the claims of the oppressed colored man, whose wrongs, being most grievous, demand a commensurate prominence, we do not ask you to stand neutral or non-committal, in your political activity, and in your votes, in respect to the wrongs, greater or smaller, of any *other* class of men. We ask your sympathy with the colored man, not for his color, but because he is a man, and your special sympathy because his incomparable wrongs demand proportionate sympathy and aid. We commend to you no cutaneous democracy, vociferous for the liberty of white men and forging fetters for colored men. On the other hand, we ask not your co-operation in any Federal, or National Republican, or Whig party, the aristocratic instincts of whose leaders are best concealed or atoned for, by profuse professions of philanthropy for the colored man. In the hands of such a democracy the liberties of the white man are not safer than those of the colored man. In the hands of their antagonists, of various names, the liberties of the colored man are equally insecure. Time, that tests all things, has sufficiently recorded these facts,

As a political party, we will hold no truce with a Northern Aristocracy for the purpose of checkmating the Southern one. We will take no shelter under the wing of a Southern aristocracy, from the spreading branches of a Northern one. Whether they choose to measure swords with each other, as rivals, as they sometimes do—or mutually court and strengthen each other, as at present inclining to do—we will wage an uncompromising and exterminating warfare with each, so long as either of them show their heads in the field, not forgetting to watch after them, if they retire. So far from their open alliance with each other, and therefore, attempting to conciliate, or avoid provoking either, we hurl open defiance at both of them—"the cotton lords" of the South, "the cotton lords of the North," and all the other incipient aristocracies of the country, few in numbers as we now are, nothing doubting and most earnestly desiring their visible and organized co-operation together, at no distant day. When all the elements of aristocracy on the one hand, and of true democracy on the other, shall thus find their latent affinities and marshal their forces, we shall have "an open field and fair play," and we ask nothing more. Instead of staving off the crisis, we will hasten it, if we can.

To those of our fellow-citizens who seek the redress of specific wrongs, we offer co-operation, on the basis we have laid down. Our assistance they *have*, of course, in the very principles of action we have espoused. To *avail* themselves of our aid, they have only to follow the golden rule of doing to others as they would have others do to them—protecting other men's rights, as they would have other men to protect theirs.

And—let us be distinctly understood. To no men, or class of men, upon any unprincipled basis of "log rolling," have we any offers to make—nor can we receive any. But to all men, and to all classes of men, who have any real wrongs to be redressed, or threatened rights to be secured, we tender, now, and henceforward, whatever of open handed and honest aid we can impart. We ask not who they are that are wronged—how few, how many—how popular, how unpopular—how rich, how poor—how black, how white—how orthodox, how heterodox—whether they vote with our party or vote against it, or not at all, but simply *whether* they are WRONGED, what *redress* justice requires—what security the case needs.

Are we taunted with our *twenty* proposed measures—mistaken for so many items of our one creed of equal rights? We answer, we are ready to swell the twenty to two hundred, whenever so many forms of oppression may need redress—equally ready to reduce them to two, or to none at all, when the occasion shall cease. Show us, at any time, which of our measures is wrong, and we will abandon it. Show us any other measure that justice requires, and we will add it. We trust to our immutable principles to give us stability, by our adherence to them. The ever onward occurrences and exigencies of human society, upon which our principles of equality and rectitude are to operate, will furnish us with all we want, of *adaptation and progress.*

With this statement—fellow citizens—of our principles—our measures and our objects, we invite your cooperation. Having organized with a view to the *benefit* of all, we ask for the *assistance* of all. Even those whose present course and position obliges us to oppose them, have no other security for their own rights, for the rights of their children, than the establishment and perpetuity of a just government. Our opposition to their *measures* involves no hostility to their *persons.* As a party *for* the whole, we seek to become the party *of* the whole—to merge *all* party in the common support by all, of the *rights* of all:—that each may feel himself secure because he sees all others secure.

If any other exposition of our principles and our views of national policy are needed, we can furnish it in the announcement of the names of the candidates we have selected to stand at the head of the Federal Government. We nominate GERRIT SMITH, of the State of New York, for President, and ELIHU BURRITT, of Massachusetts, for Vice President, of the United States.

V

Slavery and the Constitution

11

Slavery and the Constitution (1849)

William I. Bowditch

William I. Bowditch (1819–1909) was a Boston-area lawyer associated with Garrison and Wendell Phillips. He was a member of the Boston Vigilance Committee to help rescue captured fugitive slaves and his house was used by the underground railroad to hide runaway slaves. Bowditch hid one of John Brown's sons after the failed raid at Harper's Ferry and Brown's execution.

Bowditch was the leading constitutional scholar for Garrison and the radical abolitionists. In the selection that follows, Bowditch argues that the Constitution is proslavery in word, intention, and spirit—that it was a "covenant with death and an agreement with hell."

I. The Constitution Is a Pro-Slavery Instrument, According to the Necessary Meaning of Its Terms

Admitting, as we do, that the words of any written instrument constitute the only legal evidence of its meaning, we ask, What is the meaning of the following clauses in the Constitution of the United States?

Art. 1, sec. 2: "Representatives and direct taxes shall be apportioned among the several States which may be included, within this Union, according to their respective numbers, which shall be determined by adding to the whole number of free persons, including those bound to service for a term of years, and excluding Indians not taxed, three fifths of all other persons."

This section distinguishes between free persons and slaves, because to the whole number of *free* persons are to be added three fifths of *all other* persons; that is, persons not free, or slaves. By excluding from the class of free persons those bound to service for life, without—as in case of Indians not taxed—assigning a reason for such exclusion, it declares them to be slaves, within the meaning of the Constitution.

This article, therefore, recognizes slavery as explicitly as if the word *slave* itself had been used, and gives to the free persons in a slave State, solely because they are slaveholders, a larger representation, and consequently greater political power, than the same number of free persons in a free State. A BOUNTY ON SLAVE HOLDING!

Art. 1, sec. 9: "The migration or importation of such persons as any of the States now existing shall think proper to admit, shall not be prohibited by the Congress prior to the year one thousand eight hundred and eight; but a tax or duty may be imposed on such importation, not exceeding ten dollars for each person."

A person who migrates does so of his own accord; he cannot be held to be migrated by any other person. He is wholly a free agent. But a person who is imported does not import himself; he is imported by some other person. He is passive. The importer is the free agent; the person imported is not a free agent. The Virginia slave laws of 1748 and 1753 proceed on this distinction when they say *"all persons * imported * shall be slaves."* Whenever we hear an importation spoken of, we instantly infer an *owner*, and *property* imported. This distinction between the force of the words migration and importation is, then, real.

That the Constitution also makes a distinction is evident, because only persons imported can be taxed. And that it adopts the distinction we have just pointed out is also evident, because this alone can afford us a sufficient reason why persons imported may be taxed, and persons who migrate cannot be.

By this clause, therefore, Congress was prevented, during twenty years, from prohibiting the foreign slave trade with any State that pleased to allow it. But by Art. 1, sec. 8, Congress had the general power "to regulate commerce with foreign nations." Consequently, *the slave trade was excepted from the operation of the general power, with a view to place the slave trade, during twenty years, solely under the control of the slave States.* It could not be wholly stopped, so long as one State wished to continue it. It is a clear compromise in favor of slavery. True, the compromise was a temporary one; but it will be noticed, that Congress, even after 1808, was not obliged to prohibit the trade. Even now we are discussing the expediency of reopening the accursed traffic! whilst, in point of fact, until 1819 the laws of Congress authorized the States to sell into slavery, for their own benefit, negroes imported contrary to the laws of the United States! (Act Congr. 1807, c. 77, § 4, 6; 1818, c. 86, § 5 and 7; 10 Wheat. Rep. 321, 322.) So unmixed should be our satisfaction at the oft-repeated boast, that ours was the first nation to prohibit the African slave trade!

Art. 4, sec. 2: "No person held to service or labor in one State, under the laws thereof escaping into another, shall, in consequence of any law or regulation therein, be discharged from such service or labor, but shall be delivered up, on claim of the party to whom such service or labor may be due."

No one can be illegally "bound" to service, and one who is legally bound is legally "held" to that service. The expressions a person "bound" to service and a person "legally held" to service are, therefore, equivalent. This section evidently embraces, not only persons held to service for a term of years, but also those held to service for life, and therefore includes not only free persons, but those who are declared to be slaves within the meaning of the Constitution. (Art. 1, sec. 2.)

That the expression used in this section legally includes slaves is also evident on other grounds. The ordinance of 1787 calls a slave a person "from whom labor or service is lawfully claimed." (Art. 6.) It is a criminal offence in all the States, except Maryland, Virginia, and Texas, to entice a slave to leave his master's "service." In Maryland, and Virginia, and other States, the owner has a civil action for damages against the person who thus entices away his slave. And the laws of all the States recognize the master's right to enforce the labor of the slave.

If, however, it is a crime to entice a slave to leave his master's "service," and if such act subject a man to an action for damages by the owner, it is evident that the master must have a legal right to the "service" of his slave; for it is the infringement of this right which makes the crime and gives ground to claim damages. The slave is, therefore, a person legally held to service or labor. And as if to remove all doubt, the very expression is applied to slaves in the laws of all the States except Tennessee, Georgia, Alabama, and Texas.

By this section, therefore, it is provided that no person held as a slave in one State under the laws thereof; escaping into another, shall, in consequence of any law or regulation therein, be discharged from his slavery, but shall be delivered up on claim of his owner. The laws of one State, whether they support slavery or any other institution, have no power in another State. Consequently, if a slave escape into a free State, he becomes free. This is the general rule of law. In virtue of it, thousands of slaves are now free on the soil of Canada. In virtue of it, a fugitive slave from South Carolina would be free in this State, were it not for this section in the Constitution. But this section declares that he shall not thereby become free, but shall be delivered up. Again: *the Constitution makes an exception from a general rule of law in favor of slavery.* It gives to slaveholders and slave laws a power which the general rule of law does not give. It enables a South Carolina slaveholder to drag from the soil of Massachusetts a person whom the general rule of law pronounces free, solely because South Carolina laws declare the contrary. IT MAKES THE WHOLE UNION A VAST HUNTING GROUND FOR SLAVES!

Art. 1, sec. 8: "Congress shall have power * * * to provide for calling forth the militia * * * to *suppress insurrections.*"

Art. 4, sec. 4: "The United States shall guaranty to every State in this Union a republican form of government, and shall protect each of them against invasion, and, on application of the legislature, or of the executive, (when the legislature cannot be convened,) against *domestic violence.*"

All insurrections and *all* cases of domestic violence are here provided for. To constitute an insurrection there must be a rising against those laws which are recognized as such by the Constitution; and, to make out a case of domestic violence, the violence must be exerted against that right or power which is recognized by the Constitution as lawful. But by Art. 1, sec. 2, and Art. 4, sec.2, the Constitution admits that some persons may be legally slaves. Consequently, if these persons rise in rebellion, or commit acts of violence contrary to the laws which hold them in slavery, their rising constitutes an insurrection; such acts are acts of violence within the meaning of the Constitution, and consequently must be suppressed by the national power.

The self-styled owners are not the only slaveholders. All persons who voluntarily assist or pledge themselves to assist in holding persons in slavery are slaveholders. *In sober truth, then, we are a nation of slaveholders!* for we have bound our whole national strength to the slave owners, to aid them, if necessary, in holding their slaves in subjection!

II. The Framers of the Constitution Intended to Make a Pro-Slavery Instrument

On the 17th of September, 1787, the Philadelphia Convention adopted the plan of the present Constitution. The draft thus made was submitted to the people, assembled in State Conventions, "for their assent and ratification." President Madison has preserved a record of the debates in the Philadelphia Convention; and we have also published accounts of the debates in several of the State conventions. We draw our evidence mainly from these sources.

Apportionment of Representatives (Const., Art. 1, sec. 2)

Rufus King, of Massachusetts, one of the framers, said of the expression "three fifths of all other persons." "These persons are the slaves." Alexander Hamilton, of New York, another of the framers, referring to this clause "which allows a representation for three fifths of the negroes," said, *"without this indulgence no union could possibly have been formed."* Luther Martin, also a delegate to the Philadelphia Convention, objected to this clause because "it involved the absurdity of increasing the power of a State in making laws for freemen, in proportion as that State violated the rights of freedom." William R. Davie, a delegate from North Carolina, says that the Southern States, "to acquire as much weight as possible in the legislation of the Union," insisted "that a certain proportion of our slaves should make a part of the computed population." General Charles C. Pinckney, another of the framers of the Constitution, said, "We determined that representatives should be apportioned among the several States by adding to the whole number of free persons three fifths of the slaves."

Permission of the African Slave Trade (Const., Art. 4, sec. 9)

Luther Martin, speaking of this section, says, "The design of this clause is to prevent the general government from prohibiting the importation of slaves; but the same reasons which caused them to strike out the word 'national,' and not admit the word 'stamps,' influenced them here to guard against the word 'slaves.' They anxiously sought to avoid the admission of expressions which might be odious in the ears of Americans, although they were willing to admit into their system those things which the expressions signified." * * *

"The Eastern States, notwithstanding their aversion to slavery, were very willing to indulge the Southern States, at least with a temporary liberty to prosecute the slave trade, provided the Southern States would in their turn gratify them, by laying no restriction on navigation acts."

Mr. Madison says, *"The Southern States would not have entered into the Union of America without the temporary permission of that trade."* Mr. Spaight, of North Carolina, one of the framers, says that the Southern States would not consent to exclude the importation of slaves absolutely; that South Carolina and Georgia insisted on this clause as they were now in want of hands to cultivate their lands; that in the course of twenty years they would be fully supplied; that the trade would be abolished then, and that in the mean time some tax or duty might be laid on. Hon. Rawlins Lowndes, of South Carolina, thought it almost inhuman to put any limit to the trade. General Charles C. Pinckney said, "By this settlement we have secured an unlimited importation of negroes for twenty years; nor is it declared that the importation shall be then stopped; it may be continued; we have a security that the general government can never emancipate them."

Restoration of Fugitive Slaves (Const., Art. 4, sec. 2)

In the Virginia Convention, Mr. Madison said,—

"Another clause secures us that property which we now possess. At present, if any slave elopes to any of those States where slaves are free, he becomes emancipated by their laws; for the laws of the States are uncharitable (!) to one another in this respect. But in this Constitution, [then he quotes Art. 4, sec. 2.] *This clause was expressly inserted to enable owners of slaves to reclaim them.* This is a better security than any that now exists."

In the North Carolina Convention, Mr. Iredell begged leave to explain the reason of this clause:—

"In some of the Northern States they have emancipated all their slaves. If any of our slaves," said he, "go there, and remain there a certain time, they would, by the present laws, be entitled to their freedom, so that their masters could not get them again. This would be extremely prejudicial to the inhabitants of the Southern States; and *to prevent it this clause is inserted in the Constitution.* Though the word *slave* be not mentioned, this is the meaning of it. The northern delegates, owing to their particular scruples on the subject of slavery, did not choose the word *slave* to be mentioned."

In the South Carolina Convention, General Pinckney thus expresses his gratification at this Clause:—

"We have obtained a right to recover our slaves in whatever part of America they may take refuge, which is a right we had not before. In short, considering all circumstances, we have made the best terms for the security of this species of property it was in our power to make. We would have made better if we could; but, on the whole, I do not think them bad." (!)

Suppression of Slave Insurrections (Const., Art. 1, sec. 8; Art. 4, sec. 4)

In the Virginia Convention, Mr. George Nicholas said,—

"Another worthy member says there is no power in the States to quell an insurrection of slaves. Have they it now? If they have, does the Constitution take it away? * * * No; but it gives an additional security; for, besides the power in the State governments to use their own militia, *it will be the duty of the general government to aid them with the strength of the Union, when called for.* No part of this Constitution can show that this power is taken away."

Mr. Madison, respecting these clauses, says,—

"On application of the legislature, or executive, as the case may be, the militia of the other States are to be called to suppress domestic insurrections. Does this bar the States from calling forth their own militia? No; *but it gives them a supplementary security to suppress insurrections and domestic violence."*

III. The Constitution Has Been Treated as a Pro-Slavery Instrument, by the Government, in Practice

Apportionment of Representatives (Const., Art. 1, sec. 2)

In every census which has been taken by the government, the only distinction sanctioned has been between freemen and slaves; and on every occasion of apportioning representatives, according to the representative or federal number, such number has been invariably determined by adding to the whole number of free persons three fifths of the slaves. *If this, the pro-slavery interpretation of this section of the Constitution, be not right, then, since March 3, 1793, there has not been a single House of Representatives constitutionally elected, or a single statute or resolve constitutionally passed!* Who is ready to make this admission?

Permission of the African Slave Trade (Const., Art. 1, sec. 9)

On the 13th of May, 1789, in Congress,—

"Mr. Parker, of Virginia, moved to insert a clause in the bill, imposing a duty on the importation of slaves of ten dollars each person. He was sorry that the Constitution prevented Congress from prohibiting the importation altogether; he thought it a defect in that instrument that it allowed of such actions; it was contrary to the revolution principles, and ought not to be permitted; but, as he could not do all the good he desired, he was willing to do what lay in his power."

Messrs. Sherman, of Connecticut, and Schureman, of New Jersey, thought the subject should be taken up independently. Mr. Madison thought otherwise:—

"I conceive the Constitution, in this particular, was formed in order that the government, whilst it was restrained from laying a total prohibition, might be able to give some testimony of the sense of America with respect to the African trade. We have liberty to impose a tax or duty upon the importation of such persons as any of the States now existing shall think proper to admit; and this liberty was granted, I presume, upon two considerations. The first was, that, until the time arrived when they might abolish the importation of *slaves*, they might have an opportunity of evidencing their sentiments on the policy and humanity of such a trade."

The motion of Mr. Parker was afterwards withdrawn.

In 1794, "An Act to prohibit the carrying on the slave trade from the United States to any foreign place or country" was passed, (Stat 1794, c. 11.) In 1800, an act in addition to the last was passed, (Stat. 1800, c. 51.) That both these laws were framed with reference to this section of the Constitution is apparent, because the latter act expressly refers to it. sec. 6 reads thus: "That nothing in this act contained shall be construed to authorize the bringing into either of the United States any person or persons, the importation of whom is, by the existing laws of such State, prohibited."

See also Stat. 1803, c. 63.

And, not to multiply proof, on the 2d day of March, 1807, President Jefferson approved (Stat. 1807, c. 77) "An Act to prohibit the importation of *slaves* into any port or place within the jurisdiction of the United States from and after the *first day of January*, in the year of our Lord *one thousand eight hundred and eight*." That is, at the very earliest day allowed by the Constitution (Art. 1, sec. 9) for the passage by Congress of an act prohibiting the importation of persons, a law is passed totally prohibiting the *importation of slaves*.

Restoration of Fugitive Slaves (Const., Art. 4, sec. 2)

That the fugitive slave law of 1793, (Stat. 1793, c. 7,) entitled "An Act respecting fugitives from justice, and persons escaping from the service of their masters," and the act of Sept. 18, 1850, "to amend, and supplementary to" this act, are both framed to carry out this clause of the Constitution, is too apparent to need comment.

Suppression of Slave Insurrections (Const., Art. 1, sec. 8, Art. 4, sec. 4)

The "Act to provide for calling forth the militia, to execute the laws of the Union, suppress insurrections, and repel invasions," (Stat. 1792, c. 28, sec. 1,) provides that, *"In case of an insurrection in any State* against the government thereof, it shall be lawful for the President of the United States, on application of the legislature of such State, or of the executive, (when the legislature cannot be convened,) to call forth such number of the militia of any other State or States as may be applied for, or as he may judge sufficient to suppress such insurrection." Precisely the same language is made use of in Stat. 1795, c. 101. By act, approved March 3, 1807, (Stat. 1807, c. 94,) the President is authorized, "in *all* cases of insurrection," when it is lawful for him to call forth the militia for the purpose of suppressing the same "to employ for the same purpose such part of the land or naval force of the United States as shall be judged necessary."

That these laws have been held to include an insurrection of slaves is indisputable. On receipt of the intelligence of Nat Turner's insurrection in Southampton, Va., Colonel House, then commanding at Fortress Monroe, set out with three companies of United States troops, for the purpose of suppressing the revolt. He was reinforced by a detachment from the United States ships Warren and Natchez, amounting in all to about three hundred men. With *our* troops and *our* officers, we have actually aided the slaveholder in holding his fellow-man in slavery! We have actually done what our fathers engaged in the Constitution that we should do, namely, aid with the national strength in keeping the slaves in subjection!

IV. The Constitution Is Pro-Slavery, According to the Exposition of Its Final Interpreter

The Constitution declares itself to be "the supreme law of the land," (Art. 6, sec. 2.) It cannot possibly be such unless there is a final interpreter of its meaning. Now, to expound what the law is is a judicial act. "The judicial power extends to *all* cases arising under the Constitution, and laws, and treaties, (Const., Art. 3, sec. 2.) It therefore extends to the exposition of the meaning of the Constitution, when the case before the court properly calls for such exposition. This judicial power, and, consequently, this power to expound the meaning of the Constitution, is "vested in one Supreme Court," (Const., Art. 3, sec. 1.) The decision of this court, being supreme, must be final.

Apportionment of Representatives (Const., Art. 1, sec. 2)

In Hylton *vs.* United States, (3 Dallas's Rep. 177,) Mr. Justice Paterson, delivering the opinion of the Supreme Court, says that the provision contained in this clause, that direct taxes shall be apportioned between the States according to their federal numbers, "was made in favor of the Southern States," and to prevent Congress from taxing "slaves at discretion, or arbitrarily." He also says, (p. 178,) "The rule of apportionment is radically wrong; it cannot be supported by any solid reasoning. Why should slaves, who are a species of property, be represented more than any other property?"

Permission of the African Slave Trade (Const., Art. 1, sec. 9)

In the great case of Gibbons *vs.* Ogden, 9 Wheaton's Reports, pp. 206 and 207, (1824,) Chief Justice Marshall, delivering the opinion of the Supreme Court, says that the act of Congress, (1803, c. 63,) "prohibiting the importation of slaves into any State which shall itself prohibit their importation," was passed in virtue of power conferred by this clause in the Constitution.

Restoration of Fugitive Slaves (Const., Art. 4, sec. 2)

The following extracts are taken from the opinion of the Supreme Court in the well-known case, Prigg *vs.* The Commonwealth of Pennsylvania, (16 Pet. Rep. 609, &c.) Judge Story delivered the opinion.

"Historically, it is well known that the object of this clause was to secure to the citizens of the slaveholding States the complete right and title of ownership in their slaves, as property, in every State in the Union into which they might escape from the State where they were held in servitude. The full recognition of this right and title was indispensable to the security of this species of property in all the slaveholding States; and, indeed, was so vital to the preservation of their domestic interests and institutions, that *it cannot be doubted that it constituted a fundamental article, without the adoption of which the Union could not have been formed,"* (p. 613.) "We have not the slightest hesitation in holding, that, under and in virtue of the Constitution, the owner of a slave is clothed with entire authority, in every State in the Union, to seize and recapture his slave, whenever he can do it without any breach of the peace, or any illegal violence. In this sense, and to this extent, this clause of the Constitution may properly be said to execute itself, and to require no aid from legislation, state or national."

Suppression of Slave Insurrections (Const., Art. 1, sec. 8; Art. 4, sec. 4)

We are not aware of any decision of the Supreme Court upon the meaning of these clauses; but it seems difficult to conceive that they would hold that the word "insurrections" did not include all insurrections.

Such is the Constitution, according to the plain, obvious, and common meaning of its terms; such it was intended to be made by its framers; such has been the interpretation constantly followed in the practice of the government, from the time of its adoption until now; and such it is according to the decision of the final interpreter of its meaning. As reasonable men, seeking the truth, we cannot say that there is the slightest doubt whatever on the subject. THE CONSTITUTION VERY MATERIALLY SUPPORTS SLAVERY.

"Yes! it cannot be denied—the slaveholding lords of the south prescribed, as a condition of their assent to the Constitution, three special provisions TO SECURE THE PERPETUITY OF THEIR DOMINION OVER THEIR SLAVES. The first was the immunity for twenty years of preserving the African slave trade; the second was the stipulation to surrender fugitive slaves—an engagement positively prohibited by the laws of God, delivered from Sinai; and thirdly, the exaction, fatal to the principles of popular representation, of a representation for slaves—for articles of merchandise, under the name of persons, * * * in fact, the oppressor representing the oppressed! * * * To call government thus constituted a democracy, is to insult the understanding of mankind. It is doubly tainted with the infection of riches and slavery. Its reciprocal operation upon the government of the nation is to establish an artificial majority in the slave representation over that of the free people, in the American Congress; and thereby to make the *preservation, propagation, and perpetuation of slavery, the vital and animating spirit of the national government."—John Quincy Adams.*

IT IS BECAUSE THE CONSTITUTION IS THUS A PRO-SLAVERY INSTRUMENT THAT THE RADICAL ABOLITIONISTS REFUSE TO VOTE OR TAKE OFFICE UNDER IT. CAN YOU, READER, GIVE IT COUNTENANCE OR SUPPORT, BY VOTING OR ACCEPTING OFFICE UNDER It?

12

"The Constitution of the United States: Is It Pro-Slavery or Anti-Slavery?" (1860)

Frederick Douglass

By the late 1840s, Frederick Douglass broke with Garrison for a variety of personal, intellectual, and tactical reasons. After Douglass left Boston and the reach of Garrison's influence, he began to read non-Garrisonian abolitionist literature. Over time, Douglass became increasingly disturbed by Garrison's doctrine of "No Union With Slaveholders." The turning point for Douglass was his reinterpretation of the Constitution as antislavery in word, intention, and spirit. Not only was the Constitution devoid of its so-called compromises with slavery, Douglass argued that its interpretive spirit gave Congress the authority and power to actually begin the process of eliminating slavery in the Old South.

... I proceed to the discussion. And first a word about the question. Much will be gained at the outset if we fully and clearly understand the real question under discussion. Indeed, nothing is or can be understood till this is understood. Things are often confounded and treated as the same, for no better reason than that they resemble each other, even while they are in their nature and character totally distinct and even directly opposed to each other. This jumbling up things is a sort of dust-throwing which is often indulged in by small men who argue for victory rather than for truth. Thus, for instance, the American Government and the American Constitution are spoken of in a manner which would naturally lead the hearer to believe that the one is identical with the other; when the truth is, they are as distinct in character as is a ship and a compass. The one may point right and the other steer wrong. A chart is one thing, the course of the vessel is another. The Constitution may be right, the Government wrong. If the Government has been governed by mean, sordid, and wicked passions, it does not follow that the Constitution is mean, sordid, and wicked. What, then, is the question? I will state it. But first let me state what is not the question. It is not whether slavery existed in the United States at the time of the adoption of the Constitution; it is not whether slaveholders took part in framing the Constitution; it is not whether those slaveholders, in their hearts, intended to secure certain advantages in that instrument for slavery; it is not whether the American Government has been wielded during seventy-two years in favour of the propagation and permanence of slavery; it is not whether a pro-slavery interpretation has been put upon the Constitution by the American Courts—all these points may be true or they may be false, they may be accepted or they may be rejected, without in any wise affecting the real question in debate. The real and exact question between myself and the class of persons represented by the speech at the City Hall may be fairly stated thus:—1st, Does the United States Constitution guarantee to any class or description of people in that country the right to enslave, or hold as property, any other class or description of people in that country? 2nd, Is the dissolution of the union between the slave and free States required by fidelity to the slaves, or by the just demands of conscience? Or, in other words, is the refusal to exercise the elective franchise, and to hold office in America, the surest, wisest, and best way to abolish slavery in America?

To these questions the Garrisonians say Yes. They hold the Constitution to be a slaveholding instrument, and will not cast a vote or hold office, and denounce all who vote or hold office, no matter how faithfully such persons labour to promote the abolition of slavery. I, on the other hand, deny that the Constitution guarantees the right to hold property in man, and believe that the way to abolish slavery in America is to vote such men into power as will use their powers for the abolition of slavery. This is the issue plainly stated, and you shall judge between us. Before we examine into the disposition, tendency, and character of the Constitution, I think we had better ascertain what the Constitution itself is. Before looking for what it means, let us see what it is. Here, too, there is much dust to be cleared away. What, then, is the Constitution? I will tell you. It is no vague, indefinite, floating, unsubstantial, ideal something, coloured according to any man's fancy, now a weasel, now a whale, and now nothing. On the contrary, it is a plainly written document, not in Hebrew or Greek, but in English, beginning with a preamble, filled out with articles, sections, provisions, and clauses, defining the rights, powers, and duties to be secured, claimed, and exercised under its authority. It is not even like the British Constitution, which is made up of enactments of Parliament, decisions of Courts, and the established usages of the Government. The American Constitution is a written instrument full and complete in itself. No Court in America, no Congress, no President, can add a single word thereto, or take a single word therefrom. It is a great national enactment done by the people, and can only be altered, amended, or added to by the people. I am careful to make this statement here; in America it would not be necessary. It would not be necessary here if my assailant had showed the same desire to set before you the simple truth, which he manifested to make out a good case for himself and friends. Again, it should be borne in mind that the mere text, and only the text, and not any commentaries or creeds written by those who wished to give the text a meaning apart from its plain reading, was adopted as the Constitution of the United States. It should also be borne in mind that the intentions of those who framed the Constitution, be they good or bad, for slavery or against slavery, are to be respected so far, and so far only, as we find those intentions plainly stated in the Constitution. It would be the wildest of absurdities, and lead to endless confusion and mischiefs, if, instead of looking to the written paper itself, for its meaning, it were attempted to make us search it out, in the secret motives, and dishonest intentions, of some of the men who took part in writing it. It was what they said that was adopted by the people, not what they were ashamed or afraid to say, and really omitted to say. Bear in mind, also, and the fact is an important one, that the framers of the Constitution sat with closed doors, and that this was done purposely, that nothing but the result of their labours should be seen, and that that result should be judged of by the people free from any of the bias shown in the debates. It should also be borne in mind, and the fact is still more important, that the debates in the convention that framed the Constitution, and by means of which a pro-slavery interpretation is now attempted to be forced upon that instrument, were not published till more than a quarter of a century after the presentation and the adoption of the Constitution.

These debates were purposely kept out of view, in order that the people should adopt, not the secret motives or unexpressed intentions of any body, but the simple text of the paper itself. Those debates form no part of the original agreement. I repeat, the paper itself, and only the paper itself, with its own plainly written purposes, is the Constitution. It must stand or fall, flourish or fade, on its own individual and self-declared character and objects. Again, where would be the advantage of a written Constitution, if, instead of seeking its meaning in its words, we had to seek them in the secret intentions of individuals who may have had something to do with writing the paper? What will the people of America a hundred years hence care about the intentions of the scriveners who wrote the Constitution? These men are already gone from us, and in the course of nature were expected to go from us. They were for a generation, but the Constitution is for ages. Whatever we may owe to them, we certainly owe it to ourselves, and to mankind, and to God, to maintain the truth of our own language, and to allow no villainy, not even the villainy of holding men as slaves—which Wesley says is the sum of all villainies—to shelter itself under a fair-seeming and virtuous language. We owe it to ourselves to compel the devil to wear his own garments, and to make wicked laws speak out their wicked intentions. Common sense, and common justice, and sound rules of interpretation all drive us to the words of the law for the meaning of the law. The practice of the Government is dwelt upon with much fervour and eloquence as conclusive as to the slaveholding character of the Constitution. This is really the strong point, and the only strong point, made in the speech in the City Hall. But good as this argument is, it is not conclusive. A wise man has said that few people have been found better than their laws, but many have been found worse. To this last rule America is no exception. Her laws are one thing, her practice is another thing. We read that the Jews made void the law by their tradition, that Moses permitted men to put away their wives because of the hardness of their hearts, but that this was not so at the beginning. While good laws will always be found where good practice prevails, the reverse does not always hold true. Far from it. The very opposite is often the case. What then? Shall we condemn the righteous law because wicked men twist it to the support of wickedness? Is that the way to deal with good and evil? Shall we blot out all distinction between them, and hand over to slavery all that slavery may claim on the score of long practice? Such is the course commended to us in the City Hall speech. After all, the fact that men go out of the Constitution to prove it pro-slavery, whether that going out is to the practice of the Government, or to the secret intentions of the writers of the paper, the fact that they do go out is very significant. It is a powerful argument on my side. It is an admission that the thing for which they are looking is not to be found where only it ought to be found, and that is in the Constitution itself. If it is not there, it is nothing to the purpose, be it wheresoever else it may be. But I shall have more to say on this point hereafter.

The very eloquent lecturer at the City Hall doubtless felt some embarrassment from the fact that he had literally to *give* the Constitution a pro-slavery interpretation; because upon its face it of itself conveys no such meaning, but a very opposite meaning. He thus sums up what he calls the slaveholding provisions of the Constitution. I quote his own words:—"Article I, section 9, provides for the continuance of the African slave trade for 20 years, after the adoption of the Constitution. Art. 4, section 9, provides for the recovery from other States of fugitive slaves. Art. I, section 2, gives the slave States a representation of three-fifths of all the slave population; and Art. I, section 8, requires the President to use the military, naval, ordnance, and militia resources of the entire country for the suppression of slave insurrection, in the same manner as he would employ them to repel invasion." Now any man reading this statement, or hearing it made with such a show of exactness, would unquestionably suppose that the speaker or writer had given the plain written text of the Constitution itself. I can hardly believe that he intended to make any such impression. It would be a scandalous imputation to say he did. And yet what are we to make of it? How can we regard it? How can he be screened from the charge of having perpetrated a deliberate and point-blank misrepresentation? That individual has seen fit to place himself before the public as my opponent, and yet I would gladly find some excuse for him. I do not wish to think as badly of him as this trick of his would naturally lead me to think. Why did he not read the Constitution? Why did he read that which was not the Constitution? He pretended to be giving chapter and verse, section and clause, paragraph and provision. The words of the Constitution were before him. Why then did he not give you the plain words of the Constitution? Oh, sir, I fear that that gentleman knows too well why he did not. It so happens that no such words as "African slave trade," no such words as "slave representation," no such words as "fugitive slaves," no such words as "slave insurrections," are anywhere used in that instrument. These are the words of that orator, and not the words of the Constitution of the United States. Now you shall see a slight difference between my manner of treating this subject and that which, my opponent has seen fit, for reasons satisfactory to himself, to pursue. What he withheld, that I will spread before you: what he suppressed, I will bring to light: and what he passed over in silence, I will proclaim: that you may have the whole case before you, and not be left to depend upon either his, or upon my inferences or testimony. Here then are the several provisions of the Constitution to which reference has been made. I read them word for word just as they stand in the paper, called the United States Constitution, Art. I, sec. 2. "Representatives and direct taxes shall be apportioned among the several States which may be included in this Union, according to their respective numbers, which shall be determined by adding to the whole number of free persons, including those bound to service for a term of years, and excluding Indians not taxed, three-fifths of all other persons; Art. I, sec. 9. The migration or importation of such persons as any of the States now existing shall think fit to admit, shall not be prohibited by the Congress prior to the year one thousand eight hundred and eight, but a tax or duty may be imposed on such importation, not exceeding ten dollars for each person; Art. 4, sec. 2. No person held to service or labour in one State, under the laws thereof, escaping into another shall, in consequence of any law or regulation therein, be discharged from such service or labour; but shall be delivered up on claim of the party to whom such service or, labour may be due; Art. I, sec. 8. To provide for calling for the militia to execute the laws of the Union, suppress insurrections, and repel invasions." Here, then, are those provisions of the Constitution, which the most extravagant defenders of slavery can claim to guarantee a right of property in man. These are the provisions which have been pressed into the service of the human fleshmongers of America. Let us look at them just as they stand, one by one. Let us grant, for sake of the argument, that the first of these provisions, referring to the basis of representation and taxation, does refer to slaves. We are not compelled to make that admission, for it might fairly apply to aliens—persons living in the country, but not naturalized. But giving the provisions the very worst construction, what does it amount to? I answer—It is a downright disability laid upon the slaveholding States; one which deprives those States of two-fifths of their natural basis of representation. A black man in a free State is worth just two-fifths more than a black man in a slave State, as a basis of political power under the Constitution. Therefore, instead of encouraging slavery, the Constitution encourages freedom by giving an increase of "two-fifths" of political power to free over slave States. So much for the three-fifths clause; taking it at its worst, it still leans to freedom, not to slavery; for, be it remembered that the Constitution nowhere forbids a coloured man to vote. I come to the next, that which it is said guaranteed the continuance of the African slave trade for twenty years. I will also take that for just what my opponent alleges it to have been, although the Constitution does not warrant any such conclusion. But, to be liberal, let us suppose it did, and what follows? why, this—that this part of the Constitution, so far as the slave trade is concerned, became a dead letter more than 50 years ago, and now binds no man's conscience for the continuance of any slave trade whatever. But there is still more to be said about this abolition of the slave trade. Men, at that time, both in England and in America, looked upon the slave trade as the life of slavery. The abolition of the slave trade was supposed to be the certain death of slavery. Cut off the stream, and the pond will dry up, was the common notion at that time.

Wilberforce and Clarkson, clear-sighted as they were, took this view; and the American statesmen, in providing for the abolition of the slave trade, thought they were providing for the abolition of slavery. This view is quite consistent with the history of the times. All regarded slavery as an expiring and doomed system, destined to speedily disappear from the country. But, again, it should be remembered that this very provision, if made to refer to the African slave trade at all, makes the Constitution anti-slavery rather than for slavery, for it says to the slave States, the price you will have to pay for coming into the American Union is, that the slave trade, which you would carry on indefinitely out of the Union, shall be put an end to in twenty years if you come into the Union. Secondly, if it does apply, it expired by its own limitation more than fifty years ago. Thirdly, it is anti-slavery, because it looked to the abolition of slavery rather than to its perpetuity. Fourthly, it showed that the intentions of the framers of the Constitution were good, not bad. I think this is quite enough for this point. I go to the "slave insurrection" clause, though, in truth, there is no such clause. The one which is called so has nothing whatever to do with slaves or slaveholders any more than your laws for the suppression of popular outbreaks has to do with making slaves of you and your children. It is only a law for suppression of riots or insurrections. But I will be generous here, as well as elsewhere, and grant that it applies to slave insurrections. Let us suppose that an anti-slavery man is President of the United States (and the day that shall see this the case is not distant) and this very power of suppressing slave insurrection would put an end to slavery. The right to put down an insurrection carries with it the right to determine the means by which it shall be put down. If it should turn out that slavery is a source of insurrection, that there is no security from insurrection while slavery lasts, why, the Constitution would be best obeyed by putting an end to slavery, and an anti-slavery Congress would do that very thing. Thus, you see, the so-called slave-holding provisions of the American Constitution, which a little while ago looked so formidable, are, after all, no defence or guarantee for slavery whatever. But there is one other provision. This is called the "Fugitive Slave Provision." It is called so by those who wish to make it subserve the interest of slavery in America, and the same by those who wish to uphold the views of a party in this country. It is put thus in the speech at the City Hall:—"Let us go back to 1787, and enter Liberty Hall, Philadelphia, where sat in convention the illustrious men who framed the Constitution—with George Washington in the chair. On the 27th of September, Mr. Butler and Mr. Pinckney, two delegates from the State of South Carolina, moved that the Constitution should require that fugitive slaves and servants should be delivered up like criminals, and after a discussion on the subject, the clause, as it stands in the Constitution, was adopted. After this, in the conventions held in the several States to ratify the Constitution, the same meaning was attached to the words. For example, Mr. Madison (afterwards President), when recommending the Constitution to his constituents, told them that the clause would secure them their property in slaves." I must ask you to look well to this statement. Upon its face, it would seem a full and fair statement of the history of the transaction it professes to describe and yet I declare unto you, knowing as I do the facts in the case, my utter amazement at the downright untruth conveyed under the fair seeming words now quoted. The man who could make such a statement may have all the craftiness of a lawyer, but who can accord to him the candour of an honest debater? What could more completely destroy all confidence in his statements? Mark you, the orator had not allowed his audience to hear read the provision of the Constitution to which he referred. He merely characterized it as one to "deliver up fugitive slaves and servants like criminals," and tells you that that provision was adopted as it stands in the Constitution. He tells you that this was done "after discussion." But he took good care not to tell you what was the nature of that discussion. He would have spoiled the whole effect of his statement had he told you the whole truth. Now, what are the facts connected with this provision of the Constitution? You shall have them. It seems to take two men to tell the truth. It is quite true that Mr. Butler and Mr. Pinckney introduced a provision expressly with a view to the recapture of fugitive slaves: it is quite true also that there was some discussion on the subject—and just here the truth shall come out. These illustrious kidnappers were told promptly in that discussion that no such idea as property in man should be admitted into the Constitution. The speaker in question might have told you, and he would have told you but the simple truth, if he had told you that the proposition of Mr. Butler and Mr. Pinckney—which he leads you to infer was adopted by the convention that framed the Constitution—was, in fact, promptly and indignantly rejected by that convention. He might have told you, had it suited his purpose to do so, that the words employed in the first draft of the fugitive clause were such as applied to the condition of slaves, and expressly declared, that persons held to "servitude" should be given up; but that the word "servitude" was struck from the provision, for the very reason that it applied to slaves. He might have told you that that same Mr. Madison declared that that word was struck out because the convention would not consent that the idea of property in men should be admitted into the Constitution. The fact that Mr. Madison can be cited on both sides of this question is another evidence of the folly and absurdity of making the secret intentions of the framers the criterion by which the Constitution is to be construed. But it may be asked—if this clause does not apply to slaves, to whom does it apply?

I answer, that when adopted, it applies to a very large class of persons—namely, redemptioners—persons who had come to America from Holland, from Ireland, and other quarters of the globe—like the Coolies to the West Indies—and had, for a consideration duly paid, become bound to "serve and labour" for the parties to whom their service and labour was due. It applies to indentured apprentices and others who had become bound for a consideration, under contract duly made, to serve and labour. To such persons this provision applies, and only to such persons. The plain reading of this provision shows that it applies, and that it can only properly and legally apply, to persons "bound to service." Its object plainly is, to secure the fulfilment of contracts for "service and labour." It applies to indentured apprentices, and any other persons from whom service and labour may be due. The legal condition of the slave puts him beyond the operation of this provision. He is not described in it. He is a simple article of property. He does not owe and cannot owe service. He cannot even make a contract. It is impossible for him to do so. He can no more make such a contract than a horse or an ox can make one. This provision, then, only respects persons who owe service, and they only can owe service who can receive an equivalent and make a bargain. The slave cannot do that, and is therefore exempted from the operation of this fugitive provision. In all matters where laws are taught to be made the means of oppression, cruelty, and wickedness, I am for strict construction. I will concede nothing. It must be shown that it is so nominated in the bond. The pound of flesh, but not one drop of blood. The very nature of law is opposed to all such wickedness, and makes it difficult to accomplish such objects under the forms of law. Law is not merely an arbitrary enactment with regard to justice, reason, or humanity. Blackstone defines it to be a rule prescribed by the supreme power of the State commanding what is right and forbidding what is wrong. The speaker at the City Hall laid down some rules of legal interpretation. These rules send us to the history of the law for its meaning. I have no objection to such a course in ordinary cases of doubt. But where human liberty and justice are at stake, the case falls under an entirely different class of rules. There must be something more than history—something more than tradition. The Supreme Court of the United States lays down this rule, and it meets the case exactly—"Where rights are infringed—where the fundamental principles of the law are overthrown—where the general system of the law is departed from, the legislative intention must be expressed with irresistible clearness." The same court says that the language of the law must be construed strictly in favour of justice and liberty. Again, there is another rule of law. It is—Where a law is susceptible of two meanings, the one making it accomplish an innocent purpose, and the other making it accomplish a wicked purpose, we must in all cases adopt that which makes it accomplish an innocent purpose. Again, the details of a law are to be interpreted in the light of the declared objects sought by the law. I set these rules down against those employed at the City Hall. To me they seem just and rational. I only ask you to look at the American Constitution in the light of them, and you will see with me that no man is guaranteed a right of property in man, under the provisions of that instrument. If there are two ideas more distinct in their character and essence than another, those ideas are "persons" and "property," "men" and "things." Now, when it is proposed to transform persons into "property" and men into beasts of burden, I demand that the law that contemplates such a purpose shall be expressed with irresistible clearness. The thing must not be left to inference, but must be done in plain English. I know how this view of the subject is treated by the class represented at the City Hall. They are in the habit of treating the Negro as an exception to general rules. When their own liberty is in question they will avail themselves of all, rules of law which protect and defend their freedom; but when the black man's rights are in question they concede everything, admit everything for slavery, and put liberty to the proof. They reverse the common law usage, and presume the Negro a slave unless he can prove himself free. I, on the other hand, presume him free unless he is proved to be otherwise. Let us look at the objects for which the Constitution was framed and adopted, and see if slavery is one of them. Here are its own objects as set forth by itself:— "We, the people of these United States, in order to form a more perfect union, establish justice, ensure domestic tranquillity, provide for the common defence, promote the general welfare, and secure the blessings of liberty to ourselves and our posterity, do ordain and establish this Constitution for the United States of America." The objects here set forth are six in number: union, defence, welfare, tranquillity, justice, and liberty. These are all good objects, and slavery, so far from being among them, is a foe of them all. But it has been said that Negroes are not included within the benefits sought under this declaration. This is said by the slaveholders in America—it is said by the City Hall orator—but it is not said by the Constitution itself. Its language is "we the people"; not we the white people, not even we the citizens, not we the privileged class, not we the high, not we the low, but we the people; not we the horses, sheep, and swine, and wheel-barrows, but we the people, we the human inhabitants; and, if, Negroes are people, they are included in the benefits for which the Constitution of America was ordained and established. But how dare any man who pretends to be a friend to the Negro thus gratuitously concede away what the Negro has a right to claim under the Constitution? Why should such friends invent new arguments to increase the hopelessness of his bondage? This, I undertake to say, as the conclusion of the whole matter, that the constitutionality of slavery can be made out only by disregarding the plain and common-sense reading of the Constitution itself; by discrediting and casting away as worthless the most beneficent rules of legal interpretation; by ruling the Negro outside of these beneficent rules; by claiming everything for slavery; by denying everything for freedom; by assuming that the Constitution does not mean what it says, and that it says what it does not mean; by disregarding the written Constitution, and interpreting it in the light of a secret understanding. It is in this mean, contemptible, and underhand method that the American Constitution is pressed into the service of slavery. They go everywhere else for proof that the Constitution is pro-slavery but to the Constitution itself. The Constitution declares that no person shall be deprived of life, liberty, or property without due process of law; it secures to every man the right of trial by jury, the privilege of the writ of habeas corpus—that great writ that put an end to slavery and slave-hunting in England—it secures to every State a republican form of government. Any one of these provisions, in the hands of abolition statesmen, and backed up by a right moral sentiment, would put an end to slavery in America. The Constitution forbids the passing of a bill of attainder: that is, a law entailing upon the child the disabilities and hardships imposed upon the parent. Every slave law in America might be repealed on this very ground. The slave is made a slave because his mother is a slave. But to all this it is said that the practice of the American people is against my view. I admit it. They have given the Constitution a slaveholding interpretation. I admit it. They have committed innumerable wrongs against the Negro in the name of the Constitution. Yes, I admit it all; and I go with him who goes farthest in denouncing these wrongs. But it does not follow that the Constitution is in favour of these wrongs because the slave-holders have given it that interpretation. To be consistent in his logic, the City Hall speaker must follow the example of some of his brothers in America—he must not only fling away the Constitution, but the Bible. The Bible must follow the Constitution, for that, too, has been interpreted for slavery by American divines. Nay, more, he must not stop with the Constitution of America, but make war upon the British Constitution, for, if I mistake not, that gentleman is opposed to the union of Church and State. In America he called himself a Republican. Yet he does not go for breaking down the British Constitution, although you have a Queen, on the throne, and bishops in the House of Lords.

My argument against the dissolution of the American Union is this: It would place the slave system more exclusively under the control of the slaveholding States, and withdraw it from the power in the Northern States which is opposed to slavery. Slavery is essentially barbarous in its character. It, above all things else, dreads the presence of an advanced civilisation. It flourishes best where it meets no reproving frowns, and hears no condemning voices. While in the Union it will meet with both. Its hope of life, in the last resort, is to get out of the Union. I am, therefore, for drawing the bond of the Union more closely, and bringing the Slave States more completely under the power of the Free States. What they most dread, that I most desire. I have much confidence in the instincts of the slaveholders. They see that the Constitution will afford slavery no protection when it shall cease to be administered by slaveholders. They see, moreover, that if there is once a will in the people of America to abolish slavery, there is no word, no syllable in the Constitution to forbid that result. They see that the Constitution has not saved slavery in Rhode Island, in Connecticut, in New York, or Pennsylvania; that the Free States have increased from one up to eighteen in number, while the Slave States have only added three to their original number. There were twelve Slave States at the beginning of the

Government: there are fifteen now. There was one Free State at the beginning of the Government: there are eighteen now. The dissolution of the Union would not give the North a single advantage over slavery, but would take from it many. Within the Union we have a firm basis of opposition to slavery. It is opposed to all the great objects of the Constitution. The dissolution of the Union is not only an unwise but a cowardly measure—15 millions running away from three hundred and fifty thousand slaveholders. Mr. Garrison and his friends tell us that while in the Union we are responsible for slavery. He and they sing out "No Union with slaveholders," and refuse to vote. I admit our responsibility for slavery while in the Union, but I deny that going out of the Union would free us from that responsibility. There now clearly is no freedom from responsibility for slavery to any American citizen short of the abolition of slavery. The American people have gone quite too far in this slaveholding business now to sum up their whole business of slavery by singing out the cant phrase, "No union with slaveholders." To desert the family hearth may place the recreant husband out of the presence of his starving children, but this does not free him from responsibility. If a man were on board of a pirate ship, and in company with others had robbed and plundered, his whole duty would not be performed simply by taking the longboat and singing out "No union with pirates." His duty would be to restore the stolen property. The American people in the Northern States have helped to enslave the black people. Their duty will not have been done till they give them back their plundered rights. Reference was made at the City Hall to my having once held other opinions, and very different opinions to those I have now expressed. An old speech of mine delivered fourteen years ago was read to show—I know not what. Perhaps it was to show that I am not infallible. If so, I have to say in defence, that I never pretended to be. Although I cannot accuse myself of being remarkably unstable, I do not pretend that I have never altered my opinion both in respect to men and things. Indeed, I have been very much modified both in feeling and opinion within the last fourteen years. When I escaped from slavery, and was introduced to the Garrisonians, I adopted very many of their opinions, and defended them just as long as I deemed them true. I was young, had read but little, and naturally took some things on trust. Subsequent experience and reading have led me to examine for myself. This has brought me to other conclusions. When I was a child, I thought and spoke as a child. But the question is not as to what were my opinions fourteen years ago, but what they are now. If I am right now, it really does not matter what I was fourteen years ago. My position now is one of reform, not of revolution. I would act for the abolition of slavery through the Government—not over its ruins. If slave holders have ruled the

American Government for the last fifty years, let the anti-slavery men rule the nation for the next fifty years. If the South has made the Constitution bend to the purposes of slavery, let the North now make that instrument bend to the cause of freedom and justice. If 350,000 slaveholders have, by devoting their energies to that single end, been able to make slavery the vital and animating spirit of the American Confederacy for the last 72 years, now let the freemen of the North, who have the power in their own bands, and who can make the American Government just what they think fit, resolve to blot out for ever the foul and haggard crime, which is the blight and mildew, the curse and the disgrace of the whole United States.

VI
Free-Soil and Fugitive Slaves

13

"The Two Altars; Or, Two Pictures in One" (1851)

Harriet Beecher Stowe

Harriet Beecher Stowe (1811–1896) is best known today as the author of Uncle Tom's Cabin, *which helped galvanize the abolitionist cause and contributed to the outbreak of the Civil War.* Uncle Tom's Cabin *was a best seller of its day. Legend has it that when Abraham Lincoln met Stowe in 1862, he said, "So you're the little woman who wrote the book that started this Great War!"*

The purpose of the "The Two Altars" is to contrast the meaning of liberty and the responsibility assumed by Americans to protect it in 1776 with status of liberty in the light of the 1850 Fugitive Slave Law. These two simple portraits evoke a powerful sense of the rise and fall of American liberty.

I. The Altar of Liberty, or 1776

The well-sweep of the old house on the hill was relieved dark and clear, against the reddening sky, as the early winter sun was going down in the west. It was a brisk, clear, metallic evening; the long drifts of snow blushed lilac in the hollows; and the old wintry wind brushed shrewdly along the plain, tingling people's noses, blowing open their cloaks, puffing in the back of their necks, and showing other unmistakable indications that he was getting up steam for a real roistering night.

"Hurrah! How it blows!" said little Dick Ward, from the top of the mossy wood-pile.

Now Dick had been sent to said wood-pile, in company with his little sister Grace, to pick up chips, which, everybody knows, was in the olden time considered a wholesome and gracious employment, and the peculiar duty of the rising generation. But said Dick, being a boy, had mounted the wood-pile, and erected there a flagstaff, on which he was busily tying a little red pocket-handkerchief, occasionally exhorting Grace "to be sure and pick up fast." "Oh, yes, I will," said Grace; "but you see the chips have got ice on 'em, and make my hands so cold!"

"Oh, don't stop to suck your thumbs! Who cares for ice? Pick away, I say, while I set up the flag of liberty."

So Grace picked away as fast as she could, nothing doubting but that her cold thumbs were in some mysterious sense an offering on the shrine of liberty; while soon the red handkerchief, duly secured, fluttered and snapped in the brisk evening wind.

"Now you must hurrah, Gracie, and throw up your bonnet," said Dick, as he descended from the pile.

"But won't it lodge down in some place in the wood-pile?" suggested Grace thoughtfully.

"Oh, never fear; give it to me, and just holler now, Gracie, 'Hurrah for liberty!' and we'll throw up your bonnet and my cap; and we'll play, you know, that we are a whole army and I'm General Washington."

So Grace gave up her little red hood, and Dick swung his cap, and up they both went into the air; and the children shouted, and the flag snapped and fluttered, and altogether they had a merry time of it. But then the wind—good-for-nothing, roguish fellow!—made an ungenerous plunge at poor Grace's little hood, and snipped it up in a twinkling, and whisked it off, off, off,—fluttering and bobbing up and down, quite across a wide, waste, snowy field,—and finally lodged it on the top of a tall, strutting rail, that was leaning, very independently, quite another way from all the other rails of the fence.

"Now see, do see!" said Grace; "there goes my bonnet! What will Aunt Hitty say?" and Grace began to cry.

"Don't you cry, Gracie; you offered it up to liberty, you know: it's glorious to give up everything for liberty."

"Oh, but Aunt Hitty won't think so."

"Well, don't cry, Gracie, you foolish girl! Do you think I can't get it? Now, only play that that great rail is a fort, and your bonnet is a prisoner in it, and see how quick I'll take the fort and get it!" and Dick shouldered a stick, and started off.

"What upon 'arth keeps those children so long? I should think they were making chips!" said Aunt Mehetabel; "the fire's just a-going out under the tea-kettle."

By this time Grace had lugged her heavy basket to the door, and was stamping the snow off her little feet, which were so numb that she needed to stamp, to be quite sure they were yet there. Aunt Mehetabel's shrewd face was the first that greeted her as the door opened.

"Gracie—What upon airth!—wipe your nose, child; your hands are frozen. Where alive is Dick?—and what's kept you out all this time?—and where's your bonnet?"

Poor Grace, stunned by this cataract of questions, neither wiped her nose nor gave any answer, but sidled up into the warm corner where grandmamma was knitting, and began quietly rubbing and blowing her fingers, while the tears silently rolled down her cheeks, as the fire made the former ache intolerably.

"Poor little dear!" said grandmamma, taking her hands in hers; "Hitty shan't scold you. Grandma knows you've been a good girl,—the wind blew poor Gracie's bonnet away"; and grandmamma wiped both eyes and nose, and gave her, moreover, a stalk of dried fennel out of her pocket, whereat Grace took heart once more.

"Mother always makes fools of Roxy's children," said Mehetabel, puffing zealously under the tea-kettle. "There's a little maple sugar in that saucer up there, mother, if you will keep giving it to her," she said, still vigorously puffing. "And now, Gracie," she said, when, after a while, the fire seemed in tolerable order, "will you answer my question? Where is Dick?"

"Gone over in the lot to get my bonnet."

"How came your bonnet off?" said Aunt Mehetabel. "I tied it on firm enough."

"Dick wanted me to take it off for him, to throw up for liberty," said Grace.

"Throw up for fiddlestick! Just one of Dick's cut-ups, and you was silly enough to mind him!"

"Why, he put up a flagstaff on the wood-pile, and a flag to liberty, you know, that papa's fighting for," said Grace more confidently, as she saw her quiet, blue-eyed mother, who had silently walked into the room during the conversation.

Grace's mother smiled, and said encouragingly, "And what then?"

"Why, he wanted me to throw up my bonnet and he his cap, and shout for liberty; and then the wind took it and carried it off, and he said I ought not to be sorry if I did lose it,—it was an offering to liberty."

"And so I did," said Dick, who was standing as straight as a poplar behind the group; "and I heard it in one of father's letters to mother that we ought to offer up everything on the altar of liberty and so I made an altar of the wood-pile."

"Good boy!" said his mother; "always remember everything your father writes. He has offered up everything on the altar of liberty, true enough; and I hope you, son, will live to do the same."

"Only, if I have the hoods and caps to make," said Aunt Hitty, "I hope he won't offer them up every week,—that's all!"

"Oh, well, Aunt Hitty, I've got the hood; let me alone for that. It blew clear over into the Daddy Ward pasture lot, and there stuck on the top of the great rail; and I played that the rail was a fort, and besieged it, and took it."

"Oh, yes! you're always up to taking forts, and anything else that nobody wants done. I'll warrant, now, you left Gracie to pick up every blessed one of them chips."

"Picking up chips is girls' work," said Dick; "and taking forts and defending the country is men's work."

"And pray, Mister Pomp, how long have you been a man?" said Aunt Hitty.

"If I ain't a man, I soon shall be; my head is 'most up to my mother's shoulder, and I can fire off a gun, too. I tried, the other day, when I was up to the store. Mother, I wish you'd let me clean and load the old gun, so that, if the British should come"—

"Well, if you are so big and grand, just lift me out that table, sir," said Aunt Hitty; "for it's past supper-time."

Dick sprang, and had the table out in a trice, with an abundant clatter, and put up the leaves with quite an air. His mother, with the silent and gliding motion characteristic of her, quietly took out the table-cloth and spread it, and began to set the cups and saucers in order, and to put on the plates and knives, while Aunt Hitty bustled about the tea.

"I'll be glad when the war's over, for one reason," said she. "I'm pretty much tired of drinking sage tea, for one, I know."

"Well, Aunt Hitty, how you scolded that peddler, last week, that brought along that real tea!"

"To be sure I did. S'pose I'd be taking any of his old tea, bought of the British?—fling every teacup in his face first."

"Well, mother," said Dick, "I never exactly understood what it was about the tea, and why the Boston folks threw it all overboard."

"Because there was an unlawful tax laid upon it, that the government had no right to lay. It wasn't much in itself; but it was part of a whole system of oppressive meanness, designed to take away our rights, and make us slaves of a foreign power."

"Slaves!" said Dick, straightening himself proudly. "Father a slave!"

"But they would not be slaves! They saw clearly where it would all end, and they would not begin to submit to it in ever so little." said the mother.

"I wouldn't, if I was they," said Dick.

"Besides," said the mother, drawing him towards her, "it wasn't for themselves alone they did it. This is a great country, and it will be greater and greater; and it's very important that it should have free and equal laws, because it will by and by be so great. This country, if it is a free one, will be a light of the world,—a city set on a hill, that cannot be hid; and all the oppressed and distressed from other countries shall come here to enjoy equal rights and freedom. This, dear boy, is why your father and uncles have gone to fight, though God knows what they suffer and"—And the large blue eyes of the mother were full of tears; yet a strong, bright beam of pride and exultation shone through those tears.

"Well, well, Roxy, you can always talk, everybody knows," said Aunt Hitty, who had been not the least attentive listener of this little patriotic harangue; "but, you see, the tea is getting cold, and yonder I see the sleigh is at the door, and John's come; so let's set up our chairs for supper."

The chairs were soon set up, when John, the eldest son, a lad of about fifteen, entered with a letter. There was one general exclamation, and stretching out of hands towards it. John threw it into his mother's lap; the tea-table was forgotten, and the tea-kettle sang unnoticed by the fire, as all hands crowded about mother's chair to hear the news. It was from Captain Ward, then in the American army at Valley Forge. Mrs. Ward ran it over hastily, and then read it aloud. A few words we may extract. "There is still," it said, "much suffering. I have given away every pair of stockings you sent me, reserving to myself only one; for I will not be one whit better off than the poorest soldier that fights for his country. Poor fellows! it makes my heart ache sometimes to go round among them, and see them with their worn clothes and torn shoes, and often bleeding feet, yet cheerful and hopeful, and every one willing to do his very best. Often the spirit of discouragement comes over them, particularly at night, when, weary, cold, and hungry, they turn into their comfortless huts, on the snowy ground. Then sometimes there is a thought of home, and warm fires, and some speak of giving up; but next morning out come Washington's general orders,—little short note, but's wonderful what good it does; and then they all resolve to hold on, come what may. There are commissioners going all through the country to pick up supplies. If they come to you, I need not tell you what to do. I know all that will be in your hearts."

"There, children, see what your father suffers," said the mother, "and what it costs these poor soldiers to gain our liberty."

"Ephraim Scranton told me that the commissioners had come as far as the Three Mile Tavern, and that he rather 'spected they'd be along here to-night," said John, as he was helping round the baked beans to the silent company at the tea-table.

"To-night?—do tell, now!" said Aunt Hitty. "Then it's time we were awake and stirring. Let's see what can be got."

"I'll send my new overcoat, for one," said John. "That old one isn't cut up yet, is it, Aunt Hitty?"

"No," said Aunt Hitty; "I was laying out to cut it over next Wednesday, when Desire Smith could be here to do the tailoring."

"There's the south room," said Aunt Hitty, musing; "that bed has the two old Aunt Ward blankets on it, and the great blue quilt, and two comforters. Then mother's and my room, two pair—four comforters—two quilts—the best chamber has got"—

"Oh, Aunt Hitty, send all that's in the best chamber! If any company comes, we can make it up off from our beds," said John. "I can send a blanket or two off from my bed, I know,—can't but just turn over in it, so many clothes on, now."

"Aunt Hitty, take a blanket off from our bed," said Grace and Dick at once.

"Well, well, we'll see," said Aunt Hitty, bustling up.

Up rose grandmamma, with great earnestness, now, and going into the next room, and opening a large cedar-wood chest, returned, bearing in her arms two large snow-white blankets, which she deposited flat on the table, just as Aunt Hitty was whisking off the tablecloth.

"Mortal! mother, what are you going to do?" said Aunt Hitty.

"There," she said, "I spun those, every thread of 'em, when my name was Mary Evans. Those were my wedding-blankets, made of real nice wool and worked with roses in all the corners. I've got them to give!" and grandmamma stroked and smoothed the blankets, and patted them down, with great pride and tenderness. It was evident that she was giving something that lay very near her heart; but she never faltered.

"La! mother, there's no need of that," said Aunt Hitty. "Use them on your own bed, and send the blankets off from that; they are just as good for the soldiers."

"No, I shan't!" said the old lady, waxing warm; "'tisn't a bit too good for 'em. I'll send the very best I've got, before they shall suffer. Send 'em the best!" and the old lady gestured oratorically.

They were interrupted by a rap at the door, and two men entered, and announced themselves as commissioned by Congress to search out supplies for the army. Now the plot thickens. Aunt Hitty flew in every direction,— through entry passage, meal-room, milk-room, down cellar, up chamber,— her cap border on end with patriotic zeal; and followed by John, Dick, and Grace, who eagerly bore to the kitchen the supplies that she turned out, while Mrs. Ward busied herself in quietly sorting and arranging, in the best possible traveling order, the various contributions that were precipitately launched on the kitchen floor.

Aunt Hitty soon appeared in the kitchen with an armful of stockings, which, kneeling on the floor, she began counting and laying out.

"There," she said, laying down a large bundle on some blankets, "That leaves just two pair apiece all round."

"La!" said John, "what's the use of saving two pair for me? I can do with one pair; as well as father."

"Sure enough," said his mother; "besides, I can knit you another pair in a day."

"And I can do with one pair," said Dick.

"Yours will be too small, young master, I guess," said one of the commissioners.

"No," said Dick; "I've got a pretty good foot of my own, and Aunt Hitty will always knit my stockings an inch too long, 'cause she says I grow so. See here,—these will do"; and the boy shook his triumphantly.

"And mine, too," said Grace, nothing doubting, having been busy all the time in pulling off her little stockings.

"Here," she said to the man who was packing the things into a wide-mouthed sack; "here's mine," and her large blue eyes looked earnestly through her tears.

Aunt Hitty flew at her. "Good land! the child's crazy. Don't think the men could wear your stockings,—take 'em away!"

Grace looked around with an air of utter desolation, and began to cry. "I wanted to give them something," said she. "I'd rather go barefoot on the snow all day than not send 'em anything."

"Give me the stockings, my child," said the old soldier tenderly. "There, I'll take 'em, and show 'em to the soldiers, and tell them what the little girl said that sent them.

And it will do them as much good as if they could wear them. "They've got little girls at home, too." Grace fell on her mother's bosom completely happy, and Aunt Hitty only muttered,—

"Everybody does spile that child; and no wonder, neither!"

Soon the old sleigh drove off from the brown house, tightly packed and heavily loaded. And Grace and Dick were creeping up to their little beds.

"There's been something put on the altar of Liberty tonight, hasn't there, Dick?"

"Yes, indeed," said Dick; and, looking up to his mother, he said, "But, mother, what did you give?"

"I?" said the mother musingly.

"Yes, you, mother; what have you given to the country?"

"All that I have, dears," said she, laying her hands gently on their heads,— "my husband and my children."

II. The Altar of ———, or 1850

The setting sun of chill December lighted up the solitary front window of a small tenement on ——— Street, in Boston, which we now have occasion to visit. As we push gently aside the open door, we gain sight of a small room, clean as busy hands can make it, where a neat, cheerful young mulatto woman is busy at an ironing-table. A basket full of glossy-bosomed shirts, and faultless collars and wristbands, is beside her, into which she is placing the last few items with evident pride and satisfaction. A bright black-eyed boy, just come in from school, with his satchel of books over his shoulder, stands, cap in hand, relating to his mother how he has been at the head of his class, and showing his school tickets, which his mother, with untiring admiration, deposits in the little real china teapot, which, as being their most reliable article of gentility, is made the deposit of all the money and most especial valuables of the family.

"Now, Henry," says the mother, "look out and see if father is coming along the street"; and she begins filling the little black tea-kettle, which is soon set singing on the stove.

From the inner room now daughter Mary, a well-grown girl of thirteen, brings the baby, just roused from a nap, and very impatient to renew his acquaintance with his mamma.

"Bless his bright eyes!—mother will take him," ejaculates the busy little woman, whose hands are by this time in a very floury condition, in the incipient stages of wetting up biscuit,—"in a minute"; and she quickly frees herself from the flour and paste, and, deputing Mary to roll out her biscuit, proceeds to the consolation and succor of young master.

"Now, Henry," says the mother, "you'll have time, before supper, to take that basket of clothes up to Mr. Sheldin's; put in that nice bill that you made out last night. I shall give you a cent for every bill you write out for me. What a comfort it is, now, for one's children to be gettin' learnin' so."

Henry shouldered the basket and passed out the door, just as a neatly dressed colored man walked up with his pail and whitewash brushes.

"Oh, you've come, father, have you? Mary, are the biscuits in? You may as well set the table now. Well, George, what's the news?"

"Nothing, only a pretty smart day's work. I've brought home five dollars, and shall have as much as I can do, these two weeks"; and the man, having washed his hands, proceeded to count out his change on the ironing-table.

"Well, it takes you to bring in the money," said the delighted wife; "nobody but you could turn off that much in a day."

"Well, they do say—those that's had me once—that they never want any other hand to take hold in their rooms. I s'pose it's a kinder practice I've got, and kinder natural."

"Tell ye what," said the little woman, taking down the family strong box,—to wit, the china teapot aforenamed,—and pouring the contents on the table, "we're getting mighty rich now! We can afford to get Henry his new Sunday cap, and Mary her mousseline-de-laine dress—Take care, baby, you rogue!"

she hastily interposed, as young master made a dive at a dollar bill, for his share in the proceeds.

"He wants something, too, I suppose," said the father; "let him get his hand in while he's young."

The baby gazed, with round, astonished eyes, while mother, with some difficulty, rescued the bill from his grasp; but, before any one could at all anticipate his purpose, he dashed in among the small change with such zeal as to send it flying all over the table.

"Hurrah! Bob's a smasher!" said the father, delighted; "he'll make it fly, he thinks"; and, taking the baby on his knee, he laughed merrily as Mary and her mother pursued the rolling coin all over the room.

"He knows now, as well as can be that he's been doing mischief," said the delighted mother, as the baby kicked and crowed uproariously; "he's such a forward child, now, to be only six months old! Oh, you've no idea, father, how mischievous he grows"; and therewith the little woman began to roll and tumble the little mischief-maker about, uttering divers frightful threats, which appeared to contribute, in no small degree, to the general hilarity.

"Come, come, Mary," said the mother at last, with a sudden burst of recollection; "you mustn't be always on your knees fooling with this child! Look in the oven at them biscuits."

"They're done exactly, mother,—just the brown!" and, with the word, the mother dumped baby on to his father's knee, where he sat contentedly munching a very ancient crust of bread, occasionally improving the flavor thereof by rubbing it on his father's coat-sleeve.

"What have you got in that blue dish there?" said George, when the whole little circle were seated around the table.

"Well, now, what do you suppose?" said the little woman, delighted; "a quart of nice oysters,—just for a treat, you know. I wouldn't tell you till this minute," said she, raising the cover.

"Well," said George, "we both work hard for our money, and we don't owe anybody a cent; and why shouldn't we have our treats, now and then, as well as rich folks?"

And gayly passed the supper-hour; the tea-kettle sung, the baby crowed, and all chatted and laughed abundantly.

"I'll tell you," said George, wiping his mouth; "wife, these times are quite another thing from what it used to be down in Georgia. I remember then old mas'r used to hire me out by the year; and one time, I remember, I came and paid him in two hundred dollars,—every cent I'd taken. He just looked it over, counted it, and put it in his pocket-book, and said, 'You are a good boy, George,'—and he gave me half a dollar!"

"I want to know, now!" said his wife.

"Yes, he did, and that was every cent I ever got of it; and, I tell you, I was mighty bad off for clothes, them times."

"Well, well, the Lord be praised, they're over, and you are in a free country now!" said the wife, as she rose thoughtfully from the table, and brought her husband the great Bible. The little circle were ranged around the stove for evening prayers.

"Henry, my boy, you must read—you are a better reader than your father—thank God, that let you learn early!"

The boy, with a cheerful readiness, read, "The Lord is my Shepherd," and the mother gently stilled the noisy baby to listen to the holy words. Then all knelt, while the father, with simple earnestness, poured out his soul to God.

They had but just risen—the words of Christian hope and trust scarce died on their lips—when, lo! the door was burst open, and two men entered; and one of them, advancing, laid his hand on the father's shoulder. "This is the fellow," said he.

"You are arrested in the name of the United States!" said the other.

"Gentlemen, what is this?" said the poor man, trembling.

"Are you not the property of Mr. B., of Georgia?" said the officer.

"Gentlemen, I've been a free, hard-working man these ten years."

"Yes, but you are arrested, on suit of Mr. B., as his slave."

Shall we describe the leave-taking,—the sorrowing wife, the dismayed children, the tears, the anguish, that simple, honest, kindly home, in a moment so desolated? Ah, ye who defend this because it is law, think for one hour what if this that happens to your poor brother should happen to you!

It was a crowded court-room, and the man stood there to be tried—for life?—no, but for the life of life—for liberty!

Lawyers hurried to and fro, buzzing, consulting, bringing authorities,—all anxious, zealous, engaged,—for what? To save a fellow man from bondage? No; anxious and zealous lest he might escape; full of zeal to deliver him over to slavery. The poor man's anxious eyes follow vainly the busy course of affairs, from which he dimly learns that he is to be sacrificed—on the altar of the Union; and that his heart-break and anguish, and the tears of his wife, and the desolation of his children are, in the eyes of these well-informed men, only the bleat of a sacrifice, bound to the horns of the glorious American altar!

Again it is a bright day, and business walks brisk in this market. Senator and statesman, the learned and patriotic, are out, this day, to give their countenance to an edifying and impressive and truly American spectacle,—the sale of a man! All the preliminaries of the scene are there: dusky-browed mothers, looking with sad eyes while speculators are turning round their children, looking at their teeth, and feeling of their arms; a poor, old, trembling woman, helpless, half blind, whose last child is to be sold, holds on to her bright boy with trembling hands. Husbands and wives, sisters and friends, all soon to be scattered like the chaff of the threshing-floor, look sadly on each other with poor nature's last tears; and among them walk briskly glib, oily politicians, and thriving men of law, letters, and religion, exceedingly sprightly and in good spirits—for why?—it isn't *they* that are going to be sold; it's only somebody else. And so they are very comfortable, and look on the whole thing as quite a matter-of-course affair, and, as it is to be conducted to-day, a decidedly valuable and judicious exhibition.

And now, after so many hearts and souls have been knocked and thumped this way and that by the auctioneer's hammer, comes the instructive part of the whole; and the husband and father, whom we saw in his simple home, reading and praying with his children, and rejoicing in the joy of his poor ignorant heart that he lived in a free country, is now set up to be admonished of his mistake.

Now there is a great excitement, and pressing to see, and exultation and approbation; for it is important and interesting to see a man put down that has tried to be a free man.

"That's he, is it? Couldn't come it, could he?" says one.

"No; and he will never come it, that's more," says another triumphantly.

"I don't generally take much interest in scenes of this nature," says a grave representative; "but I came here today for the sake of the principle!"

"Gentlemen," says the auctioneer, "we've got a specimen here that some of your Northern abolitionists would give any price for; but they sha'n't have him! no! we've looked out for that. The man that buys him must give bonds never to sell him to go North again!"

"Go it!" shout the crowd; "good! good! hurrah!"

"An impressive idea!" says a Senator; "a noble maintaining of principle!" and the man is bid off, and the hammer falls with a last crash on his heart, his hopes, his manhood, and he lies a bleeding wreck on the altar of Liberty!

Such was the altar in 1776; such is the altar in 1850!

14

"Speech on Our Present Anti-Slavery Duties" (1850)

Charles Sumner

Charles Sumner (1811–1874) was the most influential and famous abolitionist statesman. Educated at Harvard College and Harvard Law School, Sumner was converted to abolitionism by Lydia Maria Child's An Appeal in Favor of that Class of Americans Called Africans. *He first joined the Whig Party, but later helped to form the Free-Soil Party in 1848 and then the Republican Party in 1854. Sumner is most famous for his 1855 speech in the U.S. Senate on "The Crime Against Kansas." The speech compared South Carolina senator Andrew P. Butler to Don Quixote, whose mistress, "though polluted in the sight of the world, is chaste in his sight. I mean the harlot, slavery." Two days later, Butler's nephew, South Carolina congressman Preston Brooks, entered the Senate chamber and brutally beat Sumner unconscious. Thereafter, Sumner was an invalid for three years, but his constituents reelected him by a large margin despite his inability to take his seat in the Senate.*

In his "Speech on Our Present Anti-Slavery Duties," Sumner provides a brief for the Free-Soil position and against the Slave Power and its passage of the Fugitive Slave Law.

Mr. President:

I HAD hoped to-day to mingle in the business of the Convention, and to listen to others, without occupying your time by any words of mine. Indeed, when I left our meeting at its adjournment this forenoon, I did not count upon being here this afternoon; but let me say frankly, I was uneasy away—I felt that I ought to be with you—I yielded to the attractions of the cause, which has drawn us together, and here I am, answering to your call, and, most grateful for this kind reception.

Let me, without delay, touch upon some topics which seem important to be borne in mind. The session of Congress, so long drawn out, has at last closed; and its members are now hurrying to their homes, to taste a brief respite from legislative labors. It becomes us to consider what has been done, and to endeavor, by an inquiry into the existing state of things, to discern our present duties. "Watchman, what of the night?" And well may the question be asked, "What of the night?" For things have occurred, and measures have passed into laws, which, to my mind, fill the day itself with blackness.

And yet there are streaks of light—an unwonted dawn—in the distant West, out of which a full-orbed sun is beginning to ascend, rejoicing like a strong man to run his race. *Video solem orientem in occidente.* By an Act of the recent Congress, California, with a Constitution forbidding Slavery, adopted in the exercise of its sovereignty as a State, has been admitted into the Union. For a measure like this, required not only by the simplest justice, but by the uniform practice of the country, and the constitutional principles of the slave-holders themselves, we may well be ashamed to confess our gratitude; and yet I cannot but rejoice in this great good accomplished. A hateful institution, which thus far, without check, had travelled with the power of the Republic, westward, is bidden to stop, and a new and rising State guarded from its contamination. Freedom—in whose hands is the divining rod, of magical power, pointing the way, not only to wealth untold, but to every possession of virtue and intelligence—whose presence is better far than any mine of gold—is now at last established in an extensive region on the distant Pacific, between the very parallels of latitude so long claimed by Slavery as its peculiar home.

Here is a moral and political victory; a moral victory, inasmuch as Freedom has secured a new foothold, where to exert her far-reaching influence; a political victory also, inasmuch as by the admission of California, the Free States have obtained a majority of votes in the Senate, and the *balance of power*, between Freedom and Slavery—so preposterously claimed by the Slave States, in forgetfulness of the true spirit of the Constitution, and in mockery of Human Rights—has been overturned. May free California, and her Senators in Congress, never fail hereafter, amidst the trials before us, in loyalty to Freedom! God forbid that the daughter should turn, with ingratitude or neglect, from the mother that bore her!

Besides this Act, there are two others of this long session, which may be regarded with satisfaction, and which I mention at once, before considering the reverse of the picture. The Slave trade has been abolished in the District of Columbia. This measure, though small in the sight of Justice, is most important. It banishes from the National Capital an odious traffic. But this is its least office. It practically affixes to the whole traffic, wherever it exists—not merely in Washington, within the immediate sphere of the legislative act—but every where throughout the Slave States, whether at Richmond, or Charleston, or New Orleans, the brand of Congressional reprobation. Yes!

The people of the United States, by the voice of Congress, have, solemnly declared the domestic traffic in slaves to be offensive in their sight. The Nation has judged this traffic. The Nation has said to it, "Get thee behind me, Satan." It is true that Congress has not, as in the case of the foreign slave trade, stamped it as *piracy*, and awarded to its perpetrators the doom of *pirates*; but it condemns the trade, and gives to general scorn those who partake of it. To this extent the Federal Government has spoken for Freedom. And, in doing this, it has asserted, under the Constitution of the United States, legislative jurisdiction over the subject of Slavery in the District; thus preparing the way for that complete act of Abolition, which is necessary to purge the National Capital of its still remaining curse and, shame.

The other measure, which I must hail with thankfulness, is the Abolition of Flogging in the Navy. Beyond the direct reform thus accomplished—after much effort, finally crowned by encouraging success—is the indirect influence of this law, especially in rebuking the use of the lash, wheresoever and by whomsoever employed!

Thus two props and stays of Slavery, wherever it exists in our country, have been weakened and undermined by Congressional legislation. Without the *slave-trade* and the *lash*, Slavery must fall to the earth. By these, the whole hideous monstrosity is upheld. If I seem to exaggerate the consequence of these measures of Abolition, let it be referred to my sincere conviction of their powerful, though subtle and indirect influence, and also to my desire to find something of good in a Congress which has furnished occasion for so much of disappointment. There are other measures, which must be regarded, not only with regret, but with indignation and disgust.

Two broad territories, New Mexico and Utah, under the exclusive jurisdiction of Congress, have been organized without any prohibition of Slavery. In laying the foundation of their governments, destined hereafter to control the happiness of innumerable multitudes, Congress has omitted the Great Ordinance of Freedom, first suggested by Jefferson, and consecrated by the experience of the North-Western Territory; it has neglected to recognize those principles of Human Liberty, which are enunciated in our Declaration of Independence,—which are essential to every Bill of Rights—and without which a Republic is a name, and nothing more.

Still further, a vast territory, supposed to be upwards of seventy thousand square miles in extent, larger than all New England, has been taken from New Mexico, and with ten million dollars besides, given to slave-holding Texas; thus, under the plea of settling the Western boundary of Texas, securing to this State a large sum of money, and consigning to certain Slavery an important territory.

And still further, as if to do a deed, which should "make heaven weep, all earth amazed," this same Congress, in disregard of all the cherished safeguards of Freedom, has passed a most cruel, unchristian, devilish law to secure the return into Slavery of those fortunate bondmen, who have found shelter by our firesides. This is the Fugitive Slave Bill—a bill which despoils the party claimed as a slave—whether he be in reality a slave or a freeman—of the sacred right of Trial by Jury, and commits the question of Human Freedom—the highest question known by the law—to the unaided judgment of a single magistrate, on *ex parte* evidence it may be, by affidavits, without the sanction of cross examination. Under this detestable, heaven-defying bill, not the slave only, but the colored freeman of the North, may be swept into ruthless captivity; and there is no white citizen, born among us, bred in our schools, partaking in our affairs, voting in our elections, whose Liberty is not assailed also. Without any discrimination of color, the Bill surrenders all, who may be claimed as "owing service or labor," to the same tyrannical judgment. And mark once more its heathenism. By unrelenting provisions it visits, with bitter penalties of fine and imprisonment, the faithful men and women, who may render to the fugitive that countenance, succor and shelter, which Christianity expressly requires! Thus, from beginning to end, it sets at naught the best principles of the Constitution, and the very laws of God!

I might occupy your time by exposing the unconstitutionality of this act. In denying the Trial by Jury, it is three times unconstitutional; first, as the Constitution declares "The right of the people to be secure in their persons against *unreasonable seizures*"; secondly, as it further declares, that "No person shall be deprived of life, *liberty*, or property *without due process of law*"; and, thirdly, because it expressly declares, that "In suits at common law, where the value in controversy shall exceed twenty dollars, *the right of trial by jury shall be preserved*." By this triple cord did the framers of the Constitution secure the Trial by Jury in every question of Human Freedom. That man can be little imbued with the true spirit of American institutions—he can have little sympathy with Bills of Rights—he must be lukewarm for Freedom, who can hesitate to construe the Constitution so as to secure this safeguard.

The act is again unconstitutional in the unprecedented and tyrannical powers which it confers upon Commissioners. These officers are appointed, not by the President with the advice of the Senate, but by the Courts of Law; they hold their places, not during good behavior, but at the will of the Court; and they receive for their services, not a regular salary, but fees in each individual case. And yet in these officers,—thus appointed and compensated, and holding their places by the most uncertain tenure—is vested a portion of that "judicial power," which, according to the express words of the Constitution, can be in "Judges" only, who hold their offices "during good behavior," who, "at stated times, receive for their services a compensation, which shall not be diminished during their continuance in office," and, it would seem also, who are appointed by the President and confirmed by the Senate. And, adding meanness to the violation of the Constitution, the Commissioner is bribed by a double fee, to pronounce against Freedom. If he dooms a man to slavery, he receives ten dollars; but if he saves him, his fee is five dollars.

But I will not pursue these details. The soul sickens in the contemplation of this legalized outrage. In the dreary annals of the Past, there are many acts of shame—there are ordinances of monarchs, and laws, which have become a bye-word and a hissing to the nations. But, *when we consider the country and the age*, I ask fearlessly, What act of shame, what ordinance of monarch, what law can compare in atrocity, with this enactment of an American Congress? I do not forget Appius Claudius, the tyrant decemvir of ancient Rome, condemning Virginia as a slave; nor Louis XIV of France, letting slip the dogs of religious persecution by the revocation of the edict of Nantes; nor Charles I of England, arousing the patriot rage of Hampden, by the extortion of Ship-money; nor the British Parliament, provoking, in our own country, spirits kindred to Hampden, by the tyranny of the Stamp Act and Tea Tax. I would not exaggerate; I wish to keep within bounds; but I think no person can doubt that the condemnation now affixed to all these transactions, and to their authors, must be the lot hereafter of the Fugitive Slave Bill, and of every one, according to the measure of his influence, who gave it his support. Into the immortal catalogue of national crimes this has now passed, drawing with it, by an inexorable necessity, its authors also, and chiefly him, who, as President of the United States; set his name to the Bill, and breathed into it that final breath, without which it would have no life. Other Presidents may be forgotten; but the name signed to the Fugitive Slave Bill can never be forgotten. There are depths of infamy, as there are heights of fame. I regret to say what I must; but truth compels me. Better far for him had he never been born; better far for his memory, and for the good name of his children, had he never been President!

I have already likened this Bill to the Stamp Act, and I trust that the parallel may be continued yet further by a burst of popular feeling against all action under it, similar to that which glowed in the breasts of our fathers. Listen to the words of John Adams, as written in his Diary for the time:—

> The year 1765 has been the most remarkable year of my life. That enormous engine, fabricated by the British Parliament, for battering down all the rights and liberties of America,—I mean the Stamp Act,—has raised and spread through the whole continent a spirit that will be recorded to our honor with all future generations. In every colony, from Georgia to New Hampshire inclusively, the stamp distributors and inspectors have

been compelled by the unconquerable rage of the people to renounce their offices. Such and so universal has been the resentment of the people, that every man who has dared to speak in favor of the stamps, or to soften the detestation in which they are held, how great soever his abilities and virtues had been esteemed before, or whatever his fortune, connections, and influence had been, has been seen to sink into universal contempt and ignominy.

Surely the love of Freedom cannot have so far cooled among us, the descendants of those who opposed the Stamp Act, that we are insensible to the Fugitive Slave Bill. The unconquerable rage of the people, in those other days, compelled the stamp distributors and inspectors to renounce their offices, and held up to detestation all who dared to speak in favor of the stamps. And shall we be more tolerant of those who volunteer in favor of this Bill—more tolerant of the Slave-Hunter, who, under its safeguard, pursues his prey upon our soil? The Stamp Act could not be executed here. Can the Fugitive Slave Bill?

And here, Sir, let me say, that it becomes me to speak with peculiar caution. It happens to me to sustain an important relation to this Bill. Early in professional life I was designated by the late Mr. Justice Story one of the Commissioners of the Courts of the United States, and, though I have not very often exercised the functions of this post, yet my name is still upon the lists. As such I am one of those before whom, under the recent Act of Congress, the panting fugitive may be brought for the decision of the question, whether he is a freeman or a slave. But while it becomes me to speak with caution, I shall not hesitate to speak with plainness. I cannot forget that I am a *man*, although I am a *Commissioner.*

Did the same spirit which inspired the fathers inspire our community now, the marshals—and every *magistrate* who regarded this law as having any constitutional obligation—would resign rather than presume to execute it. This, however, is too much to expect from all at present. But I will not judge them. To their own consciences I leave them. Surely, no person of humane feelings, and with any true sense of justice—living in a land "where bells have knolled to church"—whatever may be the apology of public station, could fail to recoil from such service. For myself let me say, that I can imagine no office, no salary, no consideration, which I would not gladly forego, rather than become in any way an agent in enslaving my brother-man. Where for me would be comfort and solace, after such a work! In dreams and in waking hours, in solitude and in the street, in the meditations of the closet, and in the affairs of men, wherever I turned, there my victim would stare me in the face; from the distant rice-fields and sugar plantations of the South, his cries beneath the vindictive lash, his moans at the thought of Liberty once his, now alas! ravished from him, would pursue me, repeating the tale of his fearful doom, and sounding, forever sounding, in my ears, "Thou art the man!"

The magistrate who pronounces the decree of slavery, and the marshal who enforces it, act in obedience to law. This is their apology; and it is also the apology of the masters of the Inquisition, as they ply the torture amidst the shrieks of their Victim. But can this weaken our accountability for an act of wrong? Disguise it, excuse it as you will, the fact must glare before the world and penetrate the conscience too, that the fetters and chains, by which the unhappy fugitive is bound, are riveted by their tribunal—that his second life of wretchedness dates from their agency—that his second birth as a slave proceeds from *them.* The magistrate and marshal of the United States do for him here, in a country, which vaunts a Christian civilization, what the naked, barbarous Pagan chiefs, beyond the sea, did for his grandfather in Congo; *they transfer him to the Slave-Hunter*, and for this service receive the very price paid for his grandfather in Congo—*ten dollars!*

Gracious Heaven! Can such things be on our Free Soil! Shall the evasion of Pontius Pilate be enacted anew, and a Judge vainly attempt, by washing his hands, to excuse himself for condemning one in whom he can "find no fault!" Should any Court, sitting here in Massachusetts, for the first time in her history, become the agent of a Slave Hunter, the very images of our fathers would frown from the walls; their voices would cry from the ground; their spirits would hover in the air, pleading, remonstrating, protesting, against the cruel judgment. There is a legend of Venice, consecrated by the pencil of one of her greatest artists, that the Apostle St. Mark suddenly descended into the public square, and broke the manacles of a slave, even before the Judge who had decreed his doom. Should Massachusetts be ever desecrated by such a judgment, may the good Apostle, with valiant arm, once more descend to break the manacles of the Slave!

Sir, I will not dishonor this home of the Pilgrims, and of the Revolution, by admitting—nay, *I cannot believe—that this Bill will be executed here.* Individuals among us, as elsewhere, may forget humanity in a fancied loyalty to law; but the public conscience will not allow a man, who has trodden our streets as a freeman, to be dragged away as a slave. By his escape from bondage, he has shown that true manhood, which must grapple to him every honest heart. He may be ignorant, and rude, as he is poor, but he is of a true nobility. The Fugitive Slaves of the United States are among the heroes of our age. In sacrificing them to this foul enactment of Congress, we should violate every sentiment of hospitality, every whispering of the heart, every dictate of religion.

There are many who will never shrink at any cost, and, notwithstanding all the atrocious penalties of this Bill, from efforts to save a wandering fellow-man from bondage; they will offer him the shelter of their houses, and, if need be, will protect his liberty by force. But let me be understood; I counsel no violence. There is another power—stronger than any individual arm—which I invoke; I mean that invincible Public Opinion, inspired by love of God and man, which, without violence or noise, gently as the operations of nature, makes and unmakes laws. Let this opinion be felt in its Christian might, and the Fugitive Slave Bill will become every where upon our soil a dead letter. No lawyer will aid it by counsel; no citizen will become its agent; it will die of inanition—like a spider beneath an exhausted receiver. Oh! it were well the tidings should spread throughout the land, that here in Massachusetts this accursed Bill has found no *servants*. "Sire, I have found in Bayonne honest citizens and brave soldiers only; *but not one executioner*," was the reply of the governor of that place, to the royal mandate from Charles IX of France, ordering the Massacre of St. Bartholomew.

But it rests with you, my fellow-citizens, by your words and your example, by your calm determinations, and your devoted lives, to do this work. From a humane, just, and religious people, shall spring a Public Opinion, to keep perpetual guard over the liberties of all within our borders. Nay, more, like the flaming sword of the cherubim at the gates of Paradise, turning on every side, it shall prevent any SLAVE-HUNTER from ever setting foot in this Commonwealth. Elsewhere, he may pursue his human prey; he may employ his congenial bloodhounds, and exult in his successful game. But into Massachusetts he must not come. And yet again I say, I counsel no violence. I would not touch his person. Not with whips and thongs would I scourge him from the land. The contempt, the indignation, the abhorrence of the community shall be our weapons of offence. Wherever he moves, he shall find no house to receive him—no table spread to nourish him—no welcome to cheer him. The dismal lot of the Roman exile shall be his. He shall be a wanderer, without *roof, fire, or water.*

Men shall point at him in the streets, and on the highways;

> Sleep, shall neither night nor day,
> Hang upon his pent-house lid;
> He shall live a man forbid.
> Weary seven nights, nine times nine,
> Shall he dwindle, peak and pine.

The villages, towns and cities shall refuse to receive the monster; they shall vomit him forth, never again to disturb the repose of our community.

The feelings, with which we regard the Slave-Hunter, will soon be extended also to all the mercenary agents, and heartless minions, who, without any positive obligation of law, became a part of his pack. They are *volunteers*, and, as such, should share the ignominy of the chief Hunter.

I have dwelt thus long upon the Fugitive Slave Bill, chiefly in the hope of contributing something to the creation of that Public Opinion, which in the Free States is destined to be the truest defence of the slave. I now advance to our more general duties.

We have seen what Congress has done. And yet in the face of these enormities of legislation—of this organization of the territories without the prohibition of Slavery; of the surrender of a large province to Texas and Slavery; and of this execrable Fugitive Slave Bill; in the face also of Slavery still sanctioned in the District of Columbia; of the Slave-trade between domestic ports under the flag of the Union; and in the face of the Slave Power still dominant over the Government of the country, we are told that the Slavery Question is settled. Yes: settled—settled—that is the word. *Nothing, Sir, can be settled, which is not right.* Nothing can be settled, which is adverse to Freedom. Nothing can be settled, which is contrary to the precepts of Christianity. God, nature, and all the holy sentiments of the heart, repudiate any such false seeming settlement.

Amidst the shifts and changes of party our DUTIES remain, pointing the way to action. By no subtle compromise or adjustment can men suspend the commandments of God. By no trick of managers, no hocus-pocus of politicians, no "mush of concession" can we be released from this obedience. It is, then, in the light of our duties, that we are to find true peace, at once for our country, and ourselves. Nor can any settlement promise peace, which is not, in harmony with those divine principles from which our duties spring.

In unfolding these I shall be brief. Slavery is wrong. It is the source of unnumbered woes; not the least of which is its influence on the Slave-holder himself, in rendering him insensible to its outrage. It overflows with injustice and inhumanity. Language toils in vain to picture the wretchedness and wickedness, which it sanctions and perpetuates. Reason revolts at the impious assumption, that man can hold property in man. As it is our perpetual duty to oppose wrong, so must we oppose Slavery; nor can we ever relax in this opposition so long as the giant evil continues any where within the sphere of our influence. *Especially must we oppose it, wherever we are responsible for its existence, or are in any way parties to it.*

And now mark the distinction. The testimony which we bear against Slavery, as against all other wrong is, in different ways, according to our position. The Slavery, which exists under other governments—as in Russia or Turkey; or in other States of our Union—as in Virginia and Carolina—we can oppose only through the influence of morals and religion, without in any way invoking the Political Power. Nor do we propose to act otherwise. But Slavery, wherever we are responsible for it, wherever we are parties to it, must be opposed, not only by all the influences of morals and religion, but directly by every instrument of Political Power. As it is sustained by law, it can only be overthrown by law; and the legislature, in which is lodged the jurisdiction over it, must be moved to undertake the work. I am sorry to confess that this can be done, only through the machinery of politics. The politician, then, must be summoned. The moralist, the philanthropist must become for this purpose a politician; not forgetting his morals or his philanthropy, but seeking to apply them practically in the laws of the land.

It is a mistake to say, as is often charged, that we seek to interfere, through Congress, with Slavery in the States, or in any way to direct the legislation of Congress upon subjects not within its jurisdiction. Our *political* aims, as well as our *political* duties, are coextensive with our *political* responsibilities. And since we at the North are responsible for Slavery, wherever it exists under the jurisdiction of Congress, it is unpardonable in us not to exert every power we possess to enlist Congress against it.

Looking at details;—

We demand, first and foremost, the instant Repeal of the Fugitive Slave Bill.

We demand the Abolition of Slavery in the District of Columbia.

We demand the exercise by Congress, in all Territories, of its time-honored power to prohibit Slavery.

We demand of Congress to refuse to receive into the Union, any new Slave State.

We demand the Abolition of the domestic slave-trade, so far as it can be constitutionally reached; but particularly on the high seas under the National Flag.

And, generally, we demand from the Federal Government the exercise of all its constitutional power to relieve itself from responsibility for Slavery.

And yet one thing further must be done. The Slave Power must be overturned; so that the Federal Government may be put openly, actively and perpetually on the side of Freedom.

In demanding the overthrow of the Slave Power, we but seek to exclude from the operations of the Federal Government a *political* influence,—having its origin in Slavery,—which has been more potent, sinister, and mischievous, than any other in our history. This Power, though unknown to the Constitution, and existing in defiance of its true spirit, now predominates over Congress, gives the tone to its proceedings, seeks to control all our public affairs, and humbles both the great political parties to its will. It is that combination of Slave-Masters, whose bond of union is a common interest in Slavery. Time would fail me in exposing the extent to which its influence has been felt—the undue share of offices which it has enjoyed,—and the succession of its evil deeds. Suffice it to say, that, for a long period, the real principle of this union was not observed by the Free States. In the game of office and legislation, the South has always won. It has played with loaded dice—*loaded with Slavery.* Like the Automaton Chess-Player, it has never failed to be conqueror. Let the Free States make a move on the board, and the South has said "Check." Let them strive for Free Trade, as they did once, and the cry has been "Check." Let them jump towards Protection, and it is again "Check." Let them move towards Internal Improvements, and the cry is still "Check." Whether forwards or backwards, to the right or left, wherever they moved, the Free States have been pursued by an inexorable "Check." But the secret is now discovered. Amidst the well-arranged machinery, which seemed to give motion to the victorious chess-player, there was concealed a *motive force*, which has not been estimated—the Slave Power. It is the Slave Power, which has been the perpetual victor, saying always "Check" to the Free States. As this influence is now disclosed, it only remains that it should be openly encountered in the field of *politics.*

Such is our cause. It is not sectional; for it simply aims to establish under the Federal Government the great principles of Justice and Humanity, which are as broad and universal as man. It is not aggressive, for it does not seek in any way to interfere, through Congress, with Slavery in the States. It is not contrary to the Constitution; for it recognizes this instrument, and, in the administration of the Government, invokes the spirit of its founders. It is not hostile to the quiet of the country; for it proposes the only course by which agitation can be allayed, and quiet be permanently established. And yet the attempt is made to suppress this cause, and to stifle its discussion.

Vain and wretched attempt! The important subject, which more than all other subjects needs careful, conscientious and kind consideration in the national counsels—which will not admit of postponement or hesitation—which is connected with most of the great interests of the country—which controls the tariff, and causes war—which concerns alike all parts of the land, the North and the South, the East and the West—which affects the good name of the United States in the family of civilized nations—the *subject of subjects*—has been now at last, after many struggles, admitted within the pale of legislative discussion. From this time forward it will be entertained by Congress. It will be, as it were, one of the orders of the day. It cannot be passed over or forgotten. It cannot be blinked out of sight. The combinations of party cannot remove it. The intrigues of politicians cannot jostle it aside. There it is, in its colossal proportions, in the very Halls of the Capitol, overshadowing and darkening all other subjects. There it will continue, till driven into oblivion by the irresistible Genius of Freedom.

I am not blind to the adverse signs. The wave of reaction, which, during the last year swept over Europe, has reached our shores. The very barriers of Human Rights have been broken down. Statesmen, writers, scholars, speakers, once their uncompromising professors, have became the professors of compromise. All this must be changed. Reaction must be stayed. The country must be aroused. The cause must again be pressed—with the avowed purpose never to moderate our efforts until crowned by success. The Federal Government, every where within its proper constitutional sphere, must be placed on the side of Freedom. The policy of Slavery which has so long prevailed, must give place to the policy of Freedom. The Slave-Power, the fruitful parent of national ills, must be driven from its supremacy. Until all this is done, the friends of the Constitution and of Human Rights cannot cease from their labors; nor can the country hope for any repose, but the repose of submission.

Let men of all parties and pursuits, who wish well to their country, and would preserve its good name, join in these labors. Welcome here to the Conservative and to the Reformer; for our cause stands on the truest Conservatism and the truest Reform. In seeking the reform of existing evils, we seek also the conservation of the principles of our fathers. Welcome especially to the young. To you I appeal with confidence. Trust to your generous impulses, and to that reasoning of the heart, which is often truer, as it is less selfish, than the calculations of the brain. Do not exchange your aspirations for the skepticism of age. Yours is the better part. In the Scriptures it is said, that "the young men shall see visions, and the old men shall dream dreams"; on which Lord Bacon has aptly remarked, that the palm is given to the young men, inasmuch as it is higher to see visions than to dream dreams.

It is not uncommon to hear persons declare that they are against Slavery, and are willing to unite in any *practical* efforts to make this opposition felt. At the same time they pharisaically visit with condemnation, with reproach, or contempt, all the earnest souls that for years have striven in this struggle. To such I would say, if you are sincere in what you declare; if your words are not merely lip-service; if in your heart you are entirely willing to join in any practical efforts against Slavery, then, by your lives, by your conversation, by your influence, by your votes—disregarding "the ancient forms of party strife"—seek to carry the principles of Freedom into the Federal Government, wherever its jurisdiction is acknowledged, and its power can be felt. Thus, without any interference with the States, which are beyond this jurisdiction, may you help to erase the blot of Slavery from our National brow.

Do this, and you will most truly promote that harmony, which you so much desire. You will establish tranquillity throughout the country. Then at last the Slavery Question will be settled. Banished from its usurped foothold under the Federal Government, Slavery will no longer enter, with distracting force, into the national politics—making and unmaking laws, making and unmaking Presidents. Confined to the States, where it was left by the Constitution, it will take its place as a local institution, for which we are in no sense responsible, and against which we cannot justly exert any political power. We shall be relieved from our present painful and irritating connection with it; the existing antagonism between the South and the North will be softened; crimination and recrimination will cease; the wishes of our fathers will be fulfilled; and this Great Evil will be left to the kindly influences of morals and religion.

To every laborer in a cause like this, there are satisfactions unknown to the common political partisan. Amidst all apparent reverses—notwithstanding the hatred of enemies, or the coldness of friends—he has the consciousness of duty done. Whatever may be existing impediments, his also is the cheering conviction, that every word spoken, every act performed, every vote cast for this cause, helps to swell those quickening influences by which Truth, Justice and Humanity will be established upon earth. He may not live to witness the blessed consummation. But it is none the less certain. Others may dwell on the Past, as secure. Under the laws of a beneficent God, *the Future also is secure*—on the single condition that we labor for its great objects.

The language of jubilee, which, amidst reverses and discouragements, burst from the soul of Milton, at the thought of sacrifices for the Church, will be echoed by every one who toils and suffers for Freedom. "Now by this little diligence," says the great patriot of the English Commonwealth, "mark what a privilege with good men and saints, to claim my right of lamenting the tribulations of the Church, if it should suffer, *when others, that have ventured nothing for her sake, have not the honor to be admitted mourners.* But if she lift up her drooping head and prosper, among those that have something more than wished her well, I have my charter and freehold of rejoicing to me and my heirs."

I have spoken of votes. Living in a community where political power is lodged with the people, and where each citizen is an elector, the vote is an important expression of our opinions. The vote is the cutting edge. It is well to have correct opinions; but the vote must follow. The vote is the seed planted; without it there can be no sure fruit. The winds of heaven may in their beneficence scatter the seed in the furrow; but it is not from such accidents that our fields wave with the golden harvest. He is a foolish husbandman who neglects to sow his seed; and he is an unwise citizen, who, desiring the spread of certain principles, neglects to deposit his vote for the candidates who are the representatives of those principles.

Admonished by experience of the timidity, the irresolution, the want of firmness in our public men, particularly at Washington, amidst the temptations of ambition and power, the friends of Freedom cannot lightly bestow their confidence. They can put trust in men only of tried character and inflexible will. Three things at least they must require; the first is *back-bone*; the second is *back-bone*; and the third is *back-bone*. My language is homely; I hardly pardon myself for using it; but it expresses an idea which I would not have forgotten. When I see a person of upright character and pure soul, yielding, to a temporizing policy, I cannot but say, *he wants a back-bone*. When I see a person, talking loudly in private against Slavery, but hesitating in public, and failing in the time of trial, I say *he wants back-bone*. When I see a person, who cooperated with Anti-Slavery men, and then deserted them, I say *he wants a back-bone*. When I see a person, leaning implicitly upon the action of a political party, and never venturing to think for himself, I say *he wants a back-bone*. When I see a person, careful always to be on the side of the majority, and unwilling to appear in a small minority, or, if need be, to stand alone, I say also, *he wants a back-bone*. Wanting this, they all want that courage, constancy, firmness, which are essential to the support of PRINCIPLE. Let no such men be trusted.

For myself, fellow-citizens, my own course is determined. The first political convention which I ever attended was in the spring of 1845, against the annexation of Texas. I was at that time a silent and passive Whig. I had never held any political office, nor been a candidate for any. No question had ever before drawn me to any active political exertions. The strife of politics had seemed ignoble to me. My desire to do what I could against Slavery, led me subsequently to attend two different State Conventions of Whigs, where I cooperated with several eminent citizens in endeavors to arouse the party in Massachusetts to its duties on this subject. A conviction of the disloyalty of the Whig party to Freedom, and an ardent aspiration to contribute something to the advancement of this great cause, led me to leave that party, and to dedicate what of strength and ability I could command to the present Movement.

To vindicate Freedom, and to oppose Slavery, so far as might constitutionally—with earnestness, and yet, I trust, without any personal unkindness on my part—has been the object near my heart. Would that I could impress upon all who now hear me something of the strength of my own conviction of the importance of this work! Would that my voice, leaving this crowded hall to-night, could traverse the hills and valleys of New England,—that it could run along the rivers and the lakes of my country,—lighting in every humane heart a beacon-flame to arouse the slumberers throughout the land in this cause I care not for the name by which I may be called. Let it be democrat, or "loco-foco," if you please. No man who is in earnest will hesitate on account of a name. I shall rejoice in any associates from any quarter, and shall ever be found with that party which most truly represents the principles of Freedom. Others may become indifferent to these principles, bartering them for political success, vain and short-lived, or forgetting the visions of youth in the dreams of age. Whenever I shall forget them, whenever I shall become indifferent to them, whenever I shall cease to be constant in maintaining them, through good report and evil report, in any future combinations of party, then may my tongue cleave to the roof of my mouth, may my right hand forget its cunning!

VII
Impending Crisis

15

"Moral Responsibility of Statesmen" (1854)

Joshua R. Giddings

Joshua R. Giddings (1795–1864) represented Ohio's Western Reserve in the U.S. House of Representatives from 1838–59. Giddings was one of only a handful of true abolitionists to hold a seat in Congress. In 1842 he was censured by the House for his militant antislavery tactics. Giddings resigned his seat, but was immediately reelected by his district and against the opposition of his own party (Whig). At first, Giddings argued that antislavery men should work within the two-party system and not for a strictly abolitionist party. In 1848, he left the Whigs for the Free-Soil Party and then in 1855 he joined the Republicans. In 1861 President Abraham Lincoln appointed Giddings as the U.S. consul general to Canada.

In the speech that follows, Giddings elucidates the responsibility of antislavery statesmen in the face of the Kansas–Nebraska Act and the repeal of the Missouri Compromise.

Mr. Chairman: The long-pending contest between Liberty and Oppression, under this Government, is rapidly approximating a distinct issue. This consideration renders the days in which we live, the scenes which are transpiring in this Hall, important, indeed, *historic*, in their character. I look upon them with deep interest—with peculiar emotions. I have long watched the progress of the great question of humanity, now so suddenly precipitated upon us; and I tender my thanks to those who have forced us into a discussion of the great and fundamental principles on which our political fabric has been reared.

And now, sir, what is the question before us? In the far West, midway between the two great oceans which bound our Republic, is a vast and fertile Territory. Its eastern border is washed by the American "Nile," and its western terminus is on the lofty peaks amid the perennial snows of the Rocky Mountains. Latitudinally it extends from the parallel of 36° 30' to the British possessions on the north.

Long since, our predecessors consecrated this immense Territory to Freedom. More than a generation has passed away since they proclaimed that from it *"Slavery and involuntary servitude be, and the same is hereby,* FOR-EVER *prohibited."* That dedication was *just* and *right.* It was in accordance with God's "higher law." It is right, and just, and proper, *now*, and will remain so while a God of justice shall rule the destiny of nations. It was then binding and obligatory upon all men in all places, is so now, and will remain so in all coming time.

I am not about to argue the propriety or the constitutionality of the other portion of that compromise, which rendered up Missouri to the curse of Slavery. That surrender was *wrong* of itself, *unjust*, opposed to the dictates of our consciences, to God's law, and to the rights of mankind. It remains unjust and criminal, and will continue so eternally. No time can change it; no argument, no sophistry, can modify it. The Northern men who voted for it were rejected by their constituents, and some of them hanged and burned in effigy. But the transaction was perfected and placed beyond recall. It passed into history, and no Northern man, nor statesman, nor jurist, has, by bill, resolution, or speech, denied its force or attempted its repeal. And when gentlemen charge the North with seeking its repeal, or denying its force, they presume too much upon our forbearance.

To this period we have regarded that extensive region as the home of freemen. For more than one-third of a century it has stood like the "bow of promise" in the political heavens, giving assurance that the waves of oppression should never spread over it. Now, sir, we are asked to repeal this prohibition of Slavery, and permit human servitude to curse its soil.

But, before I go further, I propose to define, so far as I can, the institution which is now sought to be extended into that beautiful region: yet there is in our language no terms by which it be properly characterized. The best definition I have seen, is that given by a distinguished Southern jurist, Judge Ruffin of North Carolina, who, on a case which came before him, said: *"A slave is one doomed in his own person and posterity, to live without knowledge, to toil that another may receive the fruits of his labor. The end is the profit of the master; the* MEANS, *the perfect subjection of the slave."*

The first process is to rob the slave of his *intellect*; to shut out from his mind the hope of eternal felicity; seal up the scriptures of truth; draw an impenetrable veil between him and the Gospel; keep from him all knowledge of the duties he owes to himself, his wife, his children, his God; commence the operation in his childhood; dwarf his infant mind; prevent it from expansion, as he increases in years; render his body a machine, as far as possible, without a soul. In short, rob him of his *manhood*. This crime is the most aggravated offence that we are capable of conceiving. It is perpetuated to a greater or less extent on every slave; daily and hourly, from his birth to his death, he is deprived of knowledge; and when he enters the future state, he does so with a mind rendered sterile, unsuited and unprepared for future life. The crime, committed against him reaches into eternity—is carried to the bar of Omnipotence.

The slave must *"toil that another may reap the fruits of his labor."* He is robbed of his labor, from childhood to his grave. Every year, every month, every week, every day, and every hour, he is robbed, of his earnings; though he toil under the lash, the avails of his labor go to enrich his despotic owner. His wife is at all times liable to be sold, from him; his children, handed over like swine to the slave-dealer; and himself transferred from owner to owner, like the brutes that perish.

"The *end*," or object, says the judge, "is the profit of the master; the *means*, the perfect subjection of the slave." The master flogs him at pleasure. Scourges him, and renders him perfectly subject to his own will. To this insult the slave must submit. If, in obedience to the first law of nature, he resist, the master may slay him on the spot. If he run from the master's brutality, the master may shoot him as if he would a dog. The case to which I referred is a good illustration of this point. A female slave had done some slight wrong. Her master attempted to flog her. She ran from him, and he shot her. The master was indicted, and, the Judge, in obedience to the law of Slavery, but against his own feelings, which revolted at the proposition, decided it was the duty of the woman to have submitted to her owner's barbarity; and as she ran from him, he had a right to shoot her.

Will Northern members vote to legislate such murders, such barbarous practices, into Nebraska? Let them answer to God and their constituents.

But the end, the object, of Slavery, is the profit of the master. To render that greater, he may work the slave to the farthest point of endurance; or he may sell him, to be sent to our *American Golgotha,* where an early death awaits him.

We all recollect the case of a man, his wife and child, imprisoned in Covington, Kentucky, some two or three years since, intended for the Southern market. In their lonely dungeon, with no eye upon them but that of God, they contemplated the miseries to which they and their infant were doomed. They preferred death to the slave market. They first murdered the child of their affections, and then, laying violent hands on their own persons, put an end to their earthly existence, and rushed to the presence of their final Judge, and there made an appeal against this institution that we are called on to extend into Nebraska.

Will Northern members vote for such a proposition? Will they bathe their hands in the blood of innocence; participate in "crimes which smell to Heaven," and call for vengeance on this guilty land?

Mr. McNair, (interrupting.) In the event that Slavery should never be carried to Nebraska, what will become of the speech of the gentleman from Ohio?

Mr. Giddings. I answer, that those Northern members who vote for the bill, will, in such event, be stultified on the record. They will have voted to permit these crimes to be committed. They will have incurred the moral guilt and the disgrace of consenting and aiding the commission of these crimes, although the slaveholders should shrink from consummating them, and mankind prove better than gentlemen now think them to be. [Laughter.]

But, I was describing the institution of Slavery, which we are solicited to extend into the Territory in question, and I do not wonder that my friend starts back with affright at the revolting spectacle. Humanity shudders as she contemplates the horrid barbarities of that institution, and Christianity hides her face as she beholds its iniquities; yet, sir, we are asked to repeal the law which prohibits its existence in Nebraska. Will Northern members vote for it? Will my friend from Pennsylvania [Mr. McNair] vote for it?

The illustrations which I have cited are from slave States; cases of public notoriety; reported through the press; never contradicted; and gentlemen will permit me to give one more case, reported through the public press of Mississippi, received as true, and ever, to my knowledge, doubted or denied. If, however, any error has occurred in the report, I see gentlemen from that State present, who will correct it.

A planter was afflicted with a loathsome disease. So offensive were his ulcers, that he was deserted by his white friends; and while thus afflicted and forsaken, a girl whom he owned as a slave kindly and patiently waited upon him, dressed his ulcers, cleansed his person, nursed him, and watched over him until he eventually recovered. With gratitude and affection to his benefactress, he took her to Cincinnati, in our State, executed a deed of manumission, had it recorded, returned to Mississippi, and there married her in legal form. They lived together affectionately for many years; reared a family of children; and, as he lay upon his death-bed, by will he divided his property between his wife and children. His friends, I think his brothers, hearing of his death, came forward and demanded the property. The widow and children were indignant at the demand. They, too, were seized, and the validity of that marriage and will was tried before Judge Sharkey, of that State, who decided that the whole matter was a fraud upon the law of Slavery; that the property belonged to the collateral heirs. His widow was sold by the surviving brothers, the children were bid off at public auction, and both mother and children now toil in chains, or sleep in servile graves.

Gentlemen of the free States: Are you prepared to give your voice in favor of permitting such outrages upon humanities in Nebraska? Let those Northern members who sustain this proposition stand forth before the world, and avow their infidelity to freedom. Let them say boldly that they are willing to assume the infamy of consenting to the perpetration of such iniquities.

These cases are merely specimens of what continually occurs in slaveholding communities. But they show that Slavery is the legalization of every crime known in the catalogue of offences. Yet no language can convey a correct idea of its atrocity. That is beyond description. It arose in a barbarous age, and has come down to us attended with the crimes of a darker period of the world.

As already observed, it is excluded by the act of 1820 from this Territory. It cannot be carried there without the consent, without the votes of *Northern Representatives.* No argument, no sophistry, no evasion, can avoid this obvious fact. To vote for the repeal of the Missouri compromise, is to vote for the abolition of Freedom, and in favor of permitting these crimes in Nebraska. It will involve those who vote for it in all the guilt attending that institution. It will be in vain for gentlemen to say they leave the people of Nebraska to commit the crime if they choose! If you, gentlemen, stand by, and consent that your fellow man may, if he choose, commit murder, you will be hanged with him. You will deserve the same fate he receives. If you consent that slave markets shall be opened up in that Territory; that men shall there be bought and sold, robbed of their toil, their intellects brutalized, shot down and murdered; if you vote to repeal this Missouri prohibition for the very purpose of enabling others to commit these offences, will you be less guilty before Heaven than those by whose hands these murders and other crimes are committed? Will not the blood of these victims stain your garments?

The gentleman from New Hampshire, [Mr. Hibbard,] I thought, spoke feelingly of the people for having hanged in effigy the Northern members of Congress who consented to spread the curse of human bondage over Missouri, and also of those who now hang in effigy members of the Senate who labor to spread these God-defying crimes over that Territory. Now, sir, I am willing that the people shall act as their judgments dictate in such matters. Of the propriety of such symbolical executions, they are the proper judges. If a member here does that which the people think compares in moral guilt with legal murder, let them pass sentence, and, if they please, typify the execution by hanging the man in effigy, provided they do not violate the public peace.

The gentleman spoke of the clergy in terms of strong condemnation of this great iniquity. I shall not stop here to defend those clergymen. The blow was aimed at the doctrine of holding us responsible for our official conduct. It was aimed at *religion,* at God's "higher law," so often denied in the other end of the Capitol and in this Hall; so often sneered at and ridiculed by gentlemen who vote to legalize crimes revolting to our natures. Had the clergy of New England and other portions of the country omitted to do all in their power to prevent the consummation of this iniquitous bill, they would have shown themselves unworthy of their profession. We shall have regarded them as *"moral cowards,"* apostates from that gospel whose Divine Author offered up his life for the promulgation of truth.

We are told here, and in the other end of the Capitol, that the clergy should attend to their flocks; that they should not interfere in politics; that religion and politics are separate matters. The argument is worthy of the occasion. It is perfectly natural that men should endeavor to shield themselves from exposure. But I ask: Is it possible that, in this age, enlightened statesmen can suppose themselves shielded from moral and religious responsibility while acting here? Do they flatter themselves that their actions are hidden from the *Searcher of all hearts?* Do they regard themselves less guilty in the sight of Heaven, when they vote to permit the people of Nebraska to sell men and women, than they would be, were they to go there themselves and deal in human flesh? If they vote to permit men in Nebraska to scourge and brutalize our fellow beings, are not such members as really tyrants at heart as Nero or Nicholas? If they vote to allow men in Nebraska to shoot down and murder their slaves, are such members less guilty than those wretches who expiate less aggravated crimes upon the gallows?

I repeat, that Slavery is now prohibited in Nebraska, and if it be extended into that Territory, it must be by aid of Northern votes, given by men who *intervene* for the purpose of repealing the prohibition of 1820. No subtle logic, no vague pretences, can excuse members from this responsibility. The record of our votes will go down to those who succeed us; our children will read it with pride or with shame.

Yes, sir, we are told that the President has warmly espoused the policy of extending Slavery into Nebraska. The Senate, by a large majority, have passed the bill before us. All the Southern members of this body, aided by Northern serviles, are in favor of it. I said all the Southern members are in favor of it. I was in error. There are a few honorable exceptions—men who, in my humble judgment, possess the foresight and judgment of statesmen. They appear to foresee the evils which the passage of this bill will bring upon the Territory.

But, Mr. Chairman, as if effrontery had no limits, we are gravely told that it is *unconstitutional thus to exclude Slavery from this Territory!* I, sir, shall not occupy the time of this House to vindicate Monroe, and Calhoun, and Adams, and Wirt, and Clay, and all the venerable statesmen who approved this measure, from the charge of stupidity and ignorance now brought against them by ephemeral politicians.

Sir, to argue the unconstitutionality of the consecration of this Territory to Freedom, is an imputation upon the intelligence of the founders of our Republic, as well as upon the intelligence of the people. The framers of the Ordinance of 1787 had no scruples on this subject. They recognized the duty of Governments to protect the liberties of the people. The preamble to that ordinance says:

"*And for extending the fundamental principles of civil and religious liberty, which form the basis whereon these Republics, their laws and constitutions, are erected; to fix and establish these principles as the basis of all laws, constitutions, and governments, which forever hereafter shall be formed in the said Territory,*" "It is hereby ordained,"&c.

These doctrines are now denied. Slavery is declared by statesmen of this day to constitute the basis on which "all laws, constitutions, and governments, which hereafter shall be formed in Nebraska *ought to rest.*"

But, sir, this is a new discovery. At the last session of Congress, a bill to organize a Government in this Territory was reported from the Committee on Territories. When it came up for discussion, an honorable member from Pennsylvania [John W. Howe] called on me, as a member of that committee, to state why a special proviso had not been inserted in the bill, excluding Slavery. In reply, I read the eighth section of the act of 1820, and stated that that law excluded Slavery from the Territory in question and that its re-enactment would give it no greater validity than it then possessed. This, sir, was done openly, publicly, before the House. No one denied my doctrines, none doubted my correctness. All admitted the accuracy of my statement by their silent acquiescence; and the bill passed this body, I think, by a majority of more than two-thirds. But now they have suddenly become zealous to preserve the Constitution, by repealing this law of 1820. What new light has fallen upon them? What new views of constitutional law have they received? Where were those views obtained? Sir, I regard this pretence a sheer deception, an attempt to mislead the people, who will so regard it.

We are also told that the consummation of this outrage *will quiet agitation, and settle the slave question forever.* Gentlemen admit that its introduction has caused a deeper and more intense feeling in the free States than has ever before been manifested; yet, they urge that its *consummation* will satisfy the popular mind. Now, sir, I cannot, and will not, argue this point with gentlemen who entertain such contempt of the popular intelligence. For twenty years, this House has endeavored to silence agitation among the people, by legislation for slavery.

When they sent us their respectful petitions, we threw them back in their faces, and closed our doors against that constitutional right of the people. We next struck down the freedom of debate; and as the people became more and more aroused to the assertion and agitation of their rights, we adopted gag-rules, arraigned members like felons at the bar of the House, for daring to assert our constitutional obligations. As the people still moved in favor of liberty, we legislated more intensely for Slavery, in order to silence agitation. In 1850, we passed the most corrupt laws which ever disgraced a free Government, to *silence agitation.* I refer to the Fugitive Slave Law, under which so much blood has been shed. Yet, sir, agitation increased; and your Baltimore platforms were adopted, and both of the great political parties pledged themselves solemnly "to resist and deprecate all agitation of the slave question, here and elsewhere, in Congress and out of it." Yet, the people became more and more engaged for freedom; and now the advocates of oppression tell us, if we will but pass this bill, consummate this greatest indignity upon humanity, upon freedom, upon the constitution, that has ever been committed, the people will feel themselves sufficiently reproved, and, like the fawning spaniel, will crouch at our feet.

Sir, I repel the foul slander. I feel indignant at the proposition. It is a libel upon the people of the free States. *Who are we?* The *servants* of the people; created by their breath; sent here to do their will; and when they summon us, we surrender our political existence. Yet, sir, we are told that we must play the tyrant, to silence the popular voice. Sir, you may as well attempt to tear the sun from the heavens, or to dam up Niagara's mighty torrent with your fingers. The people will govern *us*, will silence *our* agitation, but *we* shall never control agitation among them, except by doing our duty—by obeying their will.

Mr. Chairman, who does not know that the Southern and servile presses are already proclaiming, that when this bill shall have been passed, Slavery shall next be admitted into Minnesota, Washington, and Oregon? Who does not know that the president and Cabinet are laboring to prepare the public mind for a war upon Spain, with the undisguised purpose of maintaining Slavery in Cuba?—that they are prepared to sacrifice the lives of our citizens by thousands, in order to stay the progress of civilization in that island?—that the whole Administration press of the country sustains these Executive views?—that Southern papers insist that we shall also conquer St. Domingo, and restore Slavery there; then form an alliance with slaveholding Brazil, as the only nation, besides ours, that legalizes the crimes attendant upon the "peculiar institution?"—that we shall then restore the African slave trade, and thus disgrace our Government and sink it to a piratical power for propagating oppression and crime?

While these plans are put forth through the public press, we are constrained to listen to exhortations to pass this bill, in order to *silence agitation*, again to cheat Northern men with false pretences. Sir, these efforts to defeat the objects, the ulterior designs, of those who founded this Republic, to overthrow our Constitution and trample upon the principles of humanity and justice, is a gross, flagrant, and unqualified attempt at *revolution.* It is treason to humanity, treason to liberty, treason to the Constitution. Yet, all this is doing under the disguise of attempting to *silence agitation,* again to render us dupes of the slave power. We know from official messages that the President is desirous of entering upon such a war with Spain; that he is willing to sacrifice the lives of thousands of our own people, to stay the progress of freedom under a foreign Government. He is prepared to offer up hecatombs of his countrymen, to maintain oppression and crime in other lands.

Nor are his abettors less guilty. I refer to those *"Swiss guards,"* who are ever ready to fight for oppression, for anything, if thereby they can obtain Executive favors. I know of no worse enemies to freedom, none more unfriendly or dangerous to free institutions. They are worse traitors to liberty than were the Tories of the Revolution; and the time is not far distant when they will be so branded by popular sentiment. Pass this bill; commence your war with Spain; sacrifice the commerce of the free States to this cause of Slavery in Cuba; send your army and navy there; let our men be shot down by emancipated slaves, and then tell me I have overestimated the Northern spirit. If the avowed designs of the President be carried forward, we shall not wait long to witness bloodshed in our own country. Indeed, we have seen *that,* under the compromise acts of 1850. But the excitement arising from the question before us has rendered it impossible to execute the Fugitive Slave Law in the northern portions of the free States. At this moment, I do not believe the whole army of the nation could execute that law in Northern Ohio. Sir, it is notorious, that people already bid defiance to your laws and your power. They look upon Congress with suspicion; and woe be to the public men who, in such an hour as this, shall betray this Government into a barbarous and piratical war for maintaining and extending human bondage. The remedy for these things rest with the people of the North. They must commence the work by passing sentence, and by the political *execution* of the entire *genus* called DOUGHFACES. Then, agitation may cease.

We are also told that this prohibition of Slavery interferes with the right of the people to *"govern themselves."* In other words, the logic of those who advocate this measure amounts to this: that "self-government" includes the privilege of buying, selling, flogging, and robbing, such men and women as they can subject to their power. They do not include under the term "people," those who have been so unfortunate as to be born of mothers who have been enslaved. If their fathers were the first men in the State of Virginia, if they themselves possess intellects far superior to our own, yet slaveholders and doughfaces deny that they possess any rights. They are not to be called *"people."* They insist that such persons have no right to participate in the privilege of *"self-government,"* nor of "self-protection." Sir, the very object of this prohibition was to *secure* to *all* the people who go to Nebraska the enjoyment of "equal rights;" and on this account, and no other, do gentlemen seek to repeal it. The member who votes for this bill will thereby exhibit his hatred of "popular sovereignty," of "equal laws."

As remarked, the Congress of 1787 adopted an Ordinance for the government of the Northwest Territory. There were, at that time, perhaps less than fifty electors resident there, probably about the same number now in Nebraska. Yet these few required protection. Congress was bound to give it, as we are now. They legislated, however, as much for those who were expected to go into the Territory after the adoption of the Ordinance as for those then settled there. So do we. It would not be right for fifty men now in Nebraska to legislate for ten thousand who are to go there next year. That would not be giving the ten thousand equal privileges with those now there. We give them a Legislature, with authority to pass certain laws not incompatible with the laws of the United States. We then extend over them the law to prohibit murder. While the friends of this bill are proclaiming here and through all their presses the doctrine of *"non-intervention,"* we expressly intervene to prohibit larceny; we intervene to prohibit *robbery* and all other crimes, unless committed under the law of Slavery. The law of 1820 prohibits the commission of those crimes also. This prohibition we are called on to repeal, under pretence of *"non-intervention."*

Why, sir, this bill commences, continues, and closes, with intervention. It is itself one continued series of interventions. It authorizes the President to appoint a Governor and judges for the Territory, and yet its advocates proclaim "non-intervention," the right of "self-government," as the grand distinguishing features of the bill. It prohibits the Legislature from passing any laws affecting the rights of property or of persons pertaining to the Indians. It establishes the "per diem" of the members at precisely three dollars, but does not permit them to estimate the value of their own services. This, too, is called "non-intervention." The bill establishes the salaries of the judges and other officers, but will not permit the people to do it. Yet its advocates proclaim themselves the peculiar friends of "POPULAR SOVEREIGNTY." It goes further, and under the clamor of non-intervention," of *popular sovereignty,* it prohibits the Legislature from taxing the land of non-residents beyond the amount levied on their own. But its next "intervention" is to repeal the prohibition of Slavery, in order that a portion of the people may hold in bondage such persons, either black or white, as the Legislature may see fit to enslave.

It has ever been, and is now, the plain and obvious duty of all Governments to intervene to the full extent of all their just powers for the protection of mankind from oppression, injustice, and crime.

The whole eternity of the past has brought to us no instruction more important than this duty of Governments. In the darker periods of man's existence, brute force constituted his only safety. Go to the continent of Europe; visit the ancient castles, erected at a period when moral and political darkness covered the world. Those frowning towers were erected at immense expense, for the purpose of protecting their inmates from violence. They tell us of a period when right was maintained by physical means, by massive walls, by coats of mail, by the sword, and by the lance. These were confided in as the only protection of their owners. Those mighty fortresses are now deserted; dilapidation and ruin mark the crumbling masses. The light of civilization taught mankind that reason, "just and equal laws," are more powerful than granite walls, than coats of mail, or swords, or spears. Protected by just and enlightened laws, each man may sit under his own vine and fig-tree, and there will be none to molest or make him afraid.

Sir, I repeat, it is this safety, this protection to each and every individual, which constitutes the object, the end, and design, of all Governments. Nor is this duty confined to Governments; it attaches to individuals. Wherever I am, if I see my fellow man, who is weak, beset by the strong, either for the purpose of robbery, revenge, or murder, it becomes my duty to protect him, so far as I can safely do so. The moral duty continues far beyond the reach of municipal law. I am morally bound to protect my fellow man, if in my power, from accident, from wild beasts, from storm and tempest, from cold and hunger, aye, from the machinations of slaveholders and doughfaces, from petty despots, and from those who would play the tyrant over him. But the Senate, by passing the bill before us, has clearly denied that this duty of protection extends to the people of that Territory. A portion of this body, and I think a majority, agree with the Senate. It is also said, on all sides, that the President and Cabinet unite in the opinion that "non-intervention" shall be the policy of this Government. I therefore arrive at the conclusion, that if this bill becomes a law, Congress will not protect the weak and oppressed who shall hereafter reside there. On the contrary, the bill in distinct language repeals the law which now protects them, and leaves a portion of the people who shall go there, to oppress and enslave another portion, if they choose to do so.

Now, sir, if Congress refuses such protection, by adopting the policy of "NON-INTERVENTION," it will leave to the slaves there the right and the duty to protect *themselves*. It will be the duty of other men, to the extent of their power, to aid them in the laudable work of protecting their lives and liberties.

The thousands of American citizens, of Germans, of French, of English, of Scotch, and Irish, who have come to this country to enjoy a *free* Government and "equal laws, will sympathize with the oppressed; and as they go to Nebraska and Kansas, by thousands and tens of thousands, let them go *with arms in their hands.* I would from this forum speak to them as one who is in earnest on this subject; one who deeply feels the dishonor which this bill will bring upon our country. I would say to them, Go there, prepared to defend the democratic principle of "equal laws," of *"protection to all";* go there, recognising the great truth that *"all men are endowed by their Creator with the inalienable right to life, liberty, and happiness";* go there, determined to make it a free land; determined that you will not associate with *slaves,* nor with slaveholders; that you repudiate every tyrant, every oppressor. Tell the slave who comes there, his rights; teach him his obligations to himself; put arms into his hands; instruct him in their use, and the best mode of protecting himself. Tell him that *"non-intervention"* is the policy of Congress. Were I a resident of that Territory, and slaves were held in bondage around me, I would do by them as I would have them do by me, were I in their condition. I would supply them with arms, and teach them to use all the means which God and nature has placed within their control to maintain their freedom and their manhood.

Again, Mr. Chairman, I feel some desire to expose the statesmanship of this Administration. They have openly adopted the policy of "NON-INTERVENTION": they have tied their hands, and when the Americans, and Germans, and French, and English, who emigrate to Nebraska and Kansas, shall put arms into the hands of the slaves, and the colored men shall drive back the slaveholders, killing some and frightening others, we shall have exclamations of horror from Southern members, and from the President, calling for an army to put down the civil war which will then be going on. But, sir, do you not think that one general, united exclamation of *"non-intervention"* will then come from the North? Will they not hold the chalice, which you have prepared, to slaveholding lips? Will they not hold you to your present policy?

Southern gentlemen complain of this prohibition also, for the reason, as they say, that it precludes them from carrying their *property* (meaning slaves) into the Territory. I can half excuse Southern members for thus attempting to degrade the likeness of God to the level of swine. They are bred up to the practice of calling men and women *"property."* It sounds less harshly than *slave*. But we can find no such excuse for Northern members who designate their fellow men by the term *property.*

He who bestowed on us his own image, demands that we shall maintain the dignity of our race. If we revere God, we must respect his image. Man in his rudest state has ever refused to become the property of his brother. In no age, in no clime, has man peacefully surrendered himself to become the property of his fellow man. No people have yet been found so low in the scale of moral being as to omit defending their lives and their liberties when in their power to do so. To call men property is a libel upon ourselves. The framers of our constitution rejected such abuse of language. Mr. Madison said it would be *wrong* to admit in the Constitution *"that man could hold property in man."*

We are charitaby bound to believe gentlemen acquainted with facts so familiar to us all. It is true, however, that one gentleman attempted to argue the point, and said we could not tell the origin of property in brutes. It was evident his knowledge of Scripture was limited. Had he read his Bible more carefully, he would have learned that, early in the history of our race, *"God gave to man dominion over the fish of the sea, and over the fowl of the air, and over all the beasts of the field."* But, Mr. Chairman, he never gave man dominion over his fellow man. He created us in His own image; and God, and man, and nature, must abhor these attempts to degrade that form to the level of the beasts of the field.

But perhaps the views of gentlemen ought not to be commented on with too much severity. For, if reports be true, some of these members have *sold themselves,* at prices, perhaps, below that often paid for Southern negroes. I could tell of some rare conversions to the support of this measure; some quite as sudden, if not as miraculous, as that of St. Paul. But I prefer to withhold names until the vote shall be given, and the Executive appointment made. These names will then be published. I speak of it at this time, that Northern members who vote for this bill may understand that the eye of the public is upon them. It is time that this slave trade now carried on in the bodies of members of Congress should be prohibited.

Why, sir, for the first time in the history of our Government, the President has come out through the columns of his organ, the "Union," of this city, and advertised for the purchase of members of Congress. I refer to an article in that paper some weeks since, stating, in substance, that if Northern members, by sustaining this bill, incurred the displeasure of their constituents, the President would sustain them by Executive favors. This was the substance of a long article, in which Executive appointments were unblushingly tendered, through the public press, to buy up Northern doughfaces; to purchase the very men who now designate their fellow men as *"property."* I do not wonder that they entertain low opinions of mankind, and term their brethren *"property."* But they should remember that no colored man ever degraded his race by *selling himself!*

Sir, I feel humbled as an American, when I reflect upon this disgraceful practice, now so openly followed, of buying up members by the assurance of Executive favors. Without such resort, no man would expect this bill to succeed. It is *moral bribery.* The guilt is as great, aye, greater, than it would be if both parties were subjected to punishment under municipal laws. Standing, as we do, in high official stations, no State or municipal law can punish these corruptions. We are therefore responsible only to the people and to God. Their eyes, however, are upon us, and their judgment cannot be evaded.

Again, Mr. Chairman, we are told that this prohibition of Slavery marks the slaveholding portion of this Union as lower in their moral sentiments, and inferior to the people of the free States in their sense of justice and their duties to mankind.

Gentlemen of the South must know, the civilized world must know, that we do regard slaveholders far beneath the advocates of Freedom, in their sense of moral obligations. Why, sir, the institution has been discarded from the free States solely on account of its barbarous character. For the same reason, it was repudiated by England, by France, and by nearly all the civilized world. Indeed, the semi-barbarians of Tunis, of Egypt, and other Mahometan Governments have repudiated it. The exercise of power by one man over another, the flogging of women, the selling and buying of men, the rearing of slave children for market, the shooting of slaves, are all revolting to the conscience, corrupting to public morals, and degrading to those who participate in such wickedness.

I would call the attention of gentlemen to cases, officially reported, where the slaveholder often inherits, and sells as slaves, the children of his brother. Often he inherits and sells as slaves the children of his father. And popular judgment has been in great error if men in this city, almost under the shadow of our Capitol, have not perpetrated still greater outrages on public morals. These crimes are all legalized by the law of Slavery, and no slaveholding community is protected from them.

To surrender this vast Territory to Slavery, will exclude free men from it; for, as I have said, free laborers, bred up with feelings of self-respect, cannot and will not mingle with slaves. For these reasons, it is most obvious that the character of the States to be carved out of this Territory will be determined by that of the Government now to be established. If the Territory be settled by slaveholders, the States will of course be slaveholding States. When admitted as such, they will hold an influence in this Government according to the number of their slaves; and the man who goes there with five slaves will add to the influence of his State in the Federal Government, as much as four of our educated and intelligent freemen of the North. The petty despot who holds in bondage, in ignorance, in brutal stupidity, one hundred of his fellow beings, will wield as much influence as sixty-one of our Northern freemen. Are gentlemen willing thus to bring down their constituents to the level of slaves? Are they elected here by men deserving such moral and political degradation? It is said, however, that if the slaves were free, they would increase the apportionment of Representatives; and the number of members of Congress, from the States holding slaves, would be greater than it now is. That is true; but in such case, the Representatives would exert their influence in favor of Freedom and not of Slavery. Their objects and ours would be the same—the elevation of man, and the progress of Liberty. But let them represent slaveholding constituencies, and they will, to the extent of their power, legislate for Slavery, and *against* Liberty.

Mr. Chairman, it has become obvious to all, that these conflicting institutions of Freedom and Slavery cannot flourish together under the same Government. They can never be reconciled. They ever have been, they are now, and ever will be, at war with each other. Virtue and crime will not commingle; Heaven and Hell cannot be at peace. This Federal Government must be either separated from the support of Slavery, and set apart to the maintenance of Liberty, leaving the "peculiar institution" entirely with the States in which it exists, or we must give it up to the control of the Slave Power. No proposition can be plainer. Every indication shows this to be the case. The free States have taken position. Will they re-consecrate this beautiful Territory to Freedom? Will they spread liberty, prosperity, contentment, Christianity, over it? Shall the school-house and the church be found there? Shall well-cultivated fields and beautiful dwellings greet the eye of the traveller, as he passes over it? Shall the physical and intellectual powers of our race be developed, and man exalted, throughout that immense country?

Or shall this goodly land be delivered over to oppression? Shall clanking chains, and sighs, and groans, and bitter moanings, be heard through its wide extent? Shall slave markets supply the place of churches and school-houses? Shall waste and dilapidation spread themselves over it? Shall wrong, injustice, and crime, be encouraged and protected there?

These questions are addressed to us. The responsibility of answering them must be met. Are we the men for the occasion? If we act for that which we know to be right, in accordance with our conscience, with Heaven's law, we shall hereafter enjoy the consolation of having done our duty, and the people in that Territory "will hereafter rise up and call us blessed."

But if we repeal this prohibition, and extend Slavery, with its crimes, over that beautiful country, we must expect the condemnation of mankind, and of our own consciences. Our names will go down to posterity associated with oppression, with all the moral guilt attached to an act so unjust and wicked. And as the suffering slave shall in future years bow himself to his unending toil, or shriek under the lash, or see his wife and children sold like brutes, his bitter curses upon our names and memories will mingle with his invocations for deliverance from the torments to which our votes will have consigned him.

16

"What Is My Duty as an Anti-Slavery Voter?" and "Fremont and Dayton" (1856)

Frederick Douglass

In April 1856, Frederick Douglass published an essay supporting the candidacy of Gerrit Smith of the Radical Abolitionist Party for president of the United States. The Radical Abolitionist Party was a fringe political party made up of the remnants of the old Liberty Party and Liberty League. Remarkably, four months later, Douglass reversed his decision and came out in favor of John C. Fremont and William L. Dayton, the presidential and vice-presidential candidates of the newly created Republican Party.

These two essays read together will give students a glimpse into the difficult moral and tactical dilemmas faced by abolitionists as they confronted the prospect of the extension of slavery into the territories. Douglass, and many like him, were forced to choose between fidelity to their abolitionist moral principles or temporarily setting aside those principles in order to fight a clear and present danger.

"What Is My Duty as an Anti-Slavery Voter?"

There are, and have been, for the last dozen years, a band of conscientious men in this country, who have insisted upon casting their votes at the Ballot-Box in a manner fully to indicate their earnest desire for the abolition of Slavery. To these, the old Liberty Party of eight years ago, furnished the required platform, and the natural channels of political cooperation. Under the Banner of this party, with many, or with few, they felt at home, and ready to fall or flourish. It was a noble party, and was animated by a noble spirit. That party, as such, has almost vanished. Its members are scattered, and its old armor has been borne off to a party with another name, and of another spirit. Led by the Barnburners of New York, it supported Martin Van Buren for the Presidency in 1848. Since then, it has been in the wilderness, wandering in darkness. Active, to be sure, but making little progress towards the great end which combined its original elements. A portion of those who have filled the ranks of this wandering army, are beginning to raise the enquiry which heads this article.

The aggressive front of Slavery, openly declaring for the entire mastery of the country—the ready enrollment of the Democratic and Know Nothing parties in the boldest enterprises of Slavery—the shocking outrages perpetrated in Kansas—and the evident determination of the Slave Power to make slaveholding and slave-buying and selling the law of the whole land—have suggested the propriety of giving up the more radical and comprehensive measures of Abolitionists at the Ballot-Box, and the adoption of some one measure, upon which a large and important party can be united and organized to meet the Slave Power.

It is against this suggestion that we propose to offer a few remarks—remarks which, though coming from an humble source, may yet be deemed entitled to consideration by some sincere enquirer for the right way.

1. The ultimate success of the Anti-Slavery movement depends upon nothing, under God, more than upon the soundness of its principles, the earnestness, stringency and faithfulness with which they are enforced, and the integrity, consistency and disinterestedness of those who stand forth as its advocates. The purity of the cause is the success of the cause. There can be very little necessity for sustaining this proposition by argument. We rely upon honesty, and not dishonesty, to uproot injustice and wrong. This element of power can be rallied and enlisted by its like—and only by its like.—"Men will not serve God if the Devil bid them"—and hence the necessity for purity and consistency in all who seek to leave the world better than they found it. The first duty of the Reformer is to be right. If right, he may go forward; but if wrong, or partly wrong, he is as an house divided against itself, and will fall. He will move, if he moves at all, like a man in fetters, and to no valuable purpose. To succeed against Slavery, the public must be brought to respect Anti-Slavery; and it cannot be respected unless consistent with itself, and its advocates are conscientiously consistent with it. The country must be made to feel the pulsation of an enlightened conscience, animating, supporting and directing that cause, before they will own it and bless it as a cause entitled to triumph.

2. That the National Republican party, around whose standard Abolitionists are now called upon to rally, does *not* occupy this high Anti-Slavery ground, (and what is worse, does not mean to occupy it,) is most painfully evident. From the hour that the old Liberty Party was swallowed up by the Van Buren Free Soil party in '48, the work of deterioration began, and has been continued until now. Instead of going upward, the political Anti-Slavery sentiment has been going downward. The Buffalo platform in '48 was lower than that of the Liberty Party; and the Pittsburgh platform of '56, is

lower than that of '52. But not only is this deterioration shown in the platform of the Pittsburgh Convention, recently adopted. It is painfully manifest in the spirit of the Convention itself. There was a spirit of cold calculation, of deliberate contriving, so to pair off the edge of Anti-Slavery truth, and so to arrange and dispose of Anti-Slavery principles, as to draw into the Republican ranks men of all parties and sentiments, except the men of the Administration party. No man could have been found in the Republican Convention, held in Pittsburgh four years ago, bold enough to have proposed a slaveholder—an actual man stealer—to preside over that Convention of Anti-Slavery men. Such a proposition would have been scouted as an insult to the Anti-Slavery sentiment of the North. Then the tone of the speeches made on the occasion was lower and weaker than on any former occasion. The Anti-Slavery creed, after the filtration of this Convention, came out simply a measure to restore the restriction against Slavery to Kansas and Nebraska. Nothing said of the Fugitive Slave Bill—nothing said of Slavery in the District of Columbia—nothing said of the slave trade between States—nothing said of giving the dignity of the nation to Liberty—nothing said of securing the rights of citizens, from the Northern States, in the constitutional right to enter and transact business in the slave States. There is not a single warm and living position, taken by the Republican party, except freedom for Kansas. We need not ask Radical Anti-Slavery men if this is the natural and desirable tendency of the political Anti-Slavery sentiment of the country. They instinctively recoil from it, as destructive of the great purpose of the Anti-Slavery movement of the country. They can only be induced to follow after the Republican movement under the teachings of a plausible and sinuous political philosophy, which is the grand corrupter of all reforms. The substance of this philosophy is, that the one thing needful, the thing to precede all else, is a large party; and in order to do this, we are at liberty to abandon almost everything but a name. Parties of this kind serve certain leading ones who get into office by them; but they seldom advance the cause that gave them birth.

3. We hold that the true mode to prevent this falling away from Anti-Slavery truth and duty, and to save the Anti-Slavery movement from utter destruction, is to support candidates for the Presidency and Vice Presidency, of tried Anti-Slavery character, and of decided Anti-Slavery principles. This is the true path of Anti-Slavery duty. The Anti-Slavery voters of the country must not allow themselves to be transferred from one political demagogue to another, until all vitality shall have departed from them. Nothing can be more certain, than that the habitual accommodation of Anti-Slavery men to the men opposed to them, has weakened the self-respect of the Anti-Slavery party, and awakened the contempt of their opponents. The slaveholders themselves, seeing how ready we are to chase shadows, and to fight men of straw,

are perpetually leading us away from the main issue by these trifles.—We must show the slaveholders, and the country, that we are in earnest, and cannot be drawn away from our legitimate work. For this reason, we shall look to Syracuse, rather than to Philadelphia, for the candidates to be supported in the next Presidential election. With the party at Syracuse, principles are more precious than numbers—and hence our cause is more safe there than elsewhere.

4. But it is said that by casting our votes for a man who duly represents our Radical Anti-Slavery sentiments, in the coming Presidential election, we shall probably give the Government into the hands of the Democratic Party, and thereby establish Slavery in Kansas, thus depriving the North of a Free State, and adding its power to the Slave States—the better enabling the latter to perpetuate Slavery.—This is very evidently a grave argument, and cannot be lightly disposed of. It is meet that it should be duly considered. Suppose, then, that by voting as above, the result, which is possible, should occur—Slavery should be established in Kansas, and Kansas added to the Slave States. It then becomes us to estimate the loss which freedom would sustain, not as against the saving of Kansas to freedom, but as against the evils which would arise from the policy, which it is relied on, will save Kansas to freedom. This is the only consistent and certain method by which to arrive at the path of Duty in the premise. Looking at the matter from this point then, we hold, that great as would be the misfortune to liberty should Kansas be given to Slavery, tenfold greater would be the misfortune, should Kansas be saved by means which must certainly demoralize the Anti-Slavery sentiment of the North, and render it weak and inefficient for the greater work of saving the entire country to Liberty. Keep in mind the fact that our aim is the entire abolition of Slavery; that our work is not done till this is done; and that the real importance of establishing freedom in Kansas, is to be found in its effect to establish freedom in the country at large. We deliberately prefer the loss of Kansas to the loss of our Anti-Slavery integrity. With Kansas saved, and our Anti-Slavery integrity gone, our cause is ruined. With Kansas lost, and our Anti-Slavery integrity saved, we have, at least, means left us with which to continue the war upon Slavery, and of final victory.

5. But this is arguing at great disadvantage, far greater than our position requires. We have granted more than there is any absolute necessity for granting. It is by no means certain that Kansas can be saved by the Republican Party, even with the votes of Abolitionists. Freedom in Kansas depends, less upon politics, than upon the Anti-Slavery sentiment of the North, and the Anti-Slavery integrity of those who settle that Territory from the North.—Dark indeed would be the prospect of freedom in Kansas, if it depended entirely upon the election of a Republican President for the next four years.

If that is to decide the question, Slavery has very little to fear and everything to hope. Republican enthusiasm may predict the election of a Republican President, but the calmer reason of that party must pronounce it strongly improbable. With the South united, and the North divided, it is easy to see which side will be victorious at the Polls. Republicans will have an enemy to contend with at the North, which will require all its strength, flinging the South out of the question. Again we might claim that a strong vote for Radical Abolitionists would far more certainly help freedom in Kansas than a much stronger vote for the Republicans would do.

The whole Slave population of this country whether in States, Territories, dock yards, or on the high seas, must be emancipated. For this the true friends of the Slave must toil and hope, and for nothing less than this. It is short-sighted, as a matter of policy, to aim lower than this, and it is cruel to those bleeding millions to do so. Our God, our country and the slave, alike have called us to this great work, and we cannot come down from it to mingle in a less comprehensive or a less commanding struggle. Slavery is a sin now, a sin at all times, and a sin everywhere; and as we hold all human enactments designed to sustain it as of no binding authority, and utterly contrary to the Constitution of the United States, the coast is clear for an open, and direct war upon Slavery everywhere in the United States.—But should we not do one thing at a time?—Yes, one thing at a time; but let that thing be the abolition of Slavery. It is not doing one thing at a time, in any important sense, to limit the domain of Slavery, and to leave its continuance unlimited. It is not doing one thing at a time to establish Freedom for the white citizen in Kansas, and to hunt the black citizen from it, like a wolf; and if it is doing one thing at a time to do this, we hold that a strong vote for the Radical Abolition candidate is the best way to accomplish that one thing at a time.—"Freedom for all, or chains for all."

"Fremont and Dayton"

The readers of our journal will observe that the honored names which, for some time, stood at the head of our columns, as its candidates for the president and vice-president of the United States, have been withdrawn and although no other names have been or shall be placed at the head of our columns, we deem it proper frankly to announce our purpose to support, with whatever influence we possess, little or much, John C. Fremont and William L. Dayton, the candidates of the Republican Party for the presidency and vice-presidency of the United States, in the present political canvass.

To a part of our readers, this announcement, considering our previous position, will be an unwelcome surprise. We have, hitherto, advocated the best of our ability, a course of political action inconsistent with our present course. It is, therefore, eminently fit that we should accompany the foregoing announcement with something like a statement of reasons for our newly adopted policy.

1. A step so important as to lead to a separation in action, at least, between ourselves and of loved, honored, and tried friends, should not be hastily or inconsiderately taken. In full view of this truth, we have with much care examined and re-examined the subject of our political relations and duties regarding Slavery and the colored people of the United States. Our position, as well as the suggestion of wisdom just referred to, very naturally cause hesitation. The name of Gerrit Smith has long been synonymous with us as genuine, unadulterated Abolitionism. Of all men beneath the sky, we would rather see this just man made President. Our heart and judgment cling and twine around this man and his counsels as the ivy to the oak. To differ from him, and the beloved friends who may still intend to vote for him at the approaching election, is the result only of stern and irresistible conviction, the voice of which we cannot feel ourselves at liberty to disregard.

2. The time has passed for an honest man to attempt any defence of a right to change his opinion as to political methods of opposing Slavery. Anti-Slavery consistency itself, in our view, requires of the Anti-Slavery voter that disposition of his vote and his influence, which, in all the circumstances and likelihoods of the case tend most to the triumph of Free Principles in the Councils and Government of the nation. It is not to be consistent to pursue a course politically this year, merely because that course seemed the best last year, or at any previous time. Right Anti-Slavery action is that which deals the severest deadliest blow upon Slavery that can be given at that particular time. Such action is always consistent, however different may be the forms through which it expresses itself.

3. Again, in supporting Fremont and Dayton, we are in no wise required to abandon a single Anti-Slavery Truth or Principle which we have hitherto cherished, and publicly advocated. The difference between our paper this week and last week is a difference of Policy, not of Principle. Hereafter, as hitherto, we shall contend for every principle, and maintain [mutilated] the platform of the Radical Abolitionists. The unconstitutionality of Slavery, the illegality of Slavery, the Right of the Federal Government to abolish Slavery in every part of the Republic, whether in States or Territories, will be as firmly held, and as sternly insisted upon, as hitherto. Nor do we wish, by supporting the Republican Candidate in the approaching election, to be understood as merging our individuality, body and soul, into that Party, nor as separating ourselves from our Radical Abolition friends in their present endeavors to enforce the great Principles of Justice and Liberty, upon which

the Radical Abolition movement is based. Furthermore, we here concede, that upon Radical Abolition grounds, the final battle against Slavery in this country must be fought out—Slavery must be seen and felt to be a huge crime, a system of lawless violence, before it can be abolished. In our Paper, upon the Platform, at home and abroad, we shall endeavor to bring Slavery before the People in this hateful light; and by so doing, shall really be upholding the Radical Abolition Platform in the very ranks of the Republican Party.

4. Beyond all controversy, the commanding and vital issue with Slavery at the approaching Presidential election, is the extension or the limitation of Slavery. The malign purpose of extending, strengthening, and perpetuating Slavery, is the conclusion of the great mass of the slaveholders. The execution of this purpose upon Kansas, is plainly enough the business set down for the present by the friends of Slavery, North and South. And it cannot be denied that the election either of Buchanan or Fillmore would be the success of this malign purpose of the Slave Power. Other elements enter into the issue, such, for instance, as Northern or Southern ascendency of the Slave power in the Councils of the Nation, the continued humiliation of the Northern People, the reign of Terror at Washington, the crippling of the Anti-Slavery movement, and the security and preservation of Slavery from inward decay or outside destroying influences. The fact that Slaveholders had taken a united stand in favor of this measure, is, at least, an argument why Anti-Slavery men should take a stand to defeat them. The greatest triumphs of Slavery have been secured by the division of its enemies, one party insisting on attacking one point, and another class equally in earnest bending their energies in another direction. Were it in our power, the order of battle between Liberty and Slavery would be arranged differently. Anti-Slavery in our hands, at the ballot box, should be the aggressor; but it is not within our power, or within that of any other man, to control the order of events, or the circumstances which shape our course, and determine our conduct at particular times. All men will agree, that, generally speaking, the point attacked, is the point to be defended.

The South has tendered to us the issue of Slavery Extension; and to meet the Slave Power here, is to rouse its most devilish animosity. It is to strike hardest, where the Slaveholders feel most keenly. The most powerful blow that could be given at that point would in our judgment, be the election to the Presidency and Vice Presidency of the Republic the Candidates of the Republican Party.

5. Briefly, then, we shall support Fremont and Dayton in the present crisis of the Anti-Slavery movement, because they are, by position, and from the very nature of the organization which supports them, the admitted and recognized antagonists of the Slave Power, of gag-law, and of all the hellish

designs of the Slave Power to extend and fortify the accursed slave system. We shall support them because they are the most numerous Anti-Slavery Party, and, therefore, the most powerful to inflict a blow upon, and the most likely to achieve a valuable victory over, the Slave Oligarchy. There is not a trafficker in the bodies and souls of men, from Baltimore to New Orleans, that would not crack his bloody slave whip with fiendish delight over the defeat of Fremont and Dayton. Whereas, on the other hand, the moral effect of the Radical Abolition vote, separated as it must be from the great Anti-Slavery body of the North, must, from the nature of the case, be very limited for good, and only powerful for mischief, where its effect would be to weaken the Republican Party. We shall support Fremont and Dayton, because there is no chance whatever in the present contest of electing better men than they. And we are the more reconciled to accepting them, by the fact that they are surrounded by a Party of progressive men. Take them, therefore, not merely for what they are, but for what we have good reason to believe they will become when they have lived for a time in the element of Anti-Slavery discussion. We shall support them by pen, by speech, by vote, because it is by no means certain that they can succeed in this State against the powerful combinations opposed to them without the support of the full and complete Abolition vote. Bitter indeed, would be the reproach, and deep and pointed would be the regret, if, through the Radical Abolitionists, victory should perch on the bloody standard of Slave Rule, as would be the case if Fremont and Dayton were defeated, and Buchanan and Breckenridge elected. For one, we are not disposed to incur this reproach, nor to experience this regret, and shall, therefore, vote for Fremont and Dayton. In supporting them, we neither dishonor our Principles nor lessen our means of securing their adoption and active application. We can reach the ears and heart of as great a number within the ranks of the Republican Party as we could possibly do by remaining outside of those ranks. We know of no law applicable to the progress and promulgation of Radical Abolition Principles which would act less favorably towards our Principles inside the Party, than outside of it.

6. Another reason for supporting the Republican Party at the ballot-box and thus supporting the Anti-Slavery vote as a unit, is, that such action conforms exactly to the facts of our existing relations as citizens. There is now, evidently, but one great question of widespread and of all-commanding national interest; and that question is Freedom or Slavery. In reality, there can be but two Parties to this question, and for ourselves, we wish it to be with the natural division for Freedom, in form, as well as in fact.

7. It seems to us both the dictate of good morals and true wisdom, that if we cannot abolish Slavery in all the States by our votes at the approaching election, we ought, if we can, keep Slavery out of Kansas by our vote. To

pursue any other policy is to abandon at present, practical advantage to Freedom in an assertion of more comprehensive claims, right enough in themselves, but which reason and fact assure us can only be attained by votes in the future, when the public mind shall have been educated up to those claims. We are quite well aware that to the foregoing, objections of apparent weight may be urged by those for whose conscientious convictions we cherish the profoundest respect. And although we do not propose to anticipate objections, but intend to meet them as they shall be presented in the progress of the canvass, we will mention and reply to one. Most plainly the greatest difficulty to be met with by a Radical Abolitionist in supporting Fremont and Dayton, is the fact that these Candidates have not declared and do not declare any purpose to abolish Slavery by legislation, in the States. They neither entertain nor declare any such purpose, and in this they are far from occupying the high Anti-Slavery position of the Radical Abolition Society. But let us not be unreasonable or impatient with the Republican Party. In considering this defect in the Anti-Slavery character and creed of the Republican Candidates, it should be borne in mind that they stand now in respect to this doctrine precisely where the Liberty Party stood ten years ago. The Right and duty of the Federal Government to abolish Slavery everywhere in the United States, is entirely true and deeply important; and yet, it must be confessed that this doctrine has been made appreciable but to a few minds, the dwellers in the mountain peaks of the moral world, who catch the first beams of morning, long before the slumberers in the valleys awake from their dreams. This new doctrine, we think, may very properly be left to take its turn in the arena of discussion. Time and argument will do more for its progress, and its final adoption by the people, than can be done for it in the present crisis, by the few votes of the isolated Radical Abolitionists. In further extenuation or apology, it may be very properly urged, that while the Republican Party has not at this point adopted the Abolition creed, it has laid down principles and promulgated doctrines, which in their application, directly tend to the Abolition of Slavery in the States. But the conclusive answer to all who object upon this ground is the indisputable Truth, that neither in Religion nor Morals, can a man be justified in refusing to assist his fellow-men to accomplish a possible good thing, simply because his fellows refuse to accomplish some other good things which they deem impossible. Most assuredly, that theory cannot be a sound one which would prevent us from voting with men for the Abolition of Slavery in Maryland simply because our companions refuse to include Virginia. In such a case, the path of duty is plainly this; go with your fellow-citizens for the Abolition of Slavery in Maryland when they are ready to go for that measure, and do all you can, meanwhile, to bring them to whatever work of righteousness may remain and which has become manifest to your clearer vision. Such, then, is the conclusion forced upon us by the philosophy of the facts of our condition as a nation. A great crime against Freedom and Civilization is about to be perpetrated. The Slave Power is resolved to plant the deadly Upas, Slavery, in the virgin soil of Kansas. This great evil may be averted, and all the likelihoods of the case, the election of John C. Fremont and William L. Dayton, will be instrumental in averting it. Their election will prevent the establishment of Slavery in Kansas, overthrow Slave Rule in the Republic, protect Liberty of Speech and of the Press, give ascendency to Northern civilization over the bludgeon and blood-hound civilization of the South, and the mark of national condemnation on Slavery, scourge doughfaces from place and from power, and inaugurate a higher and purer standard of Politics and Government. Therefore, we go for Fremont and Dayton.

17

"House Divided": Speech at Springfield, Illinois (1858)

Abraham Lincoln

Abraham Lincoln (1809–1865) was born the son of a Kentucky frontiersman and died as the sixteenth President of the United States. After serving four terms in the Illinois state legislature, Lincoln was first elected to the U.S. House of Representatives as a Whig in 1846. He served one term and then returned home to resume his law practice. Lincoln's declining interest in politics was renewed by the passage of the Kansas–Nebraska Act in 1854. From that moment forward, Lincoln dedicated himself to preserving the Union for freedom and to the gradual elimination of slavery. His election as president of the United States in 1860 was the precipitating event that led to the Civil War.

Lincoln's "House Divided" Speech, justly regarded as one of the great speeches in American history, was delivered June 16, 1858 at Springfield, Illinois, at the close of the Republican State convention. The convention had just nominated Lincoln as their candidate for the U.S. Senate. The theme of the speech is that a conspiracy of Southern slaveholders and their supporters in the North were conspiring to undermine freedom in America. Lincoln predicted that the nation, thanks to Stephen Douglas's "don't care" policy of popular sovereignty and the Supreme Court's recently passed Dred Scott decision, must either become wholly free or wholly slave. A crisis had been reached, and the nation would either nationalize slavery or nationalize freedom.

If we could first know *where* we are, and *whither* we are tending, we could then better judge *what* to do, and *how* to do it.

We are now far into the *fifth year*, since a policy was initiated, with the *avowed* object, and *confident* promise, of putting an end to slavery agitation.

Under the operation of that policy, that agitation has not only, *not ceased*, but has *constantly augmented*.

In *my* opinion, it *will* not cease, until a *crisis* shall have been reached, and passed.

"A house divided against itself cannot stand."

I believe this government cannot endure, permanently half *slave* and half *free*.

I do not expect the Union to be *dissolved*—I do not expect the house to fall—but I *do* expect it will cease to be divided.

It will become *all* one thing, or *all* the other.

Either the *opponents* of slavery, will arrest the further spread of it, and place it where the public mind shall rest in the belief that it is in course of ultimate extinction; or its *advocates* will push it forward, till it shall become alike lawful in *all* the States, *old* as well as *new*—North as well as *South*.

Have we no *tendency* to the latter condition?

Let any one who doubts, carefully contemplate that now almost complete legal combination—piece of *machinery* so to speak—compounded of the Nebraska doctrine, and the Dred Scott decision. Let him consider not only *what work* the machinery is adapted to do, and *how well* adapted; but also, let him study the *history* of its construction, and trace, if he can, or rather *fail*, if he can, to trace the evidences of design, and concert of action, among its chief bosses, from the beginning.

But, so far, *Congress* only, had acted; and an *indorsement* by the people, *real* or apparent, was indispensable, to *save* the point already gained, and give chance for more.

The new year of 1854 found slavery excluded from more than half the States by State Constitutions, and from most of the national territory by Congressional prohibition.

Four days later, commenced the struggle, which ended in repealing that Congressional prohibition.

This opened all the national territory to slavery; and was the first point gained.

This necessity had not been overlooked; but had been provided for, as well as might be, in the notable argument of "*squatter sovereignty*," otherwise called "*sacred right of self government*," which latter phrase, though expressive of the only rightful basis of any government, was so perverted in this attempted use of it as to amount to just this: That if any *one* man, choose to enslave *another*, no *third* man shall be allowed to object.

That argument was incorporated into the Nebraska bill itself, in the language which follows: "*It being the true intent and meaning of this act not to legislate slavery into any Territory or state, nor to exclude it therefrom; but to leave the people thereof perfectly free to form and regulate their domestic institutions in their own way, subject only to the Constitution of the United States.*"

Then opened the roar of loose declamation in favor of "Squatter Sovereignty," and "Sacred right of self government."

"But," said opposition members, "let us be more *specific*—let us *amend* the bill so as to expressly declare that the people of the territory *may* exclude slavery." "Not we," said the friends of the measure; and down they voted the amendment.

While the Nebraska bill was passing through congress, a *law case*, involving the question of a negroe's freedom, by reason of his owner having voluntarily taken him first into a free state and then a territory covered by the congressional prohibition, and held him as a slave, for a long time in each, was passing through the U.S. Circuit Court for the District of Missouri; and both Nebraska bill and law suit were brought to a decision in the same month of May, 1854. The negroe's name was "Dred Scott," which name now designates the decision finally made in the case.

Before the *then* next Presidential election, the law case came *to*, and was argued *in* the Supreme Court of the United States; but the *decision* of it was deferred until *after* the election. Still, *before* the election, Senator Trumbull, on the floor of the Senate, requests the leading advocate of the Nebraska bill to state *his opinion* whether the people of a territory can constitutionally exclude slavery from their limits; and the latter answers, "That is a question for the Supreme Court."

The election came. Mr. Buchanan was elected, and the *indorsement*, such as it was, secured. That was the *second* point gained. The indorsement, however, fell short of a clear popular majority by nearly four hundred thousand votes, and so, perhaps, was not overwhelmingly reliable and satisfactory.

The *outgoing* President, in his last annual message, as impressively as possible *echoed back* upon the people the *weight* and *authority* of the indorsement.

The Supreme Court met again; *did not* announce their decision, but ordered a re-argument.

The Presidential inauguration came, and still no decision of the court; but the *incoming* President, in his inaugural address, fervently exhorted the people to abide by the forthcoming decision, *whatever it might be*.

Then, in a few days, came the decision.

The reputed author of the Nebraska bill finds an early occasion to make a speech at this capitol indorsing the Dred Scott Decision, and vehemently denouncing all opposition to it.

The new President, too, seizes the early occasion of the Silliman letter to *indorse* and strongly *construe* that decision, and to express his *astonishment* that any different view had ever been entertained.

At length a squabble springs up between the President and the author of the Nebraska bill, on the *mere* question of *fact*, whether the Lecompton constitution was or was not, in any just sense, made by the people of Kansas;

and in that squabble the latter declares that all he wants is a fair vote for the people, and that he *cares not* whether slavery be voted *down* or voted *up*. I do not understand his declaration that he cares not whether slavery be voted down or voted up, to be intended by him other than as an *apt definition* of the *policy* he would impress upon the public mind—the *principle* for which he declares he has suffered much, and is ready to suffer to the end.

And well may he cling to that principle. If he has any parental feeling, well may he cling to it. That principle, is the only *shred* left of his original Nebraska doctrine. Under the Dred Scott decision, "squatter sovereignty" squatted out of existence, tumbled down like temporary scaffolding—like the mould at the foundry served through one blast and fell back into loose sand—helped to carry an election, and then was kicked to the winds. His late *joint* struggle with the Republicans, against the Lecompton Constitution, involves nothing of the original Nebraska doctrine. That struggle was made on a point, the right of a people to make their own constitution, upon which he and the Republicans have never differed.

The several points of the Dred Scott decision, in connection with Senator Douglas' "care not" policy, constitute the piece of machinery, in its *present* state of advancement. This was the third point gained.

The *working* points of that machinery are:

First, that no negro slave, imported as such from Africa, and no descendant of such slave can ever be a *citizen* of any State, in the sense of that term as used in the Constitution of the United States.

This point is made in order to deprive the negro, in every possible event, of the benefit of this provision of the United States Constitution, which declares that—"The citizens of each State shall be entitled to all privileges and immunities of citizens in the several States."

Secondly, that "subject to the Constitution of the United States," neither *Congress* nor a *Territorial Legislature* can exclude slavery from any United States territory.

This point is made in order that individual men may *fill up* the territories with slaves, without danger of losing them as property, and thus to enhance the chances of *permanency* to the institution through all the future.

Thirdly, that whether the holding a negro in actual slavery in a free State, makes him free, as against the holder, the United States courts will not decide, but will leave to be decided by the courts of any slave State the negro may be forced into by the master.

This point is made, not to be pressed *immediately*; but, if acquiesced in for a while, and apparently *indorsed* by the people at an election, *then* to sustain the logical conclusion that what Dred Scott's master might lawfully do with Dred Scott, in the free State of Illinois, every other master may lawfully do with any other *one*, or one *thousand* slaves, in Illinois, or in any other free State.

Auxiliary to all this, and working hand in hand with it, the Nebraska doctrine, or what is left of it, is to *educate* and *mould* public opinion, at least *Northern* public opinion, to not *care* whether slavery is voted *down* or voted *up*.

This shows exactly where we now *are*; and *partially* also, whither we are tending.

It will throw additional light on the latter, to go back, and run the mind over the string of historical facts already stated. Several things will *now* appear less *dark* and *mysterious* than they did *when* they were transpiring. The people were to be left "perfectly free" "subject only to the Constitution." What the *Constitution* had to do with it, outsiders could not *then* see. Plainly enough *now*, it was an exactly fitted *niche*, for the Dred Scott decision to afterwards come in, and declare the *perfect freedom* of the people, to be just no freedom at all.

Why was the amendment, expressly declaring the right of the people to exclude slavery, voted down? Plainly enough *now*, the adoption of it, would have spoiled the niche for the Dred Scott decision.

Why was the court decision held up? Why, even a Senator's individual opinion withheld, till *after* the Presidential election? Plainly enough *now*, the speaking out *then* would have damaged the *"perfectly free"'* argument upon which the election was to be carried.

Why the *outgoing* President's felicitation on the indorsement? Why the delay of a reargument? Why the incoming President's *advance* exhortation in favor of the decision?

These things *look* like the cautious *patting* and *petting* a spirited horse, preparatory to mounting him, when it is dreaded that he may give the rider a fall.

And why the hasty after indorsements of the decision by the President and others?

We can not absolutely *know* that all these exact adaptations are the result of preconcert. But when we see a lot of framed timbers, different portions of which we know have been gotten out at different times and places and by different workmen—Stephen, Franklin, Roger and James, for instance—and when we see these timbers joined together, and see they exactly make the frame of a house or a mill, all the tenons and mortices exactly fitting, and all the lengths and proportions of the different pieces exactly adapted to their respective places, and not a piece too many or too few—not omitting even scaffolding—or, if a single piece be lacking, we can see the place in the frame exactly fitted and prepared to yet bring such piece in—in *such* a case, we find it impossible to not *believe* that Stephen and Franklin and Roger and

James all understood one another from the beginning, and all worked upon a common *plan* or *draft* drawn up before the first lick was struck.

It should not be overlooked that, by the Nebraska bill, the people of a *State* as well as *Territory*, were to be left *"perfectly free"* *"subject only to the Constitution."*

Why mention a *State*? They were legislating for *territories*, and not *for* or *about* States. Certainly the people of a State *are and ought to be* subject to the Constitution of the United States; but why is mention of this *lugged* into this merely *territorial* law? Why are the people of a *territory* and the people of a *state* therein *lumped* together, and their relation to the Constitution therein treated as being *precisely* the same?

While the opinion of *the Court*, by Chief Justice Taney, in the Dred Scott case, and the separate opinions of all the concurring Judges, expressly declare that the Constitution of the United States neither permits Congress nor a Territorial legislature to exclude slavery from any United States territory, they all *omit* to declare whether or not the same Constitution permits a *state*, or the people of a State, to exclude it.

Possibly, this was a mere *omission*; but who can be *quite* sure, if McLean or Curtis had sought to get into the opinion a declaration of unlimited power in the people of a *state* to exclude slavery from their limits, just as Chase and Macy sought to get such declaration, in behalf of the people of a territory, into the Nebraska bill—I ask, who can be quite *sure* that it would not have been voted down, in the one case, as it had been in the other.

The nearest approach to the point of declaring the power of a State over slavery, is made by Judge Nelson. He approaches it more than once, using the precise idea, and *almost* the language too, of the Nebraska act. On one occasion his exact language is, "except in cases where the power is restrained by the Constitution of the United States, the law of the State is supreme over the subject of slavery within its jurisdiction."

In what *cases* the power of the *states* is so restrained by the U.S. Constitution, is left an *open* question, precisely as the same question, as to the restraint on the power of the *territories* was left open in the Nebraska act. Put *that* and *that* together, and we have another nice little niche, which we may, ere long, see filled with another Supreme Court decision, declaring that the Constitution of the United States does not permit a *state* to exclude slavery from its limits.

And this may especially be expected if the doctrine of "care not whether slavery be voted *down* or voted *up*," shall gain upon the public mind sufficiently to give promise that such a decision can be maintained when made.

Such a decision is all that slavery now lacks of being alike lawful in all the States.

Welcome or unwelcome, such decision *is* probably coming, and will soon be upon us, unless the power of the present political dynasty shall be met and overthrown.

We shall *lie down* pleasantly dreaming that the people of *Missouri* are on the verge of making their State free; and we shall *awake* to the *reality*, instead, that the *Supreme* Court has made *Illinois* a *slave* State.

To meet and overthrow the power of that dynasty, is the work now before all those who would prevent that consummation.

That is *what* we have to do.

But *how* can we best do it?

There are those who denounce us *openly* to their *own* friends, and yet whisper *us softly*, that *Senator Douglas* is the *aptest* instrument there is, with which to effect that object. *They do not* tell us, nor has *he* told us, that he wishes any such object to be effected. They wish us to *infer* all, from the facts, that he now has a little quarrel with the present head of the dynasty; and that he has regularly voted with us, on a single point, upon which, he and we, have never differed.

They remind us that *he* is a very *great man*, and that the largest of *us* are very small ones. Let this be granted. But "a *living dog* is better than a *dead lion*." Judge Douglas, if not a *dead* lion *for this work*, is at least a *caged* and *toothless* one. How can he oppose the advances of slavery? He don't *care* anything about it. His avowed *mission is impressing* the "public heart" to *care* nothing about it.

A leading Douglas Democratic newspaper thinks Douglas' superior talent will be needed to resist the revival of the African slave trade.

Does Douglas believe an effort to revive that trade is approaching? He has not said so. Does he *really* think so? But if it is, how can he resist it? For years he has labored to prove it a *sacred right* of white men to take negro slaves into the new territories. Can he possibly show that it is *less* a sacred right to *buy* them where they can be bought cheapest? And, unquestionably they can be bought *cheaper in Africa* than in *Virginia*.

He has done all in his power to reduce the whole question of slavery to one of a mere *right of property*; and as such, how can *he* oppose the foreign slave trade—how can he refuse that trade in that "property" shall be "perfectly free"—unless he does it as a *protection* to the home production? And as the home *producers* will probably not *ask* the protection, he will be wholly without a ground of opposition.

Senator Douglas holds, we know, that a man may rightfully be *wiser today* than he was *yesterday*—that he may rightfully *change* when he finds himself wrong.

But, can we for that reason, run ahead, and *infer* that he *will* make any particular change, of which he, himself, has given no intimation? Can we *safely* base our action upon any such *vague* inference?

Now, as ever, I wish to not *misrepresent* Judge Douglas' *position*, question his *motives*, or do aught that can be personally offensive to him.

Whenever, if *ever*, he and we can come together on *principle* so that *our great cause* may have assistance from *his great ability*, I hope to have interposed no adventitious obstacle.

But clearly, he is not now with us—he does not *pretend* to be—he does not *promise* to *ever* be.

Our cause, then, must be intrusted to, and conducted by its own undoubted friends—those whose hands are free, whose hearts are in the work—who do care for the result.

Two years ago the Republicans of the nation mustered over thirteen hundred thousand strong.

We did this under the single impulse of resistance to a common danger, with every external circumstance against us.

Of *strange*, *discordant*, and even, *hostile* elements, we gathered from the four winds, and *formed* and fought the battle through, under the constant hot fire of a disciplined, proud, and pampered enemy.

Did we brave all *then*, to *falter* now?—*now*—when that same enemy is *wavering*, dissevered and belligerent?

The result is not doubtful. We shall not fail—if we stand firm, we shall not fail.

Wise councils may *accelerate* or *mistakes delay* it, but, sooner or later the victory is *sure* to come.

VIII

Disunion and Revolution

18

"Address to the Slaves of the United States of America" (1843)

Henry Highland Garnet

Henry Highland Garnet (1815–1882) was born into slavery and escaped from bondage as a child with his family in 1824. Raised in New York City and upstate New York, Garnet was early recognized for his natural intellectual abilities and was supported in acquiring a good education. Trained to enter the ministry, Garnet quickly moved into the abolitionist movement where he served as a lecturing agent for the American Anti-Slavery Society. Late in his life during the years of reconstruction and Jim Crow, he developed an interest in colonization. In 1881, he was appointed as the American minister to Liberia.

Garnet is most famous for an 1843 speech he delivered before the National Convention of Colored Citizens in Buffalo, New York. The speech was notable because of its radical call for revolution and black resistance. The speech frightened most convention delegates and a resolution supporting its call to arms was easily defeated. Curiously, the speech represented the highpoint of Garnet's career as an abolitionist and the beginning its decline.

Brethren and fellow citizens:—your brethren of the North, East, and West have been accustomed to meet together in National Conventions, to sympathize with each other, and to weep over your unhappy condition. In these meetings we have addressed all classes of the free, but we have never until this time, sent a word of consolation and advice to you. We have been contented in sitting still and mourning over your sorrows, earnestly hoping that before this day your sacred liberty would have been restored. But, we have hoped in vain. Years have rolled on, and tens of thousands have been borne on streams of blood and tears, to the shores of eternity. While you have been oppressed, we have also been partakers with you; nor can we be free while you are enslaved. We, therefore, write to you as being bound with you.

Many of you are bound to us, not only by the ties of a common humanity, but we are connected by the more tender relations of parents, wives, husbands, children, brothers, and sisters, and friends. As such we most affectionately address you.

Slavery has fixed a deep gulf between you and us, and while it shuts out from you the relief and consolation which your friends would willingly render, it afflicts and persecutes you with a fierceness which we might not expect to see in the fiends of hell. But still the Almighty Father of Mercies has left to us a glimmering ray of hope, which shines out like a lone star in a cloudy sky. Mankind are wiser, and better—the oppressor's power is fading, and you, every day, are becoming better informed, and more numerous. Your grievances, brethren, are many. We shall not attempt, in this short address, to present to the world all the dark catalogue of this nation's sins, which have been committed upon an innocent people. Nor is it indeed, necessary, for you feel them from day to day, and all the civilized world look upon them with amazement.

Two hundred and twenty-seven years ago, the first of our injured race were brought to the shores of America. They came not with glad spirits to select their homes in the New World. They came not with their own consent, to find an unmolested enjoyment of the blessings of this fruitful soil. The first dealings which they had with men calling themselves Christians, exhibited to them the worst features of corrupt and sordid hearts; and convinced them that no cruelty is too great, no villainy, and no robbery too abhorrent for even enlightened men to perform, when influenced by avarice and lust. Neither did they come flying upon the wings of Liberty, to a land of freedom. But, they came with broken hearts, from their beloved native land, and were doomed to unrequited toil and deep degradation. Nor did the evil of their bondage end at their emancipation by death. Succeeding generations inherited their chains, and millions have come from eternity into time, and have returned again to the world of spirits, cursed and ruined by American slavery.

The propagators of the system, or their immediate ancestors, very soon discovered its growing evil, and its tremendous wickedness, and secret promises were made to destroy it. The gross inconsistency of a people holding slaves, who had themselves "ferried o'er the wave" for freedom's sake, was too apparent to be entirely overlooked. The voice of Freedom cried, "emancipate your slaves." Humanity supplicated with tears for the deliverance of the children of Africa. Wisdom urged her solemn plea. The bleeding captive plead his innocence, and pointed to Christianity who stood weeping at the cross. Jehovah frowned upon the nefarious institution, and thunderbolts, red with vengeance, struggled to leap forth to blast the guilty wretches who maintained it. But all was in vain. Slavery had stretched its dark wings of death over the land, the Church stood silently by—the priests prophesied falsely, and the people loved to have it so. Its throne is established, and now it reigns triumphant.

Nearly three millions of your fellow-citizens are prohibited by law and public opinion, (which in this country is stronger than law), from reading the Book of Life. Your intellect has been destroyed as much as possible, and every ray of light they have attempted to shut out from your minds. The oppressors themselves have become involved in the ruin. They have become weak, sensual, and rapacious. They have cursed you—they have cursed themselves—they have cursed the earth which they have trod. In the language of a Southern statesman, we can truly say "even the wolf, driven back long since by the approach of man now returns after a lapse of a hundred years, and howls amid the desolation of slavery."

The colonists threw the blame upon England. They said that the mother country entailed the evil upon them, and that they would rid themselves of it if they could. The world thought they were sincere, and the philanthropic pitied them. But time soon tested their sincerity. In a few years, the colonists grew strong and severed themselves from the British Government. Their independence was declared, and they took their station among the sovereign powers of the earth. The declaration was a glorious document. Sages admired it, and the patriotic of every nation reverenced the God-like sentiments which it contained. When the power of Government returned to their hands, did they emancipate the slaves? No; they rather added new links to our chains. Were they ignorant of the principles of Liberty? Certainly they were not. The sentiments of their revolutionary orators fell in burning eloquence upon their hearts, and with one voice they cried, LIBERTY OR DEATH. Oh, what a sentence was that! It ran from soul to soul like electric fire, and nerved the arm of thousands to fight in the holy cause of Freedom. Among the diversity of opinions that are entertained in regard to physical resistance, there are but a few found to gainsay that stern declaration. We are among those who do not.

SLAVERY! How much misery is comprehended in that single word? What mind is there that does not shrink from its direful effects? Unless the image of God be obliterated from the soul, all men cherish the love of Liberty. The nice discerning political economist does not regard the sacred right more than the untutored African who roams in the wilds of Congo. Nor has the one more right to the full enjoyment of his freedom than the other. In every man's mind the good seeds of Liberty are planted, and he who brings his fellow down so low, as to make him contented with a condition of slavery, commits the highest crime against God and man. Brethren, your oppressors aim to do this. They endeavor to make you as much like brutes as possible. When they have blinded the eyes of your mind—when they have embittered the sweet waters of life—then, and not till then, has American slavery done its perfect work.

TO SUCH DEGRADATION IT IS SINFUL IN THE EXTREME FOR YOU TO MAKE VOLUNTARY SUBMISSION. The divine commandments you are in duty bound to reverence and obey. If you do not obey them, you will surely meet with the displeasure of the Almighty. He requires you to love him supremely, and your neighbor as yourself—to keep the Sabbath day holy—to search the Scriptures—and bring up your children with respect for his laws, and to worship no other God but him. But slavery sets all these at naught, and hurls defiance in the face of Jehovah. The forlorn condition in which you are placed does not destroy your moral obligation to God. You are not certain of Heaven, because you suffer yourselves to remain in a state of slavery, where you cannot obey the commandments of the Sovereign of the universe. If the ignorance of slavery is a passport to heaven, then it is a blessing, and no curse, and you should rather desire its perpetuity than its abolition. God will not receive slavery, nor ignorance, nor any other state of mind, for love and obedience to him. Your condition does not absolve you from your moral obligation. The diabolical injustice by which your liberties are cloven down, NEITHER GOD, NOR ANGELS, OR JUST MEN COMMAND YOU TO SUFFER FOR A SINGLE MOMENT. THEREFORE IT IS YOUR SOLEMN AND IMPERATIVE DUTY TO USE EVERY MEANS, BOTH MORAL, INTELLECTUAL, AND PHYSICAL, THAT PROMISES SUCCESS. If a band of heathen men should attempt to enslave a race of Christians, and to place their children under the influence of some false religion, surely Heaven would frown upon the men who would not resist such aggression, even to death. If, on the other hand, a band of Christians should attempt to enslave a race of heathen men, and to entail slavery upon them, and to keep them in heathenism in the midst of Christianity, the God of heaven would smile upon every effort which the injured might make to disenthrall themselves.

Brethren, it is as wrong for your lordly oppressors to keep you in slavery as it was for the man thief to steal our ancestors from the coast of Africa. You should therefore now use the same manner of resistance, as would have been just in our ancestors when the bloody footprints of the first remorseless soul thief was placed upon the shores of our fatherland. The humblest peasant is as free in the sight of God as the proudest monarch that ever swayed a scepter. Liberty is a spirit sent out from God, and like its great Author, is no respecter of persons.

Brethren, the time has come when you must act for yourselves. It is an old and true saying that, "if hereditary bondmen would be free, they must themselves strike the blow." You can plead your own cause, and do the work of emancipation better than any other. The nations of the world are moving in the great cause of universal freedom, and some of them at least will, ere long, do you justice. The combined powers of Europe have placed their broad seal of disapprobation upon the African slave-trade. But in the slaveholding parts of the United States, the trade is as brisk as ever. They buy and sell you as though you were brute beasts. The North has done much—her opinion of slavery in the abstract is known. But in regard to the South, we adopt the opinion of the *New York Evangelist*—"We have advanced so far, that the cause apparently waits for a more effectual door to be thrown open than has been yet." We are about to point out that more effectual door. Look around you, and behold the bosoms of your loving wives heaving with untold agonies! Hear the cries of your poor children! Remember the stripes your fathers bore. Think of the torture and disgrace of your noble mothers. Think of your wretched sisters, loving virtue and purity, as they are driven into concubinage and are exposed to the unbridled lusts of incarnate devils. Think of the undying glory that hangs around the ancient name of Africa—and forget not that you are native-born American citizens, and as such, you are justly entitled to all the rights that are granted to the freest. Think how many tears you have poured out upon the soil which you have cultivated with unrequited toil, and enriched with your blood; and then go to your lordly enslavers and tell them plainly, that YOU ARE DETERMINED TO BE FREE. Appeal to their sense of justice, and tell them that they have no more right to oppress you, than you have to enslave them. Entreat them to remove the grievous burdens which they have imposed upon you, and to remunerate you for your labor. Promise them renewed diligence in the cultivation of the soil, if they will render to you an equivalent for your services. Point them to the increase of happiness and prosperity in the British West Indies since the Act of Emancipation. Tell them in language which they cannot misunderstand, of the exceeding sinfulness of slavery, and of a future judgment, and of the righteous retributions of an indignant God. Inform them that all you desire is FREEDOM, and that nothing else will suffice. Do this, and forever after cease to toil for the heartless tyrants, who give you no other reward but stripes and abuse. If they then commence the work of death, they, and not you, will be responsible for the consequences. You had better all die—*die immediately*, than live slaves and entail your wretchedness upon your posterity. If you would be free in this generation, here is your only hope. However much you and all of us may desire it, there is not much hope of Redemption without the shedding of blood. If you must bleed, let it all come at once—rather, *die freemen, than live to be slaves*. It is impossible like the children of Israel, to make a grand exodus from the land of bondage. THE PHARAOHS ARE ON BOTH SIDES OF THE BLOOD-RED WATERS! You cannot move en masse, to the dominions of the British Queen—nor can you pass through Florida and overrun Texas, and at last find peace in Mexico. The propagators of American slavery are spending their blood and treasure, that they may plant the black flag in the heart of Mexico and riot in the halls of the Montezumas. . . .

You will not be compelled to spend much time in order to become inured to hardships. From the first moment that you breathed the air of heaven, you have been accustomed to nothing else but hardships. The heroes of the American Revolution were never put upon harder fare than a peck of corn and a few herrings per week. You have not become enervated by the luxuries of life. Your sternest energies have been beaten out upon the anvil of severe trial. Slavery has done this, to make you subservient to its own purposes; but it has done more than this, it has prepared you for any emergency. If you receive good treatment, it is what you could hardly expect; if you meet with pain, sorrow, and even death, these are the common lot of slaves.

Fellow men! Patient sufferers! behold your dearest rights crushed to the earth! See your sons murdered, and your wives, mothers and sisters doomed to prostitution. In the name of the merciful God, and by all that life is worth, let it no longer be a debatable question whether it is better to choose Liberty or death!

In 1822, Denmark Vesey, of South Carolina, formed a plan for the liberation of his fellow men. In the whole history of human efforts to overthrow slavery, a more complicated and tremendous plan was never formed. He was betrayed by the treachery of his own people, and died a martyr to freedom. Many a brave hero fell, but History, faithful to her high trust, will transcribe his name on the same monument with Moses, Hampden, Tell, Bruce and Wallace, Toussaint L'Ouverture, Lafayette and Washington. That tremendous movement shook the whole empire of slavery. The guilty soul thieves were overwhelmed with fear. It is a matter of fact, that at that time, and in consequence of the threatened revolution, the slave States talked strongly of emancipation. But they blew but one blast of the trumpet of freedom and then laid it aside. As these men became quiet, the slaveholders ceased to talk about emancipation; and now behold your condition today! Angels sigh over it, and humanity has long since exhausted her tears in weeping on your account!

The patriotic Nathaniel Turner followed Denmark Vesey. He was goaded to desperation by wrong and injustice. By despotism, his name has been recorded on the list of infamy, and future generations will remember him among the noble and brave.

Next arose the immortal Joseph Cinqué, the hero of the Amistad. He was a native African, and by the help of God he emancipated a whole shipload of his fellow men on the high seas. And he now sings of Liberty on the sunny hills of Africa and beneath his native palm-trees, where he hears the lion roar and feels himself as free as that king of the forest. Next arose Madison Washington that bright star of freedom, and took his station in the constellation of true heroism. He was a slave on board the brig *Creole*, of Richmond, bound to New Orleans, that great slave mart, with a hundred and four others. Nineteen struck for Liberty or death. But one life was taken, and the whole were emancipated, and the vessel was carried into Nassau, New Providence. Noble men! Those who have fallen in freedom's conflict, their memories will be cherished by the true-hearted and the God-fearing in all future generations; those who are living, their names are surrounded by a halo of glory.

We do not advise you to attempt a revolution with the sword, because it would be INEXPEDIENT. Your numbers are too small, and moreover the rising spirit of the age, and the spirit of the gospel, are opposed to war and bloodshed. But from this moment cease to labor for tyrants who will not remunerate you. Let every slave throughout the land do this, and the days of slavery are numbered. You cannot be more oppressed than you have been—you cannot suffer greater cruelties than you have already. RATHER DIE FREEMEN THAN LIVE TO BE SLAVES. Remember that you are THREE MILLIONS!

It is in your power so to torment the God-cursed slaveholders, that they will be glad to let you go free. If the scale was turned, and black men were the masters and white men the slaves, every destructive agent and element would be employed to lay the oppressor low. Danger and death would hang over their heads day and night. Yes, the tyrants would meet with plagues more terrible than those of Pharaoh. But you are a patient people. You act as though you were made for the special use of these devils. You act as though your daughters were born to pamper the lusts of your masters and overseers. And worse than all, you tamely submit while your lords tear your wives from your embraces and defile them before your eyes. In the name of God, we ask, are you men? Where is the blood of your fathers? Has it all run out of your veins? Awake, awake; millions of voices are calling you! Your dead fathers speak to you from their graves. Heaven, as with a voice of thunder, calls on you to arise from the dust.

Let your motto be RESISTANCE! RESISTANCE! RESISTANCE! No oppressed people have ever secured their liberty without resistance. What kind of resistance you had better make, you must decide by the circumstances that surround you, and according to the suggestion of expediency. Brethren, adieu! Trust in the living God. Labor for the peace of the human race, and remember that you are three millions.

19

"No Compromise With Slavery" (1854)

William Lloyd Garrison

In the mid 1840s, Garrison and his associates began to argue that slavery was protected and supported by the Constitution. As such, Garrison began to argue that the Union, the federal government, and the constitution that created them could no longer be supported. In 1844, Garrison, writing for the American Anti-Slavery Society, denounced the Constitution as "a covenant with death, and an agreement with hell." The official motto of the Society thereafter became "NO UNION WITH SLAVEHOLDERS." If the North seceded from the Union and withdrew its implicit support for slavery, Garrison believed that the South's "peculiar institution" would die of moral and political asphixiation.

On July 4, 1854, standing before a large audience at an Independence Day celebration, Garrison burned a copy of the Constitution and the Fugitive Slave Law. After shocking his audience, Garrison then delivered one of his most famous speeches. "No Compromise With Slavery" provides a general overview of Garrison's principles and is an oratorical tour-de-force.

. . . Of necessity, as well as of choice, I am a "Garrisonian" Abolitionist—the most unpopular appellation that any man can have applied to him, in the present state of public sentiment; yet, I am more than confident, destined ultimately to be honourably regarded by the wise and good. For though I have never assumed to be a leader—have never sought conspicuity of position, or notoriety of name—have desired to follow, if others, better qualified, would go before, and to be lost sight of in the throng of Liberty's adherents, as a drop is merged in the ocean; yet, as the appellation alluded to is applied, not with any reference to myself invidiously, but to excite prejudice against the noblest movement of the age, in order that the most frightful system of oppression ever devised by human ingenuity and wickedness may be left to grow and expand to the latest generation—I accept it as the synonym of absolute trust in God, and utter disregard of "that fear of man which bringeth a snare"—and so deem it alike honourable and praiseworthy.

Representing, then, that phase of Abolitionism which is the most contemned—to the suppression of which, the means and forces of the Church and the State are most actively directed—I am here to defend it against all its assailants as the highest expediency, the soundest philosophy, the noblest patriotism, the broadest philanthropy, and the best religion extant. To denounce it as fanatical, disorganizing, reckless of consequences, bitter and irreverent in spirit, infidel in heart, deaf alike to the suggestions of reason and the warnings of history, is to call good evil, and evil good; to put darkness for light, and light for darkness; to insist that Barabbas is better than Jesus; to cover with infamy the memories of patriarchs and prophets, apostles and martyrs; and to inaugurate Satan as the God of the universe. If, like the sun, it is not wholly spotless, still, like the sun, without it there is no light. If murky clouds obscure its brightness, still it shines in its strength. If, at any time, it seems to wane to its final setting, it is only to reveal itself in the splendour of a new ascension, unquenchable, glorious, sublime.

Let me define my positions, and at the same time Challenge any one to show wherein they are untenable.

I. I am a believer in that portion of the Declaration of American Independence in which it is set forth, as among self-evident truths, "that all men are created equal; that they are endowed by their Creator with certain inalienable rights; that among these are life, liberty, and the pursuit of happiness." Hence, I am an Abolitionist. Hence, I cannot but regard oppression in every form—and most of all, that which turns a man into a thing—with indignation and abhorrence. Not to cherish these feelings would be recreancy to principle. They who desire me to be dumb on the subject of Slavery, unless I will open my mouth in its defence, ask me to give the lie to my professions, to degrade my manhood, and to stain my soul. I will not be a liar, a poltroon, or a hypocrite, to accommodate any party, to gratify any sect, to escape any odium or peril, to save any interest, to preserve any institution, or to promote any object. Convince me that one man may rightfully make another man his slave, and I will no longer subscribe to the Declaration of Independence. Convince me that liberty is not the inalienable birthright of every human being, of whatever complexion or clime, and I will give that instrument to the consuming fire. I do not know how to espouse freedom and slavery together. I do not know how to worship God and Mammon at the same time. If other men choose to go upon all-fours, I choose to stand erect, as God designed every man to stand. If, practically falsifying its heaven-attested principles, this nation denounces me for refusing to imitate its example, then, adhering all the more tenaciously to those principles, I will not cease to rebuke it for its guilty inconsistency. Numerically, the contest may be an unequal one, for the time being; but the Author of liberty and the Source of justice, the adorable God, is more than multitudinous, and he will defend the right. My crime is, that I will not go with the multitude to do evil. My singularity is, that when I say that Freedom is of God, and Slavery is of the devil, I mean just what I say. My fanaticism is, that I insist on the American people abolishing Slavery, or ceasing to prate of the rights of man. My hardihood is, in measuring them by their own standard, and convicting them out of their own mouths. . . .

II. Notwithstanding the lessons taught us by Pilgrim Fathers and Revolutionary Sires, at Plymouth Rock, on Bunker Hill, at Lexington, Concord and Yorktown; notwithstanding our Fourth of July celebrations, and ostentatious displays of patriotism in what European nation is personal liberty held in such contempt as in our own? Where are there such unbelievers in the natural equality and freedom of mankind? Our slaves outnumber the entire population of the country at the time of our revolutionary struggle. In vain do they clank their chains, and fill the air with their shrieks, and make their supplications for mercy. In vain are their sufferings portrayed, their wrongs rehearsed, their rights defended. As Nero fiddled while Rome was burning, so the slaveholding spirit of this nation rejoices, as one barrier of liberty after another is destroyed, and fresh victims are multiplied for the cotton-field and the auction-block. For one impeachment of the slave system, a thousand defences are made. For one rebuke of the man-stealer, a thousand denunciations of the Abolitionists are heard. For one press that bears a faithful testimony against Slavery, a score are ready to be prostituted to its service. For one pulpit that is not "recreant to its trust," there are ten that openly defend slaveholding as compatible with Christianity, and scores that are dumb. For one church that excludes the human enslaver from its communion table, multitudes extend to him the right hand of religious fellowship. The wealth, the enterprise, the literature, the politics, the religion of the land, are all combined to give extension and perpetuity to the Slave Power. Everywhere to do homage to it, to avoid collision with it, to propitiate its favour, is deemed essential—nay, is essential to political preferment and ecclesiastical advancement. Nothing is so unpopular as impartial liberty. The two great parties which absorb nearly the whole voting strength of the Republic are pledged to be deaf, dumb and blind to whatever outrages the Slave Power may attempt to perpetrate. Cotton is in their ears—blinds are over their eyes—padlocks are upon their lips. They are as clay in the hands of the potter, and already moulded into vessels of dishonour, to be used for the vilest purposes. The tremendous power of the Government is actively wielded to "crush out" the little Anti-Slavery life that remains in individual hearts, and to open new and boundless domains for the expansion of the Slave system. No man known or suspected to be hostile to "the Compromise Measures, including the Fugitive Slave Law," is allowed to hope for any office under the present Administration. The ship of State is labouring in the trough of the sea—her engine powerless, her bulwarks swept away, her masts gone, her lifeboats destroyed, her pumps choked, and the leak gaining rapidly upon her; and as wave after wave dashes over her, all that might otherwise serve to keep her afloat is swallowed by the remorseless deep. God of heaven! if the ship is destined to go down "full many a fathom deep," is every soul on board to perish? Ho! a sail! a sail! The weather-beaten, but staunch ship Abolition, commanded by the Genius of Liberty, is bearing towards the wreck, with the cheering motto, inscribed in legible capitals, "WE WILL NOT FORSAKE YOU!" Let us hope, even against hope, that rescue is not wholly impossible.

To drop what is figurative for the actual. I have expressed the belief that, so lost to all self-respect and all ideas of justice have we become by the corrupting presence of Slavery, in no European nation is personal liberty held at such discount, as a matter of principle, as in our own. See how clearly this is demonstrated. The reasons adduced among us in justification of slaveholding, and therefore against personal liberty, are multitudinous. I will enumerate only a dozen of these: 1. "The victims are black." 2. "The slaves belong to an inferior race." 3. "Many of them have been fairly purchased." 4. "Others have been honestly inherited." 5. "Their emancipation would impoverish their owners." 6. "They are better off as slaves than they would be as freemen." 7. "They could not take care of themselves if set free." 8. "Their simultaneous liberation would be attended with great danger." 9. "Any interference in their behalf will excite the ill-will of the South, and thus seriously affect Northern trade and commerce." 10. "The Union can be preserved only by letting Slavery alone, and that is of paramount importance." 11. "Slavery is a lawful and constitutional system, and therefore not a crime." 12. "Slavery is sanctioned by the Bible; the Bible is the word of God; therefore God sanctions Slavery, and the Abolitionists are wise above what is written."

Here, then, are twelve reasons which are popularly urged in all parts of the country, as conclusive against the right of a man to himself. If they are valid, in any instance, what becomes of the Declaration of Independence? On what ground can the revolutionary war, can any struggle for liberty, be justified? Nay, cannot all the despotisms of the earth take shelter under them? If they are valid, then why is not the jesuitical doctrine, that the end sanctifies the means, and that it is right to do evil that good may come, morally sound? If they are valid, then how does it appear that God is no respecter of persons? or how can he say, "All souls are mine"? or what is to be done with Christ's injunction, "Call no man master"? or with what justice can the same duties and the same obligations (such as are embodied in the Decalogue and the gospel of Christ) be exacted of chattels as of men?

But they are not valid. They are the logic of Bedlam, the morality of the

234   DISUNION AND REVOLUTION

pirate ship, the diabolism of the pit. They insult the common sense and shook the moral nature of mankind. Take them to Europe, and see with what scorn they will be universally treated! Go, first, to England, and gravely propound them there; and the universal response will proudly be, in the thrilling lines of Cowper,

> "Slaves cannot breathe in England; if their lungs
> Inhale our air, that moment they are free!
> They touch our country, and their shackles fall!"

Every Briton, indignant at the monstrous claim, will answer, in the emphatic words of Brougham: "Tell me not of rights; talk not of the property of the planter in his slaves! I deny the right—I acknowledge not the property! The principles, the feelings of our nature, rise in rebellion against it. Be the appeal made to the understanding or to the heart, the sentence is the same that rejects it." And Curran, in words of burning eloquence, shall reply: "I speak in the spirit of the British law, which makes liberty commensurate with, and inseparable from, the British soil—which proclaims, even to the stranger and the sojourner, that the ground on which he treads is holy, and consecrated by the genius of universal emancipation. No matter in what language his doom may have been pronounced; no matter what complexion an Indian or an African sun may have burnt upon him; no matter in what disastrous battle his liberty may have been cloven down; no matter with what solemnities he may have been offered upon the altar of Slavery; the first moment he touches the sacred soil of Britain, the altar and the god sink together in the dust—his spirit walks abroad in its own majesty—his body swells beyond the measure of his chains, and he stands redeemed, regenerated and disenthralled, by the irresistible genius of universal emancipation."

Again—take these slaveholding pleas to Scotland, and, from the graves of the dead and the homes of the living, they shall be replied to in thunder-tones, in the language of Burns:

> "A man's a man, for a' that."
> "Who would be a traitor knave?
> Who would fill a coward's grave?
> Who so base as be a slave?
> Let him turn and flee!"

. . . And the testimony of O'Connell, in behalf of all Ireland, shall pass from mouth to mouth: "I am an Abolitionist. I am for speedy, immediate Abolition. I care not what caste, creed or colour, Slavery may assume. Whether it be personal or political, mental or corporeal, intellectual or spiritual, I am for its instant, its total Abolition. I am for justice, in the name of humanity, and according to the law of the living God." "Let none of the slave-owners, dealers in human flesh, dare to set a foot upon our free soil." "We are all children of the same Creator, heirs to the same promise, purchased by the blood of the same Redeemer—and what signifies of what caste, colour or creed we may be? It is our duty to proclaim that the cause of the negro is our cause, and that we will insist upon doing away, to the best of our human ability, the stain of Slavery, not only from every portion of this mighty empire, but from the whole face of the earth." "Let the American Abolitionists be honoured in proportion as the slaveholders are execrated." . . .

III. The Abolitionism which I advocate is as absolute as the law of God, and as unyielding as His throne. It admits of no compromise. Every slave is a stolen man; every slaveholder is a man-stealer. By no precedent, no example, no law, no compact, no purchase, no bequest, no inheritance, no combination of circumstances, is slaveholding right or justifiable. While a slave remains in his fetters, the land must have no rest. Whatever sanctions his doom must be pronounced accursed. The law that makes him a chattel is to be trampled under foot; the compact that is formed at his expense, and cemented with his blood, is null and void; the church that consents to his enslavement is horribly atheistical; the religion that receives to its communion the enslaver is the embodiment of all criminality. Such, at least, is the verdict of my own soul, on the supposition that I am to be the slave that my wife is to be sold from me for the vilest purposes; that my children are to be torn from my arms, and disposed of to the highest bidder, like sheep in the market. And who am I but a man? What right have I to be free, that another man cannot prove himself to possess by nature? Who or what are my wife and children, that they should not be herded with four-looted beasts, as well as others thus sacredly related? If I am white, and another is black, complexionally, what follows? . . .

What if I am rich, and another is poor—strong, and he is weak—intelligent, and he is benighted—elevated, and he is depraved? "Have we not one Father? Hath not one God created us?" . . .

Such is man, in every clime—above all compacts, greater than all institutions, sacred against every outrage, priceless, immortal!

By this sure test, every institution, every party, every form of government, every kind of religion, is to be tried. God never made a human being either for destruction or degradation. It is plain, therefore, that whatever cannot flourish except at the sacrifice of that being, ought not to exist. Show me the party that can obtain supremacy only by trampling upon human individuality and personal sovereignty, and you will thereby pronounce sentence of death upon it. Show me the government which can be maintained only by destroying the rights of a portion of the people, and you will indicate the duty of openly revolting against it. Show me the religion which sanctions the ownership of one man by another, and you will demonstrate it to be purely infernal in its origin and spirit.

No man is to be injured in his person, mind, or estate. He cannot be, with benefit to any other man, or to any state of society. Whoever would sacrifice him for any purpose is both morally and politically insane. Every man is equivalent to every other man. Destroy the equivalent, and what is left? "So God created man in his own image—male and female created he them." This is a death-blow to all claims of superiority, to all charges of inferiority, to all usurpation, to all oppressive dominion.

But all these declarations are truisms. Most certainly; and they are all that is stigmatized as "Garrisonian Abolitionism." I have not, at any time, advanced an ultra sentiment, or made an extravagant demand. I have avoided fanaticism on the one hand, and folly on the other. No man can show that I have taken one step beyond the line of justice, or forgotten the welfare of the master in my anxiety to free the slave. Why, citizens of the Empire State, did you proclaim liberty to all in bondage on your soil, in 1827, and forevermore? Certainly, not on the ground of expediency, but of principle. Why do you make slaveholding unlawful among yourselves? Why is it not as easy to buy, breed, inherit, and make slaves in this State, compatible with benevolence, justice, and right, as it is in Carolina or Georgia? Why do you compel the unmasked refugee from Van Dieman's Land to sigh for "a plantation well stocked with healthy negroes in Alabama," and not allow him the right to own and flog slaves in your presence? If slaveholding is not wrong under all circumstances, why have you decreed it to be so, within the limits of your State jurisdiction? Nay, why do you have a judiciary, a legislative assembly, a civil code, the ballot box, but to preserve your rights as one man? On what other ground, except that you are men, do you claim a right to personal freedom, to the ties of kindred, to the means of improvement, to constant development, to labour when and for whom you choose, to make your own contracts, to read and speak and print as you please, to remain at home or travel abroad, to exercise the elective franchise, to make your own rulers? What you demand for yourselves, in virtue of your manhood, I demand for the enslaved at the South, on the same ground. How is it that I am a madman, and you are perfectly rational? Wherein is my ultraism apparent? If the slaves are not men, if they do not possess human instincts, passions, faculties and powers; if they are below accountability, and devoid of reason; if for them there is no hope of immortality, no God, no heaven, no hell; if, in short, they are, what the Slave Code declares them to be, rightly "deemed, sold, taken, reputed and adjudged in law to be chattels personal in the hands of their owners and possessors, and their executors, administrators and assigns, to all intents, constructions, and purposes whatsoever"; then, undeniably, I am mad, and can no longer discriminate between a man and a beast. But, in that case, away with the horrible incongruity of giving them oral instruction, of teaching them the catechism, of recognising them as suitably qualified to be members of Christian churches, of extending to them the ordinance of baptism, and admitting them to the communion table, and enumerating many of them as belonging to the household of faith! Let them be no more included in our religious sympathies or denominational statistics than are the dogs in our streets, the swine in our pens, or the utensils in our dwellings. It is right to own, to buy, to sell, to inherit, to breed, and to control them, in the most absolute sense. All constitutions and laws which forbid their possession ought to be so far modified or repealed as to concede the right.

But, if they are men; if they are to run the same career of immortality with ourselves; if the same law of God is over them as over all others; if they have souls to be saved or lost; if Jesus included them among those for whom he laid down his life; if Christ is within many of them "the hope of glory"; then, when I claim for them all that we claim for ourselves, because we are created in the image of God, I am guilty of no extravagance, but am bound, by every principle of honour, by all the claims of human nature, by obedience to Almighty God, to "remember them that are in bonds as bound with them," and to demand their immediate and unconditional emancipation. I am "ultra" and "fanatical," forsooth! In what direction, or affecting what parties? What have I urged should be done to the slaveholders? Their punishment as felons of the deepest dye? No. I have simply enunciated in their ear the divine command, "Loose the bands of wickedness, undo the heavy burdens, break every yoke, and let the oppressed go free," accompanying it with the cheering promises, "Then shall thy light rise in obscurity, and thy darkness be as the noonday. And the Lord shall guide thee continually, and satisfy thy soul in drought, and make fat thy bones; and thou shalt be like a watered garden, and like a spring of water whose waters fail not. And they that shall be of thee shall build the old waste places; thou shalt raise up the foundations of many generations; and thou shalt be called, The repairer of the breach, The restorer of paths to dwell in." Yet, if I had affirmed that they ought to meet the doom of pirates, I should have been no more personal, no more merciless, than is the law of Congress, making it a piratical act to enslave a native African, under whatever pretence or circumstances; for in the eye of reason, and by the standard of eternal justice, it is as great a crime to enslave one born on our own soil, as on the coast of Africa; and as, in the latter case, neither the plea of having fairly purchased or inherited him, nor the pretense of seeking his temporal and eternal good, by bringing him to a civilized and Christian country, would be regarded as of any weight, so, none of the excuses offered for slaveholding in this country are worthy of the least consideration. The act, in both cases, is essentially the same—equally inhuman, immoral, piratical. Oppression is not a matter of latitude or longitude; here excusable, there to be execrated; here to elevate the oppressor to the highest station, there to hang him by the neck till he is dead; here compatible with Christianity, there to be branded and punished as piracy. "He that stealeth a man, and selleth him, or if he be found in his hand, he shall surely be put to death." So reads the Mosaic code, and by it every American Slaveholder is convicted of a capital crime. By the Declaration of Independence, he is pronounced a man-stealer. As for myself, I have simply exposed his guilt, besought him to repent, and to "go and sin no more."

What extravagant claim have I made in behalf of the slaves? Will it be replied, "Their immediate liberation!" Then God, by his prophet, is guilty of extravagance! Then Thomas Jefferson, who wrote the Declaration of Independence, and all who signed that instrument, and all who joined in the Revolutionary struggle, were deceivers in asserting it to be a self-evident truth, that all men are endowed by their Creator with an inalienable right to liberty! The issue is not with me, but with them, and with God. What! is it going too far to ask, for those who have been outraged and plundered all their lives long, nothing but houseless, penniless, naked freedom! No compensation whatever for their past unrequited toil; no redress for their multitudinous wrongs; no settlement for sundered ties, bleeding backs, countless lacerations, darkened intellects, ruined souls! The truth is, complete justice has never been asked for the enslaved.

How has the slave system grown to its present enormous dimensions? Through compromise. How is it to be exterminated? Only by an uncompromising spirit. This is to be carried out in all the relations of life—social, political, religious. Put not on the list of your friends, nor allow admission to your domestic circle, the man who on principle defends Slavery, but treat him as a moral leper. "If an American addresses you," said Daniel O'Connell to his countrymen, "find out at once if he be a slaveholder. He may have business with you, and the less you do with him the better; but the moment that is over, turn from him as if he had the cholera or the plague—for there is a moral cholera and a political plague upon him. He belongs not to your country or your clime—he is not within the pale of civilization or Christianity." On another occasion he said: "An American gentleman waited upon me this morning, and I asked him with some anxiety, 'What part of America do you come from?' 'I came from Boston.' Do me the honour to shake hands; you came from a State that has never been tarnished with Slavery—a State to which our ancestors fled from the tyranny of England—and the worst of all tyrannies, the attempt to interfere between man and his God—a tyranny that I have in principle helped to put down in this country, and wish to put down in every country upon the face of the globe. It is odious and insolent to interfere between a man and his God; to fetter with law the choice which the conscience makes of its mode of adoring the eternal and adorable God. I cannot talk of toleration, because it supposes that a boon has been given to a human being, in allowing him to have his conscience free. It was in that struggle, I said, that your fathers left England; and I rejoice to see an American from Boston; but I should be sorry to be contaminated by the touch of a man from those States where Slavery is continued. 'Oh,' said he, 'you are alluding to Slavery: though I am no advocate for it, yet, if you will allow me, I will discuss that question with you.' I replied, that if a man should propose to me a discussion on the propriety of picking pockets, I would turn him out of my study, for fear he should carry his theory into practice. 'And meaning you no sort of offence,' I added, 'which I cannot mean to a gentleman who does me the honour of paying me a civil visit, I would as soon discuss the one question with you as the other. The one is a paltry theft.

> 'He that steals my purse steals trash; 'tie something, nothing;
> 'Twas mine, 'tis his, and has been slave to thousands'—

but he who thinks he can vindicate the possession of one human being by another—the sale of soul and body—the separation of father and mother—the taking of the mother from the infant at her breast, and selling the one to one master, and the other to another—is a man whom I will not answer with words—nōr with blows, for the time for the latter has not yet come.'"

If such a spirit of manly indignation and unbending integrity pervaded the Northern breast, how long could Slavery stand before it? But where is it to be found? Alas! The man whose hands are red with blood is honoured and caressed in proportion to the number of his victims; while "he who departs from evil makes himself a prey." This is true, universally, in our land. Why should not the Slave Power make colossal strides over the continent? "There is no North." A sordid, trucking, cowardly, compromising spirit, is everywhere seen. No insult or outrage, no deed of impiety or blood, on the part of the South, can startle us into resistance, or inspire us with self-respect. We see our free coloured citizens incarcerated in Southern prisons, or sold on the auction-block, for no other crime than that of being found on Southern soil; and we dare not call for redress. Our commerce with the South is bound with the shackles of the plantation—"Free-Trade and Sailors'-Rights" are every day violated in Southern ports; and we tamely submit to it as the slave does to the lash. Our natural, God-given right of free-speech, though constitutionally recognised as sacred in every part of the country, can be exercised in the slaveholding States only at the peril of our lives. Slavery cannot bear one ray of light, or the slightest criticism. "The character of Slavery," says Gov. Swain, of North Carolina, "is not to be discussed"—meaning at the South. But he goes beyond this, and adds, "We have an indubitable right to demand of the Free States to suppress such discussion, totally and promptly." Gov. Tazewell, of Virginia, makes the same declaration. Gov. Lumpkin, of Georgia, says: "The weapons of reason and argument are insufficient to put down discussion; we can therefore hear no argument upon the subject, for our opinions are unalterably fixed." And he adds, that the Slave States "will provide for their own protection, and those who speak against Slavery will do well to keep out of their bounds, or they will punish them." The Charleston Courier declares, "The gallows and the stake (i.e. burning alive and hanging) await the Abolitionists who shall dare to appear in person among us." The Columbia Telescope says: "Let us declare through the public journals of our country, that the question of Slavery is not and shall not be open to discussion; that the system is too deep-rooted among us, and must remain forever; that the very moment any private individual attempts to lecture us upon its evils and immorality, and the necessity of putting means in operation to secure us from them, in the same moment his tongue shall be cut out and cast upon the dunghill." The Missouri Argus says: "Abolition editors in slave States will not dare to avow their opinions. It would be instant death to them." Finally, the New Orleans True American says: "We can assure those, one and all, who have embarked in the nefarious scheme of abolishing Slavery at the South, that lashes will hereafter be spared the backs of their emissaries. Let them send out their men to Louisiana; they will never return to tell their suffering, but they shall expiate the crime of interfering in our domestic institutions, by being burned at the stake." And Northern men cower at this, and consent to have their lips padlocked, and to be robbed of their constitutional right, aye, and their natural right, while traveling Southward; while the lordly slaveholder traverses the length and breadth of the Free States, with open mouth and impious tongue, cursing freedom and its advocates with impunity, and choosing Plymouth Rock, and the celebration of the landing of the Pilgrims upon it, as the place and the occasion specially fitting to eulogize Slavery and the Fugitive Slave Bill! . . .

Whatever may be the guilt of the South, the North is still more responsible for the existence, growth and extension of Slavery. In her hand has been the destiny of the Republic from the beginning. She could have emancipated every slave, long ere this, had she been upright in heart and free in spirit. She has given respectability, security, and the means of sustenance and attack to her deadliest foe. She has educated the whole country, and particularly the Southern portion of it, secularly, theologically religiously; and the result is, three millions and a half of slaves, increasing at the appalling rate of one hundred thousand a year, three hundred a day, and one every five minutes—the utter corruption of public sentiment, and general skepticism as to the rights of man—the inauguration of Mammon in the place of the living God—the loss of all self-respect, all manhood, all sense of shame, all regard for justice—the Book styled holy, and claimed to be divinely inspired, everywhere expounded and enforced in extenuation or defence of slaveholding, and against the Anti-Slavery movement—colour-phobia infecting the life-blood of the people—political profligacy unparalleled—the religious and the secular press generally hostile to Abolitionism as either infidel or anarchical in its spirit and purpose—the great mass of the churches with as little vitality as a grave-yard—the pulpits, with rare exceptions, filled with men as careful to consult the popular will as though there were no higher law-synods, presbyteries, general conferences, general assemblies, buttressing the slave power—the Government openly pro-slavery, and the National District the head-quarters of slave speculators—fifteen Slave States—and now, the repeal of the Missouri Compromise, and the consecration of five hundred thousand square miles of free territory forever to the service of the Slave Power!

And what does all this demonstrate! That the sin of this nation is not geographical—is not specially Southern—bus deep-seated and universal. "The whole head is sick, and the whole heart faint." We are "full of wounds, and bruises, and putrifying sores." It proves, too, the folly of all plasters and palliatives. Some men are still talking of preventing the spread of the cancer, but leaving it just where it is. They admit that, constitutionally, it has now a right to ravage two-thirds of the body politic—but they protest against its extension. This is moral quackery. Even some, whose zeal in the Anti-Slavery cause is fervent, are so infatuated as to propose no other remedy for Slavery but its non-extension. Give it no more room, they say, and it may be safely left to its fate. Yes, but who shall "bell the cat?" Besides, with fifteen Slave States, and more than three millions of Slaves, how can we make any moral issue with the Slave Power against its further extension? Why should there not be twenty, thirty, fifty Slave States, as well as fifteen? Why should not the star-spangled banner wave over ten, as well as over three millions of Slaves? Why should not Nebraska be cultivated by Slave labour, as well as Florida or Texas? If men, under the American Constitution, may hold slaves at discretion and without dishonour in one-half of the country, why not in the whole of it? If it would be a damning sin for us to admit another Slave State into the Union, why is it not a damning sin to permit a Slave State to remain in the Union? Would it not be the acme of effrontery for a man, in amicable alliance with fifteen pickpockets, to profess scruples of conscience in regard to admitting another pilfering rogue to the fraternity? "Thou that sayest, A man should not steal, dost thou steal," or consent, in any instance, to stealing? "If the Lord be God, serve Him; but if Baal, then serve him." The South may well laugh to scorn the affected moral sensibility of the North against the extension of her slave system. It is nothing, in the present relations of the States, but sentimental hypocrisy. It has no stamina—no backbone. The argument for non-extension is an argument for the dissolution of the Union. With a glow of moral indignation, I protest against the promise and the pledge, by whomsoever made, that if the Slave Power will seek no more to lengthen its cords and strengthen its stakes, it may go unmolested and unchallenged, and survive as long as it can within its present limits. I would as soon turn pirate on the high seas as to give my consent to any such arrangement. I do not understand the moral code of those who, screaming in agony at the thought of Nebraska becoming a Slave Territory, virtually say to the South: "Only desist from your present designs, and we will leave you to flog, and lacerate, and plunder, and destroy the millions of hapless wretches already within your grasp. If you will no longer agitate the subject, we will not." There is no sense, no principle, no force in such an issue. Not a solitary slaveholder will I allow to enjoy repose on any other condition than instantly ceasing to be one. Not a single slave will I leave in his chains, on any conditions, or under any circumstances. I will not try to make as good a bargain for the Lord as the Devil will let me, and plead the necessity of a compromise, and regret that I cannot do any better, and be thankful that I can do so much. The Scriptural injunction is to be obeyed: "Resist the devil, and he will flee from you." My motto is, "No union with slaveholders, religiously or politically." Their motto is "Slavery forever! No alliance with Abolitionists, either in Church or State!" The issue is clear, explicit, determinate. The parties understand each other, and are drawn in battle array. They can never be reconciled—never walk together—never consent to a truce—never deal in honeyed phrases—never worship at the same altar—never acknowledge the same God. Between them there is an impassable gulf. In manners, in morals, in philosophy, in religion, in ideas of justice, in notions of law, in theories of government, in valuations or men, they are totally dissimilar.

I would to God that we might be, what we have never been—a united people; but God renders this possible only by "proclaiming liberty throughout all the land, unto all the inhabitants thereof." By what miracle can Freedom and Slavery be made amicably to strike hands? How can they administer the same Government, or legislate for the same interests? How can they receive the same baptism, be admitted to the same communion-table, believe in the same Gospel, and obtain the same heavenly inheritance? "I speak as unto wise men; judge ye." Certain propositions have long since been conceded to be plain, beyond contradiction. The apostolic inquiry has been regarded as equally admonitory and pertinent: "What concord hath Christ with Belial? or what fellowship hath light with darkness?" Fire and gunpowder, oil and water, cannot coalesce; but, assuredly, these are not more antagonistical than are the elements of Freedom and Slavery. The present American Union, therefore, is only one in form, not in reality. It is, and it always has been, the absolute supremacy of the Slave Power over the whole country—nothing more. What sectional heart-burnings or conflictive interests exist between the several Free States? None. They are homogeneous, animated by the same spirit, harmonious in their action as the movement of the spheres. It is only when we come to the dividing line between the Free States and the Slave States that shoals, breakers and whirlpools beset the ship of State, and threaten to engulf or strand it. Then the storm rages loud and long, and the ocean of popular feeling is lashed into fury.

While the present Union exists, I pronounce it hopeless to expect any repose, or that any barrier can be effectually raised against the extension of Slavery. With two thousand million dollars' worth of property in human flesh in its hands, to be watched and wielded as one vast interest for all the South—with forces never divided, and purposes never conflictive—with a spurious, negro-hating religion universally diffused, and everywhere ready to shield it from harm—with a selfish, sordid, divided North, long since bereft of its manhood, to cajole, bribe and intimidate—with its foot planted on two-thirds of our vast national domains, and there unquestioned, absolute and bloody in its sway—with the terrible strength and boundless resources of the whole country at its command—it cannot be otherwise than that the Slave Power will consummate its diabolical purposes to the uttermost. The Northwest Territory, Nebraska, Mexico, Cuba, Hayti, the Sandwich Islands, and colonial possessions in the tropics—to seize and subjugate these to its accursed reign, and ultimately to re-establish the foreign Slave Trade as a lawful commerce, are among its settled designs. It is not a question of probabilities, but of time. And whom will a just God hold responsible for all these results? All who despise and persecute men on account of their complexion; all who endorse a slaveholding religion as genuine; all who give the right hand of Christian fellowship to men whose hands are stained with the blood of the slave? all who regard material prosperity as paramount to moral integrity, and the law of the land as above the law of God; all who are either hostile or indifferent to the Anti-Slavery movement; and all who advocate the necessity of making compromises with the Slave Power, in order that the Union may receive no detriment.

In itself, Slavery has no resources and no strength. Isolated and alone, it could not stand an hour; and, therefore, further aggression and conquest would be impossible....

While, therefore, the Union is preserved, I see no end to the extension or perpetuity of Chattel Slavery—no hope for peaceful deliverance of the millions who are clanking their chains on our blood-red soil. Yet I know that God reigns, and that the slave system contains within itself the elements of destruction. But how long it is to curse the earth, and desecrate his image, he alone foresees. It is frightful to think of the capacity of a nation like this to commit sin, before the measure of its iniquities be filled, and the exterminating judgments of God overtake it. For what is left us but "a fearful looking for of judgment and fiery indignation"? Or is God but a phantom, and the Eternal Law but a figment of the imagination? Has an everlasting divorce been effected between cause and effect, and is it an absurd doctrine that, as a nation sows, so shall it also reap? "Wherefore, hear the word of the Lord, ye scornful men that rule this people: Because ye have said, We have made a covenant with death, and with hell are we at agreement; when the overflowing scourge shall pass through, it shall not come unto us; for we have made lies our refuge, and under falsehood have we hid ourselves: Therefore, thus saith the Lord God, Judgment will I lay to the line, and righteousness to the plummet; and the hail shall sweep away the refuge of lies, and the waters shall overflow the hiding-place: And your covenant with death shall be annulled, and your agreement with hell shall not stand; when the overflowing scourge shall pass through, then ye shall be trodden down by it."

These are solemn times. It is not a struggle for national salvation; for the nation, as such, seems doomed beyond recovery. The reason why the South rules, and the North falls prostrate in servile terror, is simply this: With the South, the preservation of Slavery is paramount to all other considerations—above party success, denominational unity, pecuniary interest, legal integrity, and constitutional obligation. With the North, the preservation of the Union is placed above all other things—above honour, justice, freedom, integrity of soul, the Decalogue and the Golden Rule—the Infinite God himself. All these she is ready to discard for the Union. Her devotion to it is the latest and the most terrible form of idolatry. She has given to the Slave Power a carte blanche, to be filled as it may dictate—and if, at any time, she grows restive under the yoke, and shrinks back aghast at the new atrocity contemplated, it is only necessary for that Power to crack the whip of Disunion over her head, as it has done again and again, and she will cower and obey like a plantation slave—for has she not sworn that she will sacrifice everything in heaven and on earth, rather than the Union?

What then is to be done? Friends of the slave, the question is not whether by our efforts we can abolish Slavery, speedily or remotely—for duty is ours, the result is with God; but whether we will go with the multitude to do evil, sell our birthright for a mess of pottage, cease to cry aloud and spare not, and remain in Babylon when the command of God is, "Come out of her, my people, that ye be not partakers of her sins, and that ye receive not of her plagues." Let us stand in our lot, "and having done all, to stand." At least, a remnant shall be saved. Living or dying, defeated or victorious, be it ours to exclaim, "No compromise with Slavery! Liberty for each, for all, forever! Man above all institutions! The supremacy of God over the whole earth!"

20

"No Rights, No Duties: Or, Slaveholders, as Such, Have No Rights; Slaves, as Such, Owe No Duties" (1860)

Henry C. Wright

Henry C. Wright (1797–1870) was a radical New England abolitionist who rose from modest origins as a hatmaker to become an ordained minister and then a leader in the abolitionist movement. Closely allied with Garrison, he was an uncompromising pacifist and "no-government" man.

By the late 1850s, some abolitionists abandoned their pacifism and allegiance to moral suasion as the only means to advance the cause of immediate abolition. In the wake of John Brown's failed raid on Harper's Ferry and his subsequent execution, a small but growing number of abolitionists began to call for armed insurrection in the South to emancipate the slaves. Wright's "No Rights, No Duties" is one of the clearest formulations of this teaching. The essay is written as an answer to a letter from the Hon. Henry Wilson, a Republican senator from Massachusetts who had criticized the doctrine of resistance to slaveholders.

What Is Well Known To Hon. Henry Wilson and the Republican Party

Sir,—A letter from you to me, through the New York Herald, has just reached me. In it you affirm, with great seeming indignation and vexation, that I know some things, which you are kind enough to mention. In answer, allow me, frankly, but with confidence, to tell you and the political party which you represent, what you and they know.

1. "You know" that individual slaveholders, as such, have no rights which any man, black or white, enslaved or free, is bound to respect.

The individual pirate, as a pirate, has no rights. No laws nor constitutions of human device can create for and secure to him any rights; and if they attempt to do so, it is the duty of all to ignore such rights, and trample all such enactments beneath their feet. This is true of all who hold and use human beings as chattels. You cannot doubt that it is wrong to recognize the moral, social or political force of any laws which secure rights to individual slave-breeders and slave-traders. Slaveholders, as such, have no right to exist for one hour; . . .

2. "You know" that a slaveholding State can have no rights which any individual, or any State, is bound to respect.

A corporate body of pirates, though called a State or nation, can have no rights. It is an organized, systematized banditti, and any individual or State is authorized to destroy it. So, a corporate body of slaveholders, though called Virginia, Maryland, Kentucky, or Missouri, is a self-incorporated body of marauders, and as such, any man or set of men is authorized to destroy it. . . .

One million and a half are banded together, and call themselves "the State of Virginia." Suppose that the basis of their existence, as a State, is man-stealing, and the source of their wealth is slave-breeding and slave-trading. The victims of their lusts and their power they obtain from Pennsylvania and Ohio. Has the State of Virginia any rights that Ohio, or Pennsylvania, or any Northern State, or any individual in any Northern State, is bound to respect? The State is a self-incorporated kidnapper, and as such, has no more rights than a midnight assassin; and it is the right and duty of the Northern people, as individuals and States, to treat Virginia as they would an assassin. You and all "who act with you" know that it would be your right and duty to treat Virginia as you would a band of assassins that should call themselves a State.

But Virginia does not kidnap the children of Ohio and Pennsylvania;—she steals and sells her own sons and daughters! She breeds and rears her own children for the human flesh shambles of South Carolina, Louisiana, and Mississippi.

As Mr. Randolph, of Albemarle county, declared in the Virginia Legislature in 1832: "Slave-breeding is a practice, and an increasing practice, in parts of Virginia. To rear slaves for the market is her staple business. How can an honorable mind bear to see this Ancient Dominion converted into a grand menagerie, where human beings are to be reared for the market, like oxen for the shambles? It is worse than the slave-trade, which the good and wise of every clime have abolished as piracy."

True, the ancestors of these Virginia slaves were stolen, not in Ohio, nor Pennsylvania, but in Africa, brought to Virginia, and enslaved. The State has directed her efforts to make the offspring of these kidnapped sons and daughters of Africa her principal source of wealth, and her staple article of trade. She is simply a slave-breeding and a slave-trading State. There is not, probably, a white man in the State, the owner or employer of female slaves, who has not children in slavery; for the child follows the condition of the mother, and the father is never asked after by Church or State. Even the posterity of

Jefferson is, this day, in slavery, bought and sold like brutes. Virginia is a huge barracoon, whose staple article of trade is, the bodies and souls of her own children. You know that, as a slaveholding State, she has no more rights than a band of buccaniers, and that it is our right and duty to treat her, as Eaton and Decatur treated the Barbary States, those self-incorporated and self-regulated bands of Algerine corsairs.

If the slaves of Virginia were your own children, and the children of your own town and State, do you think you and the people of the old Bay State would prate about "legal and constitutional" means to rescue them? Would they, in the political cant of both political parties, talk of acting "within the Union, and under the Constitution"? No; Natick and Massachusetts would rush to the rescue; and all the New England States would join them, and at once and forever blot from the record of States that corporate ruffian and bandit, setting at naught and defying all human enactments.

Should an army of fifty thousand, direct from Africa, land in Virginia, to rescue the posterity of her sons and daughters from slavery, and to wipe from the record of States that band of slave-breeders and slave-traders, self-styled a Commonwealth, would you side with the oppressed or oppressor? On which side would be Justice, Humanity, and God? "You know" where they would be; and I have too high an opinion of your moral nature and your manhood to suppose that you would be found in the ranks of kidnappers. It would be the right and duty of the North to take sides with the enslaved, and against the enslavers.

3. "You know" that slaves, as such, owe no obedience, no service, no labor, no duties, to those who enslave them.

Suppose Senator Mason had made you a slave. Could you, by any process, be made to feel that you owe him any service or duty? No law or constitution, by whomsoever made, could create in you an obligation or duty to the man who claimed and held you as a chattel. The relation itself being void, all rights and duties deduced from it are void. Rights are the basis of duties: where no rights are recognized, no duties are owed. Slaveholders declare that slaves have no rights. Of course, slaves owe no duties to their enslavers. NO RIGHTS, NO DUTIES—is the battle-cry of the "irrepressible conflict."

The assassin has no claims on any one. No man owes, or can be made to owe him any duties; for he is in a relation that is out of the pale of all law, human or divine. No power can impose on any man an obligation to respect any claim or right, which, as an assassin, he may assume. So, no power in heaven or earth can impose on you, or on any one, an obligation or duty to those who hold and use men and women as chattels.

"You know" that, so far as the laws and Constitution of the United States, or of any of the States, enjoin duties on slaves, they are wholly without moral, social or political force; and that it is the right and duty of all to resist their execution, by such means as shall seem right and expedient to each individual or State. Were your own family, your friends and neighbors the slaves, you would deem any man unprincipled and inhuman who would acknowledge their binding force, or swear to execute them. Why then do you swear to execute laws securing rights to kidnappers, when the helpless negro is the victim?

That decision of the Supreme Court of the United States, declaring that "colored people have no rights that white men are bound to respect," is unsurpassed in atrocity by any decision that human tribunals ever made. But it will be remembered in the future, and its authors get more than they bargained for. When vengeance shall arouse the negroes, and drive them to seize the sabre and torch of insurrection, as it surely will, then will the whites of the South, as they and their families are victimized to the roused wrath and passions of the slaves, remember that Dred Scott decision; and, too late, learn that, by that decision, every negro is formally and judicially released from every duty and obligation of kindness and mercy towards those who have denied to them all rights, and hold and use them as chattels.

4. "You know" it is the right and duty of slaves to assert and maintain their freedom.

Were you a slave, you cannot doubt it would be your right and duty to assert your freedom, by word and deed; by word, by telling your enslaver that you should no longer be a slave; and by deed, by running away, or by staying where you were, and refusing to work an hour or obey any command, as a slave. It would be your duty to assert your manhood, and no longer consent to live and labor as a beast. As it would be your right and duty to save yourself and family from a burning house by getting out of it, or by extinguishing the flames; so would it be your right and duty to save yourself and family from slavery, either by running away, or by defying the power that enslaved you on the spot. Were thirty millions, called the United States, combined to enslave you, this would not alter nor diminish your right and duty to defy them, and assert your freedom. So, it is the right and duty of the four millions of slaves in the South to assert their manhood, and to cease, at once and forever, to live and labor as chattels. It is the right and duty of the North to recognize and treat them as men and women, and no longer, even by silence or political relations, recognize and treat them as chattels.

"You know," too, that it is the right and duty of slaves, not only to free themselves by running away, or otherwise, but, also, to maintain their freedom after they have asserted it. The first step is, cease to live and labor one hour longer as slaves; the second is, maintain your freedom at all hazards. Were you, your wife and daughters slaves, and you had asserted your freedom by running away, you would not doubt a moment as to your right and duty to resist all attempts, by whomsoever made, to capture and return you to slavery; you, yourselves, being sole judges as to the means to be used in resisting the kidnappers. You would resist those who should seek to re-enslave you, as readily and by the same means as you would defend yourselves against a pirate or an assassin. "You know" you would, and that you would give yourselves no trouble about "political obligations," or "political unions and constitutions." You have led your wives and daughters from the hell and horrors of slavery. You would feel it your duty to resist all efforts to drag them back, whether made by presidents, marshals or judges.

So is it the right and duty of the slaves of the South, when escaping to Canada, to resist all who would capture and return them. They owe no allegiance to any laws or constitutions, and no duties to any slave-catchers, or band of slave-catchers, no matter who or by what name called, who would deprive them of their asserted freedom.

There are two millions of female slaves in the South, subjected to rape and rapine perpetrated on them by their white enslavers. They assert their freedom and the sacredness of their persons, and no longer submit to the brutality of "your countrymen of the South." Those who claim them as chattels, and who would outrage their persons, order them to submit. They refuse. The slave-breeders assail them with the lash and horse-whip. Their fathers, brothers, husbands and sons fly to their assistance. Would you, in Natick, in Washington, or in your electioneering speeches, "express regret and condemnation" at their efforts? You would not. And when I assert that you know and feel it to be the right and duty of yourself, of the Republican party, and of all the people of the North, to "incite them to resistance and to aid them," and that at no distant day you will all do so, would you consider this "base and dastardly"? No, you would consider it "unjust, unkind, base and cowardly" to say you would side with the ravishers, or refuse to aid the slaves.

"You know" it is the right and duty of these female slaves to defend themselves against the lust and brutality of their enslavers; and of their husbands, sons, fathers and brothers to incite and assist them to defend themselves; and that, too, by such means as they shall deem right and expedient.

5. "You know" that it is the right and duty of the people and States of the North to incite the slaves of the South to assert and maintain their freedom.

Were your wife and daughter, your mother and sisters, slaves, it would be your right and duty to incite and aid them to assert their freedom, and to deliver themselves from the hell of pollution in which they were held. You would regard all laws, constitutions, creeds, and religions that forbade you to do so, as utterly infamous and void; and all who should recognize such laws and constitutions, compacts or religions, as binding, and should swear to execute them, as unprincipled and inhuman.

So, in regard to the wives, daughters, mothers and sisters, held as slaves in Virginia. It is the right and duty of their husbands, sons, fathers and brothers to incite them to resist their enslavers, who violate their persons and consign them to a living death; and of all the people and States of the North to aid them.

"You know" that, so far as the laws and constitutions and religion of the United States, or of the States, forbid us to aid them, they are null and void; and that we are bound to resist their execution, as we would laws and constitutions and religions that authorize and sustain rape, rapine, and murder.

6. "You know" that, in aiding the enslaved to resist their enslavers, it is the right and duty of the Northern people and States to use such means as they would use, or wish others to use in their behalf, were they slaves.

What means would you and your fellow-republicans use to defend yourselves and families against burglars, incendiaries, and highway robbers? The same it is your right and duty to use in defending others against similar wrongs. What means would you deem it right to use to protect yourselves and families against kidnappers? The same it is your duty to use in defending others. By what means would your constituents, and the people and States of the North deem it right to defend themselves against the efforts of slaveholders to enslave them? It is their duty to use the same to resist their efforts to enslave others.

Slaveholders sought to enslave Kansas. They sent their ruffians, headed by the army and President of the United States, there for that purpose. You, your constituents, and the people of the North met them and resisted, and with Sharp's rifles and Colt's revolvers drove them off, and made Kansas a free State; even H.W. Beecher declaring Sharp's rifles of more value to Kansas than the Bible. This you and your political party approved, and assisted in it. John Brown was the leader of your party in resisting the President, the United States Government, and their titled ruffians. You honor him for resisting the officers and government in their efforts to enslave Kansas. But, when John Brown attempts to do in Virginia what he did in Kansas—i.e., to make it a free State—you call it a "mad raid," and visit upon the deed "regret and condemnation."

"You know" if John Brown was right at Lawrence and Osawatomie, he was right at Harper's Ferry; that if it was his duty and yours, and the duty of the Republican party, to resist slaveholders in Kansas, and make that a free State, it is your duty to resist them in Virginia, and make that a free State. If it was right to "kill, and slay, and destroy" the slaveholding ruffians in Kansas, "YOU KNOW" it is right to "kill, slay and destroy" them in Virginia. Whatever means it was right to use to make a free State of Kansas, it is your right and duty to use to make Virginia, Maryland, Kentucky and Missouri free States,—laws and constitutions, political compacts and unions, to the contrary notwithstanding.

Thus, it is our right and duty to use all means to free the slaves of the South, which we would use to free ourselves, or wish others to use in our behalf, were we slaves. So, were your "countrymen of the South" to attempt to make a slave State of Massachusetts, you know that you and your constituents would resist them by arms and blood, and, at all hazards, assert and maintain the freedom of that State. Slaveholders have as good a right to make Massachusetts a slave State, as they have to make or continue Virginia a slave State; and you, your party, and all the people and States of the North, know that it is your right and your duty to use the same means to make Virginia a free State, that you would use to make or continue Massachusetts a free State.

Do you think that Virginia, or any State, has a right, or can have a right, to establish slavery in its own borders? You say, "Virginia has a right to manage her own affairs." When you and your fellow-republicans say this, do you mean that Virginia has, or can have, a right to turn human beings into beasts and chattels, and to be a slave State? Do you mean that she has, or can have, a right to breed and sell slaves; and thus to exist as a slave-breeding and slavetrading State? "You know" that you do not think Virginia has a right, before God or man, to hold, breed and sell slaves, and that when, under the phrase, "a right to manage her own affairs," the people of that State infer that you admit their right to turn your fellow-beings into chattels, you do "throw glamour in their eyes," if you leave that impression upon their minds. Political ambition, and a desire to promote the interests of your party, may have greatly bewildered and obfuscated your heart and head; yet you are not a fool nor a knave, but have an enlightened conscience, and a clear perception of the true and the right. Thus endowed, "YOU KNOW" that Virginia has no more right to exist one hour as a slaveholding, slave-breeding, and slave-trading State, than the crew of a piratical ship has to exist as a band of pirates. A religion or government that confers rights on slaveholders, as such, or enjoins obedience or any duties on slaves, as such, or forbids us to incite chattelized men and women to assert and maintain, at all hazards, their manhood and womanhood, deserves the scorn and contempt of every human being; and those who sustain such a religion and government are the deadly enemies of mankind.

7. "You know" that freedom cannot be national where slavery is local.

There are one million, four hundred and sixty-four thousand, and forty-five (1,464,045) square miles in the United States. Eight hundred and fifty-one thousand, four hundred and forty-eight (851,448) are exclusively devoted to slavery. Freedom of speech, press and person cannot exist there. Six hundred and twelve thousand, five hundred and ninty-seven (612,597) are nominally, and partially, devoted to freedom. I say nominally and partially; for the free States (as they are called) have pledged themselves not to seek to free the slaves in the slave States, but to protect the enslavers against the enslaved, and to admit slavery to be represented in Congress; have pledged themselves to allow slavery special privileges in the government; and to let slaveholders have political power in proportion to the number of their slaves. Besides, slavery from the beginning has been allowed to rule the pulpit, the platform, the press, the schools and colleges of the non-slave States. Yet you and your fellow-republicans say, "Slavery is local; freedom national"!

... Slavery virtually and absolutely controls nearly one third more of the territory of the United States than freedom. Those who embody slavery are allowed to roam freely over all the territory nominally devoted to freedom, and on the soil of freedom to advocate man-stealing, slave-breeding and slave-trading; to browbeat and threaten the friends of freedom with bowie-knives and revolvers; and to kidnap and enslave the people dwelling on this nominally free soil. But, if the friends of freedom enter the slave States to plead for liberty, to sustain the Declaration of Independence, and inculcate the duty of "loving our neighbors as ourselves," of "doing to others as we would they should do to us," of "remembering those in bonds as bound with them," and of "delivering the spoiled out of the hands of the spoiler"—they are whipped, imprisoned, or hung. Witness John Brown and his associates. Knowing all this, why do you persist in saying, "Slavery is local, freedom national"?

John Quincy Adams spoke the truth when he said, "The preservation, propagation, and perpetuation of slavery constitutes the vital and animating spirit of the national government." This fact was manifested in the compromises of the Constitution; and it has been manifested from that hour to this in the administration of the government in its every department. It was apparent in the purchase of Louisiana and Florida; in the annexation of Texas and in the Mexican war; in the Fugitive Slave Law of 1850, and the efforts to execute it ever since; in the formation and abolition of the Missouri Compromise; in the effort of the national government to make a slave State of Kansas; in its efforts to obtain Cuba, and the Dred Scott decision; and, finally, in hanging John Brown for attempting to free the slaves of Virginia, and make it a free State. "You know" all these facts. Yet you persist in affirming that "Slavery is local, Freedom national"! Slavery has sole and exclusive possession of two-thirds of the great national House; and controls the religion, the politics, the education, and commerce of the other third. Yet you affirm that "Slavery is local, freedom national"! You deceive your constituents and betray their trust, when you tell them what is so manifestly false and absurd.

I am very certain you will, at no distant day, "cease to remember that slavery, in the States, is local, and not national"; and you will learn that slavery is national, and liberty hardly local; that slavery is every where, and liberty no where. If you know it not now, you will soon know that it cannot be otherwise "within the present Union, and under the present Constitution" of the United States. You will soon be made to know, that a dissolution of this slaveholding Union is a mere question of time.

8. "You know" that no power, not God himself, can reconcile slavery with liberty. They are moral antagonisms. As well attempt to compromise and harmonize a lie with truth, as slavery with liberty. The one original, fatal error of the nation is, and has ever been, this attempt to reconcile, under the same government, two moral contradictions: the admission that slaveholders, as such, may have rights; and that slaves, as such, may owe duties. In their nature, slavery and liberty are deadly enemies. Whenever and wherever they meet, each must, necessarily, seek the destruction of the other. The existence of either is a declaration of war against the existence of the other. All who attempt to make a truce between them necessarily lose the power to distinguish between them; as he who tries to reconcile what he knows to be a lie, with what he knows to be a truth, loses the power to distinguish between them.

Whenever these antagonisms meet—be it in domestic, social, ecclesiastical, political, or commercial life; be it in Congress, in the Supreme Court, or in the Presidential chair; be it in Church or State, in the pulpit or on the platform, there must be war, and that unto death, to slavery, or death to liberty. Death to one or the other is the only finality to this conflict. The people of the North have tried to meet slaveholders in peace and harmony, in every relation of life. This is their error and their crime. True to their leading idea, the slaveholders have given no rest to those who profess to embody liberty. So far and so long as the people and States of the North embody liberty, and the people and States of the South embody slavery, undying hostility must exist, and ought to exist, between them; and he is an enemy of his race who attempts to reconcile them, or recognizes the binding force of any law or any other principle than death to slavery.

Only on one condition can there be a union between the people and States of the North, and the people and States of the South—i.e., the North must cease to embody liberty in their theories, their life and institutions, or the South must cease to embody slavery. If neither will yield, and each is fixed on embodying more and more resolutely its leading, central idea of life, one of two things is inevitable—i.e., the dissolution of the Union, and the formation of a Northern Republic on the principle of "No Union with Slaveholders," or a conflict by arms on the field of death. You cannot be true to liberty, without being an irreconcilable enemy to all slaveholders, as such, and to all slaveholding States and institutions. The Republican party cannot be a true embodiment and exponent of liberty, without seeking to overthrow and annihilate all institutions that embody slavery.

All efforts to compromise with slavery and those who embody it, for any cause, is to compound with rape, robbery, and piracy; is to compound with "the sum of all villany." It is to form "a covenant with death, and an agreement with hell." Such is the American Union, and such you will see and know it to be when slavery and politics shall have ceased to darken your reason, and pervert your moral nature.

9. "You know" that, in this "irrepressible conflict" between the enslaved and their enslavers, it is the sacred duty of the people and States of the North to side with the slaves.

As in a conflict between a band of highway robbers or pirates, and those whom they would plunder and murder, it is their duty to side with the wronged and outraged; so, in this conflict between the enslaved and their enslavers, every Northern man and State are sacredly bound by their political and religious creeds, and by their allegiance to themselves and their posterity, to the slaves and slaveholders, to their country, to mankind, and to God, to stand by the slaves. In every insurrection or rebellion of the enslaved against their enslavers, our sympathies, our prayers, our words, our money, and our efforts, such as we deem it right to make, ought all to be for the slave, and against the enslaver. This "YOU KNOW," and teach by precept and example, when you, your family, or white men (as in the case of the Barbary States) are the victims.

Will you say, the Constitution and laws bind the people and States of the North to aid the enslavers against the enslaved? What if they do? In this "irrepressible conflict" between the enslaved and their enslavers, this war unto death between liberty and slavery, "There is no attribute of the Almighty that can take sides with the slaveholders." God and Humanity are against them. In your solicitude to give triumph to your political party, will you obey the "lower law," join the slave-breeders, and array yourself against the Almighty, and against the nobler instincts of your manhood? Under pretence of carrying out the compromises of the Constitution, and of maintaining what you acknowledge to be a slaveholding, slave-catching, and slave-trading Union, and of being true to this corporation of kidnappers, this great, national "brotherhood of thieves," would you do, what Edward Everett says he would do, shoulder your musket, join the slaveholders, and fight against the slaves struggling for freedom? Henry Wilson! "YOU KNOW" you would not; but that, in the death-struggle between the enslaved and their enslavers, which must come, sooner or later, (and SOONER THE BETTER,) you will be struggling for the former, and against the latter. In that conflict, you will embody liberty, and your slogan will be—DEATH TO SLAVERY! If, as a politician, you say this is doing you a great "unkindness and injustice," I am willing to lie under the imputation, until the MAN in Henry Wilson shall triumph over the POLITICIAN. When that day comes, as come it will, then you will thank me, in spite of yourself, for vindicating your manhood against the compromising, political partisan, that now, on the eve of a presidential election, overpowers and seduces the nobler and more divine elements of your nature.

10. "You know" that it is our right and duty to make our appeals to the "heart, the reason and conscience" of the slaves, to incite in them aspirations for freedom, and to animate and encourage them to be men, rather than chattels.

An assassin is hidden by the road on which you are traveling, with a view to kill and rob you. I know he is there, and that you will lose your life if you pass on. Shall I make my appeals to you, to induce you to escape the danger, or must I appeal only to "the reason, heart and conscience" of him who is lying in wait for you? The incendiary is about to fire your house, and burn you and your family. I see him. Shall I call to you to awaken, and incite you to escape from the burning house, and aid you to extinguish the flames, and secure the evil-doer, or shall I leave you and yours to your fatal slumber, and make my appeals only to the "reason, heart and conscience" of the incendiary?

Four millions of your "fellow-countrymen of the South" are at this hour in the burning hell of slavery, and, every day and hour, waylaid by robbers and murderers; by those who steal and sell their children, outrage and whip their wives and daughters, and kill the husbands and fathers if they attempt to defend their loved ones against their ravishers. They are held and used as "chattels personal, to all intents, constructions and purposes whatsoever." Thus are they beset, on all sides, with robbers, ravishers and assassins. Shall the people and States of the North make their appeals to these four millions thus beset and outraged, to vitalize their souls, and incite and help them to escape from that burning hell, and defeat the "base and dastardly" ruffians and their abettors that surround them; or must they make their appeals only to the "reason, heart and conscience" of those who plunder and enslave them?

It is the right and duty of the people and States of the North, "to remember to make their appeals to the heart, the reason and conscience" of the enslaved, as well as of the enslavers. You are conscious that no political compromises, compacts, or constitutions can ever abridge or alter this duty. To incite slaves to cease to be chattels, and to become men and women—this is the sacred duty of the people and States of the North.

11. "You know" it is the duty of the people and States of the North to invade slaveholding States to free the slaves, and annihilate the power that enslaves them.

The right to defend life, liberty and property, even by killing the aggressor, is the basis of every governmental organization in America. It is embodied in the Declaration of Independence, in the Constitution of the United States, and in the Constitution of every State in the Union. I have heard you proclaim this, on the political and anti-slavery platforms, as the only true basis and object of every government that has a rightful existence; that every human being has a natural right to defend himself, even to the killing of the aggressors, against all who shall attempt to enslave them or their children. You have often said, and do still say, that the man, or set of men, no matter by what name called, nor by what authority invested, who seek to murder, enslave, or rob us, forfeits by so doing all rights, even that of life, and that the outraged individual, alone or by the help of others, may kill him or them, if need be. You will not deny, in Massachusetts nor in Washington, that this ever has been, and is now, your opinion, and the opinion of your party. The existence of every State in the Union, and of the Union itself, is based on the right of the enslaved to resist their enslavers by arms and blood; and on the right of others to incite and aid them to resist.

The people and State of Virginia exist by daily and hourly aggressions on the persons and property of our fellow-beings; by kidnapping, enslaving and selling them as chattels; and by aggressions on the personal property and family rights of hundreds of thousands. As individuals and as a State, they live by theft and robbery; by kidnapping and enslaving men, women and children; and by ignoring and trampling down the rights and endearments of husband and wife, parent and child, brother and sister.

If all highway robbers, midnight assassins, or pirates, or all organized bands of such marauders and desperadoes, have forfeited all rights, and if any man or set of men has a right to exterminate them, then, you being witness, have slaveholders and slaveholding States forfeited all rights, and the people and States of the North have a right to exterminate them on their own territory, or wherever they may exist. Do you deny that human beings have a right to "kill, slay and destroy" all who seek to enslave them, or to continue them in slavery? You do not; it is the cherished or fixed law of your life. As a Senator, as a Republican, as a man, a husband, father, and brother, you cherish it as your own, and as the right of every human being, to exterminate from the face of the earth all who would kidnap and enslave them, their children, their friends, neighbors or fellow-beings, whether they act as individuals, or in combinations, called States or nations.

The State of Virginia, as an organized community of kidnappers and slave-traders, as a band of American corsairs, covers a territory of sixty-one thousand square miles. This day it claims, holds and uses half a million of our fellow-beings as chattels—every one of whom you acknowledge to have been born free as you were, and with the same God-given right to liberty and the pursuit of happiness. They were kidnapped and enslaved by that self-constituted and self-incorporated American corsair, styled Virginia. You admit it is the right and duty of those enslaved fellow-beings, so outraged in all their property, personal and family relations and rights, to resist their enslavers and ravishers, and, if need be, exterminate them, to effect their deliverance. You admit, too, it is their right to call on their fellow-beings to assist them, and that it is the right and duty of all of human kind, so far as they have the power and opportunity, to go to their rescue, and annihilate the piratical power that crushes them. Why do you pretend in Congress, or any where, that you do not cherish and that you never uttered these sentiments? It is "mean and dastardly" to do so. You are recreant to your soul's most cherished convictions, and a traitor to Humanity and to God, when you deny that these are your sentiments, and of the Republicans generally.

Were these five hundred thousand slaves of Virginia taken from Ohio, you acknowledge it would be the right and duty of the people and State of Ohio to invade—march into—the territory of the enslavers, and rescue their sons and daughters from the rape, rapine and outrages which that slaveholding State perpetrates upon them. And if Ohio were not sufficient to accomplish their rescue, and sweep from the earth that piratical State, and she should appeal to Massachusetts for help, would you doubt as to the right and duty of yourself and your constituents to aid Ohio? You would not. Or, if ten thousand from Africa should invade Virginia, to rescue her children from slavery, and should appeal to Massachusetts for help, where would you and the Old Bay State be found? Where Justice, Humanity, and God are; on the side of the invaders.

Invasion, invaders, indeed! So, if Gov. Wise had kidnapped your wife and daughter, and had taken them to Virginia to grace his harem, or to sell them to New Orleans, and you and Massachusetts rushed to their rescue, and did rescue them by annihilating the kidnapper, and the band that sustained him, you are the invaders, are you? You know better; you are not a fool; your heart and head assure you that you are acting purely on the defence, and that the kidnapper and his band are the invaders, the aggressors. So, when John Brown and his companions entered the territory of Virginia, to rescue their fellow-beings from slavery, and to destroy the power that enslaves them, you being witness, the Republican party being witness, and all the people and States of the North being witnesses, acted purely on the defensive, according to the universally received opinion of defensive war. Is Massachusetts the aggressor or invader, (in a bad sense,) when, by her official agents, she enters the farm or house of a murderer, and arrests him, or of a thief and robber, and secures him, and recovers the stolen property? You admit she acts purely in defence. So, when Pennsylvania, Ohio, Indiana, Illinois and Iowa enter the adjacent slave States of Maryland, Virginia, Kentucky and Missouri, to rescue their kidnapped sons and daughters, they but act on the defensive—you and the entire nation being witnesses. So, when obedient to the call of Humanity, the people and States of the North enter those slaveholding States to rescue their fellow-beings from slavery, and destroy the power that enslaves them, they do but act in defence of themselves, their children, and our common humanity, against organized bands of marauders and pirates.

I do you no wrong, but simply justice, when I say, you do approve of invasion—of armed invasion of the slaveholding States, with a view to free the enslaved, and to annihilate the power that enslaves them. You do but stultify yourself, and make yourself contemptible in your own eyes, before your own constituents, and before the slaveholders themselves, when you assert that you do not approve such invasions. You hold to armed protection to life, liberty and property. I hold you bound to fidelity to your own law of life. You deservedly become an object of pity or contempt when you so indignantly cry out against me, for thus asserting that you are and will be true to yourself.

While, as a MAN, you know, and, by word and deed, inculcate the above specified propositions as true, as a Republican, you deny them; and strenuously and persistently maintain that, within certain geographical lines, called her State boundaries, Virginia has a right, daily and hourly, to wage an inhuman, exterminating and aggressive war against Humanity; and you have promised, not only not to interfere yourself, but, also, to do all in your power to prevent any individual or State, outside of those boundaries, from interfering to protect our common nature from these outrages. As a Republican, you concede to Virginia, (and to every slave State,) any where and every where on the sixty-one thousand square miles over which she holds sway, to invade all property, personal and family rights, and outrage every relation and endearment of life,—to seize, claim, hold and use, as beasts and chattels, our innocent and helpless fellow-beings,—while you deny to all living outside of those State boundaries the right to go in, and protect them against their enslavers.

You are passing your neighbor's house. You hear a cry for help, and know that rape, rapine and murder are being perpetrated within. An agonizing cry comes to your ears. As a MAN, your heart and soul respond, and prompt you to rush to the rescue; but, as a Republican, you say, "The family that lives in that house have a right to manage their own affairs; within any and every room in that house, they have a right to commit rape, rapine, and murder, and to get their victims where they please, and I have no right to interfere; and if I do, it will be the means of defeating the Republican party. Besides, I am bound not to interfere to protect those victims by my political obligations as a Republican Senator. I will, therefore, pass by on the other side, and leave those who have fallen among ruffians and murderers to their fate."

So, Virginia seizes men and women, wherever and whenever she pleases, in Ohio, Massachusetts, or Guinea, drags them into her own dominion, and there perpetrates every possible outrage upon them; and you, Henry Wilson, as a Republican, consent to stand sentinel to prevent any individual or State beyond Virginia from entering in, to deliver those victims, and put a stop to those outrages. You denounce all as "invaders," as guilty of "robbery, plunder, treason, anarchy, and murder," who would go into Virginia to rescue those innocent and helpless victims of lust and murder. . . .

Thus you, as a Republican, allow Virginia the right to invade Humanity, but you will not allow the people and States of the North to protect their fellow-beings against her bloody and murderous raid. You threaten to hang all who shall dare to go into Virginia,—even if it be to rescue their own children and friends from the lust and brutality of their ravishers and murderers. Thus the Republican is above the MAN; the unprincipled, compromising politician is allowed to triumph over the godlike heir of immortality! What a perversion—what a fall—is there! The naturally generous, humane, and noble MAN sunk in the cowardly, scheming, sneaking, crawling, loathsome politician! A child of God merged in the spawn of a slave-breeding, slave-hunting, slave-trading political Union!

Finally, "YOU KNOW" that "Resistance to tyrants is obedience to God," and that it is the right and duty of the enslaved to resist their enslavers, and that it is the right and duty of the people and States of the North to incite (to "arouse," "animate," "encourage") them to resistance, and to aid them in it.

I affirm that you know these things, because (1) you are a man; (2) you are a son and a brother, a husband and a father; (3) you were born and educated in New Hampshire; (4) you believe in the self-evident truth that "all men are created free and equal," and "in doing to others as you would that they should do to you"; (5) I have heard and read your speeches in Congress, and on the political and anti-slavery platforms; (6) you are not a fool. . . .

21

A Plan for the Abolition of Slavery (1858)

Lysander Spooner

Lysander Spooner (1808–1887) was a natural law libertarian who made a career of opposing all government created monopolies, such as the post office. He was also a radical abolitionist in Boston, but was not associated with the Garrisonians. Spooner's most important contribution to the abolitionist cause was his legal treatise on "The Unconstitutionality of Slavery," which became a core text for the Liberty Party. Spooner argued that not only was the Constitution antislavery in letter and spirit, but that it also gave Congress the authority to abolish slavery in those states where it already existed.

The short text that follows first appeared as a broadside in opposition to the Dred Scott decision. In that case, the Supreme Court had said that blacks were so inferior "that they had no rights which the white man was bound to respect," that blacks never were nor could be citizens of the United States, and that Congress had no authority to prevent the extension of slavery into the territories. Spooner's plan called for the creation of voluntary societies to liberate—by violence if necessary—those held in bondage.

When a human being is set upon by a robber, ravisher, murderer, or tyrant of any kind, it is the duty of the bystanders to go to his or her rescue, by force, if need be.

In general, nothing will excuse men in the non-performance of this duty, except the pressure of higher duties, (if such there be,) inability to afford relief, or too great danger to themselves or others.

This duty being naturally inherent in human relations and necessities, governments and laws are of no authority in opposition to it. If they interpose themselves, they must be trampled under foot without ceremony, as we would trample under foot laws that should forbid us to rescue men from wild beasts, or from burning buildings.

On this principle, it is the duty of the non-slaveholders of this country, in their private capacity as individuals—without asking the permission, or waiting the movements, of the government—to go to the rescue of the Slaves from the hands of their oppressors.

This duty is so self-evident and natural a one, that he who pretends to doubt it, should be regarded either as seeking to evade it, or as himself a servile and ignorant slave of corrupt institutions or customs.

Holding these opinions, we propose to act upon them. And we invite all other citizens of the United States to join us in the enterprise. To enable them to judge of its feasibility before them the following programme of measures, which, we think, ought to be adopted, and would be successful.

1. The formation of associations, throughout the country, of all persons who are willing to pledge themselves publicly to favor the enterprise, and render assistance and support, of any kind, to it.
2. Establishing or sustaining papers to advocate the enterprise.
3. Refusing to vote for any person for any civil or military office whatever, who is not publicly committed to the enterprise.
4. Raising money and military equipments.
5. Forming and disciplining such military companies as may volunteer for actual service.
6. Detaching the non-slaveholders of the South from all alliance with the Slaveholders, and inducing them to co-operate with us, by appeals to their safety, interest, honor, justice, and humanity.
7. Informing the Slaves (by emissaries to be sent among them, or through the non-slaveholders of the South) of the plan of emancipation, that they may be prepared to cooperate at the proper time.
8. To encourage emigration to the South, of persons favoring the movement.
9. When the preceding preliminaries shall have sufficiently prepared the way, then to land military forces (at numerous points at the same time) in the South, who shall raise the standard of freedom, and call to it the slaves, and such free persons as may be willing to join it.
10. If emancipation shall be accomplished only by actual hostilities, then, as all the laws of war, of nature, and of justice, will require that the emancipated Slaves shall be compensated for their previous wrongs, we avow it our purpose to make such compensation, so far as the property of the Slaveholders and their abettors can compensate them. And we avow our intention to make known this determination to the Slaves beforehand, with a view to give them courage and self-respect, to nerve them to look boldly into the eyes of their tyrants, and to give them true ideas of the relations of justice existing between themselves and their oppressors.
11. To remain in the South, after emancipation, until we shall have established, or have seen established, such governments as will secure the future freedom of the persons emancipated.

And we anticipate that the public avowal of these measures, and our open and zealous preparation for them, will have the effect, within some reasonable time—we trust within a few years at farthest—to detach the government and the country at large from the interests of the Slaveholders; to destroy the security and value of Slave property; to annihilate the commercial credit of the Slaveholders; and finally to accomplish the extinction of Slavery. We hope it may be without blood.

If it be objected that this scheme proposes war, we confess the fact. It does propose war—private war indeed—but, nevertheless, war, if that should prove necessary. And our answer to the objection is, that in revolutions of this nature, it is necessary that private individuals should take the first steps. The tea must be thrown overboard, the Bastile must be torn down, the first gun must be fired, by private persons, before a new government can be organized, or the old one be forced (for nothing but danger to itself will force it) to adopt the measures which the insurgents have in view.

If the American governments, State or national, would abolish Slavery, we would leave the work in their hands. But as they do not, and apparently will not, we propose to force them to do it, or to do it ourselves in defiance of them. If any considerable number of the American people will join us, the work will be an easy and bloodless one; for Slavery can live only in quiet, and in the sympathy or subjection of all around it.

WE, the subscribers, residents of the Town of_____in the County of_____in the state of_____believing in the principles, and approving generally of the measures, set forth in the foregoing "Plan for the Abolition of Slavery," and in the accompanying address "To the Non-Slaveholders of the South," hereby unite ourselves in an Association to be called the LEAGUE OF FREEDOM in the Town of_____for the purpose of aiding to carry said plan into effect. And we hereby severally declare it to be our sincere intention to co-operate faithfully with each other, and with all other associations within the United States, having the same purpose in view, and adopting the same platform of principles and measures.

Selected Bibliography

Abzug, Robert H. *Passionate Liberator: Theodore Dwight Weld and the Dilemma of Reform.* New York: Oxford University Press, 1980.
Barnes, Gilbert. *The Antislavery Impulse, 1830–1844.* New York: Appleton-Century, 1933.
Ashworth, John, David Brion Davis, and Thomas L. Haskell. *The Antislavery Debate: Capitalism and Abolitionism as a Problem in Historical Interpretation.* Edited by Thomas Bender. Berkeley: University of California Press, 1992.
Burke, Joseph C. "The Proslavery Argument in the First Congress." *Duquesne Review* 14 (1969): 3–15.
Cain, William E., ed. *William Lloyd Garrison and the Fight Against Slavery: Selections from The Liberator.* Boston: Bedford Books/St. Martin's Press, 1995.
Campbell, Stanley W. *The Slave Catchers: Enforcement of the Fugitive Slave Law, 1850–1860.* Chapel Hill: University of North Carolina Press, 1968.
Child, Lydia Maria. *A Lydia Maria Child Reader.* Edited by Carolyn Karcher. Durham, NC: Duke University Press, 1996.
Cover, Robert M. *Justice Accused: Antislavery and the Judicial Process.* New Haven, CT: Yale University Press, 1975.
Curry, Richard O., ed. *The Abolitionists, Reformers or Fanatics?* New York: Holt, Rinehart and Winston, 1965.
Davis, David Brion. *The Problem of Slavery in the Age of Revolution, 1770–1823.* Ithaca, NY: Cornell University Press, 1975.
———. *The Problem of Slavery in Western Culture.* Ithaca, NY: Cornell University Press, 1966.
Dillon, Merton. *The Abolitionists: The Growth of a Dissenting Minority.* De Kalb: Northern Illinois University Press, 1974.
Donald, David. *Charles Sumner and the Coming of the Civil War.* Chicago: University of Chicago Press, 1960.
Dumond, Dwight Lowell. *Antislavery: The Crusade for Freedom in America.* Ann Arbor: University of Michigan Press, 1961.
Dubois, Ellen. "Women's Rights and Abolition: The Nature of the Connection." In *Feminism and Suffrage: The Emergence of an Independent Women's Movement in America, 1848–1869.* Ithaca, NY: Cornell University Press, 1978.
Elkins, Stanley. *Slavery: A Problem in American Institutional and Intellectual Life.* Chicago: University of Chicago Press, 1959.
Essays and Pamphlets on Antislavery. Westport, CT: Negro Universities Press, 1970.
Faust, Drew Gilpin. *A Sacred Circle: The Dilemma of the Intellectual in the Old South, 1840–1860.* Philadelphia: University of Pennsylvania Press, 1977.

Filler, Louis. *The Crusade Against Slavery, 1830–1860*. New York: Harper & Row, 1960.
Finkelman, Paul. *Slavery and the Founders: Race and Liberty in the Age of Jefferson*. 2d ed. Armonk, NY: M.E. Sharpe, 2000.
Fladeland, Betty. *James Gillespie Birney: Slaveholder to Abolitionist*. Ithaca, NY: Cornell University Press, 1955.
Foner, Eric. *Free Soil, Free Labor, Free Men: The Ideology of the Republican Party before the Civil War*. Oxford, UK: Oxford University Press, 1970.
Fredrickson, George M. *The Black Image in the White Mind: The Debate on Afro-American Character and Destiny, 1817–1914*. New York: Harper & Row, 1971.
———. *The Inner Civil War: Northern Intellectuals and the Crisis of the Union*. New York: Harper & Row, 1965.
Friedman, Lawrence J. *Gregarious Saints: Self and Community in American Abolitionism, 1830–1870*. New York: Cambridge University Press, 1982.
Genovese, Eugene D. *From Rebellion to Revolution: Afro-American Slave Revolts in the Making of the Modern World*. Baton Rouge: Louisiana State University Press, 1979.
———. *Roll Jordan Roll*. New York: Pantheon Books, 1974.
———. *Political Economy of Slavery*. New York: Vintage Books, 1967.
Hawkins, Hugh, and Lawrence Goodheart, eds. *The Abolitionists: Means, Ends, and Motivations*. Lexington, MA: D.C. Heath, 1995.
Jaffa, Harry V. *Crisis of the House Divided: An Interpretation of the Lincoln–Douglas Debates*. Seattle: University of Washington Press, 1959.
Karcher, Caroline. *First Woman of the Republic: A Biography of Lydia Maria Child*. Durham, NC: Duke University Press, 1998.
Kolchin, Peter. *American Slavery, 1619–1877*. New York: Hill and Wang, 1995.
Kraditor, Aileen S. *Means and Ends in American Abolitionism: Garrison and His Critics on Strategy and Tactics, 1834–1850*. Chicago: Ivan R. Dee, 1967.
Lacy, Dan. *The Abolitionists*. New York: McGraw-Hill, 1978.
Lerner, Gerda. *The Grimké Sisters from North Carolina: Rebels Against Slavery*. Boston: Houghton Mifflin, 1967.
Lerner, Ralph. *The Thinking Revolutionary: Principle and Practice in the New Republic*. Ithaca, NY: Cornell University Press, 1979.
Mabee, Carleton. *Black Freedom: The Nonviolent Abolitionists from 1830 to the Civil War*. New York: Macmillan, 1970.
Martin, Waldo E. *The Mind of Frederick Douglass*. Chapel Hill: University of North Carolina Press, 1984.
McInerney, Daniel J. *The Fortunate Heirs of Freedom: Abolition and Republican Political Thought*. Lincoln: University of Nebraska Press, 1994.
McPherson, James M. *The Struggle for Equality: Abolitionists and the Negro in the Civil War and Reconstruction*. Princeton, NJ: Princeton University Press, 1964.
Miller, William Lee. *Arguing About Slavery: The Great Battle in the United States Congress*. New York: Alfred A. Knopf, 1995.
Nelson, Truman, ed. *Documents of Upheaval: Selections from William Lloyd Garrison's The Liberator, 1831–1865*. New York: Hill and Wang, 1966.
Nye, Russel B. *William Lloyd Garrison and the Humanitarian Reformers*. Boston: Little, Brown, 1955.
———. *Fettered Freedom: Civil Liberties and the Slavery Controversy, 1830–1860*. East Lansing: Michigan State College Press, 1949.

Pease, Jane, and William Pease. *The Antislavery Argument*. Indianapolis, IN: Bobbs-Merrill, 1965.
Pease, Jane H, and William H. Pease. *They Who Would Be Free: Blacks' Search for Freedom, 1830–1861*. New York: Atheneum, 1974.
Perry, Lewis. *Radical Abolitionism: Anarchy and the Government of God in Antislavery Thought*. Ithaca, NY: Cornell University Press, 1973.
Perry, Lewis, and Michael Fellman, eds. *Antislavery Reconsidered: New Perspectives on the Abolitionists*. Baton Rouge: Louisiana State University Press, 1979.
Potter, David. *The Impending Crisis, 1848–1861*. Compiled and edited by Don E. Fehrenbacher. New York: Harper & Row, 1976.
Quarles, Benjamin. *Black Abolitionists*. New York: Oxford University Press, 1969.
Ripley, C. Peter, et al., eds. *The Black Abolitionist Papers: The United States*. 5 vols. Chapel Hill: University of North Carolina Press, 1991.
Ruchames, Louis, ed. *The Abolitionists: A Collection of Their Writings*. New York: G.P. Putnam's Sons, 1960.
Sewell, Richard H. *Ballots for Freedom: Antislavery Politics in the United States, 1837–1860*. New York: Oxford University Press, 1976.
Stampp, Kenneth M. *The Peculiar Institution: Slavery in the Antebellum South*. New York: Alfred A. Knopf, 1961.
Stewart, James B. *Holy Warriors and the Abolitionists and American Slavery*. New York: Hill and Wang, 1976.
———. *Wendell Phillips, Liberty's Hero*. Baton Rouge: Louisiana State University Press, 1986.
———. *Joshua Giddings and the Tactics of Radical Politics*. Cleveland, OH: Press of Case Western Reserve University, 1970.
Thomas, John L. *The Liberator: William Lloyd Garrison, A Biography*. Boston: Little, Brown, 1963.
———. "Romantic Reform in America, 1815–1865." In *Antebellum Reform*. Edited by David Brion Davis. New York: Harper & Row, 1967.
———, ed. *Slavery Attacked: The Abolitionist Crusade*. Englewood Cliffs, NJ: Prentice-Hall, 1963.
Tise, Larry E. *Proslavery: A History of the Defense of Slavery in America, 1700–1740*. Athens: University of Georgia Press, 1987.
Walker, Peter F. *Moral Choice: Memory, Desire, and Imagination in Nineteenth-Century American Abolition*. Baton Rouge: Louisiana State University Press, 1978.
Walters, Ronald G. *The Antislavery Appeal: American Abolitionism after 1830*. Baltimore: John Hopkins University Press, 1976.
Wiecek, William M. *The Sources of Antislavery Constitutionalism in America, 1760–1848*. Ithaca, NY: Cornell University Press, 1977.
Wyatt-Brown, Bertram. *Lewis Tappan and the Evangelical War Against Slavery*. New York: Athaneum, 1971.
Yellin, Jean Fagan. *Women and Sisters: The Antislavery Feminists in American Culture*. New Haven, CT: Yale University Press, 1992.

Index

Abolitionist, The, 46
Abolitionist movement
   anti-slavery candidate essays (1856) (Douglass), 202–6, 207–11
   Constitutional interpretation, xx–xxii, xxv
   Constitutional rights, xv, xx–xxii
   Declaration of Independence, xii, xiii
   development (1831), xi
   "House Divided" speech (1858) (Lincoln), 212–19
   immediate emancipation, xii–xv, xvi–xvii, xviii–xix, xx
   Macedon Convention address (1847) (Goodell), 116–17, 120, 121, 127–28
   moderates, xv, xxi, xxv–xxvi
   moral conversion, xiii–xiv
   moral ideology, xii, xiii, xvii
   moral suasion, xiv, xv–xviii
   natural rights philosophy, xii, xiii
   Northern doughface, xv
   Northern racism, xvii
   political action, xv–xviii, xxiv–xxvi
   political action strategy (1838) (Jackson/Phelps), 64, 65, 66, 67, 68–70, 71–72, 74
   political ideology, xii, xiii, xiv, xvii, xviii–xx
   political obligation letter (1839) (Birney), 76–78, 84, 86–87, 88–92, 94–97
   political obligation speech (1850) (Sumner), 178–84
   political revolution, xxiv–xxvi
   popular sovereignty policy, xxiii–xxiv
   radicalism, xvi, xvii, xxiv–xxvi

Abolitionist movement *(continued)*
   religious ideology, xii, xiii, xvii
   self-ownership, xii
   Slave Power, xiv, xix, xv, xxi, xxiii, xxiv, xxv
   social ideology, xiii
   Union secession, xxiv–xxvi
   See also American Anti-Slavery Society; Liberty Party
Abolitionist political party
   American Anti-Slavery Society, xvii, xviii
   Free-Soil Party, xxii–xxiii
   political action strategy (1838) (Jackson/Phelps), 67–68
   political party dialogue (1842) (Child), 99–100
Abolition plan (1858) (Spooner), 261–63
African slave trade
   American Anti-Slavery Society, 43
   congressional responsibility speech (1854) (Giddings), 194
   Constitutional framers intent, 137, 149–50
   Constitutional terminology, xxi, 134, 147–48
   "Declaration of Sentiments" (1833), 43
   government practice, 139–40
   "House Divided" speech (1858) (Lincoln), 218
   "No Compromise With Slavery" (1854) (Garrison), 237–38
   "No Rights, No Duties" essay (1860) (Wright), 247–48
   political obligation speech (1850) (Sumner), 172

African slave trade *(continued)*
  slave address (1843) (Garnet), 224, 226, 227, 228
  Supreme Court rulings, 141
  abolitionist movement, 217–19
  African slave trade, 218
  chattel slavery, 218
  Dred Scott decision (1854), 212, 213–17
  freedom ideology, 212, 214, 216–17
  freedom nationalization, 217–19
  "House Divided" speech (1858) (Lincoln)
  Illinois, 215–16, 218
  Kansas–Nebraska Act (1854), 212–17
  Lecompton Constitution, 214–15
  Missouri, 218
  perfectly free argument, 216–17
  popular sovereignty policy, 212–13, 215, 217
  Republican Party, 219
  self-government, 213
  squatter sovereignty, 213, 215
  Union dissolution, 213
Alabama, 135, 236
"A Letter on the Political Obligation of Abolitionists" (1839) (Birney). *See* Political obligation letter (1839) (Birney)
Allen, William T., 10
American and Foreign Anti-Slavery Society, xviii, 41
American Anti-Slavery Society
  abolitionist political party, xvii, xviii
  anti-slavery candidates, xvi–xviii
  anti-slavery literature, xiv, 41, 45
  anti-slavery societies, xiv, 41, 45
  break-away faction, xviii, 41
  chattel slavery, 42–43, 44–45
  conservatism, xvi–xviii
  Divine Law, 43
  equal rights, 44
  formation (1833), xiii, 41, 42
  immediate emancipation, xiii–xv, xvi–xvii, 41, 44
  labor laws, 42–43, 44, 45
  lecturing agents, xiv, xv, 41, 45

American Anti-Slavery Society *(continued)*
  Macedon Convention address (1847) (Goodell), 121, 122–23, 125
  membership qualifications, 80, 82–83, 86–89, 94
  moral conversion, xiii–xiv
  moral suasion, xiv, xv–xviii, xxiv–xxv, 41, 42, 44–45
  motto, 230
  natural law perspective, 43
  natural rights philosophy, 44
  non-violent strategy, xiii, xiv
  oppressor guilt, 43
  political action, xvi–xviii, 44–45
  political party dialogue (1842) (Child), 98–99, 101, 102
  political petitions, xiv–xv, 41, 45
  popular sovereignty policy, 44
  publication, 3
  punishment, 45
  religious ideology, 42, 43, 45
  slave expatriation, 44
  slave trade, 43, 44
  social ideology, 43
  Union secession, xxiv–xxv
  voting strategy, xvi–xviii
  See also "Declaration of Sentiments" (1833); Political obligation letter (1839) (Birney)
American Colonization Society
  formation (1816), xiii
  gradual emancipation, xiii
  Liberian colony establishment, xiii
American Slave Code, in Theory and Practice (Goodell), 114
An Appeal in Favor of that Class of Americans Called Africans (Child), 3
Anti-slavery candidate essays (1856) (Douglass)
  presidential/vice-presidential nominees
    abolitionist movement, 207–11
    Constitutional rights, 207
    freedom ideology, 207–8, 209, 211
    Kansas, 208, 209–10, 211
    Liberty Party, 210

Anti-slavery candidate essays (1856) (Douglass)
presidential/vice-presidential nominees *(continued)*
  Maryland, 210
  moral ideology, 209, 210
  Northern doughface, 211
  Northern region, 208, 209, 211
  Radical Abolitionist Party, 207–8, 209, 210
  religious ideology, 210
  Republican Party, 206–11
  Slave Power, 208–9, 211
  slavery extension, 208
  Southern region, 208, 211
  Virginia, 210
voting obligation
  abolitionist movement, 202–6
  Barnburners (New York), 202–3
  Constitutional rights, 204, 206
  Democratic Party, 203, 205
  freedom ideology, 205–6
  Free-Soil Party, 203
  fugitive slaves, 204
  Kansas, 203, 204, 205–6
  Liberty Party, 202–4
  Nebraska, 204
  Northern region, 204, 205–6
  Radical Abolitionist Party, 204, 205–6
  religious ideology, 203, 206
  Republican Party, 203–4, 205–6
  Slave Power, 203
  Southern region, 206
Anti-slavery candidates, xvi–xviii
  Macedon Convention address (1847) (Goodell), 123, 126
  political action strategy (1838) (Jackson/Phelps), 63, 67, 68–72
  political obligation letter (1839) (Birney), 77–78
  political obligation speech (1850) (Sumner), 182–83
  political party dialogue (1842) (Child), 99–103
Anti-Slavery Catechism (Child), 3

Anti-slavery literature, xiv, 3, 41, 45, 60
Anti-slavery societies, xiv, 41, 45
Aristocracy
  Liberty Party lecture (1844) (Buffum), 107, 110, 111, 112
  Macedon Convention address (1847) (Goodell), 124, 128, 129
Arkansas, 69
Armed insurrection strategy, 246, 251–52, 254, 256–60

Balch, John, 13
Baltimore Telegraph, 8
Barnburners (New York), 202–3
Bearing Upon American Slavery (Goodell), 114
Beasly, Robert, 9
Bell, Samuel, 12
Bequest laws, 17
Bible Society, 121–22
Birney, James G. (1792–1857)
  abolitionist movement, 75
  American Anti-Slavery Society, 75
  anti-slavery candidates, 75
  conservatism, xvi
  gradual emancipation, 75
  immediate emancipation, 75
  Liberty Party nominee, xviii, 75
  moral suasion, 75
  political action, xvi, 75
  radicalism, 75
  Slave Power, 75
  See also Political obligation letter (1839) (Birney)
Black, P., 9
Bowditch, William (1819–1909)
  Boston Vigilance Committee, 133
  Constitutional pro-slavery, 133
  underground railroad, 133
  See also Constitutional interpretation (1849) (Bowditch)
Bowles, Anderson, 13
Boyce, J.P., 21
Brown, John
  freedom fighters, xxvi, 253
  Harper's Ferry incident, xxv, 251

272 INDEX

Buchanan, George, 18
Buffum, Arnold (1782–1859)
   American Anti-Slavery Society, 107
   Free-Soil Party, 107
   lecturing agents, 107
   Liberty Party, 107
   New England Anti-Slavery Society, 107
   Republican Party, 107
   See also Liberty Party lecture (1844) (Buffum)
Burritt, Elihu, 130

Calhoun, John C., xi, 4, 7
California, xxiii, 171
Calvinism, 99
Canada, 135
Chambers, William, 12
Channing, William E. (1780–1842)
   abolitionist movement, 31
   natural law perspective, 31
   Unitarianism, 31
   See also Slavery (1836) (Channing)
Charleston Courier, 7
Charleston Mercury, 10–11
Charleston Work House, 12–13
Chattel slavery
   American Anti-Slavery Society, 42–43, 44–45
   congressional responsibility speech (1854) (Giddings), 198–99
   Constitutional interpretation (1860) (Douglass), 151–52
   freedom ideology, xi, xii
   "House Divided" speech (1858) (Lincoln), 218
   Macedon Convention address (1847) (Goodell), 117–18, 119–20, 122–23, 124–25
   "No Compromise With Slavery" (1854) (Garrison), 236–37, 244
   "No Rights, No Duties" essay (1860) (Wright), 246–47, 250, 252, 256
   Patriarchal Institution (1860) (Child), 10, 20, 21–22
   Slavery (1836) (Channing), 31–38
   slavery lecture (1850) (Douglass), 26

Chattel slavery *(continued)*
   slavery remedy lecture (1834) (Phelps), 53, 54, 57, 58
Child, Lydia Maria (1802–1880)
   abolitionist movement, 3
   anti-slavery literature, 3
   newspaper editor, 3
   publications, 3
   See also Patriarchal Institution (1860) (Child); Political party dialogue (1842) (Child)
Cinqué, Joseph, 228
Civil War, 159, 212
Clay, Henry, xxii–xxiii
Clay, Thomas, 16
Clothing laws, 17–18, 21, 26
Colonization Society, 71–72
Congressional responsibility speech (1854) (Giddings)
   African slave trade, 194
   chattel slavery, 198–99
   Divine Law, 201
   domestic slave trade, 194
   equal rights, 195–96, 197–98
   freedom ideology, 187–88, 190–91, 192–93, 197–98, 199, 200–1
   Fugitive Slave Law (1850), 194–95
   individual responsibility, 197
   Kansas–Nebraska Act (1854), 187–201
   Missouri Compromise (1850) repeal, 187, 191, 193, 195, 201
   moral ideology, 198–201
   non-intervention policy, 196, 197–98
   Northern doughface, 195, 199
   Northern region, 188, 190–91, 192, 195, 198, 200
   popular sovereignty policy, 195–96
   religious ideology, 188–89, 190, 191–92, 193, 198, 199, 200, 201
   self-government, 195–96
   silence agitation, 193–95
   Slave Power, 201
   slavery characteristics, 188–90
   Southern region, 188, 192, 200
Connecticut, 154

Conservatism
  American and Foreign Anti-Slavery
    Society, xviii
  American Anti-Slavery Society, xvi–xviii
  Constitutional interpretation, xx–xxi
  political action, xvi–xviii
Constitutional interpretation
  abolitionist movement, xx–xxii, xxv
  African slave trade, xxi
  anti-slavery, xx–xxii
  Congressional power, xx, xxi, xxii
  Congressional representation, xxi
  conservatism, xx–xxi
  Fifth Amendment, xxii
  freedom ideology, xxi, xxii
  Free-Soil Party, xxi
  fugitive slaves, xxi
  indentured servants, xxi
  moderates, xxi
  Northern power, xxii
  political obligation letter (1839)
    (Birney), 78, 79–81
  pro-freedom, xxi, xxii
  pro-slavery, xx, xxi, xxii, xxv
  Slave Power, xxi, xxv
  slave rebellions, xxi
  slavery extension, xxi
  Union secession, xxv
Constitutional interpretation (1849)
    (Bowditch)
  framers intent
    African slave trade, 137
    Article 1, section 2, 136–37
    Article 1, section 8, 138
    Article 1, section 9, 137
    Article 4, section 2, 137–38
    Article 4, section 4, 138
    fugitive slaves, 137–38
    representative apportionment, 136–37
    slave insurrections, 138
  government practice
    African slave trade, 139–40
    Article 1, section 2, 138–39
    Article 1, section 8, 140
    Article 1, section 9, 139–40
    Article 4, section 2, 140

Constitutional interpretation (1849)
    (Bowditch)
  government practice *(continued)*
    Article 4, section 4, 140
    fugitive slaves, 140
    representative apportionment, 138–39
    slave insurrections, 140
  Supreme Court
    African slave trade, 141
    Article 1, section 2, 141
    Article 1, section 8, 142–43
    Article 1, section 9, 141
    Article 3, section 1, 141
    Article 3, section 2, 141
    Article 4, section 2, 141–42
    Article 4, section 4, 142–43
    Article 6, section 2, 141
    fugitive slaves, 141–42
    representative apportionment, 141
    slave insurrections, 142–43
  terminology
    African slave trade, 134
    Article 6, 135
    Article 1, section 2, 133, 134–35, 136
    Article 1, section 8, 134, 135–36
    Article 1, section 9, 134
    Article 4, section 2, 134–35, 136
    Article 4, section 4, 135–36
    fugitive slaves, 134–35
    representative apportionment, 133, 134–35
    slave insurrections, 134, 135
Constitutional interpretation (1860)
    (Douglass)
  anti-slavery, 152–56
  British Constitution, 154
  Constitutional rights, 153–54
  Constitution defined, 145–46
  debate clarification, 144–45
  framers intent, 146
    African slave trade, 149–50
    Article 1, section 2, 149
    Article 1, section 8, 150
    Article 1, section 9, 149–50
    Article 4, section 2, 150–52

Constitutional interpretation (1860)
(Douglass)
    framers intent *(continued)*
        chattel slavery, 151–52
        fugitive slaves, 150–52
        indentured servants, 151
        redemptioners (Holland), 151
        representative apportionment, 149
        slave insurrections, 150
    freedom ideology, 152–53
    government-Constitution distinction, 144
    legal interpretation
        innocent versus wicked, 152
        law defined, 152
    Northern region, 154–55, 156
    Preamble, 153
    religious ideology, 154
    Supreme Court, 152
    terminology, 146–48
        African slave trade, 147–48
        Article 1, section 8, 147–48
        Article 1, section 9, 147–48
        Article 4, section 2, 147–48
        fugitive slaves, 147–48
        representative apportionment, 147–48
        slave insurrections, 147–48
    Union dissolution, 154–55
Constitutional rights
    abolitionist movement, xv, xx–xxii
    anti-slavery candidate essays (1856) (Douglass), 204, 206, 207
    Constitutional interpretation, 153–54
    fugitive slaves, xxiii
    Macedon Convention address (1847) (Goodell), 127
    political obligation speech (1850) (Sumner), 173–74
Contractual laws, 17, 22, 31, 34
Cooner, L.E., 8
Corprew, G.W., 8
Correspondence between Lydia Maria Child and Gov. Wise and Mrs. Mason of Virginia (Child), 3
Court testimony, 17, 18, 20

Dadeville Banner, 9
Davie, William R., 136
Davis, Benjamin, 11
Dayton, William L., 202, 206–11
Dean, Jethro, 12
Declaration of Independence, xii, xiii, 5, 23, 45, 110, 111, 172, 231, 233, 238, 256–57
"Declaration of Sentiments" (1833)
    African slave trade, 43
    American Anti-Slavery Society, 41–45
    chattel slavery, 42–43, 44–45
    domestic slave trade, 43, 44
    freedom ideology, 42, 44, 45
    moral ideology, 42, 44
    natural law perspective, 43
    natural rights philosophy, 44
    oppressor guilt, 43, 45
    political action, 44–45
    political obligation letter (1839) (Birney), 76–77, 78, 79–81, 82–83
    popular sovereignty policy, 44
    religious ideology, 42, 43, 45
    social ideology, 43
Democratic Party
    abolitionist party challenge, xvii
    anti-slavery candidate essays (1856) (Douglass), 203, 205
    anti-slavery candidates, xvi
    anti-slavery faction, xix, xviii, xxii
    Liberty Party lecture (1844) (Buffum), 109, 110
    Missouri Compromise (1850), xxii–xxiii
    political action strategy (1838) (Jackson/Phelps), 63, 71, 72, 73
    political party dialogue (1842) (Child), 99–103
Divine Law, 36–38, 43, 110, 111, 119, 201
"No Compromise With Slavery" (1854) (Garrison), 235–45
Domestic slave trade
    American Anti-Slavery Society, 43, 44
    congressional responsibility speech (1854) (Giddings), 194

INDEX 275

Domestic slave trade *(continued)*
  "Declaration of Sentiments" (1833), 43, 44
  Free-Soil Party, xxiii
  Liberty Party, xviii
  political obligation letter (1839) (Birney), 77, 85
  political obligation speech (1850) (Sumner), 171–72, 178
Douglas, Stephen A.
  Kansas–Nebraska Act (1854), xxiii–xxiv
  political debates, xxiv
  popular sovereignty policy, xxiii–xxiv
  Slave Power, xxiv
Douglass, Frederick (ca. 1817–1895)
  abolitionist movement, xxi–xxii, 24
  abolitionist newspaper, 24
  autobiographical narratives, 24
  Constitutional interpretation, xx–xxii
  Free-Soil Party, xxii, 24
  Liberty Party, xxii
  presidential nominee, 202
  presidential service, 24
  Radical Abolitionist Party, 202
  Republican Party, 202
  vice-presidential nominee, 202
  See also Anti-slavery candidate essays (1856) (Douglass); Constitutional interpretation (1860) (Douglass); Slavery lecture (1850) (Douglass)
Douglass, Margaret, 15, 16–17
Dred Scott decision (1854), 212, 213–17, 249, 253, 261

Education
  free schools, 6
  slavery laws, 14–15, 22, 26, 27
  unlawful assembly, 14–15
Emancipation doctrines
  efficient doctrine, 53, 54, 55–57
  false doctrine, 52, 53, 54
  slavery remedy lecture (1834) (Phelps), 51–57
  true doctrine, 54–57, 59–60
  wicked doctrine, 52–53, 54, 55–56

Emancipation Proclamation (1863), xi
Emancipator, The, 114
Equal rights
  American Anti-Slavery Society, 44
  congressional responsibility speech (1854) (Giddings), 195–96, 197–98
  gender equality, 46, 68
  Macedon Convention address (1847) (Goodell), 114–15, 127, 128, 129–30
  "No Compromise With Slavery" (1854) (Garrison), 231–32
  political action strategy (1838) (Jackson/Phelps), 68, 73
  Slavery (1836) (Channing), 33–34, 36
  slavery remedy lecture (1834) (Phelps), 57, 58
Europe, 233–35

Fitzhugh, George, xi–xii, 5
Florida, 69, 111, 241
Food laws, 17–18, 21, 26
Freedom fighters, xxvi
Freedom ideology
  anti-slavery candidate essays (1856) (Douglass), 205–6, 207–8, 209, 211
  congressional responsibility speech (1854) (Giddings), 187–88, 190–91, 192–93, 197–98, 199, 200–1
  Constitutional interpretation, xxi, xxii, 152–53
  "Declaration of Sentiments" (1833), 42, 44, 45
  Free-Soil Party, xxii
  "House Divided" speech (1858) (Lincoln), 212, 214, 216–17
  Liberty Party lecture (1844) (Buffum), 107–8, 110, 112, 113
  Macedon Convention address (1847) (Goodell), 116
  "No Compromise With Slavery" (1854) (Garrison), 230, 232, 233, 238, 239–40, 242–43, 245

Freedom ideology *(continued)*
  "No Rights, No Duties" essay (1860) (Wright), 249–50, 252–54, 256–58, 260
  political action strategy (1838) (Jackson/Phelps), 67, 68, 72, 73
  political obligation letter (1839) (Birney), 78
  political obligation speech (1850) (Sumner), 171, 172–74, 175, 178, 181, 182, 183, 184
  political party dialogue (1842) (Child), 99
  popular sovereignty policy, xxiii–xxiv
  Republican Party, xxiv
  slave address (1843) (Garnet), 223, 224–29
  slavery remedy lecture (1834) (Phelps), 50–51, 53, 57, 58, 60
  social ideology, xi–xii
  See also Patriarchal Institution (1860) (Child); *Slavery* (1836) (Channing); Slavery lecture (1850) (Douglass); "Two Altars; Or Two Pictures in One, The" (1851) (Stowe)
Freedom nationalization
  "House Divided" speech (1858) (Lincoln), 217–19
  "No rights, No Duties" essay (1860) (Wright), 252–54
Free Press, 9
Free-Soil Party
  abolitionist political party, xxii–xxiii
  anti-slavery candidate essays (1856) (Douglass), 203
  Constitutional interpretation, xxi
  demise, xxii
  domestic slave trade, xxiii
  formation (1848), xxii, 24
  freedom ideology, xxii
  free-state admission, xxiii
  fugitive slaves, xxii–xxiii
  Liberty League, xx, xxii
  Missouri Compromise (1850), xxii–xxiii

Free-Soil Party *(continued)*
  motto, xxii
  Northern anti-slavery majority, xxii–xxiii
  political platform, xxii
  popular sovereignty policy, xxiii
  presidential nominee, xxii
  Slave Power, xxiii
  slavery abolition, xxii
  slavery extension, xxii
Free trade, xx, 119–20, 239–40
Fremont, John C., 202, 206–11
"Fremont and Dayton" (1856) (Douglass). *See* Anti-slavery candidate essays (1856) (Douglass)
Friend of Man, 114
Fugitive Slave Law (1850), xxiii, xxiv, xxv
  congressional responsibility speech (1854) (Giddings), 194–95
  "No Compromise With Slavery" (1854) (Garrison), 230, 232–33
  "No Rights, No Duties" essay (1860) (Wright), 253
  political obligation speech (1850) (Sumner), 172–78, 179
  See also "Two Altars; Or Two Pictures in One, The" (1851) (Stowe)
Fugitive slaves
  anti-slavery candidate essays (1856) (Douglass), 204
  Constitutional framers intent, 137–38, 150–52
  Constitutional interpretation, xxi
  Constitutional rights, xxiii
  Constitutional terminology, 134–35, 147–48
  Free-Soil Party, xxii–xxiii
  government practice, 140
  local posses, xxiii
  "No Rights, No Duties" essay (1860) (Wright), 249–50, 253
  Northern obligation, xxiii
  Slave Power, xxiii
  Supreme Court rulings, 141–42

Garnet, Henry Highland (1815–1882)
  abolitionist movement, 223
  American Anti-Slavery Society, 223
  lecturing agent, 223
  Liberian minister appointment, 223
  ministry training, 223
  slavery experience, 223
  See also Slave address (1843) (Garnet)
Garrison, George M., 11
Garrison, William Lloyd (1805–1879)
  American Anti-Slavery Society, xiii, xvi–xviii, xxiv–xxv, 41–45, 75–76, 230
  Constitution burning, xxv, 230
  "Declaration of Sentiments" (1833), 41–45
  immediate emancipation, xiii, xvi–xvii, 41, 75–76
  Liberator, xi, 41, 77
  moral suasion, xv–xviii, xxiv–xxvi, 75–76
  non-resistance strategy, xvi–xvii, xxv
  political action, xvi–xvii, xxiv–xxvi, 75–76
  political revolution, xxiv–xxv
  radicalism, xvi, xvii, xxiv–xxvi, 75, 230
  Union dissolution, 230
  Union secession, xxiv–xxvi
  voting strategy, xvi–xviii, 75–76
  See also "No Compromise With Slavery" (1854) (Garrison); Political obligation letter (1839) (Birney)
Gender equality, 46, 68
Georgia, 135, 236, 240
Georgia Journal, 12
Georgia Messenger, 9
Gibbons v. *Ogden*, 141
Giddings, Joshua R. (1795–1864)
  Congressional responsibility, 100, 187
  Free-Soil Party, 187
  House censorship, 187
  House of Representatives (1838–1859), 187
  Republican Party, 187

Giddings, Joshua R. (1795–1864)
  (continued)
  U.S. consul general (Canada), 187
  Whig Party, 187
  See also Congressional responsibility speech (1854) (Giddings)
Gildersleeve, W.C., 18
Gilmore, Mary, 22–23
Glasgow, Kate, 8
Goodell, William (1792–1878)
  conservatism, xvi
  Constitutional interpretation, xx–xxi, 114
  Emancipator, The, 114
  Friend of Man, 114
  Liberty League, xx, 114
  Liberty Party, xix–xx, 114
  political action, xvi
  publications, 114
  See also Macedon Convention address (1847) (Goodell)
Goodshall, Samuel, 23
Gradual emancipation, xii–xiii, 50, 51–53
Great Britain, 124, 125, 154, 174–75, 225, 234, 238–39
Greenville Enterprise, 21
Grimke, Sarah M., 12–13

Hamilton, Alexander, 136
Harris, Benjamin James, 17
Henry, Patrick, 4
Homesteads, 116, 119–20
Hylton v. *United States*, 141

Illinois, 215–16, 218, 258–59
Immediate emancipation
  abolitionist movement, xii–xv, xvi–xvii, xviii–xix, xx
  American Anti-Slavery Society, xiii–xv, xvi–xvii, 41, 45
  Liberty League, xx
  Liberty Party, xviii–xix
  moderates, xv
  non-revolutionary strategy, xiii
  non-violent strategy, xiii, xiv
  Northern sentiment, xv

278   INDEX

Immediate emancipation *(continued)*
  political action strategy (1838)
    (Jackson/Phelps), 65, 68–69, 72
  political obligation letter (1839)
    (Birney), 76, 90
  slavery remedy lecture (1834) (Phelps),
    46, 48, 50–51, 52, 54–60
Indentured servants, xxi, 151
Indiana, 258–59
Iowa, 258–59
Ireland, 22–23, 29, 234–35

Jackson, Francis. *See* Political action
  strategy (1838) (Jackson/Phelps)
Jefferson, Thomas
  African slave trade, 139–40
  Declaration of Independence, 238
  gradual emancipation, xii–xiii
  Notes on the States of Virginia, xii–xiii
  slave expatriation, xiii
  Southern prophecies, 3
Jennings, Joseph, 11
J.H. Leverick & Company, 11
Jones, C.C., 16

Kansas
  anti-slavery candidate essays (1856)
    (Douglass), 203, 204, 205–6, 208,
    209–10, 211
  "No Rights, No Duties" essay (1860)
    (Wright), 251, 253
Kansas–Nebraska Act (1854), xxiii–xxiv
  congressional responsibility speech
    (1854) (Giddings), 187–201
  "House Divided" speech (1858)
    (Lincoln), 212–17
Kenny, Edmund, 13
Kentucky, 247, 251, 258–59
King, Rufus, 136

Labor laws
  American Anti-Slavery Society, 42–43,
    44, 45
  Patriarchal Institution (1860) (Child),
    17, 18, 21
  Slavery (1836) (Channing), 31, 34–35

Laws of Slave States
  American Anti-Slavery Society, 43
  Haywood's, 9
  parental relation, 13
  Stroud's, 10, 17 ʼ
  See also specific laws/states
Leavitt, Joshua, xxii
Lecompton Constitution, 214–15
"Lecture on Slavery, No. 1" (1850)
  (Douglass). *See* Slavery
  lecture (1850) (Douglass)
Lectures on Slavery and its Remedy
  (1834) (Phelps). *See* Slavery remedy
  lecture (1834) (Phelps)
Lecturing agents, xiv, xv, 41, 45, 46, 60,
  107, 223
Leftwich, William, 12, 18
Lewis, Kerkman, 8
Liberator, xi, 41, 77
Liberia, xiii, 223
Liberty League
  formation (1847), xix–xx
  free labor, xx
  Free-Soil Party, xx, xxii
  free trade, xx
  government reduction, xx
  immediate emancipation, xx
  political platform, xx
Liberty Party
  anti-slavery candidate essays (1856)
    (Douglass), 202–4, 210
  break-away faction, xix–xx, xxii
  demise, xix
  domestic slave trade, xviii
  formation (1840), xviii
  immediate emancipation, xviii–xix
  Macedon Convention address (1847)
    (Goodell), xix–xx, 116–17, 123,
    126–27, 127–30
  moral suasion, xviii–xix
  Northern appeal, xix
  Northern rights, xix
  one-idea platform, xix–xx, xviii
  political compromise, xix
  political impact, xviii
  political party alliance, xix

Liberty Party *(continued)*
  political party dialogue (1842) (Child), 99–103
  political strategy, xviii–xix
  presidential election (1848), xix
  presidential nominee, xviii
  Slave Power, xix
  slavery extension, xviii–xix
  slave-state admission, xviii
  voting strategy, xviii
  See also Macedon Convention address (1847) (Goodell)
Liberty Party lecture (1844) (Buffum)
  aristocracy, 107, 110, 111, 112
  Declaration of Independence, 110, 111
  Democratic Party, 109, 110
  Divine Law, 110, 111
  Florida, 111
  freedom ideology, 107–8, 110, 112, 113
  government policy, 107–13
  government revenue, 109
  Liberty Party necessity, 107–13
  Liberty Party principles, 111–13
  Maryland, 111
  natural rights philosophy, 110, 112, 113
  non-slaveholding states, 107–13
  Northern doughface, 107–8
  Oligarchy, 111
  political action, 107–13
  religious ideology, 110, 111, 112
  slaveholding states, 107–13
  tariff laws, 109
  third political party, 111
  Virginia, 111
  Whig Party, 109, 110
Life and Times of Frederick Douglass, The (Douglass), 24
Lincoln, Abraham (1809–1865)
  abolitionist movement, xxvi, 212
  assassination (1865), xxvi
  Civil War contribution, 212
  Emancipation Proclamation (1863), xi
  House of Representatives, 212
  political debates, xxiv

Lincoln, Abraham (1809–1865) *(continued)*
  popular sovereignty policy, xxiv, 212
  Republican Party, xxiv, xxvi
  sixteenth President, 212
  slavery extension, xxiv
  Whig Party, 212
  See also "House Divided" speech (1858) (Lincoln)
Louisiana
  "No Compromise With Slavery" (1854) (Garrison), 240
  "No Rights, No Duties" essay (1860) (Wright), 247, 253
  slavery laws, 17–18, 31
Louisiana Act of Assembly (1819), 8
Lovejoy, Elijah, xv
Lowndes, Rawles, 137

Macedon Convention address (1847) (Goodell)
  abolitionist movement, 116–17, 120, 121, 127–28
  American Anti-Slavery Society, 121, 122–23, 125
  anti-slavery candidates, 123, 126
  aristocracy, 124, 128, 129
  Bible Society, 121–22
  British government, 124, 125
  chattel slavery, 117–18, 119–20, 122–23, 124–25
  civil government, 114–15, 122, 125, 126
  conclusion, 127–30
  Constitutional rights, 127
  definitive action, 125–27
  Divine Law, 119
  equal rights, 114–15, 127, 128, 129–30
  freedom ideology, 116, 119
  free trade, 119–20
  government revenue, 115
  homesteads, 116, 119–20
  introduction, 114–16
  Liberty Party, xix–xx, 116–17, 123, 126–27, 127–30
  Missionary Society, 121

280　INDEX

Macedon Convention address (1847)
  (Goodell) *(continued)*
  monopolies, 116, 119–20, 126, 128
  moral evils, 118, 123
  moral ideology, 116, 117–18, 124–25,
    126
  moral laws, 119–20
  Moral Reform Society, 122
  moral suasion, 123–24
  natural law perspective, 115, 119–20
  natural rights philosophy, 115, 119–20,
    126–27
  Northern region, 127–28, 129
  one-idea morality, 122–23, 124
  one-idea platform, 125, 129–30
  one-idea societies, 120–22
  party obligations, 123–25, 130
  political action, 117, 126, 128
  political obligation, 116–18, 122–23
  presidential nominee, 130
  public lands, 116, 119–20
  religious ideology, 115, 116, 119–22,
    126
  republican government, 115
  self-ownership, 119–20
  social ideology, 120–22, 130
  Southern region, 115–16, 129
  tariff laws, 115, 120, 123
  Temperance Society, 121, 122
  Texas, 115–16
  Union secession, 115
  vice-presidential nominee, 130
  voluntary societies, 120–22
  voting strategy, 117, 123, 124, 126, 128
  Wilmot provisos, 126–27
Macon Messenger, 8
Madison, James, 136, 137, 139, 150
Marriage laws, 16, 21
Martin, Luther, 4, 136, 137
Maryland
  Constitutional interpretation, 135
  Liberty Party, 111, 210
  "No Rights, No Duties" essay (1860)
    (Wright), 247, 251, 258–59
*Maryland Journal and Baltimore
  Advertiser*, 9, 18

Massachusetts
  Constitutional interpretation, 135
  "No Rights, No Duties" essay (1860)
    (Wright), 248, 252, 257, 258, 260
  political obligation speech (1850)
    (Sumner), 176, 177, 183
  political party dialogue (1842) (Child),
    99–101
Massachusetts Anti-Slavery Society
  gender equality, 46
  political obligation letter (1839)
    (Birney), 78, 96–97
  See also Political action strategy
    (1838) (Jackson/Phelps)
Mayhew Bliss & Company, 11–12
McAllister, U., 13
McDuffie, George, 5
Meade, Bishop, 15–16
Military flogging, 172
Milledgeville Journal, 12
Minnesota, 194
Minter, Anthony M., 9
Missionary Society, 121
Mississippi, 247
Missouri, 218, 247, 251, 258–59
Missouri Compromise (1850), xxii–xxiii
  congressional responsibility speech
    (1854) (Giddings), 187, 191, 193,
    195, 201
  "No Compromise With Slavery"
    (1854) (Garrison), 241
  "No Rights, No Duties" essay (1860)
    (Wright), 253
Missouri Democrat, 8
Moderates
  abolitionist movement, xv, xxi, xxv–xxvi
  Constitutional interpretation, xxi
  immediate emancipation, xv
  Union secession, xxv–xxvi
Monopolies, 116, 119–20, 126, 128
Moral action, 85–86, 87
Moral conversion, xiii–xiv
Moral evils, 54–55, 59, 118, 123
Moral ideology, xi, xii, xiii, xvii
  anti-slavery candidate essays (1856)
    (Douglass), 209, 210

Moral ideology *(continued)*
  congressional responsibility speech
    (1854) (Giddings), 198–201
  "Declaration of Sentiments" (1833),
    42, 44
  Macedon Convention address (1847)
    (Goodell), 116, 117–18, 124–25,
    126
  "No Compromise With Slavery" (1854)
    (Garrison), 233–34, 236–37, 238,
    240
  "No Rights, No Duties" essay (1860)
    (Wright), 254–55
  Slavery (1836) (Channing), 32–33,
    36–38
  slavery remedy lecture (1834) (Phelps),
    49, 50, 54–56, 59
Moral laws, 119–20
Moral Reform Society, 122
Moral science principle, 36
Moral suasion
  American Anti-Slavery Society, xiv,
    xv–xviii, 41, 42, 44–45
  defined, xiv
  Liberty Party, xviii–xix
  Macedon Convention address (1847)
    (Goodell), 123–24
  political action, xv–xviii
  political action strategy (1838)
    (Jackson/Phelps), 63, 64–65, 66,
    68, 69, 74
  political obligation letter (1839)
    (Birney), 77–78, 79, 85–87, 89, 91,
    95
  political obligation speech (1850)
    (Sumner), 178–79, 182
  political party dialogue (1842) (Child),
    98–103
  Union secession, xxiv–xxvi
Muscogee Herald, 6
My Bondage and My Freedom
  (Douglass), 24

*Narrative of the Life of Frederick
  Douglass, an American Slave, Written
  by Himself* (Douglass), 24

National Anti-Slavery Standard, 3
Natural law perspective
  "Declaration of Sentiments" (1833), 43
  Macedon Convention address (1847)
    (Goodell), 115, 119–20
  political party dialogue (1842) (Child),
    100–1, 102
  Slavery (1836) (Channing), 32–34,
    36–38
Natural Rights philosophy, xii, xiii
  "Declaration of Sentiments" (1833), 44
  Liberty Party lecture (1844) (Buffum),
    110, 112, 113
  Macedon Convention address (1847)
    (Goodell), 115, 119–20, 126–27
  "No Compromise With Slavery" (1854)
    (Garrison), 238, 239–40
  "No Rights, No Duties" essay (1860)
    (Wright), 257–58
  Slavery (1836) (Channing), 33, 35–36,
    38
  slavery remedy lecture (1834) (Phelps),
    48–49, 52–53, 58
Nebraska, 204, 241, 242
  See also Kansas–Nebraska Act (1854)
New England Anti-Slavery Society, 107
New Mexico, xxiii, 172
New Orleans Bulletin, 11–12
New York, 154
New York Tribune, 14
Nicholas, George, 138
Nile's Register, 9
"No Compromise With Slavery" (1854)
    (Garrison)
  abolition principles, 231–45
  African slave trade, 237–38
  Alabama, 236
  chattel slavery, 236–37, 244
  Declaration of Independence, 231, 233,
    238
  Divine Law, 235–45
  equal rights, 231–32
  Europe, 233–35
  Florida, 241
  freedom ideology, 230, 232, 233, 238,
    239–40, 242–43, 245

"No Compromise With Slavery" (1854)
(Garrison) *(continued)*
  free trade, 239–40
  Fugitive Slave Law (1850), 230, 232–33
  Georgia, 236, 240
  Great Britain, 234, 238–39
  Ireland, 234–35
  Louisiana, 240
  Missouri Compromise (1850), 241
  moral ideology, 233–34, 236–37, 238, 240
  motto, 242
  natural rights philosophy, 238, 239–40
  Nebraska, 241, 242
  North Carolina, 240
  Northern region, 239–42, 243, 244
  religious ideology, 230–45
  Scotland, 234
  Slave Power, 232, 239, 241, 243
  slavery extension, 242
  slavery justification, 233–34
  Southern region, 236, 239–42, 244
  Texas, 241
  Union secession, 241–42
  Virginia, 240
No-government abolitionists, 79–83, 84, 86–87, 88–90, 95, 246
Non-intervention policy, 196, 197–98
Non-resistance strategy
  Garrison, William Lloyd (1805–1879), xvi–xvii, xxv, 87, 88–89, 91–95, 96–97
  political obligation letter (1839) (Birney), 79, 87, 88–89, 91–95, 96–97
  political party dialogue (1842) (Child), 99–100, 101
Non-revolutionary strategy, xiii
Non-violent strategy, xiii, xiv
"No Rights, No Duties" essay (1860) (Wright)
  African slave trade, 247–48
  armed insurrection strategy, 246, 251–52, 254, 256–60
  chattel slavery, 246–47, 250, 252, 256

"No Rights, No Duties" essay (1860)
(Wright) *(continued)*
  Declaration of Independence, 256–57
  Dred Scott decision (1854), 249, 253
  equal rights, 260
  Florida, 253
  freedom ideology, 249–50, 252–54, 256–58, 260
  freedom nationalization, 252–54
  Fugitive Slave Law (1850), 253
  fugitive slaves, 249–50, 253
  Illinois, 258–59
  Indiana, 258–59
  individual slaveholder rights, 246–47
  Iowa, 258–59
  Kansas, 251, 253
  Kentucky, 247, 251, 258–59
  Louisiana, 247, 253
  Maryland, 247, 251, 258–59
  Massachusetts, 248, 252, 257, 258, 260
  Mississippi, 247
  Missouri, 247, 251, 258–59
  Missouri Compromise (1850), 253
  moral ideology, 254–55
  natural rights philosophy, 257–58
  Northern region, 247–48, 250–51, 254, 255–56, 257, 258–59, 260
  Ohio, 247, 258–59, 260
  Pennsylvania, 247, 258–59
  religious ideology, 247–48, 250, 252, 254, 255, 257, 258, 260
  Republican Party, 250, 251, 254, 258, 259–60
  resistance strategy, 250–51, 256–60
  slave duties, 248–50
  slaveholding state rights, 247–48
  South Carolina, 247
  Southern region, 247, 250, 252, 254
  Texas, 253
  Union dissolution, 254
  Virginia, 247–48, 251, 252, 253, 257–59, 260
North Carolina, 9, 17, 240
North Carolina Standard, 11
Northern doughface, xv, 107–8, 195, 199, 211

North Star, The, 24
Notes on the States of Virginia (Jefferson), xii–xiii

Ohio, 247, 258–59, 260
Oligarchy, 111
One-idea morality, 122–23, 124
One-idea platform, xix–xx, xviii, 125, 129–30
One-idea societies, 120–22
Oppressor guilt
  "Declaration of Sentiments" (1833), 43, 45
  political action strategy (1838) (Jackson/Phelps), 65
  Slavery (1836) (Channing), 31, 32–33, 35
  slavery remedy lecture (1834) (Phelps), 52, 53, 55
Oregon, 194

Patriarchal Institution (1860) (Child)
  bequest laws, 17
  chattel slavery, 10, 20, 21–22
  children, 21–22
  clothing laws, 17–18, 21
  conclusions, 20–23
  contractual laws, 17
  court testimony, 17, 18, 20
  education, 6, 14–15, 22
  food laws, 17–18, 21
  grandchildren, 22
  labor laws, 17, 18, 21
  marriage laws, 16, 21
  Northern slave contrast, 7, 14–18
  property laws, 17, 21, 22
  punishment, 17
  religious ideology, 7, 15–16, 22
  religious worship, 14, 15–16
  slave character proofs, 10–13
  slave happiness proofs, 7–10
  slave happiness statements, 6–7
  slave moral condition proofs, 14–17
  slave physical condition proofs, 17–18
  slavery extension, 19–20

Patriarchal Institution (1860) (Child) (*continued*)
  slavery parental relation proofs, 5–6, 7, 13–14
  Southern prophecies, 3–6
    fulfillment of, 4–6
  unlawful assembly, 14–15
  wage laws, 17, 21
Peacock, Jesse, 12
Pennsylvania, 154, 247, 258–59
Petersburg Express, 15
Phelps, Amos (1804–1847)
  abolitionist movement, 46
  American Anti-Slavery Society, 46
  gender equality, 46
  immediate emancipation, 46
  lecturing agents, 46
  Massachusetts Anti-Slavery Society, 46, 63
  newspaper editor, 46
  religious ideology, 46
  See also Political action strategy (1838) (Jackson/Phelps); Slavery remedy lecture (1834) (Phelps)
Philadelphia Convention (1787), 136
Pinckney, Charles C., 136–37, 138
Pinkney, William, 3
Poe, William, 17
Political action
  abolitionist movement, xv–xviii, xxiv–xxv
  abolitionist political party, xvii, xviii
  American Anti-Slavery Society, xvi–xviii, 44–45
  conservatism, xvi–xviii
  "Declaration of Sentiments" (1833), 44–45
  Liberty Party lecture (1844) (Buffum), 107–13
  Macedon Convention address (1847) (Goodell), 117, 126, 128
  moral suasion, xv–xviii
  political obligation letter (1839) (Birney), 77–78
  political party dialogue (1842) (Child), 98–99, 102

Political action *(continued)*
  voting strategy, xvi–xviii
Political action strategy (1838) (Jackson/Phelps)
  abolitionist movement, 64, 65, 66, 67, 68–70, 71–72, 74
  abolitionist political party, 67–68
  abstract opposition, 65
  anti-slavery candidates, 63, 67, 68–72
  Congressional measures, 69
  Democratic Party, 63, 71, 72, 73
  equal rights, 68, 73
  freedom ideology, 67, 68, 72, 73
  gender equality, 68
  general strategy, 63
  geographical context, 64, 65–66, 68
  immediate emancipation, 65, 68–69, 72
  Massachusetts Anti-Slavery Society, 63–74
  moral suasion, 63, 64–65, 66, 68, 69, 74
  Northern sentiment, 65, 66, 68
  oppressor guilt, 65
  political agitation, 63, 65, 66
  political interrogation, 63, 68–71
  political party alliance, 67–68, 73–74
  political petitions, 63, 66, 68
  principles development, 63–64, 66, 67–68, 69–70, 71, 72–74
  property laws, 73
  reform principle, 64, 65–66, 73
  religious ideology, 64–65, 66, 67, 68, 72–73, 74
  slavery evil, 65
  social ideology, 64, 65, 66
  successful action, 66–67
  Union admission, 69–70, 74
  voting strategy, 63, 67, 68, 70, 71–73
  Whig Party, 63, 71–72, 73
Political ideology, xi, xii, xiii, xiv, xvii, xviii–xx
Political obligation
  Macedon Convention address (1847) (Goodell), 116–18, 122–25, 130
  party obligations, 123–25, 130
  political party dialogue (1842) (Child), 101

Political obligation *(continued)*
  See also Congressional responsibility speech (1854) (Giddings)
Political obligation letter (1839) (Birney)
  abolitionist movement, 76–78
  American Anti-Slavery Society, 76–83
  anti-slavery candidates, 77–78
  Constitutional consent, 76–77, 82–83
  Constitutional interpretation, 78, 79–81
  Constitutional principles, 76–77, 82–83
  "Declaration of Sentiments," 76–77, 78, 79–81, 82–83
  freedom ideology, 78
  Garrison rebuttal
    abolitionist inconsistency, 94–95
    abolitionist movement, 84, 86–87, 88–92, 94–97
    abolition platform, 90–91
    Constitutional consent, 84
    Constitutional principles, 92–95
    debate positions, 84–85
    "Declaration of Sentiments," 84–85, 87–88, 92–94
    false accusation, 91–92
    immediate emancipation, 90
    justice, 84, 87–88
    Massachusetts Anti-Slavery Society, 96–97
    moral action, 85–86, 87
    moral suasion, 85–87, 89, 91, 95
    no-government abolitionists, 84, 86–87, 88–90, 95
    non-resistance strategy, 87, 88–89, 91–95, 96–97
    political action, 85–87, 90, 92, 95–97
    political argument, 85–87
    political inconsistency, 89–90
    political petitions, 86–87, 89, 90
    religious ideology, 84–85, 87, 88, 89, 90–91, 92–93, 96
    self-respect, 84, 87–88
    slave trade, 85
    social ideology, 84
    Society membership, 86–89, 94

Political obligation letter (1839) (Birney)
  Garrison rebuttal *(continued)*
    voting strategy, 84, 85–87, 89–91, 95–96
    immediate emancipation, 76
    justice, 83
    Massachusetts Anti-Slavery Society, 78
    moral suasion, 77–78, 79
    no-government abolitionists, 79–83
    non-resistance strategy, 79
    political action, 77–78
    political petitions, 81–82
    popular sovereignty policy, 76
    religious ideology, 76, 78–79, 80–83, 84
    self-respect, 83
    slave expatriation, 76
    slave trade, 77
    social ideology, 79
    Society membership, 80, 82–83
    Union admission, 76–77
    voting strategy, 77–83, 84
Political obligation speech (1850) (Sumner)
  abolitionist movement, 178–84
  African slave trade, 172
  anti-slavery candidates, 182–83
  British Parliament, 174–75
  California admission, 171
  Congressional actions, 170–78
  Constitutional rights, 173–74
  domestic slave trade, 171–72, 178
  freedom ideology, 171, 172–74, 175, 178, 181, 182, 183, 184
  Fugitive Slave Law (1850), 172–78, 179
  Massachusetts, 176, 177, 183
  military flogging, 172
  moral suasion, 178–79, 182
  New Mexico, 172
  Northern region, 179, 180
  religious ideology, 176, 178–79, 182
  Slave Power, 178, 179–81
  Southern region, 175–76, 180
  Stamp Act, 174–75
  Supreme Court rulings, 173–74

Political obligation speech (1850) (Sumner) *(continued)*
  Texas, 172, 178, 183
  Utah, 172
  voting strategy, 182–83
Political party dialogue (1842) (Child)
  abolitionist political party, 99–100
  American Anti-Slavery Society, 98–99, 101, 102
  anti-slavery candidates, 99–103
  Calvinism, 99
  Democratic Party, 99–103
  freedom ideology, 99
  Liberty Party, 99–103
  Massachusetts, 99–101
  moral suasion, 98–103
  natural law perspective, 100–1, 102
  non-resistance strategy, 99–100, 101
  political action, 98–99, 102
  political obligation, 101
  pro-slavery candidates, 99–103
  Quakers, 99, 103
  radicalism, 100
  religious ideology, 99, 101, 103
  social ideology, 99
  third party, 100–1
  Unitarianism, 99, 103
  Universalism, 103
  Vermont, 100
  voting strategy, 99–103
  Whig Party, 99–103
Political petitions
  American Anti-Slavery Society, xiv–xv, 41, 45
  political action strategy (1838) (Jackson/Phelps), 63, 66, 68
  political obligation letter (1839) (Birney), 81–82, 86–87, 89, 90
Political revolution, xxiv–xxvi
Popular sovereignty policy
  American Anti-Slavery Society, 44
  congressional responsibility speech (1854) (Giddings), 195–96
  "Declaration of Sentiments" (1833), 44
  freedom ideology, xxiii–xxiv

Popular sovereignty policy *(continued)*
  "House Divided" speech (1858)
    (Lincoln), 212–13, 215, 217
  Northern morality, xxiii, xxiv
  political obligation letter (1839)
    (Birney), 76
  Political obligation speech (1850)
    (Sumner), 171
Postell, J.C., 7
Practical principle, 57, 58–59
Presbyterian Synod (Kentucky), 9–10
Prigg v. *The Commonwealth of Pennsylvania*, 141–42
Property laws, 17, 21, 22, 26, 31, 73
  See also Chattel slavery
Pro-slavery candidates, 99–103
Public lands, 116, 119–20
Punishment, 17, 26–27, 33, 45

Quakers, 99, 103

Racial diversity, 34
Racism, xii, xiv, xvii
Radical Abolitionist Party, 202, 204, 205–6, 207–8, 209, 210
Radicalism
  abolitionist movement, xvi, xvii, xxiv–xxvi, 75, 100, 246, 261
  Union secession, xxiv–xxvi
Rankin, John, 18
Redemptioners (Holland), 151
Reform principle, 52, 53, 64, 65–66, 73
Religious ideology
  abolitionist movement, xii, xiii, xvii
  American Anti-Slavery Society, 42, 43, 45
  anti-slavery candidate essays (1856)
    (Douglass), 203, 206, 210
  congressional responsibility speech (1854) (Giddings), 188–89, 190, 191–92, 193, 198, 199, 200, 201
  Constitutional interpretation, 154
  "Declaration of Sentiments" (1833), 42, 43, 45
  Liberty Party lecture (1844) (Buffum), 110, 111, 112
  Macedon Convention address (1847) (Goodell), 115, 116, 119–22, 126

Religious ideology *(continued)*
  "No Compromise With Slavery" (1854)
    (Garrison), 230–45
  "No Rights, No Duties" essay (1860)
    (Wright), 247–48, 250, 252, 254, 255, 257, 258, 260
  Patriarchal Institution (1860) (Child), 7, 15–16, 22
  political action strategy (1838)
    (Jackson/Phelps), 64–65, 66, 67, 68, 72–73, 74
  political obligation letter (1839)
    (Birney), 76, 78–79, 80–83, 84–85, 87, 88, 89, 90–91, 92–93, 96
  political obligation speech (1850)
    (Sumner), 176, 178–179, 182
  political party dialogue (1842) (Child), 99, 101, 103
  slave address (1843) (Garnet), 224–29
  slave happiness, 7
  slave moral condition, 15–16
  Slavery (1836) (Channing), 34, 35, 36–38
  slavery lecture (1850) (Douglass), 24–26
  slavery remedy lecture (1834) (Phelps), 46–47, 48, 49, 50, 51–53, 54–56, 57, 58, 59–60
  See also Divine Law
Religious worship, 14, 15–16
Representative apportionment
  Constitutional framers intent, 136–37, 149
  Constitutional terminology, 133, 134–35, 147–48
  government practice, 138–39
  Supreme Court rulings, 141
Republican Party
  anti-slavery candidate essays (1856)
    (Douglass), 203–4, 205–6, 206–11
  formation (1856), xxiv
  freedom ideology, xxiv
  Fugitive Slave Law (1850), xxiv
  "House Divided" speech (1858)
    (Lincoln), 219
  Kansas–Nebraska Act (1854), xxiv

Republican Party *(continued)*
  "No Rights, No Duties" essay (1860)
    (Wright), 250, 251, 254, 258,
    259–60
  slavery extension, xxiv
Revenge, 50, 51
Rhode Island, 154
Rhodes, Durant H., 9
Richmond Enquirer, 6, 7, 19–20
Richmond Examiner, 6
Richmond Whig, 13
Ricks, Micajah, 11
Right Way, the Safe Way, Proved by Emancipation in the British West Indies, and Elsewhere, The (Child), 3

Scotland, 234
Self-government, 195–96, 213
Self-ownership, xii, 119–20
Self-respect, 83, 84, 87–88
Slave address (1843) (Garnet)
  African slave trade, 224, 226, 227, 228
  British government, 225
  freedom ideology, 223, 224–29
  National Convention of Colored Citizens, 223–29
  religious ideology, 224–29
  resistance strategy, 226–29
Slave character, 10–13
Slave expatriation, xiii, 44, 76
Slave happiness, 6–10, 28
Slave insurrections
  Constitutional framers intent, 138, 150
  Constitutional interpretation, xxi, 8
  Constitutional terminology, 134, 135, 147–48
  government practice, 140
  Supreme Court rulings, 142–43
Slave moral condition, 14–17
Slave physical condition, 17–18
Slave population, xi
Slave Power
  abolitionist movement, xiv, xix, xv, xxi, xxiii, xxiv, xxv
  anti-slavery candidate essays (1856) (Douglass), 203, 208–9, 211

Slave Power *(continued)*
  congressional responsibility speech (1854) (Giddings), 201
  Constitutional interpretation, xxi, xxv
  Free-Soil Party, xxiii
  fugitive slaves, xxiii
  Liberty Party, xix
  "No Compromise With Slavery" (1854) (Garrison), 232, 239, 241, 243
  political obligation speech (1850) (Sumner), 178, 179–81
  popular sovereignty policy, xxiv
  Union secession, xxv
Slave resistance
  "No Rights, No Duties" essay (1860) (Wright), 250–51, 256–60
  slave address (1843) (Garnet), 226–29
Slavery and Anti-Slavery (Goodell), 114
Slavery (1836) (Channing)
  chattel slavery, 31–38
  contractual laws, 31, 34
  Divine Law, 36–38
  equal rights, 33–34, 36
  labor laws, 31, 34–35
  moral ideology, 32–33, 36–38
  moral science principle, 36
  natural law perspective, 32–34, 36–38
  natural rights philosophy, 33, 35–36, 38
  oppressor guilt, 31, 32–33, 35
  property laws, 31
  punishment, 33
  racial diversity, 34
  religious ideology, 34, 35, 36–38
  social ideology, 36–37
Slavery extension
  anti-slavery candidate essays (1856) (Douglass), 208
  Constitutional interpretation, xxi
  Free-Soil Party, xxii
  Liberty Party, xviii–xix
  "No Compromise With Slavery" (1854) (Garrison), 242
  Patriarchal Institution (1860) (Child), 19–20
  Republican Party, xxiv

Slavery institutionalization, xi, xii, xiii, xiv
Slavery lecture (1850) (Douglass), 24–30
  chattel slavery, 26
  clothing laws, 26
  education, 26, 27
  food laws, 26
  property laws, 26
  punishment, 26–27
  religious ideology, 24–26
Slavery parental relation, 5–6, 7, 13–14
Slavery remedy lecture (1834) (Phelps)
  anti-slavery literature, 60
  chattel slavery, 53, 54, 57, 58
  efficient doctrine, 53, 54, 55–57
  emancipation doctrines, 51–57
  emancipation schemes, 49–57, 58
  equal rights, 57, 58
  false doctrine, 52, 53, 54
  freedom ideology, 50–51, 53, 57, 58, 60
  general principles determination, 47–48
  gradual emancipation, 50, 51–53
  immediate emancipation, 46, 48, 50–51, 52, 54–60
  immediate repentance, 51–52
  lecturing agents, 60
  moral character, 55–56
  moral evils, 54–55, 59
  moral ideology, 49, 50, 54–56, 59
  natural rights philosophy, 48–49, 52–53, 58
  Northern expertise, 47, 60
  oppressor guilt, 52, 53, 55
  practical principle, 57, 58–59
  reform principle, 52, 53
  religious ideology, 46–47, 48, 49, 50, 51–53, 54–56, 57, 58, 59–60
  revenge, 50, 51
  right practice, 56–57, 58–59
  slavery evil, 49–50, 54–55
  social ideology, 48–49
  theoretical starting point, 54, 55–56, 57, 58
  true doctrine, 54–57, 59–60
  universal emancipation, 49, 51
  wicked doctrine, 52–53, 54, 55–56

Slave trade. *See* African slave trade; Domestic slave trade
Smith, Geritt
  conservatism, xvi
  Liberty League, xx
  Liberty Party, xix–xx
  Macedon Convention (1847), xix–xx
  political action, xvi
  presidential nominee, 130, 202, 207
Social ideology
  abolitionist movement, xi–xii, xiii
  "Declaration of Sentiments" (1833), 43
  Macedon Convention address (1847) (Goodell), 120–22, 130
  political action strategy (1838) (Jackson/Phelps), 64, 65, 66
  political obligation letter (1839) (Birney), 79, 84
  political party dialogue (1842) (Child), 99
  Slavery (1836) (Channing), 36–37
  slavery remedy lecture (1834) (Phelps), 48–49
South Carolina, 7–8, 31, 135, 247
Southern Argus, 8
Southern Christian Herald, The, 4
Southern Commercial Convention (1859), 10
Southern Standard, 13
"Speech On Our Present Anti-Slavery Duties" (1850) (Sumner). *See* Political obligation speech (1850) (Sumner)
Spooner, Lysander (1808–1887)
  abolitionist movement, 261
  abolition plan (1858), 261–63
  Constitutional interpretation, xx–xxi, 261
  Dred Scott decision (1854), 260
  Liberty Party, 261
  natural law libertarian, 261
  radicalism, 261
  voluntary societies, 261
Squatter sovereignty, 213, 215
St. Louis Democrat, The, 14
St. Louis Observer, 16

Stamp Act, 174–75
Stowe, Harriet Beecher (1811–1896)
  Civil War contribution, 159
  freedom ideology, 159
  publications, 159
  See also "Two Altars; Or Two Pictures in One, The" (1851) (Stowe)
Stuart, Alvan, 100
Sumner, Charles (1811–1874)
  Free-Soil Party, 170
  Kansas speech (1855), 170
  political election (1856), xxv
  political obligation, 170
  Republican Party, 170
  Whig Party, 170, 183
  See also Political obligation speech (1850) (Sumner)
Supreme Court rulings
  Constitutional interpretation, 141–43, 152
  Dred Scott decision (1854), 212, 213–17, 249, 253, 261
  Gibbons v. Ogden, 141
  Hylton v. United States, 141
  political obligation speech (1850) (Sumner), 173–74
  Prigg v. The Commonwealth of Pennsylvania, 141–42
Swaim, William, 4

Tappan, Arthur, xiii, xvi
Tappan, Lewis, xiii, xvi
Tariff laws, 109, 115, 120, 123
Temperance Society, 121, 122
Tennessee, 135
Texas
  Constitutional interpretation, 135
  Macedon Convention address (1847) (Goodell), 115–16
  "No Compromise With Slavery" (1854) (Garrison), 241
  "No Rights, No Duties" essay (1860) (Wright), 253
  political action strategy (1838) (Jackson/Phelps), 74
  political obligation speech (1850) (Sumner), 172, 178, 183

Thompson, Corbin, 11
Tracking dogs, 9
True Delta, 11
Turner, Nathaniel, 140, 228
"Two Altars; Or Two Pictures in One, The" (1851) (Stowe)
  liberty altar (1776), 159–65
  liberty altar (1850), 165–69

Uncle Tom's Cabin (Stowe), 159
Union admission
  free-state, xxiii
  political action strategy (1838) (Jackson/Phelps), 69–70, 74
  slave-state, xviii
Union dissolution, xxiv–xxvi
  Constitutional interpretation (1860) (Douglass), 154–55
  "House Divided" speech (1858) (Lincoln), 213
  "No Rights, No Duties" essay (1860) (Wright), 254
Union secession
  American Anti-Slavery Society, xxiv–xxv
  Constitutional interpretation, xxv
  Fugitive Slave Law (1850), xxv
  Macedon Convention address (1847) (Goodell), 115
  moderates, xxv–xxvi
  moral suasion, xxiv–xxvi
  "No Compromise With Slavery" (1854) (Garrison), 241–42
  political revolution, xxiv–xxvi
  radicalism, xxiv–xxvi
  Slave Power, xxv
Unitarianism, 99, 103
Universalism, 49, 51, 103
Unlawful assembly, 14–15
Utah, xxiii, 172

Van Buren, Martin, xxii, 202, 203
Vermont, 100
Vesey, Denmark, 228
Views Upon American Constitutional Law (Goodell), 114

Virginia
  Constitutional interpretation, 135
  Liberty Party, 111, 210
  "No Compromise With Slavery" (1854) (Garrison), 240
  "No Rights, No Duties" essay (1860) (Wright), 247–48, 251, 252, 253, 257–59, 260
  slavery laws, 14–15
Voluntary societies, 120–22, 261
Voting strategy, xvi–xviii
  Macedon Convention address (1847) (Goodell), 117, 123, 124, 126, 128
  political action strategy (1838) (Jackson/Phelps), 63, 67, 68, 70, 71–73
  political obligation letter (1839) (Birney), 77–83, 84, 85–87, 89–91, 95–96
  political obligation speech (1850) (Sumner), 182–83
  political party dialogue (1842) (Child), 99–103

Wage laws, 17, 21
Washington, 194
Washington, Bushrod, 8
Washington, George, 150
Washington, Madison, 228–29
Washington Union, 20

Weaver, Amos, 16
Webster, Daniel, xxii–xxiii
"What Is My Duty as an Anti-Slavery Voter" (1856) (Douglass). *See* Anti-slavery candidate essays (1856) (Douglass)
Wheeling Intelligencer, 13
Whig Party
  abolitionist party challenge, xvii
  anti-slavery candidates, xvi
  anti-slavery faction, xix, xviii, xxii
  Liberty Party lecture (1844) (Buffum), 109, 110
  Missouri Compromise (1850), xxii–xxiii
  political action strategy (1838) (Jackson/Phelps), 63, 71–72, 73
  political party dialogue (1842) (Child), 99–103
White, Hiram, 12
Wilmington Advertiser, 9
Wilmot provisos, 126–27
Wise, Henry A., 19, 23
Wright, Henry C. (1797–1870)
  abolitionist movement, 246
  armed insurrection strategy, 246
  no-government abolitionists, 246
  radicalism, 246
  See also "No Rights, No Duties" essay (1860) (Wright)

About the Editor

C. Bradley Thompson is a professor of history and political science at Ashland University in Ohio. He received his Ph.D. at Brown University. He has also been a visiting scholar at Harvard University, University of London, and Utah State University. Thompson is the author of *John Adams and the Spirit of Liberty*, winner of the 1999 American Political Science Association prize for "best first book in political theory." He has also edited *The Revolutionary Writings of John Adams*, and was a coeditor of the *Encyclopedia of the Enlightenment*.

For Product Safety Concerns and Information please contact our EU representative GPSR@taylorandfrancis.com
Taylor & Francis Verlag GmbH, Kaufingerstraße 24, 80331 München, Germany